P9-DNU-665

# GOD VS. THE GAVEL: RELIGION AND THE RULE OF LAW

*God vs. the Gavel: Religion and the Rule of Law* challenges the pervasive assumption that all religious conduct deserves constitutional protection. While religious conduct provides many benefits to society, it is not always benign. The thesis of the book is that anyone who harms another person should be governed by the laws that govern everyone else – and truth be told, religion is capable of great harm.

This may not sound like a radical proposition, but it has been under assault since the 1960s. The majority of academics and many religious organizations would construct a fortress around religious conduct that would make it extremely difficult to prosecute child abuse by clergy, medical neglect of children by faith healers, and other socially intolerable behaviors. This book intends to change the course of the public debate over religion by bringing to the public's attention the tactics of religious entities to avoid the law and therefore harm others. *God vs. the Gavel* will bring much-needed balance to the contemporary, heated debate about religion and its role in society.

Marci A. Hamilton is an internationally recognized constitutional authority specializing in church/state relations. She is a leading national expert on the Religious Freedom Restoration Act, which she successfully challenged before the U.S. Supreme Court, and is involved in cutting-edge First Amendment litigation involving clergy abuse (on behalf of victims) and religious land use (Religious Land Use and Institutionalized Persons Act).

# GOD VS. THE GAVEL

## RELIGION AND THE RULE OF LAW

## MARCI A. HAMILTON

### FOREWORD BY THE HON. EDWARD R. BECKER

CAMBRIDGE
UNIVERSITY PRESS

CAMBRIDGE UNIVERSITY PRESS
Cambridge, New York, Melbourne, Madrid, Cape Town, Singapore, São Paulo

Cambridge University Press
40 West 20th Street, New York, NY 10011-4211, USA

www.cambridge.org
Information on this title: www.cambridge.org/9780521853040

First published 2005

Printed in the United States of America

A catalog record for this publication is available from the British Library.

Library of Congress Cataloging in Publication Data

Hamilton, Marci.
God vs. the gavel : religion and the rule of law / Marci A. Hamilton.
    p.   cm.
Includes bibliographical references and index.
ISBN 0-521-85304-4 (hardcover)
1. Corporations, Religious – Law and legislation – United States – Criminal provisions.
2. Tort liability of religious corporations – United States.   3. Clergy – Malpractice – United States.
4. Rule of law – United States.   I. Title: God versus the gavel.   II. Title.
KF9434.H36   2005
342.7308'52 – dc22                                                    2005003344

ISBN-13   978-0-521-85304-0 hardback
ISBN-10   0-521-85304-4 hardback

*This book is dedicated to*

my beloved Peter, Will, and Alexandra,
whose loving encouragement has been a godsend.

# CONTENTS

# ACKNOWLEDGMENTS

This book could not have been written without the assistance of my chief research assistant and third-year law student at Benjamin N. Cardozo School of Law, Rachel Steamer. She did a tremendous job, and I will be forever indebted to her for her extraordinary research skills, work ethic, and excellent judgment. I also thank Research Assistants Jodi Erickson, Rachel Lavery, Andrew Kopelman, Leo Mikityanskiy, and Philip Wellner, for their hard work and research assistance. My good friend, Kerry Ledbetter, provided invaluable line editing.

I am also indebted to John Berger, who is a brilliant editor at Cambridge University Press, and who helped me immeasurably to marshal ten years of scholarly work and practical experience into a single coherent project for a more general audience. I am very grateful to my agent, Karen Zahler, who helped me tremendously to refine my thesis and then to find the right niche for it. Sr. Karol Jackowski, who is the most spiritual person I know, was a much-needed source of inspiration and friend through it all.

Significant portions of Chapter 9 were previously published as part of the Foundations of Church Autonomy Symposium at the Brigham Young University School of Law. *See* Marci A. Hamilton, *Religious Institutions, the No-Harm Doctrine, and the Public Good*, 2004 B.Y.U. L. Rev. 1099 (2004). I am grateful to the participants of the symposium for their comments and for the excellent editorial work of BYU student editor Brigham Cannon and others.

Thanks are also due to the Benjamin N. Cardozo School of Law, Yeshiva University, for a summer grant and sabbatical in 2004, which made it possible for me to write *God vs. the Gavel*, and especially to Deans Paul Verkuil and David Rudenstine for their unflagging support for my admittedly unorthodox scholarship. Gratitude is also due to Tom Lee for his generous philanthropy that supports my chair at Cardozo School of Law, the Paul R. Verkuil Chair in Public Law. In addition, the Princeton Theological Seminary, where I was a visiting scholar during the fall of 2004, provided important research resources as well as a welcome atmosphere of open inquiry about religion and theology.

Judge Edward R. Becker, who provided the foreword, deserves lifelong gratitude. He has been the sort of mentor many people never know. He is in every sense of the term a mensch and a blessing on all those who know him.

The list of people who have taught me what I needed to know to write this book is endless, but I must express my gratitude to Jeffrey Anderson, who was helping clergy abuse victims long before the rest of us knew it was a problem, for his wisdom about clergy abuse; Ellen Mugmon and Rita Swan, for opening my eyes to the plight of children at the hands of some religious believers; Barbara Blaine and David Clohessy, of the Survivors Network of those Abused by Priests (SNAP), for their tireless dedication to the victims of childhood sexual abuse by clergy; Len Hill, who started the League of Residential Neigbhorhood Advocates, for his courage and dedication in standing up for residential neighborhoods negatively affected by ambitious religious building projects; Sarah Hart, Pam Sargent, and Todd Marti, who educated me about the abuses of religious privileges in the prisons; and the Mayor of Boerne, Texas, the Rev. Patrick Heath, whose courage as a Methodist minister in fighting the Religious Freedom Restoration Act all the way up to the Supreme Court inspires me still.

But no one deserves more credit than my husband, Peter Kuzma. He has read chapters when he needed to sleep, provided the right criticism when it was needed most (and even when I did not want to hear it), and set an example of a believer who will not tolerate the status quo if a religious entity has overstepped its bounds. He is a devoted Roman Catholic who is determined to do everything he can to make the church safe for children. His integrity, his belief in the truth, and his loving support for this book literally made it happen.

# FOREWORD

The role of religion in a free society, once a subject of benign and lofty discourse, has become a raging controversy in both the private and public arenas. While few in America challenge the multifarious benefits of religion to the individual believer and to society as a whole, there are sharply divergent views as to the extent to which notions of religious liberty immunize religious conduct from sanction when it interferes with public health, safety, and welfare.

In recent years, religious entities, often with the assistance of legislatures and courts, have advocated a presumptive constitutional right to avoid the law pursuant to the federal and state free exercise of religion guarantees, arguing that the First Amendment, the Due Process Clause, and separation of powers render them immune from some legal requirements and precepts. Opponents of these initiatives have responded that this approach is at odds with American culture and legal tradition.

In this volume, Professor Marci Hamilton, one of the nation's leading legal scholars and one of the premier authorities on the Constitution's Religion Clauses, tackles these issues in depth and with gusto. Her dominant theme is that the temptation to treat religion as an unalloyed good is a belief one can embrace only at one's peril. Building upon her already prolific body of work, she proceeds from the baseline of the "no-harm principle" – that no person or entity can act in ways that harm others without consequence – which she demonstrates was widely shared by the Framers' generation. After establishing, with impressive documentation, that, despite their generally beneficent effect, religious entities can be responsible for many harms, e.g., lethal medical neglect of children, childhood sexual abuse, the takeover of neighboring property owners' rights under the zoning laws, and the undermining of laws against discrimination, she forcefully argues that the burden rests on the religious believers demanding exemption from a law to prove that the conduct sought to be immunized is not harmful to the society and individuals within it. Referencing the precept of *Employment Division v. Smith* that "the [correct] reading [of the Free Exercise Clause] is . . . an individual's religious beliefs do not excuse him from compliance with an otherwise valid law prohibiting conduct that the State is free to regulate," Professor Hamilton engages the scholarship of Professor Laycock and Professor (now Judge) McConnell and that of others who have criticized this holding. She argues that these scholars have misconstrued the jurisprudence of the Religion Clauses and that their defense of the Religious Freedom Restoration Act (overruled by *City of Boerne v. Flores*) and the Religious Land Use and Institutionalized Persons Act (RLUIPA) is flawed.

Whatever the reader's take on these issues may be, he or she will be edified by Professor Hamilton's exegesis of the history, jurisprudence, and policy considerations that inform the debate. This is a truly important, if provocative work, which is essential reading for anyone who wishes to delve beneath the surface of the contemporary battle over religion and values.

The Hon. Edward R. Becker
United States Court of Appeals
for the Third Circuit

# GOD VS. THE GAVEL: RELIGION AND THE RULE OF LAW

PART ONE

# WHY THE LAW MUST GOVERN RELIGIOUS ENTITIES

# THE PROBLEM

The United States has a romantic attitude toward religious individuals and institutions, as though they are always doing what is right. As one scholar has quipped: "There is a long history in this country of religion being reduced to Sunday school morality in service of the common good."[1] Were religious institutions and individuals always beneficial to the public, this book would not need to be written, and they would not need to be deterred from criminal or tortious behavior. Religious liberty could be absolute. The unrealistic belief that religion is always for the good, however, is a hazardous myth. The purpose of this book is to persuade Americans to take off the rose-colored glasses and to come to terms with the necessity of making religious individuals and institutions accountable to the law so that they do not harm others.

Without a doubt many religious entities provide important benefits to society. Catholic Charities, the United Jewish Communities, and numerous other mission organizations do wonderfully good works. They feed and house the poor, counsel the addicted, minister to the downtrodden, and educate on a large scale. In 2003, religious organizations received nearly 40 percent of all charitable contributions in the United States, which translates into over $86 billion to spend on good deeds.[2] In 2005, religious relief organizations have been indispensable in helping the millions of Indonesian tsunami victims. It is nearly impossible to imagine how the United States or the world could function without the services of these groups. There would be a severe deficit in the public's welfare if they were to close their doors.

Religious belief and ritual also can be a powerful source of inspiration, comfort, and healing, as the hard sciences now acknowledge.[3] It can ease the suffering caused by disease, death of a loved one, and the other catastrophes of human life. I know this firsthand as I have turned to prayer many times in my life.

Religious beliefs and speech are also a crucial source of critique of the state, and at their best bring the human drive to power into perspective. Religion can be a liberating force. For example, believers challenged slavery in the United States as early as the 18th century, built the slave-liberating Underground Railroad in the late 19th century, and then led the civil rights marches in the 1960s. It is an undeniably powerful force.

No country, of course, can afford to ignore religion's force on the people, as China is learning with its unsuccessful attempts to eliminate Falun Gong and Christianity.[4] In today's China, burgeoning religious pluralism has translated into increasingly repressive government policies. The 2004 Report of the U.S. Commission on International Religious Freedom explained the problem: "The Chinese government's campaign against evil cults has reportedly expanded beyond the Falun Gong and similar groups to those who are not part of the officially sanctioned religious organizations. This includes both newer and long-established Protestant and Catholic churches and leaders who, for various reasons, refuse to register with the government. Religious leaders have been imprisoned and followers detained and fined for 'cultist activity.'"[5]

There could not be a gentler religion than the Falun Gong, but its existence has threatened the governing powers in China. Three values – truth, compassion, and tolerance – form the backbone of Falun Gong's philosophy. Since July of 1999, communist officials, most notably party head Jiang Zemin, have campaigned to "eradicate" Falun Gong and any support for it among the Chinese people or foreign governments. According to the Falun Dafa Information Center, as of November 2002, over 500 have died from maltreatment in custody. Sources inside China, however, place the number of deaths in the thousands. Hundreds of thousands more suffer relentless abuse in prisons, forced labor camps, and brainwashing facilities.[6] Chinese authorities have also waged an abolition campaign against Christian organizations such as the Three Class Servants Church, whose members are said to number in the millions. In 2004, a campaign of arrests, beatings, and extortion of family members resulted in the disappearances and deaths of both bishops and laypersons alike.[7] China's relentless persecution of believers has led to sanctions from the United States and other countries.[8]

Communism did not survive in Eastern Europe and has not led to true freedom for the people in other countries in part because of its inability to incorporate religious belief into its social structure.[9] Russia tried to suppress the Orthodox Church under communism, but could not stamp it out. Church members escaped to the catacombs, where they created an underground church and developed an elaborately encrypted method of communication. Despite the imprisonment and execution of church leaders in Soviet Gulags and concentration camps, the secret church survived and was shepherded through the Soviet era by priests and believers who continued to perform consecrations and religious services.[10] Religion simply cannot be denied.

Despite these many virtues, a good deal of religious conduct is not beneficial. Herein lies the problem – some religious conduct deserves freedom and some requires limitation. Ridding society of religion is no answer, and therefore the United States must grapple with religion at its worst as well as its best. *God vs. the Gavel* argues that the right balance is achieved by subjecting entities to the rule of law – unless they can prove that exempting them will cause no harm to others. There is nothing in this book that can take away these virtues, and no intention to do so. There is another side, though. Religion's force can be just another iteration of the drive to power. As such, it can wreak horrible wrongs on individuals and society. Sometimes the fight goes on for centuries, as it has in Ireland between Catholics and Protestants.[11] Christians led the horror-filled years of the Medieval Inquisition and the Spanish Inquisition.[12] Britain's Queen Mary and Queen Elizabeth executed or exiled scores of "infidels" who did not profess to the queen's religion.[13] The Hindu majority in India and the Muslim majority in Pakistan have been battling over the Kashmir border region since the British partition in 1947.[14] Israel has been in conflict with Palestinians over the West Bank for over 50 years. In the United States, the Salem witches were hung or, in one man's case, crushed to death, for religious reasons.[15] In this era, Islamic radicals, many of whom are part of a fundamentalist movement that was initiated in 1928,[16] are waging a war of terror worldwide. To this day, there are male fundamentalist polygamists in secret enclaves who enslave women and sexually and physically abuse their children.[17] Faith-healing parents let children die of agonizing deaths from easily treated medical conditions like diabetes.[18] Thousands of children have been sexually abused by clergy in many denominations. And this is only a sampling of the numerous religiously motivated actions that harm others.

Despite such facts, there has been a temptation in the United States to treat religion as an unalloyed good. It is a belief one can embrace only at one's peril. There has been an increasingly strident chorus that the United States has been secularized and that religion has lost its force in the culture. Yale Law professor Stephen Carter's widely read book, *The Culture of Disbelief: How American Law and Politics Trivialize Religious Devotion*,[19] fed into this social drive. The book portrayed religion as a diminishing influence in society. Ironically, the secularization thesis has permitted organized religion to don the garb of the underdog, when in fact its political power has been quite potent, even if usually behind the scenes. Religion's double role of downtrodden and politically powerful was ironically transparent when in 1993 Senator Orrin Hatch justified the Religious Freedom Restoration Act, which put religious individuals and institutions in the position of being able to challenge every neutral, generally applicable law in the country, by saying, "Government too often views religion with deep skepticism and our popular culture too often treats religious belief with contempt."[20]

Indeed, the *Culture of Disbelief* and the viewpoint it fostered aided religions in their lobbying efforts, because few would suspect that such "weak" political actors could be as busy and as successful as they have been in the legislative context. The truth is that the vast majority of Americans are religious believers, church attendance is higher in the United States than anywhere else in the world, higher than at any time in U.S. history, and religious viewpoints fill the public square. While Americans were reading Carter's book and being convinced that the United States was "trivializing" religion, thousands of children were being sexually abused by clergy, with no one seemingly able to help them – not the press, not the prosecutors, not their parents, and certainly not the churches. As American society has sublimated the potential risks of religious entities, it has sold out its most vulnerable.

The test of religious liberty that would fail to take into account this other side of religion guarantees suffering. Religious entities have the capacity for great good and great evil, and society is not duty bound by any constitutional right to let them avoid duly enacted laws, especially where their actions can harm others. To say that religious liberty must encompass the right to harm others is to turn the First Amendment on its head.

Part One details some of the instances where religious entities have harmed the public good and documents facts about religion that require sunshine and public debate. Some will label it perverse, and others a betrayal, but it is intended to be an education – one that is sorely needed if true liberty for all is ever to be embraced. Nor is Part One intended to be an argument for eradicating religion, as some might try to interpret it. To the contrary, the impetus for this book lies in a belief in the depthless good that religious entities can and do supply. But that belief is tempered by my deep disappointment in learning the truth of what some religious entities actually have done and continue to do. My rose-colored glasses broke years ago.

From the ivory tower, it is easy to spin abstract arguments about the high principle of protecting religious conduct. Read this:

> Having engaged in my own weighing of the value of religious diversity against the potential for anarchy and having determined that religious diversity is highly valuable while the fear of anarchy is without basis at this time in history, I would push the line to be drawn in these

cases to the farthest extreme compatible with the viability of a living democracy, which is to say that the exercise of religion should trump most governmental regulation.[21]

I'm now embarrassed to say that I wrote that. If one's theory of protecting religious conduct is based on hypotheticals, ideals, and Sunday School, as mine was, it is not difficult to concoct a theory of religious liberty that permits religious conduct to sail above the law and the people. My views have changed 180 degrees, because I have been educated and now know the severe harm religious entities can cause. Most laws should govern religious conduct, with the only exception being when the legislature has determined that immunizing religious conduct is consistent with public welfare, health, and safety.

In recent decades, religious entities have worked hard to immunize their actions from the law, either by obtaining legislative exemptions or by forcing the courts to invalidate any law substantially burdening religious conduct that was not absolutely necessary. They have always waved the banner of "religious liberty," and few Americans have thought to question them. What could be more important in a free society than religious liberty? When the question is left in the abstract, it is hard to think of anything more important. But when one operates from the ground and knows the facts, the answer to the question is that there are all sorts of interests that must trump religious conduct in a just and free society – such as the interest in preventing childhood sexual abuse, or in deterring terrorism, or in preserving private property rights. Every citizen has at least as much right to be free from harm as the religious entity has to be free from government regulation.

In effect, though never explicitly, religious entities have been lobbying for the right to hurt others without consequences. That is a severe attack on the rule of law, which is supposed to guarantee that no one becomes a law unto himself. In a republican form of democracy like this one, the laws are enacted to serve the larger public good, and no one should be permitted to harm another person without account. True religious liberty recognizes an absolute right of belief and, at the same time, society's necessary power to regulate religious conduct to serve the public good.

There are two legal tacks religious individuals and institutions (the collective of which I will refer to as "religious entities") have pursued that have led to disastrous results: legislative exemption and/or constitutional – typically First Amendment – interpretation. The first is to put pressure on the legislative process to obtain exemptions from generally applicable laws. Sometimes they are asking for the right to follow their religious beliefs. For example, the Christian Scientists have a longstanding campaign to exempt parents from having to provide their children with medical treatment, which I will address in Chapter 2.

At other times religious entities ask for exemptions that go well beyond their religiously motivated conduct to avoid liability for their misconduct. For example, the Catholic Church worked hard to prevent clergy from having to report child abuse (knowing as it did that many of its priests were in fact abusing children) – even when a report would not violate the confessional. Their religiously motivated conduct did not require the protection, but their project of keeping secret widespread child sexual abuse by its clergy did.

At other times, the exemptions requested are what I refer to as blind exemptions. Groups of religious entities have persuaded legislatures to grant them a presumptive right to trump all laws or an entire category of law, on the theory that religious liberty demands freedom from the law. Examples include the Religious Freedom Restoration Act of 1993, its counterparts in the states, and the Religious Land Use and Institutionalized Persons Act of 2000 each of which will be discussed in more detail in later chapters.

Too often, specific exemptions have been passed without the general public – and sometimes the legislators – having any idea how the exemption would affect others. In a typical scenario, a religious group would quietly approach a legislator (inside or outside the capitol), and the legislator would then slip the exemption into some bill involving a wholly different subject. There would be no hearings, no public debate, and there would be no in-depth reporting to unmask the dangers of freeing religious entities from the law. Everyone who knew about it would go home satisfied – the legislator because he had done a "good deed" that day, and the religious entity, because it would avoid liability for its actions. Yet, the secrecy meant that the entities' future victims had no idea what was coming, as it permitted legislators to mimic the hear-no-evil, see-no-evil, speak-no-evil monkeys. This was supposedly religious liberty, American style. The results, documented in Part One, are not pretty.

The blind exemptions tended not to be so secret, because they were cast in general terms. In other words, the laws themselves were bandied about for all to see, but their terms were so general, hardly anyone could comprehend how the law would affect anyone other than the religious entity getting the exemption. The Religious Freedom Restoration Act, the grand blind exemption of all time, gave religious entities the right to disobey any law unless the government could prove it was necessary. It was as opaque on its surface as they come. It would take five years for groups like the ACLU, one of its first and most ardent supporters, to discover that it had supported a law that undermined its interests – in its case, the antidiscrimination laws. The legislative history is filled with paeans to religious liberty, but precious little analysis of what was going to happen if religious individuals and institutions had the power to overcome the laws that regulate conduct.

Whether specific or blind, many of these exemptions have meant that the United States has been tolerating harms known only to those inflicting the harm and their victims. Children have been sexually abused by priests in rectories while clergy were exempt from reporting child abuse, homeowners have been told their residential neighborhoods would now host a church that would bring the kind of traffic and strangers that would force them to keep their children at home, and the prisons would become breeding grounds for terrorists.

In addition to seeking legislative exemptions, religious entities have argued vigorously and actively in the courts (and the legislatures) for a presumptive constitutional right to avoid the law pursuant to the federal and state free exercise of religion guarantees. They have foisted a definition of the First Amendment onto the American people that means, in effect, that they are immune to all but the most necessary laws. They have attempted to use the First Amendment as a shield in prosecutions involving child rape and murder. But their efforts have not stopped at the First Amendment. They have also employed due process, ex post facto, and separation of power theories to argue that the law should not apply to them, often because they are religious.

Part One describes six arenas where religious individuals and institutions have insisted on the right to avoid the law as they have harmed others: children, marriage, schools, land use in neighborhoods, the prisons and the military, and civil rights. Sometimes the exemption was consistent with the public good and no harm accrued, but too often, the exemption meant that a victim had no recourse under the law.

Part Two charts the fall of special privileges for religious conduct in Anglo-American history and the rise of the rule that religious entities have no legal right to harm others. After centuries of development, it is quite clear that harm is harm, and whoever causes it must be held to account. I will endorse the Supreme Court's unfairly maligned opinion in *Employment Div. v. Smith*, and I will argue that there is no constitutional right to harm others simply because the conduct is religiously motivated. Therefore the rule of law – which is the collection of legal principles that are duly enacted by legitimate legislatures – must be applied evenhandedly to all religious entities. Legislatures can exempt the religious from some laws, but only where the religious entities have borne the burden of proving that exempting them renders no harm.

# CHILDREN

Warning: If this chapter were a movie, it would have an NC-17 rating, because it describes horrible things that have been done to children beneath the cloak of religion in the United States. Children have been raped, beaten, and permitted to die excruciating deaths.

Young people are at risk from religious adults and institutions in two ways: (1) through the misuse of religious power to abuse the child; or (2) through their parents' religiously motivated medical neglect or physical abuse. The suffering is often unimaginable, because the children lack the ability to protect themselves from death, permanent disability, or severe abuse – at the hands of those they have been taught are here on earth to care for them.

In the first instance, some clergy, day-care providers, and religious schoolteachers use their position to take advantage of children. No person can be trusted to hold power without some check on it, and that is why we have the law – to protect the vulnerable from harm and to preserve the common good. The religious authority figure can be the most outwardly religious and pious individual, but without the law's ability to make the person accountable, he or she is capable of physical and spiritual murder. It is not just a wolf – but a lion – in sheep's clothing. Oftentimes this power-based abuse takes the form of sexual abuse, and sometimes it is physical abuse or ritualistic abuse. Many children, especially those who are already in difficult family situations, lack the life skills to be able to fend off the clergy member who seduces them with attention and affection and only then turns into a sexual predator.

In the second scenario, the parents impose sincere religious beliefs on the child that endanger him or her. The most common example is faith healing, where the parent's faith precludes medical treatment and the child suffers from easily treatable ailments, such as diabetes, which, left untreated, lead to an agonizing death. When one person's liberty to act is expansive, it is usually at the cost of another, and this is doubly true in the medical-neglect cases. This is a zero-sum game, and unfortunately, too often than not, it is the children who are sacrificed, instead of the religious conduct.[1]

No person who has ever loved a child can keep from asking the question: What kind of society permits children to be hurt like this? The answer is the United States, when it overzealously or thoughtlessly protects the right to religious conduct.

*Childhood sexual abuse by clergy*

The following stories are all true and only touch the tip of the iceberg of clergy childhood sexual abuse. Some of these are notorious; others are run-of-the-mill. There are many more reported cases, and even more unreported cases, because the shame of the acts or the threats of the perpetrators often lead the victims to prefer shadow rather than sunlight regarding their experiences. The perpetrators are clergy members – the men and women children are taught to trust with their very souls. These pedophiles and ephebophiles use their position of religious authority to lure vulnerable children into sexual molestation.[2] Although the precise details of the sexual attacks vary, the grievous harm to the victims then and later in life is the same. Victims of sexual attacks by clergy typically have no idea what has happened to them immediately after the sexual attack occurs. They are confused, ashamed, and afraid. When the clergy member tells them that they will go to hell if they tell anyone – which happens on a regular basis – the victims are almost always silent. The victims are children, after all, and this is usually their very first introduction to sex (unless they were already sexually abused by another adult). Typically, it takes decades of emotional turmoil and multiple missed dreams for them to finally realize that the acts that were done to them as children disabled some essential part of their psyche. They require intense counseling, family support, and even then may never achieve their full potential. The Roman Catholic canon law expert and hero, Father Thomas Doyle, who has dedicated his life to helping clergy-abuse victims, has accurately labeled what is done to these children as "soul murder." There is no better way to describe it.

Religious institutions have been havens for pedophiles for three reasons. First, up until now, society has so trusted clergy that no one questioned the priest or pastor or elder who volunteered to spend extra time with Bobby. Second, religion is an authoritative structure in a person's life, so that demands by clergy are oftentimes equated with commands from God and therefore are treated as imperatives. Third, religious institutions, especially those that form tight-knit communities, often succumb to the temptation to shield their public moral position by keeping internal sexual abuse secret, which ensures the authorities will not be contacted and permits the pedophile to continue to operate. The circumstances are tailor-made for the child molester. In the words of a former elder of the Jehovah's Witnesses, the religious organization can be a "pedophile paradise," especially where it features a "closed society, elder authority, [and a] masculine dominated society."[3]

As if it is not bad enough that religious institutions are magnets for pedophiles (partly because of the laws the religious institutions have endorsed), some religious institutions themselves have actively aided and abetted the abuse. The Roman Catholic Church and the Jehovah's Witnesses, among others, have handled reports of clergy abuse as though the public good was not their problem and have insisted on silence as they refused to report the crimes to authorities. There is no question that they placed the good of the organization above the needs of the child or the legitimate demands of society. Their disregard for the public good is even more sinister when one discovers that they were sacrificing the public good to elevate their earthly needs. The silence is an integral part of a twofold strategy: protect the institution's finances and protect its public image.

Twenty years ago, an internal report was offered to the U.S. Catholic Bishops that cast the phenomenon of clergy abuse in terms of an epidemic of clergy abuse cases waiting to explode.[4] It urged them to adopt a three part strategy that began with pastoral outreach to victims and included in-depth research and a crisis intervention team of experts to assist bishops with individual cases.[5] The perceived need for silence led the church to pretend publicly that it harbored no pedophiles, so that across the country cardinals, archbishops, and bishops shuffled known pedophiles from parish to parish without notice to anyone, leaving behind a trail of young victims. It was the perfect environment for the crime, which is why it happened over and over again, so that today there are thousands upon thousands of Catholic-clergy victims.[6] The same appears to be true of the Jehovah's Witnesses, and who knows who else.[7] The secrecy permitted the religious institutions to maintain a moral high ground in public and at the same time robbed vulnerable children of the forces of society that otherwise might have protected them – parents, prosecutors, the media, and civil rights groups.

The parents were often kept in the dark, even when a pedophile was assigned to their parish or children's religious school, and their lack of knowledge yielded two distinct problems. First, they had no idea they needed to act to protect their children from their own clergy in the first instance. Second, some refused to believe a child who told them about the abuse. Indeed, in some circumstances, the abused child was beaten by a parent for having the nerve to suggest a priest would do something so heinous, so abuse piled on top of abuse.

The prosecutors only heard of a small number of such cases, and therefore extrapolated to the conclusion that there must be only a small number. Since the problem appeared to be a negligible social problem, when the bishop or cardinal would ask them to let the church take care of its dirty laundry, prosecutors were all too willing.

It is somewhat of a mystery why the press did not break the story of widespread clergy abuse sooner. Perhaps they were ignorant that there were so many unspeakable crimes being committed in their jurisdictions. Or perhaps – like the prosecutors – they deferred to the bishop or cardinal, who asked them to leave the problem to them. It is not that the press has let religious entities off the hook in all circumstances. The Pulitzer Prize has been awarded many times for stories that uncovered financial misdealings in a religious institution,[8] and at least one reporter, Jason Berry, was focused on the Catholic Church's clergy-abuse problem as early as the 1980s.[9] But until 2003, no newspaper had won an award as a result of covering a national news story about clergy abuse, despite its obvious sensationalistic element.

1984 was a bellwether year for clergy abuse. Roman Catholic Father Gilbert Gauthe of Lafayette, Louisiana, was indicted for the abuse of 35 children.[10] The question was: "How did Gauthe get away with abusing that many children?" It was quite obvious: Gauthe had used his position in the church to obtain victim after victim.[11] Clear-headed reporting would have driven a good reporter into the internal operations of the Roman Catholic Church and its devotion to secrecy on these issues, and, in fact, there was intense interest by the press at the height of the scandal.[12] That interest was abetted by the intense emerging interest in the issue of child abuse at the same time.[13] In the same year, congressional testimony by FBI supervisory special agent Kenneth Lanning in 1984 stated that pedophiles gained access to children through their occupations and mentioned the following occupations: "teacher, camp counselor, babysitter, school bus driver . . . physician, minister, photographer, social worker, police officer, etc."[14] The same was circulated widely in an article in *Newsweek*, which referred to an alleged Methodist minister child abuser and quoted an expert as saying, "There should be a presumption that child abusers will gravitate to work with children."[15] It was common knowledge at the time that child molesters "are among the more respected members of their communities,"[16] a category that in most circumstances would include clergy. Thus, all the elements were in place for the story to break in the mid-1980s.

Yet, stories detailing a larger Church problem than just one perpetrator did not appear until 2001 in Boston when the *Boston Globe* unmasked the depth of the Boston Archdiocese's turpitude (and then won a Pulitzer Prize). The *Globe* was praised for its courage, but one must ask what took so long? For decades, children were being abused at will by pedophiles who were wearing a collar and grooming their young victims with charm and attention – across the country. To be sure, there is no one answer, but some component must be that at the end of the day, it was hard for even the jaded press to comprehend the enormity of the evil perpetrated by a single religious institution. And one cannot underestimate the lengths to which the Catholic Church went to keep its ugly secrets to itself. One lay Catholic described it as follows: "Their structure and social chemistry is almost identical to the Mafia. There is a deep secrecy and a fierce loyalty to the organization."[17]

Father Andrew Greeley, sociologist and well-known novelist, hypothesized at least 100,000 victims in 1993.[18] In 2004, the church's lay review board conducted an internal audit of the dioceses and concluded that there were roughly 10,000 victims, which is the very minimum number.[19] It runs against the grain of the post–World War II society to believe that religious institutions do wrong, which means religious institutions' victims have stayed under the social radar longer than other institutions' victims.

Moreover, children have been politically powerless. Children don't vote, to quote many a child advocate. To be sure, there are dedicated organizations like the American Academy of Pediatrics and CHILD, Inc. and individuals who push hard for children's rights,[20] but in this society at this time religious interests are too often granted "rights" at the expense of children.

The civil liberties groups have not been focused on the plight of children, unless they were vehicles for larger agendas. State civil liberties organizations often turn down children's advocates who ask for their support. For example, despite protestations from children's and women's groups, the Utah Civil Rights and Liberties Foundation recently spearheaded a lawsuit in Utah to defend polygamy as a constitutionally protected religious practice, and in the face of widely circulated accounts of underage marriage and statutory rape.[21] The American Civil Liberties Union supported the Religious Freedom Restoration Act, which worked against children's interests and is discussed in Part Two, and only withdrew support for that type of religious liberty legislation when its leadership realized it undermined antidiscrimination laws. The children's issues, despite being pressed by various groups, in the end did not move the ACLU.

The crimes and tortious acts described in this chapter have occurred in every state – and in many countries around the world. This is not a phenomenon limited to the United States. Every victim has a unique story, so that it is impossible to generalize to a single paradigm. Pedophiles as a general matter do share certain characteristics, however. The foremost authority in the country on the topic is Kenneth Lanning from the FBI. In 1984, he testified before the Senate Judiciary Committee's Subcommittee on Juvenile Justice and in prepared testimony described the pedophile:

> He typically nonviolently seduces children that he has befriended through the use of attention, affection and gifts. The pedophile is skilled at recognizing and then temporarily filling the emotional and physical needs of children. He is usually willing to spend as much time as it takes to seduce the targeted child.[22]

In most instances, he is a "nice guy," for the obvious reason that it furthers his schemes.[23] Pedophiles seek children through various means, but the primary avenue is occupation, which permits them "to impose authority and control on the child and thus make the seduction process easier and more secure."[24]

Despite law enforcement's ability to profile pedophiles, individual clergy-abuse stories need to be told for the public to truly understand what has been done to children and the public good by these religious individuals and institutions, who when confronted by the law furiously wave the First Amendment – in hopes the public will not focus on the evil. The criminal clergy and the religious institutions that knew about the pedophiles in their midst routinely invoke both the First Amendment and religious liberty legislation to avoid liability for the harm. For example, after the *Boston Globe* dropped the dime on the Boston Archdiocese's practice of shuffling pedophile priests around parishes, and unveiled its most heinous pedophiles – including John Geoghan, who abused at least 130 children,[25] and Paul Shanley, who openly advocated the North American Man-Boy Love Association[26] – the Church tried to block discovery by claiming it had free-exercise rights not to disclose its files.[27] It was a tactic that did not work there, but is being duplicated in thousands of abuse cases in the United States, and not just by the Catholic Church.

It is a favored tactic for any religious organization that has known about the pedophiles in its ranks and done nothing.

HAYWARD, CALIFORNIA. The following facts are taken from a video made prior to trial by lawyers for a brave childhood sexual abuse victim to document her experience so that others could learn about clergy abuse.[28] After grooming her with loving words and attention over several months, Monsignor George Francis took a five-year-old parishioner by the name of Jennifer Chapin into his rooms in the rectory and digitally penetrated her. He called her his "little princess." Then on weekends, he would take her to a hotel, where he ritualistically and sexually abused her. First, he taught this barely school-age child how to make manhattans, and then he tied her arms above her head and forced her legs apart so that he could fondle and rape her while he commanded her to tell him, "I love you." When he was done, he said she was "Satan's child," because she had tempted a priest. He then turned to ritualistic abuse to "purify" her by sprinkling her with holy water, inserting a scepter into her vagina, and hitting her while she was still tied to the bed.[29] Then he undressed and proceeded to rape her in a "loving style," as opposed to a ritualistic manner. If she told anyone, he declared that one of her family members would be killed by God. This ritualistic and sadistic abuse continued for five years. A neighbor who suspected abuse notified the diocese, but nothing was ever done.

As is usually the case, Chapin was not the only victim. Terrie Light was abused by Francis when she was seven years old,[30] and she claims that she has spoken to five other women, besides Chapin, who were victims of Francis.[31]

When Chapin's attorneys asked the church to release Francis's files to the public, the archdiocese refused and asserted that the First Amendment protected it from discovery in the case and that supposed privacy concerns for other victims prevented disclosure of the files. Both sides decided to forego a trial. On January 24, 2004, the Roman Catholic Church's Oakland diocese agreed to pay $3 million in damages and up to $50,000 in counseling and to add (at her request) her video to its program of educating parishioners, priests, and diocesan employees on the prevention of childhood sexual abuse.[32] Francis's files were not released at that point, but other victims are suing.

MIDDLETON, MASSACHUSETTS. In Massachusetts, Christopher Reardon was hired as a youth worker at the parishes of St. Agnes in Middleton and St. Rose's in Topsfield, Massachusetts. At the same time, he was hired to teach swimming at the YMCA in Danvers. During the 1990s, he abused scores of boys, aged 11 to 13, some of whom later attempted suicide, many of whom saw As and Bs on their report cards turn into failing marks, and virtually all of whom suffered extreme emotional scarring.[33] After being arrested in June 2000, Reardon pleaded guilty of 75 counts of abuse, including rape, of 24 boys, and received up to 50 years in prison for his crimes. The YMCA quickly settled the boys' claims against it; but the church held out for another year.[34] The Boston Archdiocese finally paid $85 million to settle the claims of 552 victims, including Reardon's, in September 2003.[35]

Part of the horror of the Reardon story is that it appears that St. Agnes parish priest Jon C. Martin knew about the abuse well before Reardon was arrested, and therefore could have stopped it. Victims alleged in their lawsuit that when he discovered two boys in Reardon's office in 1998, he simply warned Reardon that it might not look right. Even after a retired priest from St. Rose's parish contacted Martin to tell him he had seen a young boy go into Reardon's office, Martin took no action, which made it possible for Reardon to continue to commit crime after crime.[36] This has been a repetitive pattern in the United States, where the Roman Catholic Church, the Jehovah's Witnesses, and other denominations have had evidence that one of their own was a predatory pedophile, yet they responded by ignoring the problem, ultimately endangering thousands of children.

ST. FRANCISVILLE, ILLINOIS. Gina Trimble Parks was a teenage girl, who in the 1970s helped out with the cleaning at the local rectory. The following are the allegations of abuse that appeared in the court's published decision. One day, while cleaning Father Raymond Kownacki's bedroom, the priest said he would show her a voodoo trick. He had her close her eyes and chant, and then he raped her. She became his sexual slave after he persuaded her parents to let him take her to a "better" school in a different parish. She was set up in the rectory with him and was required to do his sexual bidding. When she tried to break away by dating a boy her own age, and she became pregnant, Kownacki (who claimed to have had a vasectomy) became enraged and abused her physically and verbally. He gave her a dose of quinine, which he believed would cause an abortion, and then while she was unconscious, he manually aborted the fetus.

When the family sued Kownacki for what he had done to their daughter, he successfully defended himself on the ground that they had missed the statute of limitations, which was only two years long.[37] The brevity of the statutes of limitations has been a significant and persistent hurdle to clergy-abuse victims finding justice. If future children are to be protected, these statutes need to be abolished. The sad truth is that religious entities have not jumped on this bandwagon for kids. Instead, they have either been silent or, worse, lobbied to keep the statutes of limitations just as they are in order to protect their purse and their image. They have been especially effective in preventing amendment where the proposal is to make civil claims retroactive so that existing victims have some means of gaining some justice.[38]

Of course, Kownacki did not have only one victim. Other claims against him have been widely reported, and he was barred from active ministry in 1995.[39] In 2003, an Illinois man who wanted to remain anonymous filed a suit against Kownacki for abusing him during a three-year period between 1979 and 1982.[40] In 2004, the diocese fought release of Kownacki's files in this case and was fined by an Illinois Court for failure to comply with the court's order. This is typical stonewalling, and the case is still pending.

**HILDALE, UTAH.** In the late 19th century in the United States, the Church of Jesus Christ of Latter-day Saints, also known as the Mormons, practiced polygamy, which was a divine mandate. The practice was formally renounced in 1890, roughly 30 years after Congress placed a general ban on all polygamous practices.[41] Today, the mainstream Mormons do not practice polygamy, though it does feature in their views of the afterlife.[42] Various splinter sects have refused to accept the Mormons' reversal on polygamy, however, and still practice it today – despite the fact it is illegal under state and federal law.

One such group, the Fundamentalist Church of Jesus Christ of Latter-day Saints, the FLDS, is currently led by Warren Jeffs, who is the prophet and president and who rules the sect with complete authority. His nephew, Brent Jeffs, has filed suit against the prophet and the FLDS for compensatory and punitive damages alleging that when Brent was between the ages of four and six, Warren Jeffs and his brothers Leslie and Blaine Jeffs took Brent out of Sunday School, into a lavatory, and sodomized him. They allegedly told him that the abuse was "God's work," done so that he would "become a man," and told him he would suffer "eternal damnation" if he ever told anyone.[43] Brent allegedly was regularly passed around between the men during these sessions.[44] Although the leadership of the church knew about the abuse for years, the complaint alleges the leadership did nothing to stop it.[45] The church has strongly denied all the allegations, and no doubt will respond that it has a First Amendment right to avoid discovery and the legal theories alleged. This is a cloistered group that lives outside the bounds of society already, and therefore is not likely to acquiesce to the application of the law lightly. Abuse is abuse is abuse, though, and if Brent Jeffs's allegations turn out to be true, the defendants deserve both compensatory and punitive damages assessed against them.

In a similar vein, Arvin Shreeve of the polygamous Zion Society of Ogden, Utah, pleaded guilty in 1991 to sodomy and sexual abuse of underage girls. In addition, 12 members of his sect, including several women, were prosecuted and put on the Utah sex offender list, because they used underage girls as models for their homemade lingerie.[46]

**THE UNITED STATES AND BRITISH COLUMBIA, CANADA.** There is evidence that the FLDS has been transporting underage girls across the Canadian border to Bountiful, British Columbia, where they are joined in marriage with much older men in polygamous unions.[47] If these facts are true, it would be a violation of the federal Mann Act, which prohibits anyone from "knowingly transport[ing] an individual who has not attained the age of 18 years in interstate or foreign commerce... with intent that the individual engage in prostitution, or in any sexual activity for which any person can be charged with a criminal offense." The Department of Justice does not appear to have taken any action to stop the practice.[48] Complaints to parliament, government tribunals and press reports allege that girls are quickly married to men sometimes three times their age, forced to have sex, and impregnated as soon and as often as possible. Because the wives that follow the first wife are not legal, typically the girl-wives are left to care for their numerous children with no support from the husband, no education, and no means of earning a living; many have no option but to turn to public assistance.⁴⁹

The local authorities in Bountiful, Canada, entered into a pact with the FLDS in the early 1990s entitled the Child Protection Protocol Agreement.⁵⁰ It allegedly provided that any child-abuse allegations would have to be screened by Rulon Jeffs (Warren's now-deceased father) and his successor, Winston Blackmore, before local authorities would have to be contacted, and the elders held the power to decide whether to report alleged child abuse. As one might have expected, there have been no reports. As with other sexual misconduct within religious institutions, the rule in Bountiful apparently has been silence. One person testified before the Hansard Legislative Assembly that, "[S]ilence is the code word in Bountiful. No one, under fear of harm, is allowed to talk. The kids are taught to keep quiet; the women are taught to keep quiet."⁵¹

The FLDS was not the only entity to maintain silence on the issue, however. For decades, the government in British Columbia paid little heed to the complaints by women who had escaped from Bountiful. There appears to have been some misguided thinking that the community's violation of the laws was protected by the constitutional right to the free exercise of religion.⁵² In 2004, a number of women filed allegations with the British Columbia Human Rights Tribunal, charging the government with permitting "massive contraventions of females' and children's human rights . . . which reduce women and children to chattel status and oppress their lives, [and which] prevent Bountiful's women and children from participating fully in Canada's economic and social life, as is their right."⁵³ The complaint describes the fate of one Deborah Palmer, who was in the commune between 1957 and 1988. At 15, she was given to Ray Blackmore, 57, to be his sixth wife, or "concubine," in the terms of the complaint, and later to two more husbands. She eventually escaped with her eight children. Given the alleged inbreeding within Bountiful, she is stepmother, sister-in-law, and niece all to the same man, Winston Blackmore. Women are taught to obey the men, or "their souls will burn for all eternity in Hell," and that their life's purpose is to assist the men in reaching "godhood," which is attained if the man has many concubines. Merrill Palmer, who is the principal of the Bountiful Elementary-Secondary School; James Oler, the current bishop of Bountiful; Winston Blackmore, the former bishop of Bountiful; and the Ministries of the Attorney-General and Education were the named defendants. Seven women who escaped Bountiful are allegedly willing to come forward, but only if they are protected by complete anonymity from the FLDS's practice of "blood atonement," which their complaint alleges is violence against those who dare to challenge the sect.[54] In a turnaround from the government's previous permissive stance toward Bountiful, the tribunal has agreed to hear the case, which is still pending.

**COLORADO CITY, ARIZONA, AND HILDALE, UTAH.** Another arm of the organization has also established an enclave in the border cities of Colorado City, Arizona, and Hildale, Utah, where the church need not worry about the fact that child abuse and polygamy violate state law, because local law enforcement belong to the church, and acquiesce in the violations.[55] The complete disregard for state and federal law and the arrogation of the right to make and enforce its own law is about as anarchical as an organization can get. These groups are discussed in further detail in Chapter 3. The FLDS's attitude, though, is just a more extreme version of the pervasive belief in the United States that religion is above the law.

**MONTREAL, CANADA.** A 52-year-old man is being tried on charges of sexual assault of a girl who was 10 years old at the time (and is now 15). His defense is religious liberty! He claims that he married the girl under the aegis of the evangelical Christian sect he started. Therefore, to his way of thinking, he had a legal marriage, the prosecution imposed on his free exercise of religion and therefore he could not be charged with sexually assaulting his wife.[56] The girl tells a very different story of childhood sexual abuse, lasting for several years, while the mother apparently knew nothing of the abuse. The story is a typical clergy pedophile story, which started out as charity and ended in tragedy. The family was in dire straits, with the mother homeless and the children taken from her. Acting the Good Samaritan, the man helped the mother find employment and then restore her custody of her children. He paid for utilities and dental bills and even took vacations and shared the holidays with them. He even attended parent-teacher conferences at the girl's school. They were needy, and apparently he took advantage of every angle to supply himself with a trusting mother, who worked long hours, and a young, vulnerable girl.

WOODLAND, CALIFORNIA. For those not familiar with the Jehovah's Witnesses, they are the individuals who are seen handing out the *Watchtower* publication in public places. They are a closely knit organization. Read how one member explained the group on national television:

> [A]s a Jehovah's Witness, you associate only with members in good standing. And that leaves you in a position where everybody you know, everybody you trust, everybody you've ever known or trusted, is somebody who's inside that organization. The threat of being thrown out of that and shunned from them is one powerful enough [to keep victims of abuse silent when told to do so by the organization].[57]

There has been a rule that no charge of abuse would be believed unless there were two eyewitness accounts,[58] a standard that is usually impossible to satisfy when the crime is adult-on-child sexual abuse.

In a complaint filed in 2003, Daniel West and two others alleged that Timothy Silva, a leader of a Jehovah's Witnesses "adolescent book studies", sexually abused them. By the time the three alleged victims were ready to file charges, the criminal and civil statute of limitations had long since expired. Fortunately, they were able to take advantage of California's one-year window during 2003 that repealed the statute of limitations for civil actions involving childhood sexual abuse, no matter when the abuse occurred.[59] According to the complaint, West was 13 years old when the molestation occurred, and while the church knew about it, it did nothing and did not notify the authorities. Indeed, the church appears to have taken the offensive and accused him of "participating in homosexual activity."

Another one of Silva's alleged victims, Shane Pence, claimed to have been sexually attacked for five years, starting at the tender age of seven. When his mother reported the abuse to the church, the family was warned not to contact the authorities and assured that the church would deal with the issue. The church, in a fashion prototypical of other churches in these cases, did not notify the police, according to the complaint, which is still pending.[60]

The same pattern was evident in the abuse cases of Heidi Meyer and Amber Long, who told Connie Chung that the Witnesses threatened "excommunication," or as they call it, "disfellowship," if they told the police.[61] When Meyer filed suit, the congregation and Watchtower, the Witnesses' parent organization, raised the First Amendment as a defense, and the court ruled in their favor. Employing reasoning that is indefensible in an ordered society, the court ruled that neither the congregation nor *Watchtower* had a duty to protect the children, because they had "acted within their constitutional right to religious freedom, which includes the authority to 'independently decide matters of faith and doctrine' and 'to believe and speak what it will.'"[62] A church does have a right to speak and believe at will, but it has no right to use those beliefs to justify illegal conduct. In effect, this reading of the First Amendment immunizes actions that display callous disregard for society's most important norms.

One former elder, Bill Bowen, now runs www.silentlambs.org, a website to assist victims of childhood sexual abuse within the Jehovah's Witnesses. Bowen claims to have spoken to over 6,000 victims of abuse by the Witnesses. He says there is a pattern in the abuse cases: When victims went to the elders, they were told to keep the abuse secret, and the abusers were permitted to remain in the fold.[63] Sometimes the girls reporting the abuse were banished from their close-knit congregations and denied contact with fellow members thereafter.[64] Those outside the Witnesses' world are considered part of Satan's world, so these girls were thrown into a society they had been taught is evil and debased.[65] Despite the lurid facts involving defenseless children, the Witnesses typically argue that the institution has a First Amendment right to avoid criminal and civil liability. Along with other religious organizations, they have succeeded to date in Maine[66] and Connecticut[67] in persuading courts that applying neutral principles of law to their actions would require them to inquire into the defendants' beliefs. They have also won the right, purportedly under the First Amendment, to shun disfavored members.[68]

I will explain in Part Two how erroneous this reasoning is, but suffice to say, the courts that have reached these conclusions have felt that they were backed into a corner by the reality of the harm and a misunderstanding of free-exercise guarantees. The Supreme Judicial Court of Maine clearly stated that it understood the "enormity" of the harm done to children where sexual abuse is "inflicted in the context of religious activities," followed by a rote recitation of the principle that judicial examination of a religious organization's conduct is "wholly forbidden by the Free Exercise Clause of the First Amendment."[69] The good news, as I will discuss in Part Two, is that an increasing majority of the state courts contemplating the weighty evidence of massive misconduct by religious institutions has figured out that the First Amendment is not a haven for scoundrels, but rather consistent with the rule of law and the rule of no harm.

SPRINGFIELD, MISSOURI. A Roman Catholic Church priest, Rev. Michael Brewer, hosted Michael Gibson and a friend for a sleepover to watch movies in the rectory. Michael alleged that, at some point in the morning, Brewer fondled him sexually. When Michael's parents contacted the diocese to complain, they were allegedly told that "this happens to young men all the time." The diocesan authorities added that Michael "would get over it," and suggested the Gibsons work it out with Brewer themselves. When they heard about other boys suffering the same treatment from Brewer, and complained again, the diocese told them that Brewer had done no more than give Michael "an innocent pat on the butt," that they should "forgive and forget," and that they should move on. The Gibsons filed a lawsuit against Brewer and the diocese that cited nine neutral principles of law that would have been invoked and applied to the defendants were they a teacher who fondled a child and a school that knowingly placed children in the reach of a pedophile: "battery, negligent hiring/ordination/retention, negligent failure to supervise, negligent infliction of emotional distress, intentional infliction of emotional distress, breach of fiduciary duty, conspiracy, agency liability, and independent negligence of the Diocese."[70] The defendants denied the allegations and sought the protection of the First Amendment.

In one of the more extreme and unfortunate decisions in the country, the Missouri Supreme Court held that the First Amendment immunized the defendants from the law. According to the court, the action could not go forward, because the courts were not permitted to "[a]djudicat[e] the reasonableness of a church's supervision of a cleric – what the church 'should know'–... this would create an excessive entanglement, inhibit religion, and result in the endorsement of one model of supervision."[71] Thus, a pedophile and a religious institution covering for him were relieved of any civil liability for their actions on the basis of supposed First Amendment principles.

PORTLAND, OREGON. Franklin Richard Curtis was an 87-year-old high priest of the Church of Jesus Christ of Latter-day Saints when he allegedly sexually abused Jeremiah Scott in 1990 and 1991. Scott was 11 years old at the time, which yields a 76-year difference between the two. Scott sued the church in 2001, alleging that the church knew that Curtis had abused a minimum of five other children in one ward but had not warned anyone.[72] Nor were the police notified, according to the complaint. In another ward, the bishop also allegedly knew of Curtis's pedophilic tendencies, but remained silent, because Curtis repented. The worst part of the story is next: the complaint alleges that when Curtis asked to live with a family during his last days, Jeremiah's mother, Sandra Scott, offered her home, and the bishop who knew Curtis's past told her only that it was not a good idea – not that she was bringing a pedophile into her home. Because of a shortage of bed space, Curtis ended up sleeping in Scott's bed with him, and for six months, Curtis allegedly abused Scott on a nightly basis.

The court hearing Scott's case ordered the church to produce any and all records involving childhood sexual abuse in its files. In what seems like a scripted response by a U.S. religious organization to claims of internal childhood sexual abuse, the church declared it had a First Amendment right to keep its records secret. Before it had to produce the records, the church settled the case for $3 million. The church's lawyer, Von G. Keetch, declared that the case "lacked merit" and the settlement reflected only a desire to end costly litigation.[73] One can only wonder at the temerity of religious institutions that have been accused of such specific crimes and torts yet insist they are settling individual *nuisance* suits for millions of dollars.

NEW YORK, NEW YORK. This is a classic case of pedophilic behavior by a trusted clergy member – where the law worked as it should. Seventh Day Adventist pastor Brian N. Savage was charged with aggravated criminal sodomy, two counts of criminal sodomy, two counts of aggravated indecent solicitation of a child, and aggravated indecent liberties with a child for the sexual crimes he committed against a 13-year-old boy, whom he had groomed to be his victim. At the time of the molestation, Savage was 44, and the victim was one of his parishioners. Savage was friendly with the victim and began to take on a fatherly demeanor with him. They emailed each other, with Savage writing, "You are like a son to me," and signing off, "Love, Dad." In the midst of this love and affection, he sodomized the boy. Some of the sexual abuse occurred in the church. He pled guilty and was sentenced to 200 months, or roughly 16.6 years, in prison.[74] Of course, there were other victims. For those victims, Savage pled guilty and was sentenced to an additional five years.[75]

SALT LAKE CITY, UTAH. Lynette Earl Franco was allegedly abused in 1986 when she was seven years old by 14-year-old boy. They were both members of the same local ward of the Church of Jesus Christ of Latter-day Saints. For seven years, she repressed the memory, but when she reached her teens, she needed counseling. She and her parents sought assistance from the local ward, where they were allegedly told to "forgive, forget, and seek Atonement." When they asked for a referral to a mental health professional, the parents claim their local bishop, Dennis Casaday, and president, David Christensen, suggested a "doctor," whose business card included the phrases, "Individual, Marital, and Family Counseling" and "General Psychiatry." The problem with the doctor, according to the Francos, was that he was not a psychiatrist, and his advice to Lynette and her parents was to forgive the perpetrator, forget the incidents, and to avoid going to the police. When they independently found a mental health professional, that person reported the sexual abuse to the police, after which their fellow Mormons "ostracized and denigrated" Lynette. They left the Church, and sued the Church, Casaday, Christensen, and Browning (along with the Bountiful Health Center where he "practices") for clerical malpractice, gross negligence, negligent infliction of emotional distress, breach of fiduciary duty, intentional infliction of emotional distress, and fraud.[76]

The church and other defendants won on all theories. The Supreme Court of the State of Utah found that the first three claims were barred by the First Amendment's Establishment Clause, on the theory that it would have required the court to delve into LDS beliefs. The court was right that clerical malpractice is not a legitimate theory, because it invites the courts to determine the standards of care for a clergy member of a particular religious order. Courts are not allowed to determine or set beliefs within a religious organization, and clerical malpractice is too close for comfort under the First Amendment. On the other theories, however, the court's reasoning was far less persuasive. The court read the various negligence theories as duplications of the clergy malpractice claim, but that is a fundamental misunderstanding of the law. Clerical malpractice claims would force the courts to ask what the religious entity would have its clergy do, but negligence requires a determination of what the "reasonable person" in the circumstances would do. If the person acts unreasonably and has a duty to act reasonably, he or she is liable for damages. The reasonable person here would not have aided in perpetrating a fraud against a vulnerable sex-abuse victim. At least one hopes that is true! The court would not have needed to determine the church's beliefs to reach a negligence holding, but rather would have had to apply neutral principles to factual action, regardless of motivation.

The court also rejected the other claims, because the defendants' actions were not sufficiently "outrageous," and because the complaint failed to allege that Casaday and Christensen knew that Browning was not a licensed psychiatrist. Not every state would have ruled the same way, but the moral to this case is "believer beware." Courts can bend over backward to make sure the religious are protected from accountability for their bad actions.

**VIRGINIA, MARYLAND, PENNSYLVANIA.** The scariest pedophiles are not the "Stranger Danger" many of today's adults were warned about as children, but rather "nice" guys who know how to operate at a child's level. Religious pedophiles, like all pedophiles, exploit whatever pathways they can to obtain victims, and the Internet is a favored path. In this case, a Seventh-day Adventist pastor, Barry William Katzer, lured a Virginia boy to meet him in person after spending four weeks conversing with him in an Internet chat room. Katzer picked up the boy and took him to a Maryland motel, where he sexually abused the boy amidst pornographic magazines and tapes.[77] Only an anonymous call to the police about suspicious activity at the hotel stopped the abuse. Katzer was sentenced to 11 months in jail after admitting he had sex with the boy.[78] Every abused child should have such a guardian angel.

There has not yet been a religious organization that has defended internal childhood sexual abuse on the ground that it believed in such abuse. Rather, these cases are about adults misusing their positions of authority to prey on trusting children and religious institutions turning a blind eye to heinous crimes, immoral actions, and the victims' deforming pain. There is no good argument to treat either the perpetrators or their institutional aides and abettors any differently than any other

entity harming children. The First Amendment was not intended to foster social irresponsibility by religious institutions.

The medical neglect cases discussed next are quite different. In these
cases, children sometimes die of untreated medical ailments, but the parents defend themselves on the ground that their actions were compelled
by their belief in prayer over modern medicine. The question is posed
whether parents can make martyrs of their children.

*Medical neglect*

Religions like the First Church of Christ, Scientist, commonly known
as Christian Science, that rely on faith rather than medicine to cure illness have obtained a number of exemptions in the states from laws that
normally protect children. For example, all states except Mississippi and
West Virginia permit parents to refuse to vaccinate their children on religious grounds.[79] Many have exemptions from newborn testing.[80] There
are also many exemptions from the requirement of providing medical
care to a sick child.

The federal government is partly at fault for the many state exemptions permitting the medical neglect of children. From 1974 to 1983,
the states were required to enact such exemptions to qualify for federal funding related to children.[81] In other words, the states would not
receive federal funding unless they instituted exemptions. It was a classic carrot-and-stick approach, and roughly 30 states plus the District of
Columbia now have exemptions for religious parents from the medical
neglect laws. In effect, this means that faith-healing parents need not obtain medical care for their children unless the children are near death or
permanent disability,[82] and even then, in some states, the parents may be
immunized from manslaughter or felonious murder charges. From the
children's perspective, the harm is even more imminent than it would
be if the parents were acting out of secular motivation, because in too
many circumstances, the parents either do not recognize serious illness
and imminent death, or they hold the misguided belief that they should
not be subject to the law. Whether they see imminent harm or state interference, they may be motivated to hide their extremely ill children
from the authorities whose job it is to ensure that children do not die or

suffer permanent disability from medical neglect. The result is suffering, unnecessary death, and the martyrdom of children who have not been permitted to reach adulthood when they could make an informed choice to live or die for their religious beliefs.

Some may argue that parents have a right to teach their children any religious belief they choose, and they would be correct. But parents do not have an unfettered right to act in ways that harm their children, even if they are acting on religious beliefs. It is now well settled that religious motivation is no defense to illegal conduct. In addition, the Supreme Court has explained that children have rights independent of their parents:

> Parents may be free to become martyrs themselves. But it does not follow that they are free, in identical circumstances, to make martyrs of their children before they have reached the age of full legal discretion when they can make that choice for themselves.[83]

The preeminent right is the right to live, so the exemptions do raise some interesting constitutional questions whether a child might well have a constitutional (as well as a statutory) right to receive medical treatment despite the parents' beliefs. At the very least, the Constitution does not prohibit the states from mandating medical treatment for seriously ill children of faith-healing parents. The religious entities' capacity to avoid the child-welfare laws is derived from their political power and moxie, not any constitutional right.

Despite the value normally placed on life in this society, and the many laws that deter individuals from causing or permitting others to die, states frequently provide religious exemptions when the victim is a child. While abortion has the attention of the American public, deaths of children arising from religiously motivated conduct have not galvanized the people. The problem is education. Few – other than those who benefit and the legislators that grant the benefit – know about or understand the exemptions or their consequences. Yet, exemptions for medical neglect are pervasive. A total of 32 states provide a defense for felonious child neglect, manslaughter, or murder, where the child's life was sacrificed for religious reasons, as well as a religious defense for misdemeanors arising from physical harm to children resulting from medical neglect.[84] When a child dies as a result of the parents' religious motivation, at least one court has taken the position that the contrast between civil exemption from abuse and generally applicable homicide laws creates enough uncertainty to deny the religious defendant due process of law.[85] In other words, the current rule in Florida is that an exemption from civil or lesser causes of action for medical neglect entails an exemption from related crimes. To be clear, these exemptions are not benign grants of religious liberty with no victims. They mean that religious parents and caretakers may not be charged with the crimes specified when their child dies from lack of readily available medical treatment. The exemptions erase the deterrence function of the criminal laws and enable devout adult believers who would martyr their children for the parents' faith to remain a serious risk to children. They also send a message that it is acceptable to let one's child die, if the death is the result of the parents' belief, which is to say, the child's life is not all that valuable. These exemptions are particularly ironic in states with strong antiabortion measures. It is a familiar lament among children's advocates that many in the United States value a fetus's right to live more than a child's.

The Christian Scientists have put significant pressure on state and federal legislatures for the purpose of obtaining exemptions from the medical neglect laws,[86] although they are not always the only religious entity that benefits.[87] As the number of exemptions shows, they have been quite successful. Christian Science theology teaches that modern medicine is unnecessary, because "[h]ealth is not a condition of matter, but of Mind," and that illness is evidence of sin that needs to be treated by prayer.[88] Yet, Christian Science leaders claim that their theology does not prohibit medical care, which implies that believers have a choice between medical care and prayer alone.[89] Indeed, when challenged, they will defend their faith by saying that prayer is not the only option, just the preferred option. For example, a teenage girl had a broken ankle and was asked by her parents what she "wanted to do – pray or go to a hospital. [She] felt prayer was reliable."[90]

If one follows the logic of this supposed choice, it also seems to imply that deaths by medical neglect are not the responsibility of the church.[91] The Church can and will say the parents had a choice. Yet, the failure to rely on prayer alone is looked upon as a serious spiritual failing, and Christian Science practitioners often chide worried parents not to give into the temptation to obtain medical attention and to pray more fervently, which translates into a message that those who face the most dire medical emergencies are holier if they avoid medical treatment.[92] An editor of the *Christian Science Sentinel* wrote that the "most impressive and persuasive ways [to show their children God loved them] often had to do with turning to God for *healthcare*. Children remember being healed, thanks to prayer alone, of children's diseases, organic problems, hernia, mononucleosis, serious sports injuries."[93] In Mary Baker Eddy's words, "The habitual struggle to be always good is unceasing prayer,"[94] a sentiment that has been translated by contemporary Christian Scientists to mean that "[d]isease really has mental roots. If you go to the root of the problem in thought – and fear is usually a factor – you'll eliminate it."[95] Moreover, the institution supports, trains, and provides faith-healing caretakers to offer end-of-life care. These caretakers are deemed "practitioners" and "nurses," although they may have no medical training, and if they do, must renounce it.[96] Christian Science treatment centers are, in fact, hospices where no medical science is practiced and no pain medication is provided, but minimal bodily needs are tended to as the patient expires.[97] They are supported in no small part through medicare funding.

Historically, Christian Scientists have put a great deal of effort into seeking exemptions from federal and state laws that would otherwise hold faith-healing parents accountable for harm done to their children.[98] They testified and argued in favor of the federal Regulation – now repealed – that forced states to enact medical neglect exemptions in order to obtain federal aid.[99] They also have been active in state legislatures.[100] At least one of their former members is trying to put a stop to the Christian Scientists' efforts. Rita Swan, a former Christian Scientist whose 16-month-old son, Matthew, died of spinal meningitis as a result of religiously motivated medical neglect, now lobbies to protect children from faith healing. She and Seth Asser, M.D. (Dept. of Pediatrics at U.C.S.D. School of Med.), cowrote an article detailing the deaths of more than 200 children from medical neglect during the years 1975–95.[101]

Even when there is an exemption for faith healing, the state typically will intervene to protect the child if they know about the child's situation. That does not mean children survive faith healing. A religious exemption permits the religious parent to initiate care on the basis of prayer alone, and getting the parent to move off that path onto the path of medical care can be difficult. Thus, if the untreated child of faith-healing parents noticeably starts to decline, it is often the case that the believers will actively attempt to keep the child from view so as to avoid state intervention.

When a child dies of a treatable medical ailment resulting from faith healing, practitioners (and churches) often raise a First Amendment defense, even to criminal charges. There are two legal regimes governing medical neglect across the states – those that treat religious parents like other citizens, and hold them accountable, and those that exempt the faith-healing parent or church and therefore make them unaccountable for the harm they inflict on an untreated ill child. The first illustrates the principles of the rule of law and the no-harm principle I will develop in Part Two. The second shows overzealous state legislatures that have confused liberty with lawlessness and sacrificed children on the altar of religious anarchy.

Oregon, beginning in 1995, exempted faith-healing parents from its criminal laws, which is to say religiously motivated parents could raise an affirmative defense to criminal liability simply by proving their belief in prayer alone to heal.[102] In 1997 and 1998, the Followers of Christ Church in Oregon City, Oregon, allowed three children to die of medical neglect. During the subsequent investigation, authorities discovered a cemetery of 78 children, and the alarm bells began to ring. Medical authorities estimated that 21 of the deceased children could have been saved by routine medical care, and 38 died before their first birthday.[103] Prosecutors were determined to convict those responsible for the infant deaths, but were stymied by Oregon law that allowed individuals who let their children die as a result of their religious beliefs to use their faith as a defense in homicide and child abuse prosecutions.[104] "It is an affirmative defense to a charge of [criminal homicide by neglect or maltreatment] that the child or dependent person was under care or treatment solely by spiritual means pursuant to the religious beliefs or practices of the child or person or the parent or guardian of the child or person."[105] Prosecutors, and the public, were outraged. Children were dying for no good reason. Yet, a bill that was introduced to make religious parents accountable for the death of a child failed in most regards. Despite the overwhelming amount of factual evidence, Oregon continues to maintain a religious exemption for felony murder, which means the most serious available charge against a parent who lets a child die of a treatable medical ailment is second degree manslaughter.[106] Oregon's failure to repeal the affirmative defense for the most serious crimes devalues the lives of children who die at the hands of their religious parents.

In contrast, California legislation places religious parents and care-takers on a level playing field with all others who commit manslaughter. Laurie Grouard Walker, who was a Christian Scientist, treated her four-year-old daughter for bacterial meningitis solely with prayer, and the child died. When the Sacramento District Attorney's Office filed criminal charges against the mother, she argued that she was "absolutely protected" from criminal liability by the religion clauses of the federal and California constitutions. The mother and the church (which was not a defendant, but filed a friend-of-the-court brief in support of the mother) also claimed that the court must consider the least restrictive alternative for punishing her. They argued that criminal liability was too burden-some on religious belief and that civil dependency proceedings would further the government's interest in a way that was less burdensome on the mother's religious beliefs. In other words, the mother argued that she need not be criminally liable for the preventable death of a child, because the death was a result of religiously motivated conduct, and that civil penalties would be sufficient. In other words, the sole frame of ref-erence was supposed to be the adult believer's faith, rather than the best interests of the child. The court rejected these arguments, because the interest in deterring the death of children was so high, and held that there is no less restrictive or more effective way to deter parents from letting their children die.[107] Even so, the mother reached an agreement with the district attorney that amounted to no jail time, less than five years' probation, a $300 fine, and community service. In addition, her teenage daughter was to be permitted to choose between her mother's beliefs and modern medical science.[108] Considering she permitted a child to die, the failure to sentence this mother to any jail time is troubling,[109] but at least criminal liability attached to a parent's actions that culminated in the death of her child.

Similar arguments were raised in a suburban Minneapolis, Minnesota, case where a divorced, Christian Science mother let her son die the ag-onizing death of an untreated diabetic. Had he been seen by a medical professional during the last weeks of his life, Ian Lundman's symptoms would have been easily diagnosed as diabetes. Insulin, administered as late as a few hours before death, would have saved him. Yet, his mother entrusted him to Christian Science caretakers, who cared for him by "reading hymnals to him." His condition worsened to the point that his mother knew she should seek outside help, but she did not. The boy died after three days of excruciating suffering. The father, who no longer subscribed to the Christian Science faith, had left the family before Ian became ill. When he learned of his son's death, he sued his wife, the church, and the practitioners who treated Ian for wrongful death. Following a seven-week trial, a jury awarded the father $14.2 million – $5.2 million in compensatory damages and $9 million in punitive damages, an award that had tremendous deterrence potential.[110]

Compensatory damages are awarded to redress the actual harm to the victim, while punitive damages are granted for reprehensible behavior that deeply offends U.S. values. The defendants raised a religious defense to the award, arguing that the damages were precluded by their free-exercise rights. While the court properly found that the mother and the Christian Science practitioners did not have a free-exercise right to avoid damages for their conduct, it absolved the church. The appellate court held that the church had no duty to Ian, because "[t]o rule otherwise would make too much of the consequences of the church's adherence to and promotion of its core tenet." The church that inculcated the dangerous beliefs was held harmless, while the mother and the practitioners did have a duty to the child. In other words, the court ruled that a sect's beliefs can immunize it from responsibility for the natural consequences of its members' actions. Though it would not hold the church accountable for the death, the court found that it was perfectly proper for "disputes involving the consequences of religious-based conduct [to] be brought before the civil courts where, as here, the underlying lawsuit is not a vehicle for attacking religious belief."[111] With respect to the church, this was a pyrrhic victory, at best.

The Minnesota Supreme Court reversed the punitive damage award, but allowed the compensatory damages (then reduced by the trial court to $1.5 million) to stand. The punitives were rejected because of the religious character of the neglect: "We do not grant churches and religious bodies a categorical exemption from liability for punitive damages. But under these facts, the risk of intruding – through the mechanism of punitive damages – upon the forbidden field of religious freedom is simply too great."[112] This is indefensible reasoning. In effect, the court ruled that religiously motivated individuals who let children die extremely painful deaths do not need to be deterred. The opposite is in fact true. Religious conduct occupies no "forbidden field," but rather stands shoulder-to-shoulder with all other conduct that engenders the same harm. The question was whether the behavior was so reprehensible as to deserve punitives. Obviously, a jury thought so.

Sometimes the state gives up, even when the child is in plain danger. While the Church of Jesus Christ of Latter-day Saints does not endorse faith healing alone, some adherents disfavor medical treatment.[113] During the fall of 2003, a drama began in the state of Utah involving Mormon parents, and their 12-year-old son, Parker Jensen, who was diagnosed with Ewing's sarcoma, which is a lethal cancer. Doctors recommended chemotherapy, and gave him a 70 percent chance of surviving with the treatment, and only 20 percent without it.[114] His parents, Daren and Barbara Jensen, refused the treatment, saying he did not have cancer[115] and several days later asserted that the treatment would make him sterile and impede his growth.[116] They fled Utah and were wanted for kidnapping, but when they voluntarily returned, the state announced it would not seek custody of the boy for medical purposes, because the Jensens agreed to abide by the recommendations of an oncologist. When the state backed out of the picture, and the oncologist recommended nearly a year of chemotherapy and a bone marrow test, they once again asserted the cancer did not exist and refused to follow the doctor's recommendation. The Utah legislature has responded to the drama by pursuing a bill that would increase parents' rights to deny medical treatment to their children.[117]

Infants have no chance when their religiously motivated parents do not feed them. There is a recurring belief on the part of a small but significant number of religious parents that a baby should not be defiled by ordinary sustenance. One pregnant mother, Karen Robidoux, who was a member of a cult called "The Body," submitted to her sister-in-law's "vision from God" that required her to take her infant son Samuel (who was the son of the cult's leader, Jacques Robidoux) off of solid food and to revert back to breast milk only. "Dubbed The Body, the isolationist group believes in paddling children as young as one and rejects the authority of the government and doctors."[118] The mother was relegated to the basement and threatened with losing her unborn child if she did not follow the prophecy. When her body stopped producing adequate milk for him, baby Samuel wasted away and eventually died just before his first birthday. The mother was acquitted by a jury of second-degree murder, because she claimed that she had been brainwashed and lacked the requisite intent. Instead, the jury convicted her of assault and battery. Her sister-in-law pled guilty to being an accessory to assault. In contrast, a jury convicted the baby's father of first-degree murder, and he received life in prison for the death of his son.[119] That was precisely the right result for the father. Prosecutors are still shaking their heads, however, over the fact that the mother received only assault and battery for letting her son die day-by-day of starvation.[120]

*Abandonment*

Sometimes religiously motivated neglect takes the form of abandonment. There is no better example than the practices of the polygamous FLDS community, the older members of which routinely leave their compounds to take teenage boys to large cities, where they are dropped off on a corner with no money and no means of surviving. They have been dubbed the "lost boys."[121] The abandonment is necessary to ensure that the older men can successfully obtain numerous younger women as their wives. It is pure math: If the young boys stay, they will compete for the available women. If the boys are abandoned, the older men's odds increase dramatically. Some of the boys have sued, and the FLDS's response has been the First Amendment, with one of the church's legal representatives telling one reporter, "There is no exception in the First Amendment for minors."[122] Nor is there an exception in family law for the religious abandonment of children. In fact, there is no First Amendment principle that protects any organization, religious or not, from discarding its children at will. Parents have responsibilities to their underage children, and any interpretation of the First Amendment that says otherwise has hijacked fundamental principles in an ordered society. The Utah attorney general, Mark Shurtleff, has considered filing charges against the parents, but no charges have yet been filed.[123] In this era, one can never overestimate the likelihood that an elected official will fail to hold religious entities accountable.

*Physical abuse*

There are times when spiritual care is in fact physical abuse, and children are severely hurt. In the following case, an exorcism led to a child's death. In Milwaukee in 2003, a storefront church of few members in Milwaukee gathered around 8-year-old Terrance Cottrell, Jr., during extended services with the intention of exorcising his autism. The child fought the members' (including his mother's) hands that restrained him, while the pastor, Ray Anthony Hemphill, pressed his knee against the boy's chest. After three weeks of meetings, the child quieted down, but when the 12th ceremony ceased, the boy could not be revived, because he had died of suffocation. Hemphill defended himself on the grounds that he was engaging in a religious practice to no avail, but his religious motivation seems to have softened the prosecutor's will. A jury convicted him of child abuse, and he was sentenced to 30 months in prison and barred from performing exorcisms for 10 years without formal training in the practice.[124] He should have been charged with reckless homicide at the least, but the prosecutor did not have whatever it takes to do what is right: this man's deeds killed this boy, and their religious quality does not alter that fact one iota.

It is tempting to trust one's own clergy with one's child, but clergy, like anyone else offering care for a child, can be hazardous. A pastor at the Third Christian Church in Overbrook in Philadelphia, the Rev. Javan McBurrows, opened his home to Erika Daye's four-year-old son, Michael, and two siblings at a time when she was having difficulties coping.[125] She was one of his parishioners. Known as a man who believed in strict discipline, McBurrows had certain house rules, including a rule that children had to close their eyes when they entered the bathroom. When Michael did not close his eyes one day and saw another child on the toilet, McBurrows responded with a vicious beating. He swung a metal-edged carpenter's level (which is a straight metal bar hollowed out on the inside like a long, thin rectangle) at Michael 6 to 10 times, and then forced the toddler to walk on his injured legs. He then commanded the boy to walk outside and rubbed snow in his face, according to testimony by his wife. That night, Michael died of multiple traumas. McBurrows immediately packed up his family and drove to Stone Mountain, Georgia, where he was arrested. The initial charge was first-degree murder, which could have led to the death penalty. At a nonjury trial, he was convicted of third-degree murder and then sentenced to 22 to 45 years in prison.[126] Anyone – religious or not – who does that to a child deserves to be in prison at least that long. Life would have been more appropriate.

Choosing a religious camp rather than a secular camp does not necessarily increase the odds that a child will be safe. Discipline, in particular, can be harsh. A summer Bible camp in Texas put a 12-year-old boy, Louie Guerrero, in the intensive care ward for a week with near kidney failure and in need of a blood transfusion. Camp operators Joshua and Caleb Thompson severely beat the boy with a switch from a tree to "get the devil out of [him]."[127] A jury convicted the men of serious injury to a child and aggravated assault. At the sentencing phase, the two men argued they should receive probation rather than prison time. Properly, Joshua received 26 years for beating the boy and Caleb received 14 years for holding him down.[128] Whatever their motivation, the boy's injuries justified stiff sentences for the abuse.

Although most of American society has moved away from it, corporal punishment is still a tenet of some religious organizations. Neil E. Edgar and Christy Y. Edgar, the leaders of a small Kansas City church, God's Creation Outreach Ministry, disciplined their nine-year-old son, Brian, by wrapping him in duct tape, only leaving space for his nose. He died by suffocation, as a result of choking on his own vomit.[129] Mother, father, and babysitter all received life sentences.[130] Further investigation into the storefront church led investigators to bring abuse charges against five more women who abused the ministers' children and a family friend. At least two of the women pled guilty and received probation.[131]

Preacher Arthur R. Allen, Jr., was convicted of beating children in the early 1990s and then again in 2002.[132] In the latter case, he engaged in the whippings of two boys, in a ceremony within the church.[133] At trial, he and other members of his House of Prayer congregation refused legal counsel on the ground that they believed corporal punishment was permissible in Georgia and the Bible, and necessary to shore up struggling families. He served three months in jail and was released on ten years' probation. The terms of his probation "allow[ed] him only to hand spank his own children and forbid him from encouraging others to punish their children."[134] Almost immediately upon his release, Allen made it clear he had no intention to follow the conditions of his probation.

Allen declared that he and his fellow believers follow the biblical teaching that "sparing the rod spoils the child." He was rearrested and found guilty of violating his probation, for which he received two additional years in jail.[135] Obviously, the civil authorities had made no impression on him. So long as he demonstrated an intent to abuse children, the state had an obligation to incarcerate and to monitor him.

Religious boot camps typically minister to "at-risk" or "troubled" youth, and are often the last resort for parents desperate to correct their wayward children. In Scottsdale, Arizona, Teen Reach, a faith-based evangelical youth facility that charges approximately $35,000 per year for drug and alcohol rehabilitation, was ordered to close for child abuse when a child was seriously bruised from religiously motivated spanking in 2004. In another instance, four or more adults allegedly held a child, while a fifth lay across his back, in order to deliver a spanking, which is a practice grounded in the organization's textual reading of the Bible. The administrator who ordered the closing, David Matthews of the Arizona State Department of Economic Security, quite correctly reasoned that the religious motivation for the child abuse was irrelevant. "There is no agency in the state that is permitted to beat a child."[136] Teen Reach responded aggressively to the closing, and filed a lawsuit against the state for violating its First Amendment right to the freedom of religion, as well as other claims. It also resolutely refused to obtain a license for its operations. A state judge rejected the argument that Teen Reach was not a child welfare agency, which means it will have to be licensed to reopen. Teen Reach is appealing. At roughly the same time it defied the state's licensing requirement, a bill was introduced into the Arizona legislature that would have exempted faith-based agencies from having to be licensed,[137] which would permit religiously motivated abuse of children to go forward without state knowledge or oversight.

Missouri, which does not regulate faith-based child-care homes, has been home to other troubling religious boot camps, which physically abused their residents, intentionally deprived them of sleep, and even disciplined a child by tying him to the back of a moving vehicle, an ATV, so that he would have to run behind it, and dragged if he fell.[138] These abuses have not been forestalled by Missouri's system of letting religious entities police themselves. "Any child-care facility maintained or operated under the exclusive control of a religious organization" is exempt from state licensing requirements. Instead, the facilities are required to notify parents in writing, for example, that the facility is in compliance with "fire, health and sanitation requirements," that all employees have been subject to background checks, and about the "disciplinary philosophy and policies of the child-care facility; and [t]he educational philosophy and policies of the child-care facility." The facility must undergo annual fire and safety inspections, and submit copies of its written notice to parents to the state, but that is the extent of the state's oversight in the interest of children.[139] It is a system wherein parents either have no helping hand to ensure their children are safe or are complicit in the religiously motivated abuse. The statute operates from a parents' rights perspective, at the expense of children.

A Baker County, Florida, church camp for troubled youth has been cited more than once by children as a place where they suffered abuse. Pastor Wilford McCormick sets strict rules for the campers – little family contact, a minimum year stay, dress codes, no medical or dental treatment unless there is an emergency or it is specially requested by a camp employee, and a five-minute limit on incoming calls with no outgoing calls permitted. The camp was investigated by the state of Florida in 1983 after three runaways charged there was abuse. It was investigated again by a grand jury in 1987, and is now the subject of at least two civil lawsuits. Kirk Griffin and Jason Berglund filed lawsuits in 2003, each saying that they were subjected to repeated demands for oral and anal sex and to cruel physical abuse.[140] Berglund alleged that he was threatened with physical harm if he spoke of the extreme abuse he suffered in 1993 at the age of 12.[141] Griffin alleged he had been abused from 1989 to 1992.[142] Both Berglund and Griffin claimed the alleged abuse occurred after a Baker County grand jury already had disapproved of Camp Tracey for its corporal punishment methods involving handcuffs and ropes. The grand jurors objected to: the use of ropes and handcuffs to restrain children, the fact that the children were forced labor for a private farmer, the limited parental contact, and the inclusion of a convicted felon on the staff.[143] No charges were filed, however, because the existing law was inadequate to hold the camp accountable. McCormick denigrated the report as "bureaucratic harassment,"[144] as though he was the relevant victim.

Instead of amending Florida law to make such camps accountable for the well-being of the children who attend, Florida took the opposite tack.

After the camp complained about having to submit to state licensing, including health and fire inspections, in a classic case of bending to religious interests regardless of the effect on children, Florida exempted religious organizations from those requirements.[145] Children who attend a camp that has been alleged to have permitted child abuse in the past and is not even required to undergo routine fire and safety inspections that any fast-food restaurant would have to permit, are being placed at risk. It is really that simple, and the state of Florida should be castigated for elevating the religious entities' convenience above children's welfare. Any legislator who responds by saying that religious institutions are good for children, and therefore should not have to bear the monetary burden and inconvenience of state inspections of their premises, needs to read this chapter carefully, maybe more than once.

*Failure to provide a safe environment for children*

In the 1970s, states began to require that child-care centers be licensed. Three factors were at work: the growing number of mothers entering the workforce, in-depth studies about the importance of early childhood education, and licensing was a condition of receiving government funds. Areas of coverage included child-to-staff minimum ratios, space requirements (i.e., square footage/child), prohibitions on smoking, certain nutritional guidelines, and minimal health and safety requirements, for example, smoke alarms or sprinklers in large facilities.[146] In recent years, some religious organizations have lobbied to avoid such requirements. Their primary argument – in a nutshell – is that they should not be forced to pay for such requirements, because they are tight on funds and have other priorities for the money. In essence, they are saying that they should be trusted with the health and safety of children, even though they are fighting the laws passed for the intention of protecting children from foreseeable harms.

A church-run day-care center in Antioch, Tennessee, was notified in 2004 that it was not in compliance with the state's neutral, generally applicable licensing requirements for child-care centers. Not only was the center out of compliance, but it also had no intention of obtaining a license, because it claimed to do so would suppress its free-exercise rights.[147] Harold Frelix, Sr., continues to fight the state agency and has vowed to fight the licensing requirements all the way to the U.S. Supreme Court. Such First Amendment arguments often fall on deaf ears, however, luckily for children. A significant number of state agencies have stood behind their licensing requirements, and their courts have supported them.[148] Even so, one can only hope that Frelix does take the issue all the way to the top, and that the Supreme Court takes the case so that it can reiterate one more time that *everyone* must adhere to neutral, generally applicable laws, including regulations enacted for the health and safety of children. It would be helpful for state regulators, and even better for children.

What would not be a victory for children would be if Tennessee were to follow Florida's lead and provide faith-based child-care providers like Frelix a pass on the typical licensing requirements for the health and safety of children. There are a number of states who have done just that.

Three legal regimes make it possible for religious entities to run child-care centers without having to abide by the usual state licensing requirements. First, some states have exempted religious child-care centers from their licensing system altogether. For example, Missouri exempts "[a]ny child-care facility maintained or operated under the exclusive control of a religious organization[,]" so long as the facility receives no state or federal funding.[149] Second, some states require religious child-care centers to register rather than obtain a license. The registration approach typically means that the state is not monitoring the child-care center to ensure the safety and health of children, but rather accepting a registration and taking action only if a complaint is filed. It is passive regulation. The licensing system thus is preventive, while the registration system is reactive at best, which means it may well be too late to protect any particular child.[150] Third, other states require all child-care facilities to meet state standards, religious or not.[151] The first two schemes displace the state's responsibility to ensure the well-being of children with blind deference to religious entities.

As I hope this book makes abundantly clear, that is an assumption that abdicates the welfare of society. It is not that every religious day care will harm children, but some may, and given the prevalence of religious day care recalcitrance to state safety and health regulation, one cannot be certain about child safety. Nor can anyone be certain that any particular denomination or religious leader is safe for children without some licensing requirements. General licensing requirements are neutral and necessary to ensure children's safety is not being sacrificed for budget reasons or other such priorities. When the state acts as a check on abuse or neglect or danger and prescribes reasonable licensing requirements, it is doing precisely what the public good demands.

Other states have enacted religious liberty acts (typically called religious freedom restoration acts, as I will discuss in Part Two), that make it impossible for the state to apply its laws to religious entities unless the law was passed for a compelling purpose and it is the least restrictive means of regulating the child-care center.[152] While only the most extreme defender of religious liberty would argue the state does not have a compelling interest in protecting children from physical harm at day-care centers, legal disputes are likely to center on what is the "least restrictive means" of ensuring that the centers are safe. For example, a large center might argue that even though fire safety is a very strong state interest, the requirement that it install sprinklers is far more restrictive than smoke detectors, because of the cost. This is a theme that runs through much of church/state litigation. If the religious entity has to bear the cost of a legally imposed duty (whether it is criminal or tort liability or regulation), it will argue that its religious mission is undermined. Yet, it is the state's obligation to assess what is necessary to ensure children are safe – and that value transcends whether the owner of the operation is religious or secular.

The problems for children under the state religious liberty acts are still not fully apparent, because the laws have been in place for a relatively short time. None of the states that have taken this route have preserved the laws that protect children, with the lone exception of Pennsylvania, which exempts day care licensing and the duty to report child abuse. Every other Pennsylvania law affecting children is impaired by the act, which is to say that children's rights to life, liberty, and protection from harm by religious entities are at risk in Pennsylvania and every state with a religious liberty protect act.

*Why has U.S. law and society failed these children so miserably?*

This chapter has described a lot of suffering. To those who would argue that these are just the bad apples, that is simply not the case. These are only a very small number of the many, many instances of religious entities putting children's interests second, or even worse. But even if these are only the bad apples, these bad apples are precisely whom the law is intended to deter and punish. Even one child's life sacrificed for an adult's religious beliefs is one too many, and to be sure, there are far more than one.

From the 1960s through the 1980s, during the Chief Justice Earl Warren and Chief Justice Warren Burger Supreme Courts, the religious institutions were coddled to believe that they had special rights under the First Amendment to avoid general laws. Thus, the Supreme Court deserves some of the blame here. As I will discuss in Part Two, there was a brief period in the history of the Religion Clauses where the Supreme Court toyed with permitting religious entities to avoid any law that was not necessary. That encompasses a lot of law. Worse, legislators were led to believe by the high-flying rhetoric that accompanied the Court's free-exercise cases that it was appropriate to exempt religious entities without inquiring into the harm they might cause. This false understanding of free exercise in this ordered society led courts and legislatures down errant and ultimately dangerous paths. It cannot be that the Constitution was intended or crafted in such a way that there is no means for society to deter, redress, or halt child abuse in religious settings. The First Amendment is about freedom from government overreaching, not about finding loopholes for criminals to avoid paying what they owe society. It is a false and dangerous understanding of free-exercise rights to believe that religious entities sit above the society. They are part of it and therefore must be accountable for the harm they cause. The Supreme Court in 1990 clarified its free-exercise doctrine and explained that neutral, generally applicable laws certainly can be applied to religious conduct.[153] There can be no other rule if children's interests are to be adequately protected.

Some states continue down the wrong path and let religious entities off the hook when what is needed is stronger deterrence. For example, a handful of state courts have held fast to the Supreme Court's errant jurisprudence from the 1960s, 1970s, and 1980s, despite the Court's plain and persuasive rejection of the notion that any and all laws that substantially burden religious entities are presumptively unconstitutional. They include: Massachusetts,[154] New York,[155] Minnesota,[156] Alaska,[157] Wisconsin,[158] Washington,[159] Ohio,[160] Maine,[161] North Carolina,[162] and Kansas.[163]

But legal doctrine has not been the only cause of harm to these children. There has also been a long era, at least since 1950, during which the people of the United States have believed as a general matter that religion is always moral and that it is as innocuous as apple pie. This view was fostered in the latter 20th century by Stephen Carter's widely read book, *The Culture of Disbelief*. This Pollyanna understanding of religion sold these children short and cannot be sustained in the face of these facts.

It was also a mistake for prosecutors to permit religious institutions to handle their own "dirty laundry," which happened too often. When that was combined with the typical difficulties attendant upon removing molesters out of the way of children, the deficiencies of the law and its enforcement – from a child's perspective – become apparent.[164] With rare exceptions, the media also gave religious entities a pass. That dirty laundry was the public's problem and needed public airing, and if either had fulfilled their appropriate roles, more children might have been saved from such harm. Blind trust in any human, whether religious or not, is misplaced trust.

It is also a profound fact that power protects power. The religious leaders that were on the A-list, with the influential newspaper editors, and with the powerful legislators, were capable of asking for favors that should not have been granted, but were. The press has been dogged in pursuit of stories about religious institutions' financial improprieties.[165] The children deserve that same devotion from every corner of society.

In the end, society pays when religious entities place themselves above or beyond the law, and thus all of us are victims. When the churches hid the facts about child molesters, they kept these monsters out of prison in the first instance and then permanently when the statute of limitations expired during their prolonged secrecy. When they let a clergy member go, they typically did not alert anyone outside their closed circle that a pedophile would now be on the loose, free to groom and seduce other children at will. That means that former priests can now be found performing karaoke or pumping gas, and living lives with plenty of access to children.[166]

Society is also severely burdened when polygamous sects deprive women of education at the same time they saddle them with multiple children, and society, at large, is further hindered when these same sects abandon their boys to keep the ratio of girls-to-men optimal for the older men. Public assistance too often becomes necessary in both instances – which means the average taxpayer is being forced to prop up the illegal polygamous society. Finally, when faith healers permit children to die or to become permanently disabled, or when fundamentalist disciplinarians permanently injure or kill children, they deprive society of the talent and the good those children could have brought into the world. The cost is enormous, and it is the result of an abundance of religious license, as opposed to liberty. It is also proof positive that religious individuals and institutions cannot be permitted to act as though they have no obligations to the rest of us.

# MARRIAGE

Recent wars of religious power have been intense on the subject of marriage – whether the issue is gay marriage or polygamy. Both topics have earned headlines in the early part of the 21st century, with religious entities intent on imposing their religious viewpoint on public policy. The religious have every right to contribute their religious viewpoints to the public debate and to try to persuade leaders and fellow citizens that their ideas about social problems have merit; wisdom can be found in many corners. But they do not have a right in the United States to mold public policy to their beliefs, and their beliefs alone. The hard choices depend on a more broad-ranging inquiry than any one religious worldview encompasses (even when that perspective is shared by a significant number of individuals and institutions).

The complication in the debates over marriage in 21st century America is that few in government seem to understand or be willing to shoulder their role, which demands significantly more than deference to religious entities. Citizens may speak to them from the heart and soul, but it is up to our elected officials to contextualize the debate by adding the scope of the public good to all public consideration. That is not secularization, as those who would employ religious rhetoric to drown out all discourse might insist, but rather the hallmark of a successful representative democracy. If government officials do not move the conversation off of its solely religious bottom, they have shortchanged everyone, because they have abdicated their responsibilities. To be sure, it is easier to react to religious voices and to give them what they demand. They are, after all, typically quite passionate. But that is no excuse for elected representatives to abandon the public good.

The controversy over marriage has stretched from coast to coast. On the eastern side of the United States, the Supreme Judicial Court of Massachusetts in February 2004 held that the state was required to permit same-sex couples to get married. Fourteen homosexual couples in long-term relationships had challenged Massachusetts's heterosexual-only marriage law.[1] Their argument, which was reflected in the court's opinion, was in a nutshell that their unions were not distinguishable from heterosexual unions. They were monogamous and dedicated, and they nurtured their children. The purposes of Massachusetts's marriage laws were served by their unions, and therefore, Massachusetts's distinction between gay and traditional marriages rested on invidious discrimination on the basis of sexual orientation.[2] The Massachusetts Senate asked the court whether the Massachusetts Constitution would permit it to enact Senate No. 2175, which accorded homosexual couples civil union – but not marital – status. The answer was, "No." After paying lip service to the importance of deferring to legislative judgment in this arena, the court said, "[T]he traditional, historic nature and meaning of civil marriage in Massachusetts is as a wholly secular and dynamic legal institution, the governmental aim of which is to encourage stable adult relationships for the good of the individual and of the community, especially its children. The very nature and purpose of civil marriage, the court concluded, renders unconstitutional any attempt to ban all same-sex couples, as same-sex couples, from entering into civil marriage."[3]

The response from some conservative religious organizations to the original opinion was swift and fierce.[4] To quote: "This decision is on an order of magnitude that is beyond the capacity of words. The court has tampered with society's DNA, and the consequent mutation will reap unimaginable consequences for Massachusetts and our nation."[5] Part of the opposition arose out of deep-seated disapproval of homosexuality, not just of homosexual marriage. For example, according to the Christian Coalition of America, the Massachusetts decision was wrong, because "marriage is one of the last obstacles to the complete normalization of homosexuality in America."[6]

President George W. Bush, who typically has echoed his fundamentalist conservative base on social issues, declared that "Marriage is a sacred institution between a man and a woman."[7] The blame for the decision, according to Bush, lay in an activist judiciary. "If activist judges insist on re-defining marriage by court order, the only alternative will be the constitutional process. We must do what is legally necessary to defend the sanctity of marriage."[8]

Many demanded from a religious standpoint that the federal government take action, which was their right. Unfortunately, some members of Congress followed suit – employing those same religious perspectives – by introducing a (dead-on-arrival) Marriage Protection Amendment (MPA) (formerly known as the Federal Marriage Amendment) that would have banned all gay marriages in the United States, as well as various court-stripping laws that would keep the issue from the "activist" federal courts.[9] Representative Marilyn Musgrave (R – Colo.) spoke more like a pastor in support of the MPA than an elected official:

> The very foundational document of our nation assumes that our rights exist within the context of God's created order. The self-evident differences and complementary design of men and women are part of that created order. We were created as male and female, and for this reason a man will leave his father and mother and be joined with his wife, and the two shall become one in the mystical spiritual and physical union we call "marriage."[10]

Former Rep. William Dannemeyer of California supported a court-stripping bill to protect heterosexual marriage in equally religious language: "Decisions of the federal judiciary over the last half century have resulted in the theft of our Judeo-Christian heritage."[11] For these politicians, their interpretation of the Bible, which for them is the only interpretation, blesses only heterosexual marriage. The snag is that they are (or were) elected representatives charged with serving all Americans, not just those who have a Christian heritage that they believe needs to be preserved.

Religious organizations were not shy about using political muscle in support of pro-traditional marriage proposals. On September 24, 2004, the *Baptist Press* published an editorial in which members were urged to contact members of Congress who were "undecided or who live in districts where the amendment likely would be popular" to urge support of the measures. It appended a list of "high priority" members and their phone numbers, which was compiled by the Family Research Council, for Baptists to contact.[12] Rev. Jerry Falwell initiated a "Save the Sanctity of Marriage" campaign on his ministry's website, where he urged supporters to sign and send a petition to their congressional representative reading:

> I am greatly concerned over recent Canadian and American liberal court rulings in favor of homosexual "marriage," the legalization of sodomy, and other actions damaging the traditional family.
>
> As a voting taxpayer, I fully support Rep. Marilyn Musgraves's proposed Federal Marriage Amendment (H.J. Res. 56) and urge your unwavering support for this legislation.[13]

Catholic ethicist and Princeton professor Robert P. George, writing in the *Wall Street Journal*, insisted that there was a natural law justification for fighting same-sex marriage, when he justified a ban on same-sex marriage on the basis of the self-evident "nature of marriage as a 'one-flesh union' of sexually complementary spouses" and the corresponding self-evident entitlement of mixed-sex marriages to receive "benefits, privileges, rights or immunities" because the spouses are of the opposite sex.[14] Apparently, the physical characteristics of males and females predetermines the law of marriage. His circular reasoning implies that no legislature should consider the issue other than to reach his religiously based conclusion, a conclusion once again that is an argument from theocracy, not public policy. Accordingly, he promoted the idea of a federal constitutional amendment to ban all marriages other than those between a man and a woman, without entering into the debate over what forms of marriage are best for children, the economy, or the public good. His is a revealed legal regime, not a reasoned one.

Once the presumed invincibility of heterosexual marriage was pierced by the Massachusetts decision, and it became necessary to articulate why one man/one woman marriage is important (or not), the subject of polygamy was reintroduced into the public square as well. Some have tried to link the two issues by saying that opening the door to one opens the door to the other, but they have fundamentally missed the point of the legislative role. Constitutional principles can be subject to what is called a "slippery slope" effect, where the granting of one right logically entails the granting of another; those who have argued that judicial recognition of gay marriage demands recognition of polygamy are employing slippery-slope reasoning. For example, the Liberty Counsel in a letter in support of the Federal Marriage Amendment asserted as fact that "[i]f same-sex marriage were sanctioned it would be virtually impossible to ban polygamy."[15] They are speaking to the wrong branch of government, though. In most states, this is a policy and not a constitutional issue. There is no such slippery slope when it comes to crafting public policy on marriage. The legislature is required to determine what elements of marriage best serve the common good, and they must take into account how the arrangement affects children, inheritance, and the culture at large, just for starters. From that perspective, the two challenges to traditional marriage, which are factually quite distinct, are also, for public policy purposes, separate topics for legislative consideration.

In the Western United States, fundamentalist Mormons are actively challenging the laws that ban polygamy.[16] Polygamist Tom Green, who was convicted of bigamy,[17] asked the Supreme Court to hear his constitutional defense of polygamy. The Utah Civil Rights and Liberties Foundation[18] defended the right to polygamous marriage when a couple that sought to add an additional wife were denied a license.[19] They claimed that the three adults had a right to the free exercise of religion to be exempt from the federal and state antipolygamy laws. Their arguments have fallen on deaf judicial ears, as they should, but they provide an excellent example of religious conduct that cannot be vouchsafed by the First Amendment – which incorporates the need to deter and punish conduct that harms individuals and society.

Their arguments belong in the legislative sphere, where many voices – religious, secular, activist, and traditional – can contribute to finding the optimal public policy. If they can persuade a legislature that opening the definition of marriage to include polygamy is consistent with the public good, it can be done. Similarly, if gay rights groups and others can persuade state legislatures that same-sex marriage is in the public interest while those opposed express their views, the legislature has the power to expand the definition of marriage. In response to the Massachusetts decision mandating same-sex marriage, the Alliance for Marriage advocated returning the debate "to the democratic process at the state level authority that is currently being usurped by courts at the request of activist organizations."[20] They are right to look to state legislatures, but they will not avoid the actions of "activist" organizations by removal to the legislature. Indeed, one of the advantages of dealing with these issues in the legislatures rather than the courts is that more voices can be heard. If proponents cannot persuade the legislature that their proposals are consistent with the public good, then neither the First Amendment nor the legislature offer refuge.

Although the resolution of each issue is ultimately a matter for the legislatures, which I will explain in more detail in Part Two, these two social issues represent the two paradigmatic ways religion interacts with the culture. In the gay marriage context, fundamentalist religions have been insisting quite loudly in the public square that their biblical values mandate a particular form of marriage and that their belief should in fact be the law. They are intent on using what political power they have to ensure the law matches their religious worldview.

The polygamy debate is quite different, at least from a constitutional perspective. The polygamists are not trying to impose their beliefs on everyone else. Rather, they are asking for relief from the law that governs everyone else. It is typical, therefore, to hear polygamists talk in libertarian terms and to dwell on the right to be left alone by the government. In contrast, those trying to forestall gay marriage talk in terms of the "Christian tradition" and the necessity of maintaining social order. Despite the differences, though, in the end, both religious entities are trying to shape the law to their religious conduct, and it is the government's obligation to persistently reframe the issues in light of public interest.

*The gay marriage debate: religious liberty is not religious hegemony*

A powerful, mainstream religious voice composed of numerous denominations has denounced the Massachusetts Supreme Judicial Court's decision that the state could not distinguish between homosexual and heterosexual couples to define marriage. The issue was framed as an equality principle, but it charged into the public forum as a debate over morality and religion. Opponents of gay marriage are actually arguing that their religious worldview should determine the country's constitutional law.

The religious opponents of gay marriage would have the country determine the definition of marriage solely by reference to their religious beliefs and traditions, which are typically taken literally from the Bible and their own religious tradition. Relying on the Bible, human biology, and Catholic tradition, a 2003 Vatican document declared that "[t]here are absolutely no grounds for considering homosexual unions to be in any way similar or even remotely analogous to God's plan for marriage and family.... Marriage is holy, while homosexual acts go against the natural moral law."[21] For Orthodox Rabbi Jonathan Rosenberg, whose congregation is in Bexley, Ohio, homosexuality and therefore same-sex marriage is wrong, and "[w]e'll never change our position, based on the Torah... which we consider to be divine; it wasn't manmade."[22] For the Orthodox Jew, according to Rosenberg, same-sex marriage is just one of many public policy issues that are to be addressed through Jewish laws.[23]

Christian fundamentalists, who believe in reading the Bible literally, believe first that homosexuality is a sin and second that gay marriage is as well.[24] One televangelist, Frederick K.C. Price of California, has said that he has "nothing against homosexual individuals," but the Bible is clear that "marriage is a union [between a man and a woman] created and recognized by God" and that "homosexuality is an abomination."[25]

There has been a concerted attempt by those opposed to gay marriage on religious grounds to set up an us-against-them political scene. The "us" is every true American with the right view against same-sex marriage. The "them" are the infidels who believe in same-sex marriage. One of the most active groups against it, the Alliance Defense Fund, which was founded "for the legal defense and advocacy of religious freedom"[26] believes that "God has defined marriage as one man married to one woman . . . [and that] radical activist groups in the U.S. are attempting to twist the law to change the definition of the family to include same-sex 'marriage,' polygamy, and other structures."[27] The Alliance for Marriage, which fights gay marriage, claims to incorporate a broad swath of believers, saying it "cuts across traditional party lines and includes Catholic, Jewish and Muslim leaders as well as ministers in historically black Protestant denominations."[28] In short, the Alliance (note the name) hopes to convey the image that all Americans stand shoulder-to-shoulder with them. Others joining the chorus of disapproval have included Catholics and Orthodox Jews,[29] and "the Southern Baptist Convention, Focus on the Family, several Catholic dioceses, and the Traditional Values Coalition."[30] It is an impressive array, but it does not encompass every Christian or believer in the United States by a long shot.

At the same time, a significant cadre of religious and secular groups opposes the federal amendment, for example, the Human Rights Campaign.[31] Certain Reform and Conservative Jewish groups also are opposed.[32] Thus, the fight over same-sex marriage cannot be drawn on "Christian" or even "Judeo-Christian" lines and certainly does not include all those who would consider themselves part of that tradition. Once the debate cannot be framed by one religious tradition, the door has been opened to a more appropriate public debate over the common good.

In the midst of this debate, there has been a growing refrain that this is a "Christian country." The Supreme Court's decision in *Lawrence v. Texas*, which held that private, consensual sex between adults is protected by the constitutional right to privacy,[33] and the specter of same-sex unions have prompted some religious leaders to pine for what they believe is the "soul" of the country. Theology Professor Harold O. J. Brown put it this way:

[T]here are many vestiges of authentic Christianity still to be found in our nation. But it would be a disaster for Christians and other God-fearers not to recognize that we've reached a turning point in our cultural history, and to go on dreaming that we can gradually change this formerly more or less Christian country for the better.[34]

The "Christian country" claim in this era faces an uphill battle. Harvard Professor of Comparative Religion and Indian Studies Diana L. Eck has written a book entitled, *A New Religious America: How a "Christian Country" Has Become the World's Most Religiously Diverse Nation*,[35] which captures the evolution of religious diversity in the contemporary United States. She describes a Cambodian Buddhist temple opening in the Minnesota farmlands and the Sikh gurdwara in Fremont, California.[36] Despite the attempts to paint this as a solely or predominantly or properly a Christian country, Eck's work, as well as others', leads to the irrevocable conclusion that it is no such thing. If it ever was, it is not now. "Christian country" is a mantra that has become more insistent as the gay marriage battle has raged, indicating that its speakers are not only asserting what they believe as fact, but also attempting to hold onto a vision of the United States that even they, in their most reflective moments, must admit is no longer accurate. For example, Lee Duigon, a freelance writer and contributing editor for the Chalcedon Foundation, said, "many of us have been wondering how, in a supposedly Christian country, we find ourselves watching helplessly, dazedly, as our whole way of life is dismantled, piece by piece, by liberal judges, lawsuit-happy atheists, alleged 'entertainers,' so-called 'educators,' and even out-of-control elected officials."[37] The whole culture has turned against him, it seems. The problem may be, though, not in the country, but rather in the fact that there is no reliable content to the phrase, "Christian country." Those words might have described Britain when the monarchy imposed a religious set of beliefs on the people (Catholic or Protestant), but it does not capture the miraculous blossoming of many varieties of religious beliefs in the United States.

The "Christian country" declaration hides the ball and begs the public policy question all at the same time.

**HIDING THE BALL.** The primary problem with the "Christian country" claim in this context is that it is factually misleading. In truth, not all Christians or Jews oppose same-sex marriage and many are undecided. For example, the Unitarian Universalist Church and the Reconstructionist [Jewish] Rabbinical Association perform same-sex marriages.[38] At the same time, various mainstream dominations have had divisive and spirited arguments over the issue, with the parent organization banning gay unions while individual congregations and pastors have performed them in defiance. For example, a national Episcopalian committee recommended a compromise that would bless same-sex unions at the same time that the church was at odds over the issue of whether or not to confirm an openly gay bishop in New Hampshire.[39] More recently, an Anglican Church commission chastised the Episcopal Church USA for condoning both, but it did not censure the Episcopalians. Indeed, the report sent a double message: on the one hand, there was a "real danger" the two churches would split apart, but on the other hand, the Anglican commission wanted to try "dialogue" before taking any definitive action.[40] Presbyterian Church representatives at their annual meeting only narrowly sustained the rule against same-sex unions, while ministers have openly defied the ban and expressed their intention to bless gay couples in their churches.[41] The Methodists are hardly a united front either. As a body, they have voted to reject same-sex marriages and affirmed their belief that homosexuality is inconsistent with the Bible. Meanwhile, many individual congregations continue to support same-sex unions with dozens of pastors in California presiding over such unions. In the face of that kind of internal rebellion, the church withdrew its original decision to sanction the California pastors.[42] Like the Christians, the Jews are all over the place on this issue, and one cannot always use the believer's denomination to be certain what they believe. Most Reform Jews favor same-sex unions, Conservatives are split, and most Orthodox are adamantly opposed. For instance, at the nation's largest gay and lesbian synagogue, Congregation Beth Simchat Torah in Manhattan, Rabbi Sharon Kleinbaum, issued a call to all clergy, but particularly to rabbis, "to solemnize weddings without a marriage license."[43] When Conservative rabbi Jack Moline, whose synagogue is outside of Washington, D.C., explained the contradictory outlook of his faith, he said:

> [M]y confusion about gay marriage is . . . a conflict between two sets of values. If homosexuality is an orientation and not something that is environmentally conditioned or a matter of choice, then there must be a way for a sacred expression of intimacy for gays and lesbians, as there is for heterosexuals. On the other hand, you can't deny that the weight of our tradition is heavily against such an arrangement.[44]

While Conservative Jews have no provisions to sanctify gay marriage, ceremonies have been performed by individual rabbis. At the opposite end of the spectrum, Orthodox Jewry not only prohibits such expressions, but also supports the federal marriage and court-stripping bills.[45] All of which is to say that a so-called Judeo-Christian tradition has not led to an ineluctable conclusion on the issue of same-sex marriage for millions of believers in the United States. Religion simply cannot resolve this public debate.

Those resting on the "Christian country" formula may reply that they mean "Christian" in their sense, and that all others are not "true" Christians. Yet, that is simply incoherent in the United States' public arena, where the many Protestants (and Catholics) who in fact support gay unions are Christian in any normal sense of the term. No matter how diverse the group claiming that same-sex marriage is opposed to "Christian values," it obviously does not speak for all Christians on this issue. Therefore, the "Christian country" assertion is a nonstarter.

**BEGGING THE QUESTION.** "Christian" has so many connotations that invoking it leads to no particular theological and certainly no public policy conclusion. "Christian" can refer to the set of beliefs that are Catholic, or those that are Protestant, or those that are evangelical, or all of these beliefs taken together. It encompasses disparate cultural worldviews. For example, the Irish Catholics are Christian and so are the white Anglo-Saxon Protestants. "Christian" contains within itself powerful contradictions: The South African Dutch Reformed Church, which supplied the theology on which apartheid was built,[46] is Christian, and so was the Rev. Martin Luther King, Jr., who led the civil rights movement in the United States in the 1960s on religious principles. Slavery in the United States was enforced with Christian maxims, like the following by Jefferson Davis, president of the Confederate States of America: "[Slavery] was established by decree of Almighty God . . . it is sanctioned in the Bible, in both Testaments, from Genesis to Revelation . . . it has existed in all ages, has been found among the people of the highest civilization, and in nations of the highest proficiency in the arts."[47] Truth be told, one can find individual biblical passages that support the practice. For example, Ephesians says:

Slaves, be obedient to the men who are called your masters in this world, with deep respect and sincere loyalty, as you are obedient to Christ: not only when you are under their eye, as if you had only to please men, but because you are slaves of Christ and wholeheartedly do the will of God. Work hard and willingly, but not for the sake of men. You can be sure that everyone, whether a slave or a free man, will be properly rewarded by the Lord for whatever work he has done well.[48]

At the same time, Christians constructed the Underground Railroad that brought thousands of former slaves and their families to freedom.[49] The term "Christian" can equally refer to the harrowing torture of the Inquisition, the impetus behind the Salem witch trials, or Mother Teresa's work in Calcutta. Christianity is present in every one of these examples, which means it is an amorphous term that carries more political punch than one identifiable meaning. In fact, its current political force is built on an assumption that the Unites States is a monolithic and united Christian nation. There is no such thing – America has always been a collection of sects, not a homogeneous people of faith.

The United States is still not a Christian country in the sense those using the phrase want it to mean, because even if every possible meaning were packed into the term, it still would not encompass what this republican form of government aspires to. That is the achievement of the highest public good, which in turn, is determined by representatives who are delegated the responsibility to consider and then determine it in light of current knowledge and experienced problems – not a particular religious viewpoint or writing. It is not an overstatement to say that the phrase "Christian country" in the same-sex marriage context is no more and no less than a political grab for power, rather than a description of any single set of values that could or should determine public policy.

The hard work of this republican form of government cannot be avoided by posting a sign declaring "Christian" on the front lawn of the White House. Representatives, in dialogue with the people, must forge the hard policy choices for every citizen, believer or nonbeliever, Jew, Muslim, Christian, or Wiccan. Their job is to define the social construct of marriage in a way that best serves the needs of the public, and all those who are affected by the marriage law, which is part of an intricate social web. The issues are extraordinarily complex: inheritance, legitimacy, children's rights, property ownership, and taxation, to name a few, and the task is unfortunately quite difficult. Resorting to phrases like "Christian country" does not begin to answer the question.

We in the United States are sometimes blind to what the world already sees. It is a simple fact that those fundamentalists that are insisting that marriage be determined in whole by their religious faith are, at base, trying to drive toleration and pluralism into an oncoming train of a one-faith society. They advocate their own beliefs; everyone else should simply be happy that they are Americans, or perhaps they should just move. This is the sort of parochialism that makes what is a noble constitution in theory the laughing stock of the world. We look hypocritical, and naive.

There is also great inconsistency in the devotion to a one-Christian culture. Ironically, the same groups that push for their faith to determine public policy have pushed for federal commissions to chastise foreign governments like China for their intolerance of a wide variety of religious faiths.[50] The Catholic Church, which has frequently asserted that public policy (including public servants) should be shaped by its religious principles, expressed deep concerns about China's suppression of religious liberty as follows:

> The tools of U.S. diplomacy need to be brought to bear in a broad way to make China's religious prisoners of conscience an undeniable priority in U.S.–China relations. Forming policy to respond to China's violation of religious liberty is not just a matter of utilizing the sanctions available under the International Religious Liberty Act. Rather, it is a matter of making religious liberty a first-level concern of our whole diplomatic effort. Our European friends should be encouraged by all our ambassadors on a daily basis to join the U.S. initiative before the U.N. Human Rights Commission. Trade representatives and business travelers, under State Department or other government auspices, ought to raise the concerns as their own in private talks with their counterparts. The U.S. ambassador to China should pose a question in his every meeting with the Chinese government, and so should his staff, whatever their formal role, whether military attache or commercial officer.[51]

Those who would define marriage solely by the light of their religious belief clearly are not proposing, but rather are trying to impose a theocracy, with their faith at the helm of public policy. Whether intentionally or not, they are dictating a certain governing order that is antithetical to what the Constitution was intended to accomplish. There were Christian theocracies not long before the founding of the United States, in particular in Britain, and they were the negative backdrop against which colonies were established here.[52] Queen Mary forced everyone to be Catholic and then Queen Elizabeth I forced everyone to be Protestant, and they took care of dissent by exterminating those who would not follow their belief mandate. The era when the definitions of Catholic and Protestant could be so pure as to draw an either/or distinction is long past. To now seek a "Christian" culture through the imposition of one religious viewpoint is only a small step from the history intended to be set behind forever.

Many of the early American colonists departed Britain to escape the either/or theological choices posed to them as well as the theocracies that blended sovereign and religious power to control the people's beliefs. To claim that a set of beliefs is Christian is not to immunize oneself from the charge of theocracy. Indeed, in this pluralist society, the pressure by a subset of Christians to push for a single moral vision under the heading of "Christian" cannot be characterized other than as a drive to institute a theocracy in their own image. In short, their arguments, which are intended to summon references to the flag, mom, and apple pie, in fact are quite dangerous to a free America.

In any event, it is a request no legislature in the United States can honor, either in form or content, because the Constitution forbids elected representatives to act solely for religious purposes. The country cannot craft social institutions on the basis of a particular belief system, even if it is some form of Christianity. The government has to look more broadly than the religious views of some citizens to see whether the social construction of marriage is consistent with the public good.

The theocratic arguments against gay marriage will not wash in the United States, and the religious entities opposed will either learn this through self-education or the expensive route of pursuing the issue through the courts. This, however, is not to say that gay marriage must be embraced as a constitutional matter across all states. The states have wide latitude.

First, the U.S. Supreme Court, when it held that private consensual sexual conduct between consenting adults was protected by the right of privacy in *Lawrence v. Texas*,[53] explicitly stated that the decision did not extend to same-sex marriage: "[The case] does not involve whether the government must give formal recognition to any relationship that homosexual persons seek to enter."[54] Justice Sandra Day O'Connor's concurrence also emphasized her conviction that distinguishing between homosexual and heterosexual sexual practices violated equal protection, because it was an irrational distinction between two similarly situated sets of adults. But that did not "mean that other laws distinguishing between heterosexuals and homosexuals would similarly fail." On her reasoning, the state may well assert a legitimate state interest in "preserving the traditional institution of marriage."[55] Justice Antonin Scalia, though, muddied the waters in his dissent, when he declared that "State laws against bigamy, same-sex marriage, adult incest, prostitution, masturbation, adultery, fornication, bestiality, and obscenity are . . . called into question by [the Court's] decision; the Court makes no effort to cabin the scope of its decision to exclude them from its holding."[56] His apoplectic statements triggered alarm bells across the country, and generated some rather extreme claims.

Professor Brown spun Justice Scalia's reasoning into a claim that with *Lawrence*, the Supreme Court "has in effect declared the nation pagan."[57] His reasoning is a classic illustration of the religious individual who judges public policy solely according to his own religious reference, and who expects it to reflect his particular religious worldview. The only possible government for him is a Judeo-Christian theocracy. On *Lawrence*, he wrote:

> What were those justices thinking? The man who wrote the majority opinion [Justice Anthony Kennedy] is a Roman Catholic. Does he not know that his church, his spiritual leader the pope, the Bible, and all of the church fathers up to the present, consider the behavior that he now protects an abominable sin? . . . Do the two Jewish justices not know that their Torah rejects sodomy as an abomination? . . . And the two women on the Court: by what perverted logic do they mock the role that God and nature have given to their sex in conjunction with the male – to bring children into the world in a matrimonial union. . . .[58]

Thus, religious leaders were capable of transforming the *Lawrence* decision's judgment regarding private, adult sexual conduct into a moral travesty and an attack on traditional marriage. The power of state legislatures to demarcate the boundaries of marriage were hindered not one iota by the decision, either explicitly or implicitly, but this sort of religious argumentation almost always sets aside the proper role of the branches in order to impress its religious demands on the culture. When they do that, they waste their effort, because they are speaking to the wrong branch. The courts do not exist to set public policy.

Second, the social construct of marriage is a state law question, and no other state constitution has been interpreted to require gay marriage. Indeed, in decisions since Massachusetts' landmark decision, courts have declined to follow its reasoning.[59] The states are free to have an open and ongoing debate about the shape of marriage, which can take into account the religious views of every citizen, but the public policy discussion cannot be dictated solely by any religious viewpoint.

Beyond the courts and the legislature, there is also the option of a constitutional amendment, which was attempted and failed in Congress. The citizens of eleven states, however, voted in 2004 to amend their state constitutions to ban gay marriage.[60] It is a more extreme answer to the political question, and may have prematurely suspended debate, but at least it does not feature the government imposing one religious viewpoint on the people.

In the case of same-sex marriage, a vocal coalition of religious organizations has demanded that marriage be constructed to reflect their worldview, even though they certainly do not constitute all religious viewpoints. Far from it, but they feel entitled to have the law of marriage determined by their own lights.

The issue of polygamous marriage presents both a different and a similar issue. In the case of polygamous marriage, there are very few religious sects that advocate the practice. They are small in number and even smaller in political power; they lack the close relationships with those in power that the same-sex marriage opponents enjoy. Nor do they argue that the law should reflect their religious teaching. They do not suggest, as do the opponents to gay marriage, that every marriage should reflect their particular beliefs. Rather, they argue that the First Amendment gives them the right to practice polygamy, despite the laws against it.

In the end though, the two sets of arguments by religious entities are quite similar. Both expect religious belief to direct public policy, and neither has a sufficient appreciation for the role of the legislature in achieving the public good, or in the content of the public good, for that matter. Their horizons are defined by their religious belief, and they transport those horizons into the public square as though they should delineate good and bad public policy by themselves. Yet, religious belief, no matter who holds it, or even how many hold it, cannot be the sole measuring rod for U.S. policy. This pluralist society is the result of the Constitution's best aspirations and for those who claim that they share the faith of the Framers to argue that the fruit of those aspirations – religious diversity – is intolerable should be treated with some skepticism. The drive to power can wear religious garb just as easily as secular.

*The polygamy question: demands for accommodation vs. the public good*

Well over a hundred years ago, when the Church of Jesus Christ of Latter-day Saints believed that polygamy on earth paved the way to heaven, the federal government outlawed the practice.[61] Polygamy is "[t]he condition or practice of having more than one spouse at one time."[62] The most common form of polygamy is polygyny, which is "the condition or practice of having more than one wife at one time."[63] The laws, however, outlawed multiple spouses of either gender. For purposes of this discussion, I will use "polygamy" to mean just that. It does not mean, by the way, "polyamory," the practice of having multiple sexual partners. When the Supreme Court decided *Lawrence v. Texas*, it made it rather clear that personal sexual relations between consenting adults were protected by the right of privacy.[64] Thus, polyamory has been left to private choice. That does not mean it is the right choice from a moral perspective, but it does mean it is beyond the government's purview. "Polygamy," by contrast, implicates the larger social construct of marriage, not the sexual relations between adults. For these purposes, the two universes need to be kept distinct.

George Reynolds, a polygamist Mormon, challenged the federal law outlawing polygamy in the 1870s, arguing that because his actions in taking two wives were the result of religious belief, they were outside the force of the law. In other words, the antipolygamy law might be okay as applied to someone who took two wives simply because he liked two women equally, but where a man's religious beliefs required taking multiple wives, then the government was powerless.

Essentially, Reynolds asked the Court to interpret the First Amendment to mean that belief and conduct are the same thing. That religious belief should be protected was not contested. The Court certainly had no problem in protecting the absolute freedom of conscience, but it refused to extend that unassailable protection to conduct.[65] In *Reynolds v. United States*, it uttered one of the most famous lines in free exercise cases: "Can a man excuse his practices to the contrary because of his religious belief? [To] permit this would be to make the professed doctrines of religious belief superior to the law of the land, and in effect to permit every citizen to become a law unto himself."[66] And common sense requires this reasoning. Religious individuals harm the public good by violating the law no less (and no more) than any other entity breaking the law. As I will explain in chapter 10, the touchstone in conduct cases must be harm or damage, not the perspective of the religious entity. No proper democracy exists that permits individuals to harm others at will simply because of their beliefs. The principle is often repeated in federal and state cases. One particular case comes to mind: a 1944 Utah decision upholding a conviction for cohabitation with more than one member of the opposite sex avowed, "when the offense consists of a positive act which is knowingly done, it would be dangerous to hold that the offender might escape punishment because he religiously believed the law which he had broken ought never to have been made."[67]

As Chapter 2 shows, a parent who lets a child die of a medically treatable ailment does an identical harm to society as a parent who does it out of spite. In either case, society is robbed of that child's potential and talents. And society's quantum of suffering has increased, because a child has been permitted to suffer while there were means to stop it. Just as no parent should be permitted to act to make a child a martyr, no adult is permitted to redefine marriage unilaterally. Marriage is a social construct that must be determined in light of the common good, not by the reflection of any particular group's religious beliefs. Here is where the polygamists' line of reasoning starts to look like the fundamentalists' argument that would ban gay marriage. They expect to shape public law according to a religious litmus test, without reference to larger public good.

Canadian officials, whose constitution typically shares U.S. free exercise principles, have indirectly intimated in the last several decades that polygamy may be constitutionally protected and therefore the polygamy laws were unenforceable.[68] "Former Prime Minister Pierre Trudeau told us it wasn't the state's business and he implied that the rest of us shouldn't poke our noses in either."[69]

The contention raised by *Reynolds* was no different from the pervasive argument in present times that religious conduct should be privileged vis-à-vis the law – simply because the cause is religious. The U.S. Supreme Court has not embraced this precept then or now, as I will discuss in more detail in Part Two, and it is not likely the Supreme Court of Canada ultimately will either.[70] For present purposes, *Reynolds* initiated a series of cases implementing a remarkably consistent and persistent principle: one's actions are measured by their effects and the law, not by their motivation. No one's conduct, with its capacity to harm others, is immune. In 1971, the U.S. Supreme Court in *Gillette v. United States*,[71] stated it as clearly as it has ever been stated: "Our cases do not at their farthest reach support the proposition that a stance of conscientious opposition relieves an objector from any colliding duty fixed by a democratic government."[72] Mr. Reynolds's actions directly collided with the law, and the resultant crash was not averted simply because of his beliefs.

There is no question in the United States that polygamy is not constitutionally mandated, and the current challenges coming out of Utah, where the most polygamists reside, do not change that fact.[73] The arguments were rejected first in 1879 and that rejection has been cemented in multiple federal and state decisions, including in Utah, ever since.[74] One 1955 Utah decision put it as plainly as possible:

> It was never intended or supposed that the amendment could be invoked as a *protection against legislation for the punishment of acts inimical to the peace, good order, and morals of society*. . . . However free the exercise of religion may be, it must be subordinate to the criminal laws of the country, passed *with reference to actions regarded by general consent as properly the subjects of punitive legislation.*[75]

But to say there is no constitutional right to polygamy is not to say that the religious accommodation discussion is necessarily over. The Constitution does not force the government to abandon its policy goals in the face of individuals' religious beliefs. It equally does not require that polygamy (or same-sex marriage) be banned. The question is not whether polygamists may trump the law, but rather whether polygamy can coincide with the public good.

To date, in the United States, the answer has been a rather resounding "no." There is never any harm, though, in a free society reexamining the bases of public policy, even when that which is being examined has been entrenched since the beginning of the country. Tradition by itself cannot and should not determine whether the common good has been adequately served. When polygamy was first outlawed in the United States, it was considered, along with slavery, to be one of the "twin relics of barbarism,"[76] and there is some modern evidence that at least in religious polygamous households, wives are servants of the husband. There was a strong sense in that era that humankind had moved beyond it, to a better social order,[77] and that may be true. But the debate is not off limits.

In this era, the polygamists are challenging the traditional marriage model, and saying essentially, "no harm, no foul." If consenting adults are willing to enter into polygamous relationships, it is a victimless crime, the reasoning goes. It is the classic libertarian position that holds that government should involve itself in the lives of individuals as minimally as possible, and is enormously attractive in an era when the Supreme Court has recognized a private right to choose sexual practices and partners in *Lawrence v. Texas*. But the link between *Lawrence* and polygamy is far more tenuous than it appears at first blush. Consensual practices involving adults constitute a category decidedly distinct from the definition of marriage, which determines legitimacy, inheritance, and numerous other legal consequences. The private sexual act can stay in the bedroom; the shape of marriage is an external decision, far removed from the bedroom – even if most marriages involve sex between the partners. The sex is simply not the marriage.

Until recently, and this may be because of the Supreme Court's muddling of free exercise doctrine between 1963 and 1990 (discussed in Chapters 8 and 10), government officials in Canada and the United States have been extraordinarily diffident in prosecuting the crime of polygamy or even child or spouse abuses within such communities. For example, the Department of Justice has not pursued what would seem to be tailor-made Mann Act violations where underage girls have been exchanged between polygamous colonies in Utah, Arizona, and Canada.[78] Nor have they followed up on those situations involving polygamous husbands taking underage and multiple wives across state borders in order to avoid prosecution in Utah or Arizona. Nearly 60 years ago, the U.S. Supreme

Court held that the transport of girls and women in such circumstances violated the Mann Act, and maintained that a free exercise "defense claims too much. If upheld, it would place beyond the law any act done under claim of religious sanction."[79] Yet, the succeeding Departments of Justice have not seen fit to pursue such prosecutions. Even so, the federal government has been unable to ignore the publicity surrounding such violations. While no prosecutions appear imminent, the Department of Health and Human Services announced in July 2004 that it was providing grants for victim outreach programs.[80] In other words, it appears that the federal government concedes there is a problem, yet finds it politically unpalatable to prosecute, and so is throwing money at the problem. In contrast, there have been prosecutions for Mann Act violations that did not involve religion.[81] The federal government's weak stance on such trafficking when it is done by a religious entity sends a (false) message from the federal government that religious belief can immunize otherwise illegal conduct. No prosecutor should choose between available prosecutions according to the religious status of the actor.

Arizona's governor, Janet Napolitano, skirted the issue in face-to-face meetings with leaders of the Church of Jesus Christ of Latter-day Saints,[82] who many believe have turned a blind eye themselves to the abuses of the polygamous practices that were initiated by their founder, Joseph Smith, in the 1830s. The persistent publicity and the growing voice of groups like Tapestry Against Polygamy have gotten the attention of Arizona legislators, however. Twenty-seven legislators asked the Arizona attorney general to prosecute criminal violations by polygamous communities, including rape, incest, and bigamy.[83] To respond to that kind of political pressure, within months, a multi-use facility was established in the Arizona/Utah enclave, which will be staffed by local and state officials and will be a place for victims to report abuse.[84]

In Utah, it took the revelation of child abandonment discussed in chapter 2 for Attorney General Shurtleff even to say he would consider taking action.[85] When the office distributed a manual for polygamy's victims, Tapestry Against Polygamy refused to assist in the distribution of the book, because it depicted polygamy as a "unique lifestyle," rather than a criminal act.[86] In early September 2004, however, action was taken through the Justice Department's Office of Violence Against Women, which established a grant of approximately $700,000 to assist domestic violence victims in rural and polygamous communities.[87]

The same phenomenon seems to be at work in British Columbia, Canada, where authorities have left the Fundamentalist Church of Jesus Christ of Latter-day Saints (FLDS)'s Bountiful commune to its own devices for decades,[88] though social forces seem to be moving toward some means of redressing abuses. British Columbia officials announced an investigation into abuse, sexual exploitation, and forced marriage in Bountiful, although, interestingly enough, the investigation will ignore the issue of polygamy.[89] The mayor near Bountiful endorsed an investigation, mentioned in chapter 2, into practices at the FLDS commune there.[90] The government's decades of studious avoidance were brought under a spotlight by the civil rights suit recently filed by former polygamous wives against British Columbia government ministries for permitting extreme discrimination against women and girls in the polygamous compound in Bountiful.[91] Despite persistent reports of serious abuse, the British Columbia Civil Liberties Association has urged "the government not to browbeat the community's leaders on the polygamy issue,"[92] as though prosecutors should backpedal prosecutions involving extremely serious charges, on the ground that the actors are religious.

Civil liberties groups, civil authorities, and other proponents of "religious liberty" for conduct seem to operate from the premise that a democratic society is obligated to ensure the perpetuation of religious groups. After the *Salt Lake Tribune* published an editorial saying "polygamy is inherently destructive,"[93] a letter to the editor argued that laws against polygamy in the 1800s might have obliterated the early Mormon Church, as though public policy should be chosen to preserve religious groups.[94] Government regulation is not supposed to ensure or foster the development of certain religions; the United States has fostered a busy marketplace in religion, in part because the government has been constitutionally deterred from supporting or undermining religious institutions. A religious organization that has declining membership may not and should not be able to demand government assistance or regulation to sustain itself. Andrea Moore-Emmett rightly responded to the letter, saying that religion has proven remarkably resilient in the face of government regulation regulating certain actions,[95] and therefore such concerns cannot drive the public policy determination. Rather, the government's obligation is to persist in choosing the public good over all other concerns.

As the issue has become a front-page story, at least one academic has defended polygamy on First Amendment grounds, and his reasoning nicely illustrates what is wrong with the current debate over marriage. Professor Jonathan Turley in USA *Today* called the arguments against polygamy by conservative groups fighting gay marriage hypocritical: "Given this history and the long religious traditions [that had recognized polygamy at some point in history], it cannot be seriously denied that polygamy is a legitimate religious belief . . . if we yield to our impulse and single out one hated minority, the First Amendment becomes little more than hype and we become little more than hypocrites."[96] That the belief is "legitimate," means nothing as a legal matter, because under the First Amendment, all religious beliefs – no matter how outlandish – are legitimate, and the government may not draw such a distinction between beliefs. He then declares, "The First Amendment was designed to protect the least popular and least powerful among us."[97] This is the kind of overgeneralization that too often substitutes for considered discussion of the First Amendment in the United States, regrettably. The First Amendment was not crafted to protect conduct that harms others, even if the actor is unpopular or powerless. A small polygamous and incestuous California sect was no doubt unpopular and politically powerless, but the cult leader who is now accused of murdering his wives and children (some of whom were both) was no more defensible than any other mass murderer.[98] The First Amendment is simply irrelevant to the legality of his conduct. If the government had directed the cult to cease believing in polygamy or to stifle its speech about it because the government found it unpalatable, Turley's analysis might have had some bite, but it is completely beside the point when the issue is conduct, like polygamous marriage. Turley's main mistake was that he substituted the view of the religious individual for legal reasoning, and therefore lost sight of the only relevant question: is the conduct harmful or beneficial? Indeed, his focus on the religious is so intense that he fails to take into account that bigamy and polygamy are not just religious practices, and that even the secular bigamists may harm society.[99] He frames the question incorrectly. The legal issue is not whether the religious viewpoint of certain believers is internally inconsistent, or even what any one group of believers holds true. The question for public policy is whether the practice of polygamy is consistent with what is best for society, period. As with so many public officials and representatives, he confuses a debate over belief with the debate over public policy. Both debates are welcome at the public round-table. Only the latter properly shapes the law. The government may not enter the former, but it is duty-bound to address the latter.

In the last decade in the United States, there has been a growing rumble from formerly polygamous wives, who criticize the notion that polygamy is a victimless crime. Tapestry Against Polygamy was founded by a group of formerly polygamous wives who decided to fight polygamy. It describes its mission as advocating "against the human right violations inherent in polygamy and provides assistance to individuals leaving polygamous cults."[100] Journalist Andrea Moore-Emmett has taken an in-depth look at the problems expressed by formerly polygamous wives across a range of polygamous religious communities, and concluded that religiously based marriages involving one man and multiple women frequently entail spousal and child abuse.[101] Canadian Nancy Mereska formed an email network campaign dubbed "Stop Polygamy in Canada" after learning of the abuses that seem to be endemic in many of the known polygamous communities.[102]

Former polygamous wives argue that the typical religious polygamy community elevates certain men over all others, and that women and children are nothing more than property to accumulate. In chapter 2, I described polygamy's impact on children; it has also harmed women. When underage girls are forced into marrying much older men in these communities, they are taken out of school, deprived of any means of future earning or self-support, and burdened with the expectation of bearing as many children as possible. The cost of such enormous families can prove to be too much for any one man, leading some polygamist men to support only their first wives, leaving all later wives (and their children) no option but state support.[103] Moreover, home schooling is favored in order to avoid the public school system, which could lead to discovery of their criminal acts. So mothers who have marginal educations themselves are teaching their children. These children would appear to be destined to be as undereducated as their mothers, despite federal legislation that purports to leave no child behind. When government refuses to prosecute the legal violations within these polygamous enclaves, it further isolates the women and leaves their children far behind the standardized goals set by the federal legislation.[104]

There is some debate whether this describes the natural propensities of polygamy, or whether only the bad polygamous actors get the attention of the public. Some of the wives from the FLDS Bountiful commune have defended their lifestyle, saying that they enter the marriages freely, that the women are educated, and that there is no abuse.[105] There is also a Utah organization of polygamous women in Utah, Principle Voices of Polygamy, which defends the practice.[106]

Polygamy's defenders are not only Mormon fundamentalists. Mark Henkel is a self-proclaimed spokesman for a Christian polygamy advocacy group in Maine, who "cites biblical scripture and the polygamists' lifestyle of such Old Testament biblical figures as Abraham and King David as justification." He asserts he does not, however, support forced marriages and believes in the free choice of women to enter the arrangement.[107]

Legislators who take up the issue, though, must consider whether the unbalanced numbers in a polygamous marriage institute an inherently unequal situation. While there are a certain number in the United States who argue that the above abuses are simply perversions of what can be a productive and happy relationship, others have seen in polygamy an internal contradiction with the rule of law and democracy. At the very least, polygamy sends the message that only one man need satisfy multiple women, so that the women are not equal to the man. Naomi Schaefer Riley, who is a Fellow at the Ethics and Public Policy Center, in Washington, D.C., believes the latter, saying that it "corrupt(s) civil society as a whole, destroying education, individual rights and the rule of law – in other words the foundations of democratic governance."[108] Others, like political science professor Thomas Flanagan at the University of Calgary, Canada, are more blunt, arguing that polygamous societies are highly unequal and a deadly foe of constitutional government. He offers as proof that constitutional democracies have arisen only from monogamous societies.[109]

The facts of religious polygamy are the proper focus of any social and legislative reconsideration of marriage. The victims of polygamy should be heard, as should the continuing practitioners who would defend the practice. The typical defense by the men is that their religion demands it, and the government should have no power to regulate their religion.

"[M]embers of the Fundamentalist Church of Jesus Christ of Latter-day Saints . . . believe that men must have at least three wives to reach heaven's highest echelon."[110] One leader elaborated by pointing out that it was a blessing for the women, because "the only way she could ever be happy was – that she would let her husband, a faithful man, rule over her. That was the only way back to Heavenly Father for the woman."[111] He was not quite as subtle when dealing with recalcitrant wives: "You can either live here and live in hell, and then when you die have eternal happiness. Or else, you can go out into the world and live in hell and die and even have more eternal hell."[112]

It is not as though the United States is the first culture to deal with polygamy. Although, to be quite frank, the United States is always sorely tempted to assume it stands alone and ahead of others on issues adressing religious practice. Many countries in the world permit it, and it does have some political clout. For example, in Afghanistan's 2004 elections, the Afghanistan Supreme Court demanded one candidate be prohibited from the election, because he had publicly criticized polygamy.[113] Even so, its legality has not meant that it is widely followed. In East Malaysia, for example, where the practice is legal, there were only 168 polygamous marriages recorded between 1999 and 2003, amounting to only .6 percent of marriages recorded.[114]

In other underdeveloped regions of the world where polygamy is still widely practiced the issues are more complex. Florence Butegwa, former regional director of Women in Law & Development in Africa (WiLDAF) has commented on the contradicting views of polygamy in Uganda, where women have organized "to demand the abolition of polygamy as a necessary step for protecting women's rights in marriage." At the same time, Muslim women, "either on their own volition or on the demands of their Islamic leaders," opposed the movement. "They liked polygamy, they [didn't] want it to go away." Their claims "provided the government with an escape route."[115] Similar campaigns against polygamy have been started in other African nations, especially Nigeria, where The Campaign Against Polygamy & Women Oppression In Nigeria and Africa (CAPWONA), and the Total World Women Freedom Alliance (TOWWFA), believe that polygamous marriages are inherently unequal and lead to unhappiness for the women, but they also see a larger issue involving the building blocks of the society.[116] Given the multitude of issues surrounding women's rights in Africa, including access to healthcare, child custody issues and basic property laws, Professor Mojubaolu Olu-funke Okome of Brooklyn College, CUNY, put it this way: "I don't think that many women in Nigeria think polygamy is a problem in and of itself. . . . [it is the] the unjust treatment of a woman under the polyga-mous system may be a problem."[117]

However, without addressing polygamy, it will be virtually impossible to address the other concerns of these women. If the family is a group unit, how can courts decide custodial issues? If a man has more than one wife, which wife should inherit his property when he dies without a will? If a man can marry as many women as he wants, will there ever be a solution to the endemic problem of AIDS in Africa? Indeed, some believe the culture of polygamy has contributed to the spread of AIDS in Africa.[118]

While United States officials have been apt to turn the other way, international treaties have labeled polygamy as an inherently unequal relationship that violates fundamental principles of equality. For exam-ple, following the creation of the Convention for the Elimination of All Forms of Discrimination Against Women (CEDAW), the United Na-tions offered the following analysis: "Polygamous marriage contravenes a woman's right to equality with men, and can have such serious emo-tional and financial consequences for her and her dependents that such marriages ought to be discouraged and prohibited."[119]

All of this is proper fodder for legislative consideration, including the experiences of those in the United States who have lived within the institution, the views of those who have left it, and the knowledge of the international community. And the focus needs to be on polygamy, religious and secular, not just religious. There may be those polygamous situations that do not entail the severe civil rights abuses apparent in the religiously motivated polygamy that has been at the forefront of the debate. Those individuals should be encouraged to make their case to their legislators. But in the end, it is the obligation of the legislators to determine what is in the best interests of all the people – men, women, children, and society as a whole. And the debate belongs in the legislature, not the courts.

It is simply incoherent to argue that the First Amendment should determine the parameters of marriage. The First Amendment is solidly available when it protects the right of anyone to believe in polygamy, and when it protects the right of those believers to speak about the practice, and even to urge the legislature to deregulate marriage. Consideration of conduct and its impact is the legislature's correct role, which permits wide-ranging and wide-eyed factual inquiry, consultation with experts here and abroad, and consideration of what this society wants marriage to accomplish.

To the extent the religious polygamists insist that the Constitution mandates permission for their practices, they are on quicksand. The argument has no foundation. If they are arguing instead that polygamy is a socially beneficial practice that is capable of serving the public good, then they should make the case.

Here, as elsewhere, legislators need to be reminded that they are not in their positions of power to roll over for religious organizations that demand rights to do whatever their beliefs dictate. It is never enough for representatives to assert they are furthering religious liberty. They must also always ask whether the conduct in question comports with the public good, and that means they must examine with some care how the conduct impacts others. The victims of polygamy need to be taken into account in such a calculus, just as the victims of clergy abuse and medical neglect need to be in the forefront of legislators' minds when they determine statutes of limitations on childhood sexual abuse and child abuse reporting laws. The legislative mantra needs to be that conduct always has the potential to harm, and that as legislators, they are obligated to identify, forestall and deter harm.

# RELIGIOUS LAND USE AND
# RESIDENTIAL NEIGHBORHOODS

Religious landowners face daunting needs for buildings and property, which means their residential neighbors are often affected by their plans. The worship space needs to be large enough to accommodate weekly gatherings of a significant percentage of their members and even bigger assemblies for holidays. Thus, a small building with minimal parking is ordinarily not adequate to the task. In the era when these buildings were only used for worship and maybe a choir practice, despite their size, houses of worship were attractive residential neighbors. Church properties were like miniature parks of peaceful tranquility in residential neighborhoods – the grounds were pretty, the building was tasteful, and they were excellent neighbors. Parking, traffic, lights, and noise were not typical problems. That is no longer true.

*The paradigm shift in houses of worship*

There has been a paradigm shift in houses of worship in the United States. Unfortunately for their neighbors, although favorable for the recipients of their services, contemporary houses of worship are not the sleepy institutions they once were. They are now a locus for social services, as well as a center for worship and entertainment. The thriving religious entities have sizeable buildings, with seating for hundreds – maybe thousands, along with heavy traffic, intense parking needs, and even bus transportation into the neighborhood from off site. If they are starting from scratch, they usually (though not always) search for a large parcel of land that is along a major thoroughfare. Problems arise, though, when established houses of worship situated in residential neighborhoods attempt to compete with these new multipurpose churches or when large or growing congregations try to wedge a new campus into a neighborhood. The established church may seek to transform its existing grounds into parking lots as it adds buildings and services, or a new church may enter the real estate market and purchase five or six neighboring homes – often without telling the neighbors. A homeowner can go to sleep in a quiet residential enclave and wake up next door to a proposed 150-car parking lot.[1] The result of church expansion is too often that neighborhood streets where children once played roller hockey are now so busy that the parents are uneasy letting the children play in the front yard. Minimal traffic and the atmosphere it creates, after all, attract many families to their homes in the first place.

Sometimes the size of the congregation can dwarf the surrounding community. In Rolling Hills Estates, California, the Rolling Hills Covenant Church's congregation numbers 3,700 adults and children and seeks to build a huge church to accommodate its growing membership. The city has been concerned about the project's scope and increased traffic, because the congregation amounts to half of the city's population and has a budget that exceeds the city's. The conflict between homeowners and such a large religious project should be apparent; the city expects the homeowners to sue as the project goes forward and the church to sue if the city government does not approve the proposal. City Manager Doug Prichard, says, "Our goal is to find a project that will meet the church's needs that will not negatively impact the neighbors and [will] keep everybody out of court."[2] That is often a tall order.

The size of the congregation alone does not dictate how the house of worship will affect residential neighborhoods. There is also the question of what services will be provided. "Church on Sunday" is no longer the rule. The model of church use that is carved into the memories of so many adults in the United States is gone. Houses of worship are, in fact, multiple-use social centers. The typical congregation may use its property for schools, weddings, receptions, social services like Alcoholics Anonymous and soup kitchens, and weekly religious study. The worship program may include numerous elements as well, such as a summer religious camp; services on days other than the Sabbath; youth groups for elementary, junior high, and high school students; and multiple choirs. Hours of use skyrocket from less than a dozen to well over 60 in a single week, with the use generating a traffic pattern more evocative of a grocery store than a home. "When viewed from an objective land-use perspective (considering only the level of activity, not its substance) or from a traffic perspective, such a use begins to look more like a commercial facility than like the traditional neighborhood church."[3]

The more recent phenomenon of the "megachurch" in the United States takes this trend to its logical extreme, with some campuses including child and senior day care, recreation centers, health clubs, bowling alleys, bookstores, coffee houses, hotels, home-repair assistance, and motion picture theaters.[4] There is one religious institution in Houston, Texas, that has a McDonald's.[5] These complexes are, in fact, self-contained communities for believers to go after work and on the weekends, where social and religious needs are satisfied simultaneously.

The final factor in this house-of-worship expansion is that many congregations have come to think of themselves as ministers to all, not just their own members, so there is competition among religious entities to provide panoply social services to those outside the congregation. The menu of services also serves to entice new members. According to one expert, "'American churches of all kinds are trying to do everything they can to enlarge their tent, be seen, be accessible.'"[6] It is a formula that seems to be working, because nondenominational, nontraditional churches are the fastest growing religious groups in the United States.[7]

When size and intense use combine to affect those who reside nearby, previously friendly neighbors can become hostile enemies. There are two conflicting dynamics happening at once. The religious entity is experiencing a heady and exciting period of expansion, and may well see earthly hurdles as contrary to its divinely inspired religious movement. The neighbors are in a very different place. Typically, they have lived in the neighborhood for a long time, or they chose the neighborhood for its residential qualities, so the new building project is a serious threat to their quality of life. To make matters worse for everyone concerned, a home is often a family's largest financial, and emotional, investment; thus, when the character of the neighborhood and, therefore, property values are threatened, homeowners understandably object. They really do not care if the expansion project will result in a bakery or a temple. "You could be a car dealership, a hospital, a university; it doesn't matter – especially if it is in your neighborhood."[8]

Either way, they are losing what they value most in their homes. Yet, given the demographics of religion in the United States, the two sides are almost always religious, so any implied condescension from the leader of the project can really hit a nerve and even a whiff of a holier-than-thou attitude from the members can lead to a conflagration of bad feelings. Conversely, objections by the homeowners are too often translated as somehow anti-religious.

Local government has found itself quite literally between a rock and a hard place on these issues. These intensely used properties wedged into residential neighborhoods are often the result of imprudent decision making by city governments, which follow the tendency of all U.S. politicians to defer to requests by religious entities without adequate independent analysis. It is as if whatever the religious institution requests is good for everyone. A recent study concluded, "It is extraordinarily uncommon for congregations to be denied permission by government authorities to engage in the activities in which they wish to engage."[9]

It can take little for government officials to be swayed to the religious entities' side, especially if the religious applicant pulls the discrimination card. If there is one thing local governments do not want, it is constitutional litigation in the federal courts accusing them of religious or racial discrimination, and whenever they can avoid it, they will. If that means bending the land-use rules to grant a religious entity's request, that is often what will happen.

This is not to say that local governments always blindly rule in a religious entity's favor. They don't. They are quite capable of sticking to their land-use guns, especially when the result of applying their law is quite clear. But in this era it does not take much for the balance to tip in favor of the religious entity. I speak from experience as one who has been contacted by dozens, if not hundreds, of homeowners around the United States who have had remarkably similar experiences, and one who represents some of the cities involved in these disputes.

### A *home becomes a synagogue*

In Los Angeles's beautiful Hancock Park neighborhood, an Orthodox Jewish shul, or synagogue, operated for decades out of Rabbi Chaim Baruch Rubin's home. The neighborhood is roughly 75 years old, and many of the homes have a distinctive Mediterranean look.

For many years, the shul was attended by a small number of men, and the neighbors had no reason to complain. But then the rabbi passed away and the rabbi's son, Rabbi Chaim Baruch Rubin, took over and had a grander vision, which led to the current dispute. First, he expanded the use of his father's home from a daily prayer meeting to a synagogue with a congregation attending weekly Sabbath services and holding bar and bat mitzvahs. Then, when this new and intense use triggered resistance from the neighbors, he requested a variance to construct and operate what amounted to a full-service synagogue on another nearby property in the neighborhood. Under existing law, there was virtually no question that this project was inconsistent with the surrounding neighborhood. On the first round in 1996, the city council affirmed the zoning board of appeals and declared that the use would have been unprecedented in Hancock Park:

> There are no other church or institutional uses on the residentially zoned properties within the notice radius for this action, this use would be precedent setting and compromise the 75 year maintenance and recognized quality and sought after ambience of this historical residential neighborhood.[10]

The Los Angeles Superior Court wholeheartedly agreed, saying that the synagogue "'would be a precedent setting encroachment of an institutional use in a single family area . . . [that could] destabilize what has been a long standing, quality single-family residential neighborhood that has through constant efforts maintained its stable, high quality residential character.'"[11]

In response to the argument that the synagogue was convenient for its members, and therefore should receive this unprecedented treatment, the court held, "There are other locations within a reasonable walking distance from the subject site which could be used as a synagogue by right without the potential to impact and disturb the quiet enjoyment of the existing residential community."[12] The California Court of Appeals affirmed.[13]

In federal court, where the congregation appealed the city's decision on constitutional grounds, the court rejected all of their constitutional arguments and was ready to dismiss. Yet, when the Religious Land Use and Institutionalized Persons Act of 2000 (RLUIPA), which granted special privileges to religious landowners and which I will discuss in the next section, became law, the city did an about-face on its settled and affirmed land-use principles by entering into a Settlement Agreement that "accomplished the purpose sought by the Congregation in its 1996 conditional-use permit application – gaining official approval for property uses then taking place in violation of the Los Angeles Municipal Code."[14]

In other words, this new federal law, which carried with it the threat of continuing federal court litigation, persuaded the City of Los Angeles that it should abandon its land-use code and grant the religious entity most of what it requested.

Los Angeles put a few conditions on the use. For example, it required the synagogue to maintain the "residential character" of the neighborhood. That proved futile, as neighbors watched the small house on the new property being razed and then replaced with a building twice the size on the same land, which looks like a synagogue and overshadows its neighbors. It is so close to the property line that the homeowner to the side no longer keeps her curtains facing the synagogue open.

The neighbors were outraged that their city's settled land-use law could be discarded so abruptly and their neighborhood taken in precisely the opposite direction from what the law required. A significant number of them formed the League of Residential Neighborhood Advocates and filed a federal lawsuit, which is a highly unusual step for a homeowner's organization. They are now in federal court challenging the reversal as an abdication of the city' responsibility to follow its own laws, and therefore violating due process.[15] In the interest of full disclosure, I represent them. For purposes of this book, I seek only to describe the facts.

Neighborhood disputes also have the capacity to creep beyond their borders. The Hancock Park dispute is a classic example of the challenges imposed when a religious use increases in intensity and scope. Unfortunately, the ugliness of the dispute is typical as well. When the neighbors objected to the opening of this new, intense use, the congregation took offense. A press release was distributed in the neighborhood accusing those opposed to the building project as "anti-Jewish" and "anti-Semitic." The congregation's response got the attention of other Jewish leaders, including a leading museum curator, who wrote a letter accusing the neighborhood of "hate." After he met with the synagogue's neighbors, he claimed he was not calling the neighbors anti-Semitic, only intolerant. No homeowner walks away from such an exchange without feeling less happy about his or her choice of neighborhood.

This case is especially ironic, because Rabbi Rubin testified before Congress:

> Congregation Etz Chaim ("Congregation" or "Etz Chaim") is a small group of Orthodox Jewish residents of Hancock Park who, for the last 30 years, have gathered together in one of two residences in Hancock Park for communal prayer. Orthodox Judaism requires that worshipers pray together, and that they walk to services on the Sabbath and on other holy days. Thus, in order to comply with the dictates of their faith, Orthodox Jews must have a house of worship within walking distance of their homes. Over the years, Etz Chaim has come to serve the needs of many elderly and disabled Hancock Park residents, who, because of their disabilities, are physically unable to walk the mile or more round-trip to synagogues located in the commercial zone outside of Hancock Park. For years, these faithful congregants have attended services at Etz Chaim using their canes and walkers.[16]

He then described the current use as involving "40 members (with a high of sixty (60) members ... [and] four bar mitzvah ceremonies," and claimed that "[t]he only activities which take place at the residence are prayer services."[17] If one were inclined to read the testimony for its facts, one would quickly see that a minyan had become a full-service synagogue catering to families with children. That is a dramatic change in use, and for it to be characterized any other way is disingenuous at best.

Yet, the truth rarely impedes those religious interests intent on obtaining special benefits from Congress and their willing accomplices, the members. In spite of its incomplete character, Rabbi Rubin's testimony has been repeatedly invoked as evidence of rank discrimination against benign neighborhood religious uses. Senators Orrin Hatch (R, UT) and Edward Kennedy (D, MA), in their joint statement, asserted that, "[s]ometimes, zoning board members or neighborhood residents explicitly offer race or religion as the reason to exclude a proposed church, especially in cases of black churches and Jewish shuls and synagogues. More often, discrimination lurks behind such vague and universally applicable reasons as traffic, aesthetics, or 'not consistent with the city's land use plan.'"[18] In other words, it was the rare instance where overt discrimination could be indentified in the land use process, but discrimination supposedly could be implied on the basis of "universally applicable reasons" for land use determinations. Thus, Congress pulled the discrimination rabbit out of the hat and transformed all homeowners into bigots.

Despite no overt proof of discrimination, a city's decision to follow its settled land-use law could be twisted into a pretext for invidious discrimination, while the typical concerns of homeowners about traffic, aesthetics, and maintaining the city's land-use plan were supposedly so base that to invoke them led to the ineluctable conclusion that discrimination must be at play. It's a disturbing claim for two U.S. senators to make about millions of their constituent homeowners without concrete proof, but it had legs, because it became *the* element of all of the hearings before Congress that undergirded RLUIPA in the eyes of the courts.

Professor Douglas Laycock went even further than the senators, claiming overt and not just implied religious discrimination, when he wrote that Los Angeles's "express reason for excluding a place of worship was that it wanted to exclude places of worship!"[19] Nothing but an overactive imagination intent on finding discrimination because it suits one's purposes can explain this characterization of Los Angeles's decisions in the Hancock Park case. It was the increasing intensity of use that engendered the original denial, which was affirmed by the California courts, not the religious character or identity of the gathering.

If there is one thing that is sacrosanct in the United States, it is the belief that one's home is one's castle, and therefore these disputes pit one cherished ideal – religious liberty – against another – the American Dream of a nice home in a quiet suburb, where children can be safe. In 1974 the Supreme Court put it this way:

> A quiet place where yards are wide, people few, and motorcycles restricted are legitimate guidelines in a land-use project addressed to family needs. . . . The police power is not confined to elimination of filth, stench, and unhealthy places. It is ample to lay out zones where family values, youth values, and the blessings of quiet seclusion and clean air make the area a sanctuary for people.[20]

Religious groups lobbying for preferential land-use rights seem to have an odd blind spot on this core American value. They live in the culture, and surely many live in just such a setting. Yet, they seem surprised – or bemused – when their preferential statutes render neighborhoods war zones, although they will admit it is problematic in certain states where there is a "greater emphasis on land."[21] Anthony Picarello of the Becket Fund, which supports such legislation and provides free legal assistance to churches in these types of suits, said it like this: "RLUIPA does not create 'two classes of citizens' across religious lines. Instead, it creates two classes of activities – land use that involves religious exercise, and land use that does not – and then reinforces the constitutional protection for all citizens who choose to use their land for religious exercise."[22] The problem is that the word "reinforces" in fact means "adds to," and therefore religious entities have been granted extra-constitutional rights that make religious landowners first-class citizens to their lesser residential neighbors.

Keep in mind, however, that these lobbying groups on behalf of religious institutions have never *legislated* special privileges for religious landowners; that was done by legislators. And these legislators are the ones who need to be brought to account on these issues. It is one thing for an interest group to fail to see the other side of an issue, but it is a severe failure of responsibility for Congress to miss the other side altogether. Moreover, in the land-use arena, virtually every one of them has owned or owns a home, so it is not as though they needed special expertise to be able to foretell how private homeowners would feel when their religious neighbors could destroy the residential quality of their neighborhoods.

The failure of Congress to investigate these issues is shameful. When the Religious Liberty Protection Act (RLPA) was under consideration in Congress in 1999 (and those hearings were then said to support RLUIPA), only religious entities with vested interests were permitted to testify. I testified, but solely on constitutional issues (to get on the record that Congress had considered constitutionality in light of the Court's recent rebukes of Congress's cavalier enactment of laws for which they may or may not have had the power). Groups like the National League of Cities and the International Municipal League of Cities asked to testify, but they were never invited. Mayor Rudolph Giuliani asked to testify regarding New York City's concerns with the bill, but he was not invited. Sen. Patrick Moynihan (D.-N.Y.), other land-use officials, and zoning authorities who might have been able to give Congress the benefit of another side of the issue were not invited either. Certainly no homeowner or homeowners' association that had tangled with an ambitious religious building project was permitted to get on the record, but that is probably because Congress simply did not bother to ask whether relieving religious entities of land-use laws might well affect one's neighbors. It's an obvious question, but was never posed throughout the hearings for RLPA.

The record contains many religious entities complaining about garden-variety land-use laws along with anecdotes of discriminatory treatment. The problem with the discrimination claims was that there are virtually no cases to support their argument that Congress needed to intervene to help these landowners. In fact, the only secular – as in unbiased – study done to date supports the view that the claims to discrimination before Congress do not hold water, because discrimination simply is not a typical feature in the land-use process when religious entities are involved.[23] In the face of religious representatives from the Mormon Church, the Presbyterian Church, and the Roman Catholic Church, the congressional members basically accepted what was being alleged, as though it were gospel truth, and once the testimony was recorded in the *Congressional Record*, courts deferred to the claims as well, because Congress had accepted them.[24] The first court to uphold RLUIPA's constitutionality simply quoted the conference report delivered by Senator Hatch (who has yet to see a pro-religious bill he will not support), as though independent, disinterested review of the record to ensure constitutional requirements were followed was not the court's business (even though it is). It engaged in the following "analysis," which merely parrots Senators Hatch and Kennedy's joint statement: "The hearing record compiled massive evidence that this right is frequently violated."[25]

Thus, interest group politics builds on gossamer threads, and voila, religious landowners have the ability to get around the land-use laws that make neighbors good neighbors. As I said previously, the deficiency in the political process here is not with the interest group's distorted or self-interested perspective. That is to be expected. But there is every reason to criticize elected representatives who kowtow to religious interests, and, as a result, fail to ask the simplest questions: for example, how does your land use proposal affect others, like your neighbors? Had the question been posed, it might have occurred to a member to ask others besides the religious groups (and a handful of scholars) to testify. Then there might have been some fact finding, as opposed to opinion expressing.

When any landowner – religious or secular – receives or seemingly receives preferential treatment, there are bad feelings in the United States. Because city governments are supposed to ensure that residential neighborhoods remain peaceful and attractive to families, when they abandon their principles for religious entities, homeowners feel betrayed.[26] The impact of these large operations on property values and residential character turn homeowners against religious entities all too often.[27] In the words of one reporter, although RLUIPA was only "intended to ease city zoning restrictions for religious institutions, the civil rights law has pitted neighbor versus neighbor and church versus state in areas nationwide."[28]

Religious entities often view their property as serving a higher purpose, which can translate into insensitivity to the "earthly" values of their neighbors. The message is sent loud and clear that increased traffic is a negligible burden on the neighborhood when compared to their religiously motivated plans. When homeowners object to bringing homeless into the neighborhood for social services, because they fear for the safety of their children and the impact on property values, they are told that their values are misplaced. From the religious perspective, the religious mission transcends these mortal concerns. Sometimes a pastor will spearhead an ambitious building project, on the basis of a vision for the future, not current numbers. For example, in Greensboro, North Carolina, Senior Pastor Jerry Shetler of the First Presbyterian Church said in 1995 that his plan to raze historic homes set on tree-lined streets for a parking lot and a hall large enough to accommodate basketball as well as banquets was not "necessitated by the congregation's growth in numbers, [but rather] the growth of the congregation in terms of its understanding of what it ought to be."[29]

At one conference I attended, a representative for a religious organization declared that he simply could not comprehend residential homeowners' objections to cars parked on the street on a regular basis. At the same time, a scholar declared that concerns about traffic and parking are simply pretexts for discrimination against religion, as though it is inconceivable that homeowners would take those issues seriously.[30]

The ingrained American prejudice in favor of the religious projects was evident at a 1999 conference at the University of California, Davis School of Law, where Professor Douglas Laycock asserted the following as a fact: some neighbors to a new church "are hostile to religion and to churches, either in general or in certain manifestations. Some Americans are hostile to all religion. They believe it is irrational, superstitious, and harmful." He immediately qualified the statement, though, because it could not stand on its own: "This is the view of a small minority."[31]

Religious hostility, however, does not, in fact, describe the attitudes of the vast majority of residential neighbors. For Laycock, the homeowners objecting to a law that would let churches off the hook for land-use laws "brought a remarkable intensity and sense of entitlement to their desire to prevent the construction of churches."[32] The intensity is not remarkable at all. Had he attended just about any public hearing involving a building project affecting private homes, he would have witnessed the same passion, which is motivated by these homeowners' love of their neighborhood and families, not any hatred for any or all religions.

What is remarkable in the religious-building debate is that those on the side of the religious entities have been so far removed from the emotional, economic, and even spiritual value that American families invest in their homes. It is neither a de minimis nor a throwaway value. This is where the family meets, where children live, and where personal traditions are built.[33] If the family is the fundamental building block in American society – as so many are claiming in the same-sex marriage debate – the home is simply an extension of those values. Yet, page after page of congressional testimony in support of federal religious liberty legislation can criticize how religious landowners are treated in the United

States, without a single witness called to ask about the impact these religious building projects have on private homeowners. That is a severe
failure of representation.

Part one includes many arenas wherein religious entities act as though
the public interest pales in comparison to their agendas. In many circumstances, though, the average American has little idea how religious
entities are harming others. Here, the disputes are literally in Americans'
own backyards.

Given their worldview, there is a tendency for religious landowners to
characterize run-of-the-mill zoning regulations and the costs of securing
property and building as an unacceptable burden on their free exercise
of religion. Until recently, their land use was treated according to its
impact, not the identity of the owner. For example, in Miami Beach,
Florida, Naftali and Sarah Grosz lived in their home on property zoned
for single-family residential use for a number of years. They bought the
property with a deed restriction that explicitly limited their use to residential purposes and did not request rezoning. But they did have an
"accessory structure" for which they asked and received permission to re-
model for what they called "playroom use." As part of its approval, among
other particulars, the city told them that the structure could not be used
as a "religious institution." While the external features of the structure
were not changed, the couple installed "benches to seat over 30 persons,
Torahs, Arks, a Menorah, skull caps, an eternal light, numerous books,
shawls, and other items of religious significance," all of which violated
the city's ordinance against religious institutions in residential neighborhoods without permission.[34] The Grosz's sued the city in federal court,
claiming the ordinance was an unconstitutional burden on their free-
exercise rights.[35] The U.S. Court of Appeals for the 11th Circuit rightly
rejected their claims in 1983, because there is no justification in a residential neighborhood to treat the impact of a religious use as though it is
any different from the impact of a nonreligious use. Here, a "playroom"
would have had extremely light use, while the shul was in constant use.
The court quite rightly found there was no substantial burden on their
free exercise of religion, saying:

> [W]e note that Miami Beach does not prohibit religious conduct per
> se. Rather, the City prohibits acts in furtherance of this conduct in

certain geographical areas. . . . Appellees' home lies within four blocks of such a district. Appellees do not confront the limited choice of ceasing their conduct or incurring criminal liability. Alternatively, they may conduct the required services in suitably zoned areas, either by securing another site away from their current house or by making their home elsewhere in the city. We cannot know the exact impact upon Appellees, in terms of convenience, dollars or aesthetics, that a location change would entail. The burden imposed, though, plainly does not rise to the level of criminal liability, loss of livelihood, or denial of a basic income sustaining public welfare benefit. In comparison to the religious infringements analyzed in previous free exercise cases the burden here stands towards the lower end of the spectrum.[36]

This is the sort of common sense reasoning that permeated the cases before the Religious Freedom Restoration Act (RFRA) and RLUIPA entered the picture.

Religious landowners are unique, because they are often persuaded that their building mission is transcendent, and therefore, in the order of things, they should take precedence over competing earthly demands. Developers frequently have a "vision" for a project, but when religion enters the picture, that vision can become freighted with a sense of entitlement. For example, in the Rolling Hills Estates dispute described above, the church has sought permission to build an enormous worship center. Pastor Virgil Best couched the project in terms of religious mission, saying that it was their "mission that our congregation should be able to worship together."[37] The lawyer for the Grace United Methodist Church in Cheyenne, Wyoming, that sought to add a 100-child day-care center to its building in a residential neighborhood pointed to testimony from a church leader that "God called the group to build the day-care center."[38] Broward County's Primera Iglesia Bautista Hispana believed that its building plans were a "Godly mission" that was stymied by the county's zoning and land-use restrictions, which they blamed for undermining the growth they sought.[39]

As a constitutional matter, generally applicable, neutral zoning laws are just as much the religious landowner's responsibility as any other landowner's, and this is as it should be, because land use inescapably affects neighbors, the community, and the state. Zoning and land-use laws exist to minimize the negative effects of any landowner's use of their property. "One of the general purposes of zoning is to ameliorate the impact of development on neighboring land and on the community as a whole."[40] Zoning law, which is a 20th-century phenomenon, was made necessary to mediate disputes from increasingly concentrated populations, as the Supreme Court explained in 1926:

> Until recent years, urban life was comparatively simple; but with the great increase and concentration of population, problems are developed, and constantly are developing, which require, and will continue to require, additional restrictions in respect of the use and occupation of private lands in urban communities. . . . Such regulations are sustained, under the complex conditions of our day, for reasons analogous to those which justify traffic regulations, which, before the advent of automobiles and rapid transit street railways, would have been condemned as fatally arbitrary and unreasonable.[41]

In contrast to the application of everyday land-use laws to religious organizations, discrimination against a religious landowner is a free-exercise violation. For example, if a zoning board or city intended to rid the community of a religious group, and therefore denied an otherwise appropriate variance simply because they disliked the landowner's beliefs, the purpose would violate the Establishment Cause, which prohibits laws that do not "have a secular legislative purpose."[42] It would also violate the Free Exercise Clause, which the Supreme Court has employed to invalidate laws governing a religious entity based on animus or hostility.[43] As I will discuss in more detail below, religious lobbyists continually argue that they are often subjected to discriminatory land-use decisions, but "[t]he nearly universal experience of American congregations seeking government authorization to do something they want to do is one of facilitation rather than roadblock."[44]

For those familiar with the typical relationship between religious entities and the government in the United States, this should come as no surprise. In my experience at least, it is the rare city, town, or municipality that will not go out of its way to help a religious project go forward. The government will not turn its back on the community's master plan, ordinarily, but religious landowners seem to do significantly better than secular developers with similarly burdensome projects. As the *Employment Division v. Smith* Court said:

Values that are protected against government interference through enshrinement in the Bill of Rights are not thereby banished from the political process. Just as a society that believes in the negative protection accorded to the press by the First Amendment is likely to enact laws that affirmatively foster the dissemination of the printed word, so also a society that believes in the negative protection accorded to religious belief can be expected to be solicitous of that value in its legislation as well.[45]

There is a strong hint of entitlement in the religious landowners' drive to avoid the typical expenses and hurdles faced by any ambitious building project, especially if that project seeks to insert itself into a residential neighborhood. The United States has fed into such a view by giving religious landowners property tax exemptions, which despite the enormous financial benefit, were upheld against Establishment Clause attack in 1970, because the practice had been in place since the beginning of the country.[46]

Historical preservation has been treated as a bur in religious entities' saddles, because they often own older buildings that are eligible for historical designation. In New York City in 1986, St. Bartholomew's Church challenged the city's historical preservation laws, but the court found that there was no free-exercise defense.[47] That decision spurred religious entities to lobby for exemptions from historical preservation and land-use regulations, which they argue never serve a compelling interest.[48] Religious landowners also have been assisted by exemptions from historical preservation laws in California,[49] Pittsburgh,[50] and Rockwall, Texas, which revised its historic district boundaries to specifically exclude four churches so that they would not be burdened by the designation.[51] In 1992, the Washington Supreme Court, applying state constitutional law, determined that Seattle could not impose landmark designation on a church, where it would have to seek approval for alterations, and the ordinance granted the city the right to determine which changes were religious in nature. Because the law was not neutral on its face, strict scrutiny applied, and the government failed to prove that historical preservation is a compelling interest.[52]

This is one of the more curious features of American society, actually. No one in Europe would dream of asserting that history is a second-class interest. There is history on every corner, oftentimes in the form of a cathedral, but in this relatively new country, there is little respect for history, and even less for preserving historical buildings. Thus, courts tend to have little difficulty declaring that historical preservation is comparable to aesthetic preference, and that beauty is a second-order value as well. For example, one Oregon court flatly stated that "zoning for aesthetic purposes alone is not a valid exercise of police power, as land use restrictions designed solely for improvement of appearance of community do not tend to promote public health, safety, morals or general welfare of community."[53] A Washington state court also set the value of historic preservation and aesthetics well below the religious landowner's interests: "The City's interest in preservation of aesthetic and historic structures is not compelling and it does not justify the infringement of First Covenant's right to freely exercise religion. The possible loss of significant architectural elements is a price we must accept to guarantee the paramount right of religious freedom."[54]

In this environment, churches presume that historical preservation is not their responsibility. When the Trinity United Methodist Church in Opelika-Auburn, Alabama, was given the century-old Frederick-Whatley-Chapman house, it saw "it as a white elephant," which it hoped to sell to someone to move it from the lot.[55] If no one was willing to pay for the move, they planned to demolish it, even though the house has been described as one of the city's "most majestic and historic homes."[56] This is a story repeated frequently – the religious institution sees no moral or social problem with treating historical properties as throwaways and treats those who do place value in historical preservation as enemies of the good. Good government would inject the idea of the public good into this competition of interests and find means of serving everyone's interest. The best result in every land use dispute is the win-win result.

### From RFRA to RLUIPA: religious landowners obtain preferential treatment under the land-use laws

The political clout of organized religions in 20th-century America permitted them to obtain even more preferential treatment in the land-use process. Congress passed the Religious Freedom Restoration Act in 1993, which treated every law in the country, including land-use laws, as presumptively unconstitutional, which means no governing authority could impose land-use laws under RFRA unless it could prove the law was passed for a compelling interest and was tailored as narrowly as possible.[57]

I will discuss RFRA in some detail in Part Two, but suffice it to say for now that RFRA was an enormous boon for religious entities intent on avoiding the law. In an interesting turn of events, it was a land-use, historic preservation case that razed RFRA. The archbishop of San Antonio, Texas, sought to demolish the St. Peter Catholic Church in Boerne, Texas, and to replace it with a box-like structure. The Boerne City Council responded by refusing to permit complete demolition, because the mission-style church, built in 1923, was located in a historic preservation district, and in fact was a focal point of the district. The two parties began to negotiate over what percentage of the front of the church would be preserved when RFRA became law in November 1993. The archbishop filed a federal lawsuit claiming that RFRA permitted the church to avoid the city's historic preservation laws. In 1997, the Supreme Court held that Congress could not usurp state and local authority by this law with its breathtaking scope, and invalidated RFRA.[58] What was the result? The parties resumed negotiating and 80 percent of the church was retained, with the facade facing the historical district preserved and a beautiful addition on the back, beyond the sightlines from the historical district.[59] All of which is to point out that land-use law is usually a matter of negotiating, and that reasonable parties typically sit on either side of the table. The federal law tipped the power balance in favor of the religious entity, and its invalidation righted the balance.

Religious entities, however, were not to be impeded by the Supreme Court's rejection of RFRA. They soldiered on to introduce the Religious Liberty Protection Act, which would have had nearly the same scope, but which did not make it to the floor of the Senate, because of growing concerns about its real-world impact, especially on children. When the vast scope of RFRA and RLPA proved unconstitutional and then unpalatable to Congress, religious groups stripped the RLPA bill down to two categories: land use and prisons. The resulting statute was the Religious Land Use and Institutionalized Persons Act.[60] The acronym, RLUIPA, rhymes with chalupa.

Before RLUIPA, religious landowners in virtually every jurisdiction were just landowners, required to abide by zoning and land-use restrictions, with the concomitant market price for property and for obtaining zoning alterations. If their project was incompatible with the district, they would have to apply for a special-use permit or a variance, just like any other landowner. When they sought to institute a building project in a residential neighborhood, they had to weigh the cost of the land and construction, the likelihood the use would be limited because it was in a residential area, and the costs of obtaining a permit. They also had to take into account the views of the homeowners regarding the impact of their proposal. In other words, they were property owners with equal rights under the land use law with all other property owners, and they had to be a good neighbor.

RFRA and then RLUIPA changed all that. In 2000, President Bill Clinton (who never met a religious cause he would not support as president),[61] signed RLUIPA, saying: "Today I am pleased to sign into law S. 2869, the 'Religious Land Use and Institutionalized Persons Act of 2000,' which will provide important protections for religious exercise in America." Then he praised the usual suspects behind such legislation, Senators Hatch and Kennedy. (It has not been done yet, but one could write a book about their partnership benefiting religious entities). Not skipping a beat, he then thanked the religious groups, a group of which called themselves the Coalition for the Free Exercise of Religion, and the civil rights communities for "crafting this legislation."

President Clinton went on to say: "Their work in passing this legislation once again demonstrates that people of all political bents and faiths can work together for a common purpose that benefits all Americans."[62] To state his point a little more clearly, this was special interest legislation, drafted outside Congress and then passed because the members and the president believed the right people were behind it, not because they had determined independently that it was a good law for the people.

RLUIPA requires equal and fair treatment for religious landowners, which is not particularly remarkable, aside from the fact one can fairly question why Congress would spend its time on provisions that obviously mimic the Constitution.[63] But it also directs courts to treat land-use laws as applied to religious entities as though they were presumptively unconstitutional. Those provisions mandate the following: Where the land-use law imposes a substantial burden on a religious landowner's religious conduct, and the law is applied through an "individualized assessment," the government may not enforce its law unless it can prove the law was necessary and narrowly tailored.[64] In other words, Congress created a new "civil right" and a new forum – the federal courts – for churches burdened by land-use laws. This new regime has introduced the following scenario: A religious landowner who might not have attempted to impose an ambitious building project on a residential neighborhood, or who would not have purchased a piece of property because it needed zoning that would be difficult to obtain, will change course 180 degrees. Local zoning and planning authorities were displaced by Congress, and the federal judiciary, who have never heard land-use cases unless there was a constitutional violation charged, became zoning board review courts. This is not a good scenario for homeowners or local governments. The balance of power in residential neighborhoods shifts to the religious landowners at the expense of the residential quality of the neighborhood. The untoward result is that homeowners become second-class citizens to their religious neighbors, and federal courts meddle with constitutional land use law.

The reader may be thinking that churches might not take advantage of their superior status very often, because they are institutions of integrity or because the cost of federal litigation would lead them to bring RLUIPA claims only when the cost of the litigation could be justified. Unfortunately, they do.

The first reason – integrity – unfortunately does not wash, because the religious entities usually view their project as so superior to the needs of the neighbors that they feel justified in their elevated status. The statute sets up a terrible dynamic where religious landowners defend their special treatment on the ground that their goals are religious, as though the neighbors are all atheists (the likelihood of which, in this society, is low – only about 14 percent claim to be atheists or agnostics).[65] When the neighbors balk at the projected plans on neutral grounds, such as increased traffic, noise, and light, they are accused of being anti-xxx (the reader should fill in the blank of the religious affiliation of the landowner), invoking RLUIPA. RLUIPA has turned neighbor against neighbor and is one of the most religiously divisive laws ever enacted in the United States.

Nor does the cost of RLUIPA litigation typically deter religious landowners. The drafters of RLUIPA (the American Civil Liberties Union, the Department of Justice, and others) did not stop at providing "a legal weapon" no secular landowner could wield.[66] RLUIPA contains what is called an "attorneys' fees" provision, which forces the government to pay the attorneys' fees for both sides if the government loses.[67] The attorneys' fees provision has magnified the special quality of RLUIPA for religious landowners, literally enticing them to file federal lawsuits they would not have dreamed of filing in the past. In these times of tight budgets for cities and states, the prospect of having to pay for federal litigation, which is always expensive, is daunting enough. But the specter of having to pay both sides' fees could break the community bank, especially where the locality's insurance carrier balks at covering the cost of the litigation. Local authorities fold like a house of cards, regardless of the merits of either side's position.

The prospect of attorneys' fees also has encouraged religious interest groups like the Becket Fund (one of RFRA's and RLUIPA's most enthusiastic supporters) and the Pacific Justice Institute to bankroll land-use litigation, making the litigation free for the religious entity. No longer is cost a factor in deciding whether to go to federal court, and claims that religious landowners would never have pursued in the past suddenly become attractive. Coincidentally, RLUIPA's potential to elevate religious landowners above all similarly situated landowners becomes a reality.

The religious landowners also have a strategic advantage in the federal courts, because, as the usual claims of discrimination waft through the lawsuit, the federal court usually knows very little about typical zoning practices and rules – this has been an arena that has belonged to local and state governments in almost all circumstances until now. The churches have an uncanny ability to make standard, fair practices sound inherently prejudiced. In that poisoned atmosphere, cities then must argue that their laws were passed for a "compelling interest" by the "least restrictive means." It's a miracle if every church does not obtain whatever it seeks through RLUIPA, because the atmospherics and the church's arguments typically amount to a claim that they have a right to complete exemption from the law. RLUIPA, thus, is a win-win-win situation for religious landowners. They obtain new power against neutral, generally applicable land-use law, they have the prospect of having their attorney's fees paid by the city, and the cost is ameliorated by religious interest groups.

Remarkable religious land-use proposals have been asserted under the RLUIPA umbrella. A good number have not been winners for the religious landowners, but RLUIPA still has generated serious costs for the neighbors and the cities. Residential neighbors have had to fight incompatible land uses to keep their neighborhoods residential, and local governments have been saddled with the cost of such litigation even when the claim was not meritorious. It takes money to defend oneself in federal court, and RLUIPA does not have a corresponding attorneys' fee provision that would require the religious plaintiff to pay the city's fees in the event the plaintiff loses.

*Religious day-care centers in residential neighborhoods*

Before RFRA or RLUIPA became law, it was generally held that religious day-care centers in residential neighborhoods could be regulated as a distinct category from churches and nursery schools in churches.[68] They had to abide by density, signage, and other typical requirements for obtaining a special-use permit. For example, in Evanston, Illinois, in 1987, Love Church and its pastor, Marzell Gill, alleged that requiring them to file a detailed plan and an application fee for a special-use permit violated their free-exercise rights. The court rejected their argument, because the express purpose of these requirements was plainly secular: to protect health, safety, morals, and welfare. The court explained:

> The burden this ordinance places on Love Church is merely financial. If the price is right, landlords can be found who will be willing to agree to a contingency clause. If all else failed, plaintiffs could rent without a contingency clause. Economic burdens do not rise to a constitutionally impermissible infringement of freedom to worship.[69]

This was standard reasoning until 1993, when RFRA was passed. Then there was a return to sanity from 1997 to 2000, after RFRA was held unconstitutional. In 2000, this reasoning took another hit when RLUIPA was enacted.

Since RLUIPA was enacted, cases have turned 180 degrees. Before, a zoning decision could be made according to the intensity of the use, so churches were required to be treated like all other landowners. It worked both ways for them. In California, for example, churches had no special privilege to be in any particular zoned district. Therefore, cities could zone churches to zones other than residential zones, in part because their intense use was incompatible with residential neighborhoods.[70] In other circumstances, it meant that a zoning authority could not treat a church any less well than other landowners in the same district, e.g., by adding a day-care facility. "Churches or religious associations are recognized and treated . . . as bodies entitled under any form of government, to enjoy the benefits of property, which property, like that of all other citizens, whether individuals, associations of individuals, or corporations, should be protected and secured to them by law."[71]

In Cheyenne, Wyoming, the Grace United Methodist church proposed in 2001 to build a nonreligious 100-child day-care center in the heart of a settled residential neighborhood.[72] When the local authorities denied permission, the church appealed but the Board of Adjustment still rejected its claims, because it was not a use permitted in a residential district and it was "incompatible with community goals and the neighborhood."[73] A federal lawsuit soon followed, invoking RLUIPA. The federal trial court held that the church had failed to prove the zoning law placed a substantial burden on its religious conduct, and therefore could not rely on RLUIPA. The church has appealed to the Tenth Circuit, where the case is pending.

### Bringing the homeless into a residential neighborhood

In the Pico-Union area of East Los Angeles, the Catholic Brothers of the Missionaries of Charity, which was founded by Mother Teresa, have sought to bring a homeless shelter – operating three days a week during the day and serving approximately 40 adults – into the settled residential, historic neighborhood of Alvarado Terrace. In May 2001, neighbors started to notice beer cans on the ground and loitering by those coming to the shelter. The city did nothing on its own about the fact a homeless shelter was operating in a residential neighborhood without the necessary permits, which is typical. Cities generally do not extend themselves to find religious entities in violation of zoning laws. But when the neighbors complained, the city issued citations for zoning violations and asked the use as a homeless shelter be moved to another, more compatible area. As often happens in these cases, the city scouted out more suitable sites for the religious organization, which is not necessary, but certainly shows the city's good faith. The Brothers insisted their younger homeless needed the "safe haven" of a "residential environment." The group's leader, Brother James Walker, said, "This is how we worship . . . by helping the poorest of the poor."[74] The neighbors observed the residential quality of their neighborhood crumbling, as some witnessed drug deals near the shelter and endured the homeless knocking on their doors at night, looking for the shelter.

Instead of finding a middle ground, the Brothers filed an RLUIPA lawsuit in federal court, arguing that the city's order to move would be unduly burdensome on the homeless who came to the shelter and that such a move would be costly for them. At the trial-court level, the judge issued a tentative order finding that the city did not infringe on the Brothers' free-exercise rights, but that it created a substantial burden on the Brothers' under RLUIPA.[75] The judge set a date to hear the parties on the constitutionality of RLUIPA in the late summer of 2003, but the hearing and ruling have yet to take place.[76]

*The attempt to transform light religious use into congregational use*

In Abington, Pennsylvania, a thriving Reform Jewish congregation projected to encompass approximately 450 families, purchased a 10-acre parcel in 1999 for worship services, Hebrew classes, religious classes, the High Holy Days, religious meetings, bar and bat mitzvah services, wedding ceremonies, and other celebrations. The parking lot was to be expanded from 20 to a minimum of 137 spots.[77] The property was in a residential neighborhood, but the congregation argued it had a right to establish a synagogue at the site, because it had been previously dedicated to religious purposes. The zoning board rejected the claim, though, because the prior use was dramatically different than the proposed use: it had been a nunnery and then a monastery, and traffic was nearly nonexistent in the quiet cul-de-sac. Indeed, the monastery was so quiet some of the neighbors thought the monks had all died. Traffic studies indicated that the synagogue's proposed use would increase the number of cars daily from fewer than 10 to over 100,[78] which meant homeowner neighbors, who bought their homes thinking they would remain on a quiet cul-de-sac, faced the necessity of having to tell their children to stop playing street hockey and to watch for cars and strangers. The character of the neighborhood was about to undergo a seismic change that would affect basic aspects of the homeowners' lifestyles.

Replacing the formerly light uses with a busy congregation would have undermined the residential character of the street. Judge Clarence

Newcomer, of the district court, however, ruled initially that the congregation's constitutional rights were infringed on equal protection grounds."[79] The U.S. Court of Appeals reversed the trial court's equal protection reasoning, finding that standard land use principles had been applied. On remand in the trial court, the congregation won again, but this time under RLUIPA. That decision is now before the Third Circuit, though the Congregation reportedly has found other more suitable property.

In order for an RLUIPA claim to go forward, the religious entity bears the burden of showing that the land-use law imposes a "substantial burden" on religious conduct. "Substantial burden" is a term of art, which has been employed in free-exercise cases for decades. It means that if a law places a de minimis burden on religious conduct, there is no issue about religious liberty. Rather, the burden must "effect" grave interference with important religious tenets or . . . affirmatively compel congregants to perform acts undeniably at odds with fundamental tenets of their religious beliefs.'"[80] Expense and inconvenience are not substantial burdens.[81] The congregation argued "that preventing a church from developing a particular property is in fact a substantial burden on free exercise."[82] In effect, the Abington congregation was arguing that it had a right to choose its location, which is to say that zoning was simply inapplicable to them under RLUIPA. Amazingly, Judge Newcomer agreed: "Evaluating the instant case with the understanding that the RLUIPA changed the standard for the type of burdens on free exercise that are actionable, and under the case law applying this definition, it is clear that the Ordinance and the denial of a variance to the Plaintiffs are substantial burdens on their free exercise rights."[83]

The congregation had available to it other alternative locations within the same jurisdiction, but it succeeded in proving that its religious beliefs were somehow burdened, as if it were being forced to change, because that particular property was being made unavailable. In effect, the court ruled that inconvenience was sufficient to prove there was a substantial burden on religious conduct. The court is wrong on the interpretation of "substantial burden," but this case illustrates how religious liberty discourse can get so off track in the United States, especially when RLUIPA enters the picture.

The means by which religious land-use advocates have orchestrated the public record is quite evident in the Abington case. The neighbors objected to the changing quality of their neighborhood, but, from the beginning, the congregation's strategy was to insinuate that the denial was based on religious discrimination. The *Wall Street Journal* gave the Becket Fund space for an editorial addressing the issue in general, which also addressed the Abington case in particular: "The Philadelphia suburb of Abington Township refused to allow a Jewish congregation to move into a former Catholic convent, ruling that substituting Jewish worship for Catholic worship was not a 'continuing use' of the land."[84] Yet, the use was not continuous, because the use was dramatically different regardless of religious identity. The congregation was asking to transform a property so quiet that neighbors did not know monks still resided there into a full-service, large-scale religious complex that would multiply traffic by a factor of 15. What you have here is a religious advocate injecting interdenominational hatred into a context where it otherwise did not exist. If these are the tactics of those assisting religious landowners, presumably with their clients' consent, it is no wonder that divisive religious discord is being sown in residential neighborhoods in the wake of RLUIPA.

In the same op-ed, a pending case at the time was given the following description:

> Across the country, laws inhospitable to religious organizations . . . have become quite typical. Consider: In Castle Hills, Texas, the city, in a recent court filing, referred to a Baptist church as a "cancer." Several years ago the city ran another house of worship out of town, ultimately moving into the space, taking down the cross and transforming the building into city hall.

Sounds like a pretty awful city, doesn't it? It certainly rings of discrimination against religion. When federal judge Royal Furgeson decided the case, though, he found a very different picture. First, the city had "granted multiple special use permits to the [mentioned Baptist] Church in order to accomplish its goals for expansion." The city was not opposed to religious use at all, but rather was consistently concerned about the impact of intense uses on residential neighborhoods. In an insightful and well-written opinion, he stated that

> this City struggles against size, not religious practice. Here, the undisputed facts reveal a long-lasting antagonism between Church and City that is rooted in a struggle over size of the Church and size and character of the surrounding neighborhood. There is no evidence here that the City harbors ill-will nor that the City means by its aggressive zoning decisions to alter or impede the religion in any way. Rather, the

City means to halt this Church's growth, not spiritually, but geographically . . . [even though the] City refers to the Church as a cancer feeding
upon healthy surrounding cells, [t]he Court's review of the evidence
submitted by both parties. . . . [shows that none of the City's conduct]
rises to the level of religious discrimination or exclusion.[85]

The *Castle Hills Baptist Church v. City of Castle Hills* case illustrates
how charges of discrimination can mask actual disputes over land use,
and how RLUIPA fails to solve that very real, local problem. In the case,
the church was not permitted to add a parking lot, but was given the right
to use a fourth story in a neighborhood zoned for two stories, and because
it prevailed on that single issue, the city could be liable for attorney's fees
for the church's entire litigation.

The Guru Nanak Sikh Society of Yuba City, California, filed an application in 2001 for a conditional use permit to build a Sikh gurdwara, or
temple, in an area designed primarily for single-family residences. The
project was to be built on 1.89 acres and included a "2,000 square-foot
assembly area; 1,550 square feet dedicated to restrooms, storage and an
entryway; an additional 1,500 square feet dedicated as a dining area; and
conversion of an existing building to be used as a commercial kitchen
for temple activities. The proposed temple site would hold religious ceremonies for no more than 75 people at a time."[86] The application was
denied, and in the course of the inevitable RLUIPA lawsuit, the trial court
ruled that the county planning commission violated RLUIPA, because
"'preventing a church from building a worship site fundamentally inhibits
its ability to practice its religion.'"[87] This is extremely troubling reasoning, because the logical conclusion is that any religious entity that seeks
permission to build anywhere and is denied has already shown a substantial burden on its religious exercise – whether it is a religious school for
a 1,000 students or a megachurch landing in a residential neighborhood.

### Racing from the local land use authorities to federal court in RLUIPA cases

Before RLUIPA was enacted in 2000, cities, towns, municipalities and
their organizations asked that RLUIPA include a provision that required
landowners to exhaust the local land-use process before RLUIPA could be
invoked. Apparently, they saw the specter of early land-use rulings on any

application by a religious entity taking them straight to federal court – before they even had a chance to fully investigate the case. They did not get the provision, although the legislative history does include the following: The "Act does not provide religious institutions with immunity from land use regulation, nor does it relieve religious institutions from applying for variances, special permits or exceptions, hardship approval, or other relief provisions in land use regulations, where available without discrimination or unfair delay."[88] As RLUIPA has worked its way through the courts, one of the questions that has required resolution (because Congress failed to be clear enough) concerns when a religious landowner may go to federal court with RLUIPA. The federal courts, which rarely heard land-use proceedings before RLUIPA, have split on when a religious land use claimant can get into federal court.

In Mamaroneck, New York, a suburb of New York City, an Orthodox Jewish school's construction permit for a new school structure in a residential neighborhood was denied for environmental/neighborhood reasons in 2002.[89] The school immediately took its case to federal court, before "the possibility of approval of a resubmission with modifications designed to address the cited problems" was explored.[90] The district court granted summary judgment in favor of the school and directed immediate and unconditional approval of the school's application.[91] A panel for the U.S. Court of Appeals for the Second Circuit was not so inclined. It reversed the district court's ruling and held that the decision did not seem to be final at the local level.[92]

In Morgan Hill, California, San Jose Christian College did not even bother to file a complete application for a zoning amendment to allow for the conversion of a hospital, grandfathered into a residential community, into an educational facility. The U.S. Court of Appeals for the Ninth Circuit correctly found there was no substantial burden on the college, where it had not even initiated the proper land-use processes.[93]

*RLUIPA is not limited to religious institutions; private homeowners have invoked it as well*

In New Milford, Connecticut, Robert Murphy believes in praying at home with family and friends and has held weekly prayer meetings at his home.[94] Often, attendance reached or exceeded 50 people, and the guests stayed a number of hours every Sunday. The neighbors did not respond to the religious character of the meetings, but they did voice objections to increased traffic and parking problems. In response, Murphy asked for permission to install a parking lot on his property. He eventually withdrew the parking lot request, which made sense, given that a parking lot is not a typical accessory use for a single-family home. The Zoning Enforcement Officer counted 13 to 20 cars in the driveway, rear yard, or cul de sac on three separate occasions, and issued a cease-and-desist order for the intense use of the home to cease. This was not a "customary" use for a residential property, which is to say it was not "commonly, habitually, and by long practice established" as a use reasonably associated with a single-family home in an R-40 zone (which is a low-density, single-family zone that permits residences, farms, and associated accessory uses).

There were several options open to Murphy at that point. He could have filed an appeal with the zoning board of appeals in New Milford or he could have requested a variance. Either avenue was open. Instead, he chose to go straight to federal court on the basis of a single cease-and-desist order. On the basis of this undeveloped record and incomplete determination in New Milford, the magistrate judge, Holly Fitzsimmons, found in favor of the Murphys in 2003 in a 39-page opinion on a number of theories, and the zoning enforcement officer, Kathy Castagnetta, whom I represent, appealed. The case is now pending in the U.S. Court of Appeals for the Second Circuit. The point here is not to debate the merits, but to point out how RLUIPA could transform a single zoning action taken by a town into costly litigation that lasts years. The rational person must wonder if it is worth it, at any level.

*The problem with RLUIPA, or any law that gives neighboring landowners different rights simply on the basis of religious status*

The primary problem with RLUIPA is that it alters the balance between neighboring properties in the same zoned district. Residential homeowners who are faced with ambitious religious building plans have a strong claim that their right to the equal protection of the laws has been violated. The religious entity is attempting to do that which the homeowner may not, and in effect, there are two classes of citizens under RLUIPA or the state RFRAs. The first class is classified as "religious" and the second class envelops everyone else. It is fundamentally unfair, as any homeowner who has been in this circumstance will tell you.

Lower courts have been hoodwinked into believing that RLUIPA is just a reiteration of the Free Exercise Clause, so no harm, no foul. The significant uptick in federal litigation over religious land use since RLUIPA's passage would seem to indicate just the opposite. The law was passed because religious landowners demanded better than the status quo provided. Enterprising defenders of the law, however including some in the U.S. Department of Justice, hit upon a way to have their cake and eat it, too. Religious landowners are granted better treatment than ever before, but the law's defenders wave a wand as they chant that nothing has changed.

Here is how it works. Before RFRA and RLUIPA imposed strict scrutiny on land-use laws to the benefit of religious entities, those same entities were required to follow generally applicable, neutral laws. By strict scrutiny, I mean that the courts treat the law as though it is presumptively unconstitutional.[95] The clever trick is that RLUIPA imposes strict scrutiny on land-use laws that involve "individualized assessment,"[96] because there are some Supreme Court free-exercise cases that invalidate laws that employ "individualized assessment," or so they say. Then in every RLUIPA case, they argue that any application of a land-use law entails an "individualized assessment," in the sense that each landowner's case is decided on its own facts. Trust me, this is crazy reasoning.

The Supreme Court has never treated case-by-case analysis as presumptively unconstitutional. That is tantamount to saying that every time a court decides a case by applying the law to the facts, its decision should be presumptively unconstitutional. What's happened is that the drafters of RLUIPA ingeniously included the term "individualized assessment," but they left off its modifier. That has permitted them to argue in a huge universe of cases (virtually all land-use cases) that RLUIPA is simply replicating free-exercise law. It is masterful, wishful thinking, or just plain devious.

"Individualized assessment," by itself, means "case by case." If government making individualized assessments makes the outcome presumptively unconstitutional, then every judicial decision in the United

States is likely unconstitutional. That's just plain silly. In the cases where government regulations employed individualized assessments and the Court treated the government's action as presumptively unconstitutional, the constitutional error was not case-by-case analysis, but rather the fact that government engaged in case-by-case analysis *of the reasons* for the requested exemption.[97] Where the government was willing to exempt some from its rules for secular reasons, but would not provide any relief for religious reasons, the court was suspicious of animus toward religion, and rightly so.

For example, there was no rational explanation for the Newark Police Department's rule that no officer could have facial hair unless he had a medical condition.[98] Those with religious reasons for facial hair were not accommodated. If the department's policies were not undermined by creating an exemption for the few that had a medical problem, then they could not be harmed for the few that required a religious exemption.

Similarly, an unemployment compensation scheme that permitted people to take certain days off for secular reasons was unconstitutional when it rejected religious reasons to take those days off.[99] Again, if the general policy could tolerate the secular exceptions, it should tolerate the religious. It is the disparate treatment between secular and religious *reasons* for the exemption that justifies strict scrutiny, not the individualized assessment itself. Thus, RLUIPA goes significantly farther for religious entities than the Constitution does. Under settled constitutional principles, religious entities are bound by generally applicable, neutral laws, including land-use laws, but now those laws are presumptively illegal under RLUIPA. It is a large net win for the religious.

The lower courts that have addressed the issue so far, though, have fallen for the "individualized assessment" language. In the Eastern District of Pennsylvania, Judge Stewart Dalzell, saw the issue as obvious: "What Congress manifestly has done . . . is to codify the individualized assessments' jurisprudence in Free Exercise cases that originated with the Supreme Court's decision in *Sherbert v. Verner* [the individualized assessments' unemployment compensation case]."[100] The point was equally unremarkable to Magistrate Judge Holly Fitzsimmons, who stated that it is "'apparent that [RLUIPA] faithfully codifies the 'individual assessments' jurisprudence in the *Sherbert* through *Lukumi* line of cases.'"[101] They missed a step in the free exercise analysis.

*Religious landowners will still have special privileges in some*
*states once RLUIPA is found unconstitutional or dramatically*
*narrowed in scope*

Twelve states have some form of privilege for religious entities to transform generally applicable, neutral laws into presumptively illegal laws. They usually state that the government "may not substantially burden a person's exercise of religion, even if the burden results from a rule of general applicability, unless it demonstrates a compelling governmental interest that is 'the least restrictive means of furthering that compelling governmental interest.'" Ten states have legislative religious freedom restoration acts or state constitutional amendments that extend to land use. These are Alabama, Arizona, Connecticut, Florida, Idaho, Illinois, New Mexico, Pennsylvania, South Carolina, and Rhode Island.[102] At the same time, two states have RFRA-like laws that carve out specific exceptions to allow local governments to carry out generally applicable land-use laws. Oklahoma and Texas allow that "a governmental entity has no less authority to adopt or apply laws and regulations in a nondiscriminatory manner concerning zoning, land-use planning, traffic management, urban nuisance, or historic preservation, than the authority of the governmental entity that existed under the law prior to the passage of this act."[103]

These state laws are like ticking time bombs, which have not yet been used extensively, but that will be ready for action when RLUIPA is held unconstitutional or severely restricted in scope to make it constitutional. The home prayer case discussed above, invoked not just RLUIPA, but also the Connecticut RFRA, which (like the Alabama constitutional amendment) has the troubling provision that it is triggered by any burden on religion, substantial or not. That means that any de minimis burden on religion may trigger the special treatment and severely disable the universe of land-use regulation as applied to religious entities. Other cases have adverted to the RFRAs, as well, but there are precious few decisions, because the theory is usually duplicative of RLUIPA at this point.

The conflict between religious land use and residential owners generated by the likes of RFRA, RLUIPA, and the state RFRAs entrenches on the most fundamental beliefs of most Americans. Private property is the building block that permitted a massive middle class to be built and to have upward mobility. It broke the bonds of the aristocracy on property ownership, and equalized citizens in ways that no other innovation in the United States would. The private property norm brings into question the notion that entities should have different property rights simply because of their religious status. Real property is real property, and its use affects neighbors regardless whether the homeowner is having a Tupperware party or a prayer meeting, or a large building is hosting religious or secular child care.

It also cuts to the heart of another cherished American principle: the belief in fair dealing. When churches get special privileges, their neighbors feel (and rightly so) that they have been cheated. It is fundamentally unfair to treat property owners in the same location differently because of their identities. It's a gut instinct for Americans, and altering the balance between property owners has been divisive, to say the least.

The real property system in the United States established opportunity and equality. So long as religious entities insist on having special property rights, they will generate the backlash they are just now beginning to comprehend.

# SCHOOLS

The public school system was initiated with religious dispute, and religious accommodation conflicts continue to today. Public schools were originally instituted by a Protestant majority and reflected Protestant religious viewpoints, including mandatory daily readings from the King James Bible. In the early 1820s, New York started funding schools, and by 1840, some Catholics were objecting to the Protestant religious curriculum. As Professor Philip Hamburger recounted in his excellent book, *Separation of Church and State*, the early public schools started with indoctrination in a Protestant perspective. Moreover, they protected their turf, by denying funding to "sectarian" schools (as though the Protestant public schools were not sectarian), "including Baptist, Methodist and Catholic." Over the succeeding years, the political will to prevent funding for any schools other than the

Protestants' was distilled into an antifunding drive aimed mainly at Catholics.[1]

A significant number of Christians in the United States might be tempted to latch onto the early Protestant practices in the schools as proof that the schools should now reintroduce prayer and religion in the schools. They would argue that public education has been corrupted, because prayer and Bible reading have been excised. The Rev. Jerry Falwell, following 9/11, remarked: "We have seen the course of secularism in our schools, and it is obviously time for a change. It is high time our nation once again favors its people of faith by allowing our public-school students to be exposed to prayer and the pursuit of faith."[2] When Wingfield High School (Jackson, Mississippi) principal Bishop Knox was fired after starting the school day at the public school with the prayer, "Almighty God, we ask that you bless our parents, teachers and country throughout the day. In your name we pray. Amen," the American Family Association provided Knox an attorney to challenge his firing.[3] Mississippi Governor Kirk Fordice opined that "'[I]f we keep on with what started in Jackson, Mississippi, one day, I hope soon, it's not going to be legal to keep prayer out of public schools.'"[4] The Rev. Louis Farrakhan also has urged a return to prayer in the public schools: "Thomas Jefferson was rooted in the Gospel of Jesus Christ even though he didn't apply it to his slaves. Those Founding Fathers of this nation were God-fearing men [who would be displeased] if they could come back today and see that the children can't utter a prayer in school, that this nation has put God out and relegated God and religion to some back seat, when without God you have no government."[5]

Before embracing a return to the supposedly golden era of the public school system, though, it is worthwhile to consider how the early preference for the majority religion affected citizens. Instead of simply crafting good character among the students, it sowed religious conflict. Catholics legitimately objected to the use of the King James Bible, but Protestants "refused . . . to withdraw the King James Bible, which, although Protestant, no longer seemed to [them to] belong to any one church."[6] When the Protestants insisted on their own version, the Catholics walked away from the entire system and created their own, at their expense. The extensive Catholic parochial school system that exists today is a result of that exchange.

The early conflict between Protestants and Catholics is not an indict-ment of public education. Rather, it is an object lesson about the dangers of any one religious worldview dominating.

The more diverse the U.S. student body has become, the more extraor-dinary are the claims that have arisen. The United States is well past the era when it could be credibly claimed that the public schools catered ex-clusively to a Judeo-Christian population. School districts face a dizzying menu of challenges from Sikhs to the Amish to the United Pentecostal Church, just to name a few.

This chapter describes three areas of school regulation where religious entities have requested accommodation: antiviolence regulations, dress codes, and curriculum. Each request taken by itself may seem innocu-ous enough (leaving out the violence category), but the problem for the schools was nicely captured by U.S. Supreme Court Justice Robert Jackson in 1948:

> If we are to eliminate everything that is objectionable to any of these warring sects or inconsistent with any of their doctrines, we will leave public education in shreds. Nothing but educational confusion and a discrediting of the public school system can result from subjecting it to constant law suits.[7]

The problem is the enormous assortment of religions in the United States. The accommodation question, as in every other context, cannot be ade-quately addressed by an examination of the believer's tenets and conduct, for they are not the only ones affected by the exemption. When the issue is education, the other students, the educational mission, and the society as a whole that benefits from a well-educated citizenry all have a stake in the decision. Discipline and a controlled atmosphere necessary to educate young people would evaporate if there was slavish accommodation.

The court-ordered accommodations – under either the Religious Free-dom Restoration Act (RFRA)[8] or the *Wisconsin v. Yoder*[9] line of cases – are the most difficult to harmonize with common sense, because the court is drawn into a sympathetic, almost narcissistic, assessment of the believer and invited to discount society's interests in the light of this one believer. There is a tendency in these cases to minimize the actual impact the religious conduct has on the government interests necessary to create the conditions for a good education. For example, when a child carries a relatively small knife for religious purposes, it is easy to believe that this one accommodation will not hurt anyone – it's just a de minimis infringement of the no-weapons rule. But the child carrying the knife does not live in a vacuum, or in a constant state of grace. Here, as elsewhere, accommodation needs to be accomplished by a legislative body that can calculate the balance of harms within a broader context, not by a judge who may only consider the facts of the case before him or her.

These cases address only public and not private schools, because the First Amendment's free-exercise guarantees only limit government action. But they have tremendous impact, because 90 percent of U.S. students attend public school.[10] The same free exercise formula is necessary here as in every other context: legislative accommodation must be consistent with the public good, and the legislature needs to consider all sides, because it imposes a larger perspective than any one religious believer, faith, or administrator.

## Religious accommodation in conflict with preventing violence in the public schools

**WEAPONS.** In 1990, there were approximately 13,000 Sikhs in the United States; by 2001, there were 57,000.[11] Most of the roughly 20 million Sikhs in the world live in the Punjab region of India, which is in the northwest, near Pakistan, with significant populations in the United Kingdom and Canada, whose Sikh population now sits at over 270,000, as well.[12] The devout Sikhs are initiated into the Khalsa, and wear the 5Ks, which are Kesh (uncut hair), Kara (a steel bracelet), Kanga (a wooden comb), Kaccha (distinctive underwear), and Kirpan (sword).[13] (Other, less-doctrinaire believers have moved toward Western style dress and hair.)[14] The Sikhs believe generally in mutual tolerance and respect. Even so, it should come as no surprise that the sword, or knife, they carry has caused consternation in the schools.

In the Sikh faith, kirpan (knives) are considered to be "ceremonial," and there is no set style, which means they can be only a few inches or as long as three feet. They are worn in a sheath over or under clothing.[15] While the rule is that they are only to be drawn if the person believes himself to be in a life and death situation, they are potentially lethal weapons, at times concealed, and at the ready in volatile circumstances.[16] Human nature being what it is, the kirpan have not been simply benign symbols of the Sikh faith.

The Sikhs live in the real world where crime and drug trafficking exist. Two drug addicts (one of whom was a police officer's son) purchased some heroin in Delhi, India, and when they discovered it was mixed with other chemicals, returned, killed two of the dealers and injured a third with a kirpan.[17]

There are many Sikhs in British Columbia, Canada, and provincial authorities have had their share of kirpan-related problems. A Toronto Sikh temple's high priest, Jatinder Singh, allegedly stabbed one of his members, Sarbjit Singh Sandhar, with a kirpan in the midst of a heated exchange regarding whether a Sikh holy book was available for a blessing ceremony. After Singh said none was available, a fight ensued, and Singh allegedly stabbed Sandhar in the chest, and then attempted to stab his neck as well. The priest claimed that his turban was knocked off by the men, and therefore, he feared for his life (which would have justified the stabbing in the Sikh religion if not the secular law). The court did not find his claims credible, but later evidence was discovered that indicated someone else may have used his kirpan in the dispute, so that he was granted a new trial. Singh ultimately pleaded guilty to assault for stabbing the parishioner with his kirpan.[18]

In Toronto, Canada, Tarlochan Dhillon pulled his kirpan on a distant relative, Harvinder Virk, and stabbed him in the stomach. Dhillon was convicted of aggravated assault, but amazingly, while in custody, he objected to the prison authorities taking away his kirpan (and turban), but there was no question that an inmate could not have a knife in prison.[19] In Vancouver, fundamentalists believe in eating on the floor because it signifies all are equal, but others do not think it is necessary. The controversy (which was actually international in scope) turned into a battle royal at one Vancouver temple when a crowd gathered and some tried to bring tables and chairs into the temple. A lot of them carried kirpan, and in the resulting melee, there were six injuries before the police could pry the two factions apart. One man's throat was slit, leading to charges of attempted murder.[20]

The school problems have arisen when Sikh children wear kirpans, typically strapped to their leg, to elementary school. The kirpan that have been at issue have been approximately seven inches long.[21] Every public school in the United States has a no-exceptions weapons ban at this point, so a conflict was inevitable.

In California, the Livingston Union School District refused to permit Rajinder, Sukhjinder, and Jaspreet Cheema, who were Khalsa-baptized Sikhs, to wear their kirpan to school. Under the Supreme Court's dominant free-exercise jurisprudence, the school should have had no problem applying its neutral, generally applicable law to these children.[22] Indeed, it is highly unlikely that the case would have even been brought but for the fact that the RFRA encouraged claims to the free exercise of religion even when the customs are well beyond accepted practices. In the infamous *Cheema v. Thompson* case, the U.S. Court of Appeals for the Ninth Circuit held that the school had a compelling interest in safety, but it had not engaged in the "least restrictive means" of regulating the "ceremonial" knives, and therefore preliminarily enjoined the school district from preventing the Cheema children from coming to school with their kirpan.[23]

This is a classic case of a court with only the record of two parties before it, thinking only in terms of the needs of the believer, and letting the RFRA suspend common sense. According to judges Betty Binns Fletcher and Cynthia Holcomb Hall, the school could not ban the knives simply because other students might be frightened; rather, it could only regulate them in response to "those [threats] which are reasonably related to a real threat," implying that any children's fears would have been irrational. The school district, according to the court, had failed to prove that "any of its students are afraid of or upset by kirpans." Under the RFRA, the school district had to avoid "all unnecessary burdens" on religious believers, so the Sikhs could not be prohibited from attending school with the knives, because the record showed no "school-related violence" from kirpan to date and some school districts had permitted kirpan if they were riveted to their sheaths or the blade was blunt with a rounded tip.[24] Only a flawed legal doctrine would lead a court out on such a weak limb. Knives are knives, and children are not safe in their presence, no matter who they are.

Judge Charles Wiggins, in dissent, invoked a far more rational analysis, by thinking beyond the believer's perspective. The Sikh believer may sincerely believe that a kirpan is only a formality, not intended to be used as a weapon, but Judge Wiggins asked, not what the believer sincerely believed, but rather what was the impact of the conduct for which protection was being claimed. He identified three categories of danger arising from a kirpan, even if the average Sikh child would not be likely to draw it on other children. First, there was the "abnormal, non-law-abiding Sikh child," which is to say that one must bring one's knowledge of the human race to bear on these questions, and there is no question that some children (and adults) do not follow the mores they are taught. Second, he noted that it is not only the child carrying the weapon who is a potential threat, but also the child who could grab the kirpan to hurt others. Finally, he made the observation that the plaintiffs were children, who had only the

> maturity and judgment of children. Given that Sikhs are to use their kirpans in life-or-death situations, we would be forced to rely on school children to make the determination as to when their lives are at stake. Clearly, school officials need not knowingly expose the non-Sikh school children to such an unacceptable position of vulnerability.... [I]t is not clear that any feasible means exist to accommodate the Cheemas' need to carry kirpans.[25]

Without the RFRA, the case likely would not have been filed.

After the RFRA was invalidated, and the proper free-exercise rule was reinstated, the only legitimate forum for the Sikhs to obtain permission for their children to attend public school with kirpans was in the legislature, where the costs and benefits of exempting children from the weapons bans could be weighed, and there could be intensive investigation of how the kirpans might, perhaps, be made nonlethal. In fact, the sizable Sikh population in California persuaded the California legislature to pass just such a measure. Governor Pete Wilson, though, vetoed the exemption in 1994, saying "I am unwilling to authorize the carrying of knives on school grounds and abandon public safety to the resourcefulness of a thousand districts."[26] Thus, the system vetted the issue, and common sense prevailed.

In the Cheema case's Canadian counterpart, a trial court granted a Sikh student, Gurbaj Singh, the right to wear a wooden kirpan underneath his clothes and in a sheath with a fold that was then sealed so that it could not be drawn either intentionally or accidentally. The student was also required to maintain control of the kirpan. The appellate court reversed, because the "kirpan is intrinsically dangerous and the conditions imposed by the trial judge do not address all the risks.... [N]ot only the [school], but any students, would have to assume the risks associated with the presence of a kirpan. Firstly, the physical integrity of the entire school community is threatened by the presence of dangerous objects at school. Secondly, the perception of the climate of security can also be affected."[27] It is hard to disagree with the court's reasoning. The conduct of carrying a knife is inherently dangerous, even if the motivation is sincere religious belief.

The question on many readers' minds, I imagine, will be: What is a Sikh family to do? The kirpan has a long tradition in the faith. History gives three answers. First, the family may choose to send their children to religious schools or to home school, just as the Roman Catholics did in the United States when they disapproved of the public schools' religious bent. Second, the religion might adjust to the legal requirements, as happened with the Mormons and polygamy in the United States, by jettisoning the practice altogether. Third, there might be some attempt on the part of the faith to meet the law halfway. For example, no adult Sikh can fly or enter a federal courtroom with a kirpan. Perhaps, children might be given the same dispensation for school hours. To be clear, these are not legally enforceable suggestions and should not come from the government. It is not the business of the government to direct the Sikhs to alter their beliefs, but it is certainly within the government's purview to reject religious practices that are innately dangerous in the hands of children (and adults). The accommodation, therefore, will have to be made by the Sikh believer to conform to the law, not vice versa.

GANG COLORS AND INSIGNIA. U.S. schools have struggled mightily to eradicate gangs in the schoolhouse. They are inherently violent and when given free rein in the schools, terrorize other students, foster the drug trade, and commit other heinous crimes.

With 48 school-related violent deaths, 2003–04 was the deadliest in several years.[28] The upward trend is making the issue more important than ever. "Increases in gang membership and violent gang activities have negative effects on our nation's schools." Some 40,000 school students reported being threatened or attacked by a gang or gang member.[29] Interestingly, girls make up a significant percentage of the gangs. For example, 16,000 to 20,000 of Chicago's 100,000 gang members were female, according to the 1999 study by the Chicago Crime Commission.[30]

Schools have found that in order to remove gang activity from their halls, they need to force students to remove gang identifications, for example, gang "colors" or jewelry containing gang symbols. "The primary consensus is that a gang is a group with social, racial, or ethnic ties that acts to further a criminal purpose."[31] They alter their colors or symbols so that members are more difficult to detect. One school board explained, "clothing which is identifiable as gang related changes frequently and is, therefore, often difficult to discern."[32]

Frank Hutchins, the principal of the Horace Mann Junior High School in Baytown, Texas, expressed his alarm at the effects that gang apparel caused in his school:

> It wasn't subtle at all. . . . You'd see students dressed in black and red, for instance, clustering together in the mornings. Students said they were being told if they didn't wear a gang's 'colors', they'd be jumped. Teachers noticed the increased presence on campus and said it was becoming disruptive in the classroom.[33]

A dress code was instituted.

Horace Mann Junior High is part of a movement among public schools nationwide to institute school uniforms and rigid dress codes to minimize the impact of gangs (who are so often identified by their apparel) on the learning environment. A survey of school principals revealed that 85 percent wanted dress codes at their schools, and they cited the elimination of gang activity as one of the top motivations for instituting the policy.[34] At the beginning of the movement, President Bill Clinton urged the adoption of such policies to improve behavior and eradicate gang clothing in schools.[35] The Department of Education published a widely distributed "Manual on School Uniforms" that listed decreasing violence and gang affiliation in schools as important goals of instituting dress codes. The department further cited several "Model School Uniform Policies" that appeared to have had an impact on the school environment. For example, after requiring uniforms in all elementary and middle schools, the Long Beach, California, schools saw a 36 percent decrease in overall crime and 50 percent fewer weapons offenses. Other schools commended by the Department of Education did not detail crime statistics, but all saw marked changes in the attitudes and educational environments at their schools.[36]

When schools restrict gang symbols, they can come into conflict with other students' religiously motivated conduct. In *Levon v. O'Rourke*, the Calumet City [Illinois] School District was worried about gang activity at the school and in adjacent areas, and therefore considered a dress code. Street gangs calling themselves the Latin Kings, Black Gangster Disciples, Black P Stones, and Insane Unknowns were known to be in the vicinity near the school. During the 1995–96 school year, the District asked students to wear blue "bottoms" and white "tops," but when compliance was low, instituted a mandatory dress code for the 1996–97 school year, because "[s]tudents' choice of clothing disrupts the learning environment where it may be representative or suggestive or [sic] gang affiliation, or activities. The Board of Education recognizes that gangs are present in the District's community and pose a real threat to the disruption of the schools." The policy also contained a religious and health accommodation provision as well, which authorized the principal discretion to accommodate the student's religious- or health-motivated conduct where there was a "genuine conflict" between the policy and the conduct.[37]

When the policy was under consideration, one mother, Kathryn Levon, in 1994 objected to the school board's policy, because jeans were more durable and the cost of a uniform was beyond her means. Two years later, she argued that it violated her parental rights and that it would not solve the gang nuisance. In August 1996, she objected on numerous religious grounds, most drawn from the New or Old Testament of the Bible, one from the Rev. Martin Luther King, Jr., and another from the Rev. John Irvin. Finally, she quoted an ancient proverb, "A monkey in silk is still a monkey." The board then offered to purchase a uniform for her son, Adam, which was refused, and after Adam was expelled for refusing to follow the code, the board offered him a uniform again, home tutoring, or tutoring in the public library. The parents declined, and Adam was not educated during the fall term.

Magistrate Judge Joan Lefkow found that the Levons failed to prove there was a substantial burden on their religious conduct, because their beliefs were not being coerced. The question was whether the parents were "'being prevented from engaging in religiously motivated conduct or expression,'"[38] and under that standard, the court concluded that the burden placed by the school district was de minimis, and therefore could not rise to a free-exercise violation (under RFRA or the Constitution).

As a matter of black-letter law, the court's decision was correct, but one must wonder why Principal Chinino refused the accommodation, which seemed reasonable and de minimis. To the extent that the parents' religious beliefs dictated that the dress code be struck altogether, their claims were bound to fail. When a regulation serves an important public interest, like reducing the effect of gangs on schools, no single faith has the right to obliterate the rule for all. The closer question was whether accommodation should have been made by the school board for the Levons, in particular. From a constitutional perspective, the district policy could be applied to the Levons, but from a public policy perspective, the principal failed to explain, at least in my view, why blue jeans did not satisfy the white shirt/blue pants formula. There could be a neutral reason. Perhaps it is a slippery slope where it is too difficult to regulate which jeans will be worn and therefore the potential for gang identification arises, but on the basis of the reported opinion, it is difficult to understand why blue (not black or any other color) jeans would not have served the board's goals.

It appears the outcome was determined by a mistake by the principal. The reason he rejected the accommodation was that he found the religious objections to the code weak, because they were not voiced from the beginning,[39] and perhaps because they were so peculiarly tailored for the situation. Yet, these elements offer no justification to deny a requested accommodation. As the reviewing court rightly pointed out, the fact a sincerely held religious belief is peculiar to the believer is no reason to deny accommodation,[40] and there is no obligation to assert one's religious objections to a government policy before asserting secular objections. Thus, the principal should have proceeded from the assumption that the request was sincerely religious. It would have been at that point that the principal would have had to determine whether blue jeans were inherently different from dark blue pants for purposes of avoiding gang activity. The same result might have accrued, but it would have been better explained and therefore more legitimate.

Evenhandedness is the hallmark of a constitutional policy. No school district may choose to enforce a rule against some students and not against others. When the district permits a child to avoid any rule, it better be prepared to permit other students that are similarly situated to avoid it as well, and if it lets the policy be abridged for secular reasons, it must permit the same abridgement for sincere religious reasons. For example, in Biloxi, Mississippi, school officials refused to permit Jewish student, Ryan Green, to wear a Star of David necklace outside his clothing.[41] His grandmother had given it to him as a symbol of his heritage. On a unanimous vote, the school board supported a teacher who had ordered him to take it off, because students were forbidden from wearing any symbol that might be construed as a gang symbol. Gang insignia have included a six-pointed star, like the Star of David, as well as crosses and crucifixes.[42]

The constitutional problem arose, however, when the board decided to permit Christians to continue wearing crucifixes and crosses. Thus, not only is this a case where the rule was not so necessary that it could not be broken in some circumstances, but also the board was picking and choosing between religious symbols. That smacks of potential discrimination and justifies the courts' closest scrutiny of the school board's actions and purposes. After a lawsuit was initiated by the ACLU, the board properly reversed its position.[43]

### Dress codes in conflict with religious mandates (beyond gang issues)

Sometimes a school district will prohibit an article of clothing or jewelry because it is disruptive to the educational atmosphere. Overly short skirts, skimpy tank tops, and T-shirts with obscene messages fit into this category and show that instilling a dress code can be an appropriate means of encouraging the proper learning environment. The concept of "disruption," however, can also play into the marginalization of uncommon religions, but school districts are capable of learning from their mistakes. Rebecca Moreno was a student at the Waxahachie, Texas, High School, and her family was Wiccan. The Morenos explained Wiccan religion as a pagan religion that incorporates witchcraft, multiple gods and goddesses, and nature worship.[44] In 2001, when she was 15 years old, she wore a pentacle necklace, which is a five-pointed star that is a central symbol for the Wiccan religion. First, the school district banned it for its disruptive qualities. Then, Rebecca and the school compromised; she could wear it under her clothing. It needed to be concealed from the other students, because it scared the Christians. The school authorities said they banned the pentacle because Christians associated it with Satan worship and animal sacrifice. September 11 made everyone in the community feel like they were a united force, even if they did not all share the same religious faith. The school superintendent, Bobby Parker, told the Morenos in writing that "While the Wiccan faith may not be the majority religion in our community, our board policies protect all faiths."[45] From a situation that demanded a lawsuit, the parties were able to land on the correct constitutional and policy rule.

The Religious Freedom Restoration Act promised to reach an irrational result in this arena as well, however. The dress code and apparel regulations do serve (when applied as they should be) important ends, including safety and maintaining a nurturing educational environment. RFRA robbed school districts of their power to enforce uniform dress codes, by making it likely that "schools generally may not prohibit the wearing of [religious] items," in the words of the U.S. Secretary of Education Richard Riley and Attorney General Janet Reno memorandum to the schools on religious liberty in the schools in 1995.[46] The invalidation of RFRA makes it possible for the school district experiencing severe gang problems or drug trade to take the steps it may need to take to address the problem, even if it means not accommodating all religious clothing.

The Illinois High School Association prohibited any person playing high school sports from wearing hats or headgear (except a headband no wider than two inches). The reason was that they feared the headwear would fall off during play, and create an unsafe condition for the other players. Orthodox Jewish males challenged the rule, saying that they were required to wear a yarmulke (a small skull cap worn on the crown of the head) except when unconscious, immersed in water, or in a life-threatening situation.[47] The conflict was obvious, but because the case was decided in 1982, which was the era when the Supreme Court's doctrine handed the authority to legislate exemptions to the courts, the result was not so clear. The United States Court of Appeals for the Seventh Circuit held, in an opinion by Judge Richard Posner, that the rule was neutral and generally applicable and it violated no equal protection principles, and then he proceeded to weigh the interest of the believer against the interest of the state, which turned into a complicated calculus:

> The more valuable the benefit to the claimant and hence the greater the burden on him of forgoing it in order to continue to observe his religion, the greater must be the burden on the government of relaxing the conditions it places on that benefit for a refusal to make an exception for the claimant to survive a challenge based on the First Amendment.

> Free exercise of religion does not mean costless exercise of religion, but
> the state may not make the exercise of religion unreasonably costly.[48]

In plainer English, the court's task was to assess (1) how important the
religious conduct was to the believer, (2) the degree of the burden on
that conduct imposed by the law; and (3) what it would take for the
government to create an exemption for the conduct. At this time, when
free-exercise doctrine had gone off track, the court took it upon itself to
be the judge of a person's beliefs and to know just how the law should
have been crafted to find the right median point between "costless" free
exercise and "unreasonably costly" legislation. It is a lot to ask from a
court delimited by the Establishment Clause and its own institutional
incapacity to engage in broad-ranging social policy determinations. This
is an excellent case to show how misguided such an approach is.

First, the court speculated that the Talmud did not really require the
wearing of yarmulkes every minute other than the three exceptions permitted, pointing out that that would mean no haircuts. Further specula-
tion centered around whether the bobby pins used to hold the yarmulke
on the head, which were not very successful in keeping the yarmulke
on in sports, were required by the Talmud. The conclusion on this latter
question was that they probably were not religiously required, with Judge
Posner opining, "while we are not Talmudic scholars we are reasonably
confident, and the plaintiffs' counsel acknowledged at oral argument, that
the precise nature of the head covering and the method by which it is kept
on the head are not specified by Jewish law."[49] In other words, the court
was basing its decision on its individual assessment of Jewish law, which
was not in the record, but was confirmed at oral argument, of all places.
The court's jurisprudence at the time invited this sort of unseemly judicial assessment of the meaning of religious doctrine. While courts may
acknowledge religious doctrine as a factual element in a case, they may
not determine its contours, and this poking around Jewish belief should
ring all sorts of constitutional bells. The oral argument sounds more like a
legislative hearing than a discussion of legal principles properly addressed
by a court.

Having assessed the meaning of Orthodox Jewish law, the court then
viewed its role as divining whether there is a necessary conflict between
the sports rule and the Jewish law. In effect, the court asked itself whether

there was a way for the rule and the conduct to coexist peacefully. This essentially legislative inquiry led Judge Posner to delve into the ways in which a yarmulke might be secured to the head so that the Orthodox Jews could wear it and the association's concerns could be put at rest. In an unintentionally humorous passage, he says, "We are not the people to devise the method [of attaching the yarmulke more securely to the head], to say that yarmulkes should be equipped with chin straps or sewn to headbands or replaced by some form of head covering that fits the head more securely."[50] If they weren't the people to fix the problem, what was the second clause of that sentence doing? Maybe a mild suggestion, which just so happened to take into account that headbands were permitted? In case those who were supposed to make such decisions came to believe no accommodation could be crafted that works, the court said, "But we are reasonably sure that a secure head covering exists or can be devised at *trivial cost* without violating any tenet of [O]rthodox Judaism.... "[51] The court had by then taken on the full power of the legislative or regulatory powers – assessing the need for accommodation, the means of accommodation, and even the financial cost.

But how did the court know all this? Not because the record provided support. To the contrary, the court made it all up. It did not know for a fact whether bobby pins are required or whether another head covering could substitute for the yarmulke, that a chin strap would be feasible in any situation, or that the manufacturing of a device to keep the yarmulke on the head would be cost effective, let alone, only a "trivial cost."

But here is the most entertaining part of the opinion. After going through all of these legislative details, the court finally reached its holding, and lo and behold, the players lost. The association's no-headwear rule stood, because there was "no constitutional right to wear yarmulkes insecurely fastened by bobby pins."[52]

The resolution of the question adverse to the players normally would have been cause for dismissal of the case, but, no, not when the courts were in control of accommodation. Judge Posner ordered the district court to retain jurisdiction "so that the plaintiffs can have an opportunity to propose to the association a form of secure head covering that complies with Jewish law yet meets the association's safety concerns."[53]

In other words, the court arrogated to itself the power to order an accommodation that was not constitutionally mandated. The court further micromanaged the process by placing the "burden of proposing an alternative" on the players, because they "know so much more about Jewish law."[54] This was judicial lawmaking at its most arrogant, and the 1990 decision in *Employment Division v. Smith* decision – which held that legislatures, not courts, are the appropriate branch to decide whether to create exceptions to a neutral, generally applicable law – could not have been decided fast enough thereafter. *Smith* took the courts' unbounded power to force religious accommodation and placed it where it belonged – in the legislature – where these issues of fact and belief can be openly debated by various experts and no one need bear any particular burden of proof, because everyone involved in the process is intended to work toward an outcome consistent with the public good.

A recurring contemporary problem here and abroad has been the conflict between school prohibitions on headgear and the Islamic belief that adolescent girls and women should wear a burka, niqab, hijab, khimar, or headscarf.[55] Headgear bans in the schools exist because hats detract from the educational atmosphere, may be used as gang reinforcement, and are preferred hiding places for contraband, such as drugs and weapons.[56] Once again, one can hardly fault any school district for the policy, and the First Amendment is no defense to a neutral rule. Even though the Constitution does not mandate the accommodation, the door always remains open, and various school districts have accommodated a variety of religious headgear. For example, the Lafayette, Louisiana, school board permitted eight Rastafarian children to attend school, even though their religion required head coverings, crowns (loose-knit circular hats, which typically are knitted red, yellow and green, which represents the Ethiopian flag), worn over dreadlocks.[57] In February, 2004, a computer teacher at Antelope Valley College in Lancaster, California, ordered a student to remove her hijab, but she refused on religious reasons. When the dean backed her up, the teacher resigned.[58]

The problem has not been limited to the United States, as Canadian schools have had to deal with it as well. In 1994, Emilie Ouimet, age 12, was expelled from Ecole Louis Riel, a public high school, for wearing a hijab, but a year later, the Quebec Human Rights Commission ruled that public school dress codes banning the hijab violate the charter. The issue is rather different when the question is whether the hijab can be worn in the context of a nonpublic religious school. In 2003, Irene Waseem, 16, was expelled from College Charlemagne, a private Catholic girls' school, for wearing the hijab.[59] The different results lie in the fact that private schools have more latitude to impose beliefs and religious symbols in their schools. Dania Bali, a straight-A student at College Regina Assumpta, a private Catholic girls' school in northend Montreal, was permitted to wear her hijab for two years, but then was expelled for wearing it. Upon consideration, the parents' committee voted unanimously to retain its strict school uniform policy of banning headwear, and the school's administration agreed. Despite her fellow students' support, Ms. Bali was told to remove her scarf or shop for a new school the following year. When she chose the latter, there were no further legal consequences.[60]

There is a strong First Amendment defense where the rule is selectively enforced. A Muskogee, Oklahoma, school district had in place a rule against wearing "hats, caps, bandannas, plastic caps, and hoods on jackets inside the [school] building."[61] The policy was enforced against sixth-grader Nashala Hearn, who wore a niqab to the Benjamin Franklin Science Academy, by suspending her twice. Apparently, the school permitted some students to wear head coverings for secular purposes, at the same time it refused to let Nashala wear her niqab. The U.S. Department of Justice, which intervened after the conservative Rutherford Institute filed the lawsuit, reached a consent decree with the school district and condemned its actions, saying, the department "would not tolerate discrimination against Muslims or any other religious group.... [S]uch intolerance is un-American, and is morally despicable."[62] This is an archetypal case for explaining when the courts should strongly suspect unconstitutional purposes. Whenever the government has a rule and permits some exceptions, it cannot prefer nonreligious reasons over religious reasons. This is exactly the sort of individualized assessment of the reasons for the conduct that calls for a presumption of unconstitutionality and strict scrutiny by the courts.[63] After all, if the policy behind the hat ban is not severely undermined by those wearing hats for secular reasons, the religious individuals are not going to undermine it either. We do not have the benefit in this case of a fully developed trial record to know precisely what happened, but the existence of the consent decree speaks volumes. The decree required the district to permit Nashala to wear her niqab and to revise its dress code to permit headgear for a "bona fide religious reason." The accommodation was not absolute, however, as the district was instructed to consider requests for religious accommodation individually. The school could reject the request only where the claimed belief was not sincerely held and where to grant the accommodation would endanger "safety and security."[64] In addition, the district was ordered (1) to educate administrators, teachers, parents, and students on the new policy, which permitted head coverings in only three circumstances: doctor's orders, religious accommodation, and for a "special school activity"; (2) to certify compliance over a four-year period; and (3) to pay the Hearn family an undisclosed sum.[65] Had the school district enforced its headgear ban uniformly against all students, without reference to religion, the Department of Justice would have had no constitutional argument against the district. By its arbitrary actions, the district invited federal intervention.

France has followed a principle that forbids all religious and political symbols from the public schools, which includes head scarves. This is an apt place to show the differences between the French and the U.S. approaches to accommodation.

In the United States, there is a value placed on encouraging a free marketplace of religion. Two First Amendment principles work together to let religion operate in a free and open market. The Free Exercise Clause prevents persecution based on religious belief that would rid the market of certain religious elements and the Establishment Clause prevents the government from supporting religion, which would torque the market away from actual demand toward government-managed demand. The result is not only a truly amazing variety of religious faiths, but also a fascinating blend of a public square filled with religious talk and images, juxtaposed with a government that does not itself take positions in that square on religious belief. The celebration of religious diversity that is at the heart of the First Amendment encourages accommodation, and so a flat ban tends to appear undesirable if religious belief can be accommodated consistent with the public good. The problem in the United States is that too often the drive to accommodate religious conduct takes flight from common sense and public security.

The French appear to have the opposite inclination – a presumption against accommodation. As of March 15, 2004, it became illegal in France to wear clothing, insignia, or symbols that "conspicuously manifest a religious [or political] affiliation."[66] The directive applies across the board to all students, though some believe it was prompted by Muslim girls wearing head scarves to school,[67] at a time of large Muslim migration into France and resulting discord.[68]

The motive behind the French law would not have made it unconstitutional in the United States, because the law is neutral and generally applicable. But the culture created by the First Amendment's robust protection of belief and speech would have set the default position at accommodation. That, in turn, would have opened the door to the Islamists to persuade parliament that head scarves could be worn without harm to the public good. For those in the United States who believe that this country has reached the point of factually separating church and state and has eviscerated all traces of religion from public places, the French example provides an outstanding context for understanding that strict separation never was and likely never will capture the spirit of the Religion Clauses.

Hair length also has posed accommodation issues in the schools, especially for Native Americans. The Alabama Coushatta Tribes of Texas and 12 Native American students challenged the hair-length regulations of the Big Sandy Independent School District in east Texas. A number of the students received in-school suspensions for refusing to cut their hair, because they believed in the context of their Native American and Christian beliefs that long hair was a "symbol of moral and spiritual strength," and was an integral part of the body's "oneness."[69] The school's hair code was enacted to "minimize disruptions attributable to personal appearance," to "foster an attitude of respect for authority," and to create a favorable impression of the district when its students participated in extracurricular activities elsewhere.[70] While acknowledging that the U.S. Court of Appeals for the Fifth Circuit had previously upheld a hair policy because it did not violate any fundamental rights, the Big Sandy court distinguished that case, because it did not implicate the free exercise of religion.[71] The students prevailed, because the court believed the rule announced by the Supreme Court in *Employment Div. v. Smith*, giving legislatures the power over accommodation, rather than courts, did not apply. Because the case involved a combination of rights, free exercise, free speech, and equal protection, the court examined the rule closely and presumed that the accommodation should be permitted. Where the school had not shown that enforcing its hair-length rule against these students was the least restrictive means of achieving its goals of order, respect, and public image of the school, the regulation could not be applied to them. (The court then went on to reach the same conclusion under various other theories: the Free Speech Clause, parental rights to direct their children's upbringing, and procedural due process.)

This notion that multiple rights, which the *Smith* court called "hybrid rights," justify heightened judicial scrutiny of a law is questionable at best. Some circuits have simply thrown up their hands trying to understand or apply it,[72] because it is difficult to understand how combining rights ought to influence the constitutional conclusion. Where there are two rights, for example, and the government has not violated either individually, it makes no sense to conclude that their coexistence justifies treating the law as presumptively unconstitutional, so this decision is on shaky ground.

If there is any case, though, that argues for judicial intervention in the religious accommodation context, this might be the one. The students were not themselves disruptive, their hair did not block anyone's educational experience, and, in this day and age, surely no one was so distracted by the fact of its length so as to be unable to pay attention in class. The school district's refusal to accommodate them seems willful, if not just plain silly, and maybe the judge in this case got a whiff of discrimination that led him to find for the Native Americans under as many theories as he could. Having said all that, however, the rule was generally applicable; it was found by the court to be neutral, and the district's policy was rational, so under existing free-exercise jurisprudence today, the outcome should have been the opposite.

That would have left the tribe with the Texas legislature to obtain accommodation. Some will immediately shake their heads and assume that they have no chance, because they are a small group or because they lack political power, but exemptions for Native Americans were already in place. Religious use of peyote, which is used by the Native American Church as part of the worship service, is exempt from the Texas drug laws.[73] And where the hair-length restriction is unevenly applied, so that only one group, like the Native Americans, is being punished for the infringement, the punishment would be unconstitutional.[74]

*The challenges of choosing a curriculum to fit all*
*religious viewpoints*

My vote for the worst Religion Clause case in the United States goes to
*Wisconsin v. Yoder*, which held that the Amish could avoid Wisconsin's
compulsory education laws by removing their children from school after eighth grade, because the First Amendment required it.[75] As I will
discuss in more detail in Part Two, I would deep-six it for its romantic,
rose-colored depiction of Amish life, its assumption that parental rights
automatically trump any question about the children's needs or beliefs,
and its judicially forced accommodation, which forestalled any legislative debate and determination regarding whether permitting a significant
number of children to forego higher education was consistent with the
public good. There is good reason to question that conclusion in a society where every other citizen is required to complete 12th grade (and
therefore the Amish children are being severely disabled in terms of their
future prospects) and where the political and social welfare of the country
rests on well-educated and informed adults.

The Amish compulsory education issue is on a par with the religious
medical neglect cases. Should parents be permitted to deprive their children of medical treatment or education, when that deprivation could
disable them permanently? These are not easy questions, though I would
weigh the children's interests in health and education more weightily
than they have been to date. In any event, the issues certainly were not
resolved by the Court's love letter to the Amish in *Yoder*. For purposes
of this chapter, *Yoder* is emblematic of the entire social debate over curriculum. If students can be pulled from school altogether during the last
four compulsory years, in order to pursue a more agrarian education, it
is hard to argue that they must participate in any particular curriculum
at any stage. It would also seem to be quite difficult to argue that *any* religious organization's alternative education, including home schooling,
must be accommodated under the Free Exercise Clause. If farming can
replace the classroom, then why can't any other content just as well –
in light of the purposes of public education? The answer is that *Yoder*
was badly reasoned and wrongly decided, that it is up to the legislature to
weigh these different considerations, and that there is a very strong interest

in a well-educated public if this system of representative democracy has any chance of succeeding.

**HOMESCHOOLING.** There is a tremendous movement in the United States toward homeschooling, where parents keep their children out of public or private schools and shoulder the responsibility for education themselves.

One of the impetuses has been the ongoing debate involving the science curriculum dealing with the beginning of humankind – scientists talk about "evolution," while some believers advocate what is called "creation science," or the theory that God created the first human, as the Bible says.[76] Mainstream believers tend to be able to incorporate the evolution theory into their belief systems, while fundamentalists, who read the Bible literally, cannot. The 1987 Supreme Court, *Edwards v. Aguillard*, decision held that a school policy of banishing evolution in favor of creationism alone, or requiring denigration of evolution theory, violated the Establishment Clause, because the statute permitted government funds and power to achieve a religious purpose.[77] The decision left the door open, however, to curricula choices that permitted both to be taught, and school boards continue to struggle with that choice.[78]

For example, the school board of a Wisconsin district has revised its curriculum to allow the teaching of creationism.[79] In 2001, the Kansas State Board of Education restored the teaching of evolution to the curriculum after having controversially voted to remove it from public school science standards in 1999.[80] The existence of a middle ground in some school districts, though, does not signify the end of the power struggle between the two views. In Cobb County, Georgia (just outside Atlanta), in 2002, 2,000 parents presented a petition to school officials complaining that their science textbooks discussed evolution but not creationism. The schools responded by requiring science textbooks to contain an evolution warning sticker, that read:

> This textbook contains material on evolution. Evolution is a theory, not a fact, regarding the origin of living things. This material should be approached with an open mind, studied carefully and critically considered.

The ACLU and six parents filed an Establishment Clause challenge, saying that the stickers promote creationism and discriminate against certain religions. Federal District Court judge Clarence Cooper refused to dismiss the lawsuit, because he was not satisfied that the stickers did not have the effect of advancing or inhibiting religion. During the bench trial, Cooper asked, "How were teachers told to address questions or conflicts stemming from the disclaimer?" The school district's answer was troubling: the sticker was supposed to bring the students' attention to the fact that "there is a scientific discussion and there's a religious discussion, and we're going to have a scientific discussion." That made it sound as though the sole purpose of the stickers was to inject religion into the schools. Moreover, he tried to use the pressure by the creationists to justify the schools' action, saying that the school, "had an obligation to those who felt very strongly about this."[81] Private individuals may have any views they like, but a public school may not use those citizens' religious viewpoints to justify its actions. Accordingly, the court found the stickers unconstitutional.

However the debate over creationism resolves itself, the movement toward home schooling has taken on a life of its own, as the existence of the active and often influential Home School Legal Defense Association (HSLDA) illustrates. Homeschoolers typically are escaping from the "secular" environment and curriculum in the public schools, and thus find themselves leaving the system for religious reasons.[82] The HSLDA website makes this position quite clear:

> God has delegated the authority *and* responsibility to teach and raise children to the parents first. Parents can delegate their *authority* to teach and raise children to someone else, but they can never delegate their *responsibility* to teach their children to anyone else. God will hold parents responsible for what education their children receive (whether from teachers, books, projects, or peers). To whom much is given, much is required. We have a free choice in this country to *not* send our children to an ungodly public school – we will, all the more, be responsible. Remember, our children are dying souls entrusted to our care![83]

Two conflicts have arisen as a result. The first involves access to extracurricular programs while the second deals with how the state can ensure that each child is being adequately educated, in light of the overriding interest in an educated citizenry in a republican form of democracy.

First, homeschooled children have asked to participate in the extracurricular activities typically offered by the public schools, despite the fact they are receiving their education at home. Of the 26 states that have legislation or case law addressing access of private school or home school students to public school activities, all but seven permit access. In states without laws addressing the issue, the decision is generally left to individual schools and school districts to decide. Most states also have private sports league associations for interscholastic sports, which have adopted bylaws that usually do not permit schools to allow a student's participation in these activities unless the student is enrolled full time in the school.[84]

Second – and this is the far more difficult issue – is how to monitor each child's education. The states impose requirements on each public and private school to satisfy certain educational aims in each subject, so that the education of each child in the system is monitored and well documented. Paperwork goes back and forth between the school districts and the state, and the private schools and the state. In addition, there are state visits to each school, and there is standardized testing – which determines whether each school is teaching the necessary curriculum and whether individual students are achieving certain minimum standards. The homeschooling context poses a difficult challenge for the states, because it is so difficult to monitor such students. It's a problem of enforcing some kind of reporting requirement, having the manpower to deal with the individual education of children outside the public and private school system, and the expense associated. Homeschooling eliminates the efficiencies created by the school systems' ability to take on the administrative burdens of monitoring education child by child. In contrast, homeschooling parents find some state's reporting requirements onerous, invasive, and unnecessary. "Homeschooling parents are overburdened" says former HSLDA president Michael Farris.[85] Moreover, most believe that parents have the constitutional right to choose to educate their children as they wish. The Supreme Court has rejected the notion, however, that a child can be a "martyr" for his or her parents' faith, and held that "those who nurture [a child] and direct his destiny have the right and high duty to recognize and prepare him for additional obligations."[86]

The HSLDA is spearheading litigation in handpicked states to fight the burdens placed on parents by the states' education reporting requirements. Currently, in a pair of Pennsylvania cases, two families are fighting the state's home education law under Pennsylvania's Religious Freedom Protection Act, claiming that the home education law imposes a substantial burden on the free exercise of their religion. The plaintiffs are challenging the provisions of the statute that require parents to notify the district that they are homeschooling their children, provide a detailed curriculum, submit homeschool students to regular testing, and have their program certified annually by the superintendent.[87] The HSLDA's agenda is to deregulate education for homeschoolers, but complete deregulation is inconceivable in light of the importance of education in the United States, and the school boards and state are expected to fight the case vigorously.

From a free exercise perspective, the issue presents the typical analytical hurdle in all accommodation cases: from the perspective of the individual believer, it seems like a de minimis burden on the state, but from the state's perspective, the individualized element in it poses nearly insuperable administrative and cost barriers. In general, no matter the prevailing standard, the government has won these sorts of cases. When the Amish challenged the requirement that they pay Social Security taxes, the Supreme Court rejected the claim, saying "Congress drew a line in § 1402(g), exempting the self-employed Amish but not all persons working for an Amish employer. The tax imposed on employers to support the Social Security system must be uniformly applicable to all, except as Congress provides explicitly otherwise."[88] The same result accrued when Native American parents objected to the requirement that every child must have a Social Security number. They argued that, under their religious beliefs, the assignment of a unique Social Security number would "rob the spirit" of their daughter.[89] The Court held that the government's interest in the fair and efficient administration of the system trumped the family's interest in accommodation. Under *Employment Div. v. Smith*, the analysis is even more straightforward – education laws (except in the rare instance) are neutral and generally applicable, which means the homeschoolers' best route for accommodation is in the state legislatures. And they have not done too badly, as they have obtained exemptions for participation in interscholastic activities, truancy laws, drivers' education requirements, and the necessity of having someone trained in CPR present. Some have even enacted a special tax credit for them.

The public good calculus on this topic, though, is not limited to the state's interest in educating children, or the parents' right to determine their children's education. Children have rights as well, and in particular the right not to be made "martyrs" by their parents' religious beliefs.[90] Where their level of education is inferior to their peers', children are being disabled for later life. The state also has an obligation to protect children from abuse and neglect. Homeschooling removes one of the most effective means the state has of ensuring that children are not abused – the teachers and principals who see the children outside the home on a regular basis. Doctors are another crucial layer of protection as well, and where the home-schooling family does not believe in medical care, or does not take the child to the doctor because of the abuse, the schools are literally the last line of defense. For the state to fully deregulate homeschooling may well abdicate its responsibility toward children potentially at risk of abuse or neglect. This is not to say that homeschoolers abuse children anymore than do other parents (unfortunately, the amount of abuse never reaches zero), but rather that children who are being homeschooled do not have the additional protection of a teacher or principal who can intervene and that has a mandatory obligation to report any abuse. It is just a fact that these children are at a higher risk of abuse.[91] Many homeschoolers would respond that their children engage in extracurricular activities, so their children are seen by other adults; the question is whether they are adults with a legal obligation to report perceived abuse.

All of which is to say that the question of legislative accommodation for the homeschoolers is complicated. There are weighty issues on both sides. It should be crystal clear that no court has the tools or powers necessary to determine the right balance between the competing interests of the children, the parents, and the public.

CHOICE OF READING SERIES. There can be no more likely stage for conflict between religious parents and the schools than in the choice of a reading curriculum. It is impossible to teach reading without substantial content, and religious parents have had objections to a large range of materials, including the fantasy materials at the heart of the following case.

Parents in Wheaton, Illinois, challenged an elementary school's adoption of the Impressions Reading Series, which encourages reading skills, using the works of C. S. Lewis, A. A. Milne, Dr. Seuss, Ray Bradbury, L. Frank Baum, Maurice Sendak, and other authors, because it established a religion of "superior beings exercising power over human beings by imposing rules of conduct, with the promise and threat of future rewards and punishments." It also "indoctrinates children in values directly opposed to their Christian beliefs by teaching tricks, despair, deceit, parental disrespect and by denigrating Christian symbols and holidays"[92] and therefore deprived them of the free exercise of religion. A contrary view of the series was put forth by, among others, the Institute for First Amendment Studies, which filed an amicus brief in the case:

> The Impressions reading series employs the whole language approach to language arts instruction. Many fundamentalists believe the whole language method is a deliberate scheme on behalf of the National Education Association to produce functional illiterates, thus creating a dependent society susceptible to a one-world government. Believing that phonics is the only correct way to learn to read, they find inventive ways to reject whole language curricula.[93]

The parents lost on both Religion Clause theories, as they should have. The court listed certain types of activities in the schools that had been held to violate the Establishment Clause, and each of them involved the school sending a rather clear message to the students about what they should believe: for example, inviting clergy to offer prayers at graduation, daily Bible readings or recitation of the Lord's Prayer, distribution of Gideon Bibles to public school students, posting the Ten Commandments in classrooms, excluding evolution science or requiring it be taught along with creation science, beginning school assemblies with prayer, and "teaching a Transcendental Meditation course that includes a ceremony involving offerings to a deity." In comparison, the courts have not been eager to invalidate the use of particular books in the public schools, whether they were novels, textbooks, other reading series, or even the Bible when employed for literary or historical purposes.[94]

The court struggled to identify what religion was allegedly being established in the series, which appeared to the court to be no more than a "collection of exercises in 'make-believe' designed to develop and encourage the use of imagination and reading skills in children that are the staple of traditional public elementary school education."[95] In a refreshingly frank passage, the court vehemently rejected the notion that fantasy and make-believe amounted to a "pagan" religion, asking, "[W]hat would become of elementary education, public or private, without works such as these and scores and scores of others that serve to expand the minds of young children and develop their sense of creativity? With that off our chest, we can now properly dispose of the parents' claim within the structure of the 'Lemon' test." The court found a "clear secular purpose" in the choice of "fantasy and 'make-believe' to hold a student's attention" and develop the child's creative side, and that despite the presence of a few stories employing witches and goblins, the series "fit the norm."[96] Nor did the court find that the series had the effect of furthering a religion, because some of the stories employed imaginative characters, some were consistent with Protestantism and Catholicism, and overall the series simply improved reading skills. Finally, there was no entanglement with religion where the school board chose the series, because that is a standard school board activity.

The parents lost on their free-exercise claim as well, because there was no coercion of the parents or the children's religious beliefs and the school's interest was extremely important. The same result accrued when a mother of four challenged the Holt, Rinehart, and Winston reading series, because her children were not permitted to abstain from using the series, which is used in many schools.[97] The court distinguished Yoder in that it "rested on such a singular set of facts" that it did not announce a general rule. Unlike the Amish parents in Yoder, the parents in the present case wanted their children to acquire the necessary skills to live in modern society, and it was not impossible to reconcile the religious requirements with the aim of public education.[98]

COEDUCATIONAL CLASSES. Intellectual content is not the only arena where parents have objected to a school's curriculum. In McLean County, Illinois, children of the United Pentecostal Church objected to having to attend coed physical education classes, because of the "immodest apparel" worn.[99] The decision was predetermined by the Yoder Court's reasoning, as it evidences every bit as much concern about preserving the religious entity's future as it does the government interest at stake:

Given the abundant support in the record that modest dress is a traditional way of life of the plaintiffs, the compulsory attendance at a coeducational physical education class is in sharp conflict with the fundamental mode of life mandated by the Pentecostal religion. . . . Under the present facts there is, through coeducational physical education, daily exposure of the children to worldly influences in terms of attitudes and values of dress contrary to their religious beliefs. This exposure . . . substantially interferes with the religious development of the Pentecostal children and their integration into the way of life of the Pentecostal faith community at the crucial adolescent stage of development. These two effects of the way this Illinois statute has been construed contravenes the basic religious tenets and practice of the Pentecostal Church, both as to parents and the children.[100]

The students suggested that they be permitted to have sex-segregated physical education or individual physical education, and the court added a third option, providing them an exemption from physical education altogether. The court obviously had some discomfort about its holding, because it stated more than once that it was "not telling the school system or these defendants what they must do; only what they may not do."[101] But, like Judge Posner's yarmulke decision above, the court did indeed indicate the option it thought should be considered to adequately accommodate the religious adherents, without serious investigation into the state's interest. It expressly disavowed forcing the district to provide the students' suggested sex-segregated or individual physical education (P.E.), saying that its holding simply meant the students could not be forced to go to the coeducational P.E. In effect, the judge mandated at a very minimum, the exemption he earlier suggested. The decision is a product of its era, which placed courts in the impossible position of adjudicating constitutional rights and crafting exemptions that call for legislative judgment.

## Conclusion

Schools stand in the position of parens patriae, literally in the shoes of the parents, so they have a strong responsibility to enforce fair rules evenhandedly, to keep the atmosphere positive for learning, and to ensure the children's health and safety. It is impossible to accommodate the kirpans carried by the Sikhs; children and knives do not mix, no matter how good and pure the intentions are. At the same time, schools must guard against enforcing their dress rules unevenly. If the school is willing to wink at the kid wearing a hat for fun, it cannot then punish the girl who shows up in a hijab. The willingness to let the rule be bent speaks volumes to the actual necessity of the rule in the first place. Because most dress codes can tolerate some differences on the margins, many have and should have exemptions for religious reasons.

But those exemptions are never absolute, because there is always the possibility that the girl who is wearing the hijab is not in fact wearing it for religious reasons, but rather because it is a perfect place to hide the drugs she sells. So inquiries into sincerity are perfectly appropriate. And in schools with intractable and pervasive problems with contraband, it may be impossible to permit anyone to wear a head covering of any kind. In that situation, the no-exceptions policy is perfectly constitutional, so long as it is applied as strictly as it is intended and written.

# THE PRISONS AND THE MILITARY

Terrorist networks within United States borders before September 11, 2001, were an undetected cancer spreading through the system. Our own prisons – and the military – were potential breeding grounds for extremist Muslims who believed that the United States was evil and should be eradicated. It took the annihilation of almost 3,000 victims from abroad and the U.S., including the World Trade Center – two of the tallest buildings in the world – for Americans to realize that there was a religious movement that was intent on their destruction.

In the aftermath of September 11, it quickly became apparent that Muslim chaplains in the prisons and the military were in a strategic position to recruit, train, and indoctrinate those individuals who were open or vulnerable to an approach. Like the pedophiles discussed in Chapter 2, terrorists seek out individuals who are vulnerable to their overtures – those who are isolated from family and friends – and then they play on their insecurities. The same is true for extremist gangs. John Pistole, the head of the FBI's counterterrorism division in 2003, and now its deputy director, summarized the phenomenon in the prisons like this:

> Inmates are often ostracized, abandoned by, or isolated from their family and friends, leaving them susceptible to recruitment. Membership in the various radical groups offers inmates protection, positions of influence and a network they can correspond with both inside and outside of prison.[1]

The fact is that violent religious extremists in prisons have been a problem for ages, and this is just a new iteration. The United States (with the exception, perhaps, of the prison administrators with firsthand knowledge) was not paying special attention to the Islamic terrorists when they struck on September 11. The country as a whole, however, was becoming increasingly aware of the existence of white supremacists preaching hatred and violence, for example, the Aryan Brotherhood, Ku Klux Klan, World Church of the Creator, Arizona Aryan Brotherhood, Aryan Circle, and Aryan Brotherhood of Texas, among others. The two movements – violent gangs and terrorist recruitment – are archetypes for chaos and criminal activity in arenas where security and order is paramount.

For legal purposes, the problem with these groups is not what they believe, as distasteful as that may be. As in every other venue in the United States, they have every right to believe whatever they choose. Conduct, as usual, is the trigger for the law to enter the picture. The challenge for prison authorities and the larger society from white supremacists or extreme Muslims is that their beliefs lead them to take illegal action – either advocating the violent overthrow of the government or taking concrete steps to that end. Often, their beliefs or membership in violent societies is proof of likelihood of illegal action. Whether Muslim extremists or white supremacists are involved, the potential for violence is not hypothetical.

### The Aryan Brotherhood: intolerance and violence spread through the prisons

The Aryan Brotherhood is a particularly scary organization that started in the California prisons in the early 1960s for the purpose of protecting white inmates from the black and Mexican prison gangs.[2] In 1967, the name Aryan Brotherhood (AB) was chosen; later, it became known also as the Brand. At first, the members had to be part Irish to join – hence the identifying clover tattoo, often with the religious symbol, 666, the "mark of the beast," in the middle. Their other identifying symbol is the swastika, which designates the wearer as an outlaw. The organization originally was intended to help whites, but it eventually devolved into a racist group interested solely in its own power – to kill, deal in drugs, run prostitution rings and extortion rackets, control gambling, and dominate entire prison populations. They killed with their bare hands in maximum-security prisons and ordered hits from solitary confinement. Assistant U.S. Attorney Gregory Jessner reportedly assessed the AB as the "most murderous criminal organization in the United States," capable of dividing the prison population into "predators and prey."[3]

The AB recruited the strong and the ruthless, and demanded single-minded devotion to other members even into death. In the 1970s, when AB members started to be incarcerated for federal crimes in the federal prisons, the AB's influence spread beyond state prison boundaries. By 1982, the FBI estimated that there were about 100 AB in California's prisons and 100–160 in federal prisons, and when they came up for parole or discharge, they took their gang membership to the outside. Once out, they were obligated to look out for the interests of the others inside; otherwise, they would be killed if and when they reentered the prison system. Those interests included supplying drugs and killing people on the outside. The AB became so powerful at one point that it was thought that it controlled elements of organized crime. Its ethos was no different; an AB instruction manual said the act of killing "is like having sex" and becomes extremely rewarding, because "it's a holy cause."[4]

An extensive federal investigation of the AB has resulted in numerous arrests and a trial is expected in 2005. Their power has at least momentarily decimated, but another gang was waiting in the wings, the Nazi Low Riders, to take over the prison drug trade, the assaults and murders of black or Latino gang members, and on the outside, authorities saw a decisive escalation in drug dealing, physical assaults, and home robberies. It took four full-time police officers and four full-time agents from the FBI plus assistance from the Federal Bureau of Alcohol, Tobacco, Firearms, and Explosives; the California Department of Corrections; the county sheriff's department; and three other local police departments to slow them down.[5] The move induced members to drop out of the gang, and to cooperate. Who knows what other gang lurks in the background, waiting for its own opportunity to assert its power. There are plenty of possibilities, including the Latin Kings, Crips, and Bloods.[6]

*The evil within the prisons and the evil on the outside*

The history of the AB highlights one of the reasons that it is absolutely essential that violent gangs are suppressed in prison: Many of their members eventually get out, and when they do, they become a menace to society. The notorious and horrific killing of James Byrd, Jr., in 1998 in Jasper, Texas, is one example. Three white men picked up Byrd, who was African-American, in their pickup truck, took him to a secluded area, and used a chain to attach him to the back of their truck after spray-painting his face black. Then they dragged him until his body came apart, and he eventually died. Russell Brewer and John King were sentenced to the death penalty, while Sean Berry, the driver, received life in prison. The three of them had been in prison before, where King and Berry had joined a white supremacist gang, the Confederate Knights of America. By the time they got out, each had a number of alarming tattoos, and had become out-and-out racists. They had been misfits, and now they belonged. And when they got out, an assistant district attorney explained, "They brought their prison life out with them."[7] Prison gangs had prepared them to kill Byrd.

Both radical Muslims and white supremacist groups, like the AB, have confounded standard penological practices. In general, when a group of inmates becomes trouble, the best way to deal with the problem is to disperse them through the system. Unfortunately, that can be the equivalent of blowing on a dandelion puff in the summer, with the seeds spreading far and wide, and eventually generating more weeds. In the case of the AB, the dispersal mechanism meant that they expanded their empire from California to Texas, Illinois, Kansas, Pennsylvania, and Georgia.

French prisons have witnessed precisely the same phenomenon with the Muslim extremists, as their numbers have swelled. One inmate told *Le Monde,* the Paris daily, that French prisons had "become the cradle of the future jihad" by 2001.[8] The same is true in the United States where Muslims constitute 5.5 percent of the federal prison population and Islamic conversion appears to be outpacing other faiths.[9]

## Muslim imam recruitment in the military and federal prisons

Muslim chaplain recruitment has been worrying certain sectors in the government for a number of years now. It is not terribly difficult for an extremist to fall through the cracks of the system, especially when there is a shortage of clerics in a particular faith. In the military, official chaplains must be ordained clergy, nominated by their denomination to serve as a chaplain. They must have completed a postbaccalaureate degree in theology or a related field from an approved institution. The graduate degree must require at least 72 credit hours, and the institution must be accredited by the American Council on Education or must meet Department of Defense approval guidelines for unaccredited institutions.[10] Chaplains must meet all of the other criteria required for commission as an officer of the armed forces. Chaplains are selected from approved denominations based on quotas, which are calculated based on the needs of the services and the general population.[11] The armed services, however, are not always able to fill a need with a full-time chaplain. Under these circumstances, at least as of 1983 (when the military could not fill its requirements from the ranks of its chaplains), it relied on auxiliary chaplains who are appointed on an annual basis and whose function is purely religious. They must have ecclesiastic endorsement and must be approved by the chief of chaplains. If auxiliary chaplains are not available, then the military can contract with individual religious organizations to provide chaplain services, and these requirements are much looser. The organization is supposed to be a "recognized religious institution," and the institution can appoint the individuals who will provide the services.[12]

In the prison setting, some claim that the conduits for Muslim chaplains were, in fact, keeping moderates out and bringing only radicals within prison walls. Thus, the prisons' paid chaplains were in a position to reach the disaffected prisoners that would be susceptible to their anti-society and anti–United States rhetoric. Prisoners already are on the outs with the general society and the government, so these are fertile grounds for radical Muslim chaplains to recruit. Furthermore, conversions of recruits from non-Muslim backgrounds are crucial to the terrorists' plans, because they are more capable of "blending in" and have Western passports.[13]

According to Senator Charles Schumer D.-N.Y., "These imams flood the prisons with anti-American, pro-bin Laden videos, literature, sermons and tapes." They "seek to create a radicalized cadre of felons." The dedication of the terrorists to their cause is single-minded, and the initiation of imams into the federal prisons was accomplished by a man with connections to the extremist Muslim Brotherhood. Abdurahman Alamoudi started the American Muslim Council and was responsible for vetting chaplain candidates for the military from 1993 to 1998, even though he (1) publicly asserted that the 1993 World Trade Center attackers were treated "harshly and with vengeance, and to a large extent, because they were Muslim"; (2) defended Hamas's "good work" and its need to "resort to some kind of violence" as well as Hezbollah; and (3) in 1996, spoke to the convention of the Islamic Association of Palestine in the following terms:

> It depends on me and you, either we do it now or we do it after a hundred years, but this country will become a Muslim country. And I [think] if we are outside this country we can say, oh, Allah, destroy America, but once we are here, our mission in this country is to change it.[14]

Alamoudi was arrested in September 2003 for serving as an intermediary between Libyan officials and Saudi dissidents. Although he was not charged in connection to the alleged plot to kill Crown Prince Abdullah, the prosecutors referred to it as a reason to give him the maximum sentence.[15] He was sentenced to 23 years in federal prison after "admitting that he pocketed nearly $1 million and used it to pay conspirators in the plot, which sources said came close to succeeding before it was broken up by Saudi intelligence officials."[16]

Three organizations have been said to be responsible for placing imams in the federal prisons: the Graduate School of Islamic and Social Sciences (GSISS), the Islamic Society of North America (ISNA), and the American Muslim Armed Forces and Veteran Council. The Bureau of Prisons (BOP) has said that only ISNA has been an official endorser of imams, although the GSISS is where most of the Muslim chaplain candidates have been trained.[17]

According to the military, the government may not choose clergy, because of constitutional limitations, and therefore the religious groups choose their own representatives when a chaplaincy is open. Filling Muslim chaplaincy spots without introducing dangerous elements into the system has been more difficult than it is with other faiths, because Islam is so decentralized, which leads the government to rely on the views of "grassroots Muslim groups" rather than established leaders to fill the positions.[18]

Although the groups have denied links with terrorist networks, Professor of Islamic Studies at Harvard University Ali Asani has said that the ISNA and the GSISS are "ultraconservative, ultraorthodox," and out of touch with the moderate Muslims in the United States.[19]

And the problem has not been solely confined to federal prisons. In New York, prison authorities had to boot a longtime chaplain recruiter because he told the *Wall Street Journal* that the September 11 terrorists were actually martyrs. There was even a lawsuit brought by Shiite Muslim inmates in New York, arguing that moderate imams were not available to them.

One of the roots of the problem appears to be a shortage of Muslim clerics. Department of Justice inspector general Glenn A. Fine explained why a shortage could further the terrorist agenda: "Without a sufficient number of Muslim chaplains on staff... inmates are much more likely to lead their own religious services, distort Islam and espouse extremist beliefs."[20] After being instructed to investigate the issue, the Office of the Inspector General identified some troubling problems in the recruitment of chaplains in the federal prisons, which still persisted after the BOP tried to ameliorate concerns.

The problems identified were:

- Review of candidates did not include a review of their belief systems to see if they were inconsistent with prison security policies;
- An inadequate exchange of information between the Bureau of Prisons and the FBI;
- Since the federal government was no longer accepting recommendations from national Islamic organizations, imam hiring had come to a standstill, leading to a shortage;
- The BOP was not using imams already in the system to help screen potential candidates;
- There was inadequate supervision of the messages delivered by imams;

- There was a lack of supervision of Islamic services by BOP employees;
- There was inadequate supervision of imams by correctional officers within the prisons.[21]

The first problem the inspector general identified, that the government had not done an inquiry into the beliefs of potential imams, probably raises constitutional red flags for some. Belief, after all, is *absolutely* protected under the Constitution. The issue, however, does not involve pure belief or even pure speech. The relevant question is whether the imam advocates the violent overthrow of the U.S. government and its people. That is not mere speech; it is speech directed at inciting illegal action, and that speech can be regulated. Authorities do not have to wait for the illegal action to occur before putting a stop to it. Outside the prisons, such speech is strongly protected unless the violence is imminent, under *Brandenburg v. Ohio*,[22] which expanded the protection for speech advocating illegal action.

The prison context, however, and its strong potential for producing antisocial or criminal behavior, argues in favor of relaxing the protections required by *Brandenburg*. Arguments have been advanced that weigh against suppressing terrorist speech on websites, because it is impossible to determine whether the danger is imminent.[23] Yet, the prison context increases the likelihood of violence inside or outside the prison significantly, and therefore such speech demands monitoring and even suppression.

Some chaplains have blamed the growth in radical Muslims in the prisons on inmate as opposed to clerical persuasion. This may be true, because of the shortage of Muslim clerics. The Federal Bureau of Prisons has a rule that "inmates are not permitted to lead religious programs."[24] The problem, though, is that when there are inadequate clerics, inmates must lead religious services if they are to have them at all, and so the practice has become a staple of federal prison life.

Some might ask whether a government-sponsored chaplaincy is constitutional. It obviously features the government paying for religious worship. Perhaps it should be privatized. Numerous reasons, though, can be listed to justify it, not the least of which is that the military cannot operate securely if it is not evaluating those in close contact with their soldiers. To privatize the chaplaincy service altogether (and therefore avoid the government payment issue) would present serious problems for national security, especially in an era of terror.[25]

Whatever the source of recruitment, there is no question that prisons worldwide have become breeding grounds for the terrorists. Richard Reid, who was convicted of attempting to detonate an American Airlines flight from Paris to Miami with a bomb in his shoe, found Islam through radical clerics in a British prison, where some have said the amount of Islamic literature far outpaces Christian literature.[26] The French prisons, with half of their population Muslim, have had terrible problems with controlling terrorists. And Jose Padilla, who attempted to set off a "dirty" bomb in the United States, was converted to radical Islam in a Broward County, Florida, prison, and later drawn into al-Qaeda. Padilla's case made it to the U.S. Supreme Court, but they did not reach the merits for procedural reasons.[27]

Not only do radical Muslims appear to be recruiting new members inside the prisons, but those who are already imprisoned have also tried to orchestrate further terror from inside, not unlike the Mafia don who tries to arrange a hit while incarcerated. Abdel Rahman, who helped orchestrate the 1993 attack on the World Trade Center, and was incarcerated in a federal prison in Rochester, Minnesota, tried to foment more terror in April 2002. It is alleged that he used his attorney and translator to pass messages to his followers, including calling for the end to a cease-fire in Egypt and new terrorist attacks by his followers in a terrorist network called the "Islamic Group," which is said to be responsible for the deaths of dozens of Western tourists visiting the pyramids at Luxor in 1997.[28] The nature of extremism is such that when the criminal is arrested and put into prison, he can still generate hatred within the prison walls by writing, teaching, and inculcating new recruits. While it is a cliché in the United States that a Mafia don might be pulling the strings of his organization from inside the prison walls, the notion that terrorism can be arranged from inside is disconcerting, to say the least. It may be surprising, but it is a fact.

## The law of religious accommodation in the prisons

The U.S. Supreme Court has been extremely deferential in the prison and military contexts, because it has viewed the courts as incapable of assessing security threats and needs regarding prisons or national security. Thus, they have given the executive branches of the federal and state governments wide berth to keep order. In the Court's own words, "'courts are ill equipped to deal with the increasingly urgent problems of prison administration and reform.'"[29] In these contexts, the branch most capable of assessing the issue – the executive – has been given the power to do so, with minimal restrictions. Prison regulations have been subject to low-level scrutiny, which means the prisoner must first show that the law imposes a substantial burden on his religious practice, and then the prison administrator need only show that the regulation was created for a "legitimate penological" objective.[30] This left room for reasonable accommodations, like no-pork diets (which are required by a number of faiths), but it did not force prison authorities to either sacrifice security for any prisoner's beliefs or divert precious resources to repeated federal litigation.

That is, until the Religious Freedom Restoration Act (RFRA) and the Religious Land Use and Institutionalized Persons Act (RLUIPA) were enacted, which turned generally applicable, neutral prison regulations into presumptively illegal regulations. A hair regulation applied across the board in a prison could no longer be presumed to be legal, at least until the government litigated the issue through the federal courts and persuaded them that the grooming policy existed for a compelling interest (security) and there was no other less restrictive way to serve the same end. It is an expensive process, with questionable utility.

### The Religious Land Use and Institutionalized Persons Act

In 2000, President Bill Clinton signed RLUIPA, and launched another litigation attack on prison authorities. The prison side of RLUIPA received so little attention in the form of hearings and testimony that it is virtually impossible to divine what existing problem it was intended to redress. Two men testified in support of it: Charles Colson (the ex-con from the Nixon administration's Watergate scandal, who then found religion in prison), who founded the conservative Christian Prison Fellowship Ministries, and Isaac M. Jaroslawicz of the Aleph Institute, which assists state and federal prisons to accommodate Jewish inmates. Both emphasized how important religion can be to rehabilitation, as they assumed without stating that the religious influences helped by RLUIPA would all be beneficial. What they meant was that their religion was good for rehabilitation. If RLUIPA could constitutionally only empower those faiths that in fact further rehabilitation, that would be one thing. But as a constitutional matter, no law may impose denominational preferences. So it is all or nothing – expand rights beyond the First Amendment's requirements for the destructive as well as constructive religions, or do it for neither. Neither Colson nor Jaroslawicz dealt with the myriad problems posed by expanding free-exercise rights beyond constitutional boundaries for gangs, white supremacists, rabid racists, or terrorists. Nor did they talk about the impact on the prison system of subjecting the state and federal prison systems to the potential for lawsuits from every corner, whether the faith aided rehabilitation or impeded it. Nor did the members ask.

Neither Colson nor Jaroslawicz provided much in the way of justifying the imposition of strict scrutiny on every prison regulation. Colson objected to the Supreme Court's free-exercise jurisprudence that left accommodation to the legislatures, saying, "We *want* judges to handle these questions and we want them to use the legal standard" that imposed strict scrutiny on every prison regulation.[31] Of course he did, because then the believer is the primary focus of the case and the public good is proportionally discounted. At this point, there is no question that the Court has settled on a free-exercise doctrine that Colson does not approve, and he has the right to have his own views, but that debate is and should be settled. Religious entities are subject to neutral, generally applicable laws. As is typical in the circumstances, he did not offer actual proof of any actual religious suppression in the prisons that justified RLUIPA's imposition on the prisons. Instead, Colson invoked the need for religious liberty in the prisons as an accepted fact for which no proof to Congress was necessary. Given the members' extraordinary deference to religious entities with RFRA and RLUIPA, it was not.

The only "hard" evidence presented was by Jaroslawicz, who testified that Jewish prisoners are not adequately accommodated in the prisons. Some of the examples he raised did not justify an RLUIPA, because they involved overt discrimination against Jews, which is unconstitutional under both Religion Clauses. For example, he stated that the Michigan Department of Corrections had banned Chanukah candles at every prison, because of concerns for fire safety. If the rule against fire had been enforced against every prisoner, the inmate would not have had a free-exercise claim, but "smoking, cooking, and votive candles were all still allowed."[32] Thus, the Free Exercise Clause's entrenched rule against singling out religions would be triggered, and RLUIPA was, at best, duplicative.

He also criticized the prisons for inadequately protecting Jews from hostile anti-Semitic inmates, of which there are many. He said there were instances where a Jewish inmate was beaten and then placed in "administrative segregation," which means "solitary confinement," for his safety. But the aggressors continued to "roam free." Finally, he claimed pervasive anti-Semitic treatment from prison chaplains against Jews throughout the Texas system. All of these examples would be subject to strict scrutiny under the Religion Clauses, and therefore RLUIPA was not necessary.

But Jaroslawicz did object to at least one neutral, generally applicable practice in state prisons: the practice of providing accommodation for certain faiths only at some of the prisons. In other words, not every Michigan facility offered kosher food, but at least some would.[33] His objection was that the locations of the prisons providing the kosher food were not desirable, because they were far from family. But one is hard pressed to fully understand the objection. Prisoners have never had a right to "choose" their prison location. While a state may permit them to suggest a preference, they are assigned where the state or federal government decides. This fact was most recently seen in Martha Stewart's case, where she had requested a facility close to home in New England, but was assigned instead to a prison in West Virginia. It is also a puzzling objection in light of his earlier stated concerns about Jews being isolated and placed in danger; bringing them together is surely better than dispersing them so that they are completely isolated from others of their own faith. Essentially, he was demanding RLUIPA be passed, not because there was no accommodation, but so that Jewish prisoners (and all other faiths) could insist on having accommodation at the prison closest to their families. That would be a huge sea change in the law, and one that does not sound in free-exercise principles, but rather prisoner preferences. If that is why RLUIPA was needed, it is a slender reed on which to hang such a heavy and costly burden on the prisons.

One actual conflict between religious needs and prison security Jaroslawicz described was the refusal in Michigan to permit the Aleph

Institute to ship matzo (unleavened bread) into high-security facilities during Passover, when Jews are not permitted to eat any other kind of bread. The system's general rule was that no "outside" foods were permitted, because they open the door to contraband. At the same time, the system did not provide the matzos itself, and therefore Jewish inmates were forced to violate their religious beliefs during Passover. The rule passes constitutional muster, because it is neutral and generally applicable. Under RLUIPA, however, the state would have to explain the necessity of the prohibition on outside foods, which should not be difficult in a high-security prison context, but it would be forced to prove as well whether its plan was the least restrictive means to serve security needs. In other words, a court would have the power to second-guess and micromanage the policy from the courtroom. Forcing the prison to buy the matzos is likely a failed effort because prisons (and therefore the public) cannot be expected to bear the cost of an inmate's religious observance.

Thus, RLUIPA would drive the court to engage in the essentially legislative process of determining whether there is *any* way to get the matzo to the prisoner without undermining the security concerns. Just to take the role of the court for a moment, i.e., assessing accommodation in the absence of facts or expertise, one possibility would be to make matzos at that time of year available through the commissary, so that an inmate could purchase them, while the food would have come into the prison from ordinary delivery channels. Could a court enjoin the prison to do just that? RLUIPA seems to say so. Without further facts, though, it is hard to know what the right accommodation solution should be, which is almost always the case when the issue is decided in a courtroom rather than the legislature. Better for the legislature to gather and then weigh the facts.

Others, however, were against the prison provisions of RLUIPA. Unlike the land-use side of RLUIPA, where no government official or land-use expert was permitted to testify against RLUIPA or even to explain the operation of local land-use law vis-à-vis churches, there was a semblance of balance and fair-minded consideration of the issues on the prison side, as abbreviated as it was.[34]

Ohio solicitor Jeffrey Sutton (now a federal appellate judge) was permitted to testify that prisons should have been exempted from the Religious Liberty Protection Act, the predecessor bill to RLUIPA. The

Ohio Corrections Department's experience with RFRA led him to offer the following: The RFRA "cases included such bizarre claims as demands for recognition of the right to burn Bibles, the right to possess and distribute racist literature, the right to engage in animal sacrifices, and the right to group martial arts classes," but it also forced prison authorities to spend a great deal of time on issues that had been settled in the courts already.[35]

Even more troublesome, though, was the fact that prisoners "exploited" RFRA to "insulate illicit, even dangerous, activities from official scrutiny." Nationwide, "white supremacist inmates suddenly converted to obscure or eccentric religions, then demanded that officials recognize their religious gatherings and practices under RFRA . . . and recruited 'religious volunteers' to bring drugs and prostitutes into Lorton prison" – a District of Columbia facility located in Virginia. He cited the example of the Wyoming prison that permitted Luciferian inmates unsupervised group services to burn Bibles and hymnals, which led to significant smoke damage throughout the facilities. Sutton also pointed out that RFRA forced chaplains to shift their focus from providing religious services to litigation, because the inmates came to view the chaplains as the "enforcers" of RFRA, rather than a spiritual resource.[36] His implicit point was that prisons are already financially strapped and under siege from serious internal security problems. To add RLUIPA on top made no sense to him.

When RFRA was under consideration, Sen. Harry Reid (D-Nev.) offered an amendment on the Senate floor that would have prohibited the application of RFRA to incarcerated individuals, in part because he believed prisoners had become far too litigious. But it was too late in the process, which meant RFRA was enacted without the exception. He later expressed concerns regarding the impact of RLPA and RLUIPA on prisons, because corrections officers had contacted him and expressed sincere concern about their own and the public's security:

> AFSCME recently alerted their corrections officer membership that this legislation was coming up for a vote, and was deluged with phone calls from members expressing their distress about how this bill might affect their ability to maintain security and protect the safety of the public. As you can well imagine, getting inmates to comply with security

measures in prison is no easy task. Many prisoners will use any excuse to avoid searches and to evade security measures instituted to protect prison personnel and the general public from harm.[37]

Sen. Strom Thurmond (R-S.C.) expressed similar concerns in testimony following RLUIPA's passage by Congress but before President Clinton signed it into law on September 22, 2000, and added that "[I]nmates have used religion as a cover to organize prison uprisings, get drugs into prison, promote gang activity, and interfere in important prison health regulations. Additional legal protections will make it much harder for corrections officials to control these abuses of religious rights."[38] Despite these legitimate concerns, the members did not inquire further; no study was done to address the issue, no state prison administrator called to testify to inject some facts into the process, and apparently no concern on the part of the vast majority of the members was expressed. It is a perfect example of the phenomenon where Congress resolutely serves religious entities by deferring to a religious lobbyist (Colson) without taking into account the questions implicating the larger public good – and the many other interests implicated by these questions.

Unbelievably, Reid dropped these concerns and supported RLUIPA on a promise that Sen. Orrin Hatch (R.-Utah) would hold hearings a year *after* its enactment, to which state officials would be invited to assess how it had worked in practice. Anyone who knows anything about legislation knows that once a law is passed, it is virtually impossible to get it repealed, so the promise of postenactment hearings seems hardly adequate to Reid's concerns. He was also mollified by the notion that he and Senator Hatch would ask the General Accounting Office to conduct a detailed study of its (and the Prison Litigation Reform Act's) effect on prisons.[39] Not surprisingly, neither was ever done. September 11 intervened, and the prisons are still being sued by inmates with a dizzying array of religious requirements. The Supreme Court will decide by July 2005 whether it is constitutional. (It's not.)

It appears that, but for Colson (and Jaroslawicz to a lesser extent) and his desire to position Prison Fellowship Ministries to proselytize conservative Christianity in prisons across the country, RLUIPA might only have addressed land use, and not prisons. What is desperately needed in Congress is some member who can rise above religious lobbying to secure the larger good – members that at least ask if there is another side to an issue raised by a religious entity, without being its servant.

*The challenge of accommodating religious prisoners*

Prison wardens welcome peaceful religions within their walls, because they can assist with rehabilitation.[40] The same cannot be said for white supremacist religions that preach violence or Islamic fanatics, advocating the end of the United States. Given the high percentage of religious believers in the United States, prison officials are in all likelihood religious themselves, so the notion that there is antireligious sentiment in the prisons is hard to prove. The problem with these groups is their threat to security and order. New York City corrections commissioner Martin Horn nicely captured the difficulties faced by prison authorities: "The vast majority of inmates have genuine faith needs, and the professional standards of prison and jail administration call for the respect of honestly held faith beliefs. But there are no lack of examples of inmates who will misuse it."[41]

For those not familiar with prison administration, the requests for religious accommodation by prisoners may seem innocuous, taken one by one. This fellow needs a kosher diet, and that woman needs a crucifix, while another needs long hair. And these issues typically come up in the context of legal action, so it appears that it is a simple request by a sincere individual or small group of individuals. The global impact on the prisons is lost in the context of the particular case, but that larger context is what the prison administrator *must* take into account. Prisons can only operate successfully where each prisoner perceives he or she is being treated just like any other prisoner, where discipline is tight and predictable, and where the routine is set. And it is not just a problem of logistics; it is expensive for a significant number of inmates to be accommodated, because it requires at the least additional guards to cover various locations within the prisons.

How much trouble can religious accommodation be? The answer is that it can be enormously problematic, when one multiplies religions, religious practices, and the individual variations on each and then sets them in the context of a prison that must ensure security and order within a typically tight budget. (The First Amendment contemplates the absolute right to believe, which has no "mainstream religion" or "settled religious practice" element, so the breadth of religious belief is huge.) The following is a list of some of the requested accommodations in state and federal prisons to give the reader a sense of the scope of the issue. It is far from inclusive.

| Accommodation request | Religion |
| --- | --- |
| *Diet restrictions* | |
| • Vegan | African Hebrew Israelite |
| • Vegetarian diet | Buddhist |
| • Protein tablets | Buddhist |
| • Vegetarian diet | Jehovah's Witness (not required for most) |
| • Vegetarian (no meat/eggs) | Hindu |
| • Kosher diet* | Orthodox Jew |
| • Diet – no pork; halal[†] meat only | Muslim |
| • No pork or shellfish | Seventh-day Adventist |
| • Dairy vegetarian most of year; fast of milk and water | Ethiopian Orthodox Tewahido Church |
| • I-tal diet[‡] | Rastafarian |
| • Biblically derived diet[§] | Nation of Islam |
| • Fish and unleavened bread during Lent | Catholic |
| • Steak and sherry every Friday | CONS (Church of the New Song) |

*A kosher diet basically prohibits pork and shellfish, and the consumption of milk and meat together.

[†]"Halal" meat has been killed according to religious rituals. Kosher meat satisfies the halal requirement.

[‡]Fresh, unprocessed fruit, vegetables, fish, juices and grains.

[§]Permits whole wheat or rye bread; fruit, and fruit pies with brown sugar and whole wheat flour; navy beans, soy beans, kale, peas, collard greens, turnip greens, sweet or white potatoes, some fish, and cream cheese. No lima beans, pork, fried or hard-baked foods, cornbread, freshly cooked bread, pancakes and syrup, nuts, halibut, catfish, carp, eel, oyster, lobster, crab, clam, shrimp, and snail.

| Accommodation request | Religion |
|---|---|
| *Grooming/dress restrictions* | |
| • No haircut | Hindu, Native America |
| • No haircut; beard | Sikh |
| • Beard | Muslim |
| • Muslim cellmate | Muslim |
| • Muslim head covering in prison yard (already allowed in prayer services) | Muslim |
| • Dreadlocks and hat | Rastafarian |
| • Beard longer than allowed | Rastafarian |
| • Headband | Native American |
| • Metal cross | Protestant |
| • Religious medal | Odinis |
| • Bow ties during religious service | Nation of Islam |
| • Tallow-free soap and conditioner | Buddhist |
| • Sidelocks | Orthodox Hasidic Jew |
| • Worship in the nude | Technicians of the Sacred (Neo-African faith) |
| | |
| *Literature* | |
| • Racist literature | Christian Identity, Church of the Creater |
| • Noncensored religious texts | Hebrew Israelite Faith |
| • Texts | Taoism |
| • Religious materials | Moorish Science Temple of America |
| • Access to banned literature | Asatru, Church of Jesus Christ Christian, Wiccan, Satanist, Nation of Islam |
| • Scripture – NPKA Book of Blotar | Odinist |
| • Racist literature, redacted | Hebrew Israelite |
| • Satanic Bible | Satanist |
| • Aryan Nation literature | Aryan Nation |
| • Religious comic books | Fundamentalist Christian |

| Accommodation request | Religion |
|---|---|
| *Literature (continued)* | |
| • Literature and numerological devices | Nation of Gods and Earths, or Five Percent Nation (roots in Black Islam) |
| • Bible – specific version | Variety of Christian denominations |
| *Miscellaneous* | |
| • Evergreen tree, sauna, charm necklace with Thor's hammer, small stone altar in cell, cauldron, drinking horn, branch, Viking-type swords made of soft wood | Odinist |
| • Sweat lodge* | Native American |
| • Wild-bird feathers | Native American |
| • Permission to cast spells/curses | Wiccan |
| • Tarot cards | Wiccan |
| • Proper disposal of blood after drawn for medical testing | Jehovah's Witness (fundamentalist) |
| • Refusal to take tuberculosis test | Rastafarian, Muslim |
| • Placement only with Caucasians | Christian Separatist Church Society |
| • Worship separate from Sunni Muslims | Shi'ite Muslims |
| • Worship separate from Shi'ites | Sunni Muslims |
| • Muslim cellmate | Muslim |
| • Right not to be classified as a Security Threat Group, which designates violent prisons gangs | Five Percent Nation |
| • Medicine pouch | Native American Church |

*A building made of branches in which rocks are heated so that participants have a sauna-like effect, which is a location for medicine and pipe ceremonies and prayer.

| Accommodation request | Religion |
|---|---|
| *Miscellaneous (continued)* | |
| • Spiritual necklace | Native American Church |
| • Weekly Jumu'ah prayer | Muslim |
| • Prayer oil (in or outside cell) | Muslim |
| • Candles, incense | Muslim |
| • Religious talismans | Muslim |
| • Bible burning | Luciferian |
| • Writing paper, newspaper, more access to spiritual adviser | Wotanist |
| • Menorah for Hanukah | Jew |
| • Tefillin* | Orthodox Jew |
| • Not filling out standard form to obtain kosher meal | Orthodox Jew |
| • Wine for communion | Catholic |
| • Personal counseling, worship service, Bible study, ministers | Pentecostal |
| • Prayer rug | Muslim |
| • Spiritual adviser, well-rounded research library in cell, Bible in yard for proselytization | Fundamentalist Christian Separatist |
| • Denominational pin, shirt, separate services | Christian Identity Church |
| • Cleric from outside prison to conduct services | Muslim |
| • Weekly group meetings | Atheist |
| • Oils, powders, incense, candles, religious Botanicals, stones, Talisman, Charm bags | Voodoo/Egyptian Freemasonry |
| • Better Protestant programming | Baptist |
| • Observance of Muslim holidays not recognized by Sunni/Shi'ites | Nation of Islam |

*Small leather boxes with prayer scrolls inside that are tied with leather straps to the foreheads and forearms while praying.

| Accommodation request | Religion |
|---|---|
| *Miscellaneous (continued)* | |
| • Embrace and kiss wife | Christian |
| • Change of name after being born again | Universal Life Church |
| • Kirpan (knife) | Sikh |

Most prisons try to accommodate at least some religious diets – within the parameters of affordability, good nutrition, and feasibility. Typically, there will be a kosher option, a vegetarian option, and/or a no-pork option. The fine differences between the different versions of vegetarianism are nearly impossible to match. Some Hindus will not have any food resulting from an animal's suffering, which means no meat, eggs, animal by-products, or honey, while dairy products are acceptable. Jains add to the Hindu diet a restriction on any food resulting from the suffering of plants, for instance, root vegetables like potatoes, and microorganisms. For some Buddhists, eating meat is forbidden, and the larger the animal, the worse the karma, but fish is lower on the animal kingdom scale and therefore may be eaten. The Seventh-day Adventist believer is not a vegetarian per se and will not eat pork or shellfish, while Muslims tend not to eat pork. Putting together a nutritionally balanced diet for all of these beliefs at once is quite challenging, to say the least. That is why some systems concentrate certain faiths in certain prisons so that they can accommodate that group as efficiently as possible.

Grooming policies also come into conflict with a fair number of religious practices. Typically, prisons regulate hair length and beard length, because both, if long enough, can be used to hide contraband, including drugs and weapons. The rule is obviously passed for a compelling interest – security in the prisons. A number of faiths are burdened by such a regulation. Native Americans often believe that hair should only be cut in sorrow. Rastafarians believe in wearing long dreadlocks and beards. The Muslim faith requires men to have beards. Like long hair and beards, head coverings also are convenient places for drugs and weapons, and similarly regulated.

If the grooming policy is applied across the board, it is constitutional, despite the burdens on religious believers, under the reasoning of both

*Employment Div. v. Smith* and *Turner v. Safley*. Prison authorities get into trouble, though, if they do not apply the principle evenhandedly. If the policy can be abridged by one prisoner, the claim to security has lost a great deal of its force.

Religious objects are a very difficult category for the prison authorities to handle. The key problem is that prisoners are unbelievably clever at crafting just about anything in their cells into a weapon. The metal from crosses and crucifixes can be shaped, if one spends enough time, into a shank. One or two headbands can be an effective garrote. Whether wood or metal, a menorah can be fashioned into an offensive weapon. And the sweat lodge requested by some Native Americans involving a fire within a structure built with branches, with fire's obvious potential for harm, has been accommodated, though it requires additional guards and ample grounds on which to place it. When a Wyoming prison gave Satan worshipers – called Luciferians – a Bible and a match, the ritual burning of the Bible caused smoke damage throughout the prison.[42]

Space requirements – the need for a place for worship, or to be near or away from certain other groups – can be especially difficult when the variety of religions in the prison reaches a certain quantum of faiths. Prisons have to scramble to find enough worship spaces, appropriate rooms for each particular group, and additional guards.

Each of these practices can be the basis of a federal lawsuit under RLUIPA. So long as the inmate is sincere about the belief, the court must consider the request for accommodation of the prison's regulation under a standard that presumes that regulation is illegal.

These sincere requests are difficult enough, but the prisons also face an uphill battle against the creativity, some would say cunning, of prisoners in coming up with new "religions."

*New religions in prison*

One of the more serious problems for prisons facing broad religious liberty guarantees for their inmates, which admittedly can also be entertaining, is that a significant number of prisoners are sorely tempted to claim religious privilege for what is, in fact, a secular desire. It is not out of the realm of possibility that a Christian inmate who thinks the kosher food looks better than what he was eating will insist that he has had a sudden conversion to Judaism. Or that a prisoner will claim that his religion requires an exercise mat and free time every day at 4:00 P.M. But the prize has to go to the Church of the New Song (CONS).

The CONS was founded in the early 1970s by a federal inmate, Harry Theriault, who said it was a "game." And what a game it is. This "religion" requires a prisoner to be served Harvey's Bristol Crème and steak every Friday at 5:00 P.M.[43] As one can imagine, it quickly gained recruits. This is a classic case of a group testing the waters with insincere claims of religious devotion. Common sense should have sent their free-exercise claims packing.

Unfortunately, though, their original claims aired in the 1970s when the Supreme Court's free-exercise jurisprudence bent over backward for believers to the detriment of the public good, and a court actually held that CONS was a religion deserving protection under the First Amendment.[44] It is, to be sure, an embarrassing moment for the U.S. Court of Appeals for the Eighth Circuit, which reasoned as follows:

> After careful consideration of the entire record we are satisfied that the district court's judgment that The Church of the New Song is a religion within the ambit of the First Amendment is based on findings that are not clearly erroneous and that no error of law appears. Further there is insufficient evidence in this record to establish [the] contention that [CONS'] beliefs are not sincere and genuinely felt. It also appears that [CONS] have not been allowed a fair and meaningful opportunity to freely exercise their religion in the same degree as other inmates, Protestant and Catholic.[45]

The good news (if one thinks of common sense as a virtue) is that another court refused to fall for the legal ploy, and held that:

> The beliefs professed by [CONS] are not sincerely held and do not in their own scheme of things constitute a 'religion' nor are they sincerely of a 'religious' character. . . . The so-called 'Church of the New Song' does not meet the criteria adopted by this Court in its analysis above to entitle it to First Amendment protection as a religion. It is clearly a sham designed and calculated to obtain favored treatment for its members incarcerated in various prisons and has no measurable following outside Federal Penitentiaries.[46]

Hear, hear.

Thirty years after the Eighth Circuit recognized CONS as a religion, the church brought a new free-exercise claim. The lawsuit was brought when prison authorities at the Iowa State Penitentiary in Fort Madison, Iowa, refused to deliver trays of food for the CONS' "celebration of life" to inmates who were in lock-up during the banquet. Apparently, the other believers were able to eat their "celebration-of-life" feast together, so the only CONS believers at issue were in lock-up. In any event, a federal lawsuit was filed on behalf of these locked-up inmates who were denied participation in the "celebration of life." Thirty years into this charade, the judges of the Eighth Circuit were bound by the previous decision, but they seemed to have gotten some perspective. Judge Pasco M. Bowman, writing the opinion for himself and Judges William Jay Riley and Lavenski R. Smith, had to "suspend disbelief" to get through the case.[47]

When prisoners create religions, there can be some chaos in the institution of their traditions. CONS is an excellent example. During the Iowa litigation, at first, the "celebration of life" (1) was a spring festivity, saluting nature's renewal of life; (2) then it was a party to celebrate the day CONS was founded; (3) and then it was the same as the Sacred Unity Feast mentioned in their religious text, the Paratestament. The court perused the Parastatement carefully, and was forced to conclude that it could not be the same as the Sacred Unity Feast, because the latter only happens after "the hundred and forty-four thousand Revelation ministers have been sealed as prophesied." Since it was "apparent" to the court that the hundred and forty-four thousand Revelation ministers had not yet been sealed," no Sacred Unity Feast could be held.[48] Further perusal of the scripture led the court to conclude that this was not a religiously mandated celebration and therefore no free-exercise rights would accrue.

But on the off chance that the Supreme Court might consider reversing its reasoning, I suppose, the court persevered to explain why, even if the celebration were religiously mandated, the prison authorities could refuse to deliver the trays of food to lock-up. The penitentiary argued that there was no way for it to prevent contraband from traveling in or on the trays, in part because health regulations prohibited them from handling the food. In fact, CONS helped to make the penitentiary's case, because before the celebration of life denial, CONS members "sent contraband into the lock-up unit through a variety of illicit methods."[49] So the court had to conclude the state had more than carried its burden, and, besides, the "celebration-of-life" feast itself had no particular dietary requirements, so the deprivation of the trays did not affect the CONS's beliefs.

It is a silly "church" and a funny case, to be sure. But it is also deeply troubling. The CONS's testimony regarding the meaning of the so-called "celebration of life" was confused and muddled, probably because they were making it up as they went along. When that first court declared them a legitimate, protected religion, they won. They successfully played the system. The fact that they won recognition as a religion from a federal court taught them that conning the correctional system works, and that the Constitution protects the con game. That's some rehabilitative message, and it shows the folly that results when courts are as muddle-headed about religion as legislators often are. Demanding proof of sincerity about religious belief and practices is not antireligious, as perhaps the first court believed; rather, it keeps the system honest, the results just, and the First Amendment legitimate.

### A new phenomenon: Religious prisons

Two cultural forces have come together to create "religious prisons" in the United States. First, there has been a persistent belief that religion, as a whole, is good for people, and inmates in particular.[50] There appears to be an increasing amount of evidence that suggests that some religious programming in the prisons can reduce the recidivism rate.[51]

Second, certain religious entities have gained remarkable power in the political sphere, which leads politicians to desire to be identified with religious projects and to grant religious entities what they request. The combination of a Pollyanna-like attitude regarding religion and religion's political power make it an opiate for elected representatives. It is an addictive mix that paralyzes their common sense and disables their otherwise natural cynicism about lobbyists in general. When Chuck Colson importuned a Republican-dominated Congress to include prisons under RFRA and RLUIPA, the members were all too happy to oblige. At one point, there was even a rumor that the goal was to get RLUIPA passed by Easter! To state the matter modestly, the temptation to make religion a centerpiece of the prison experience is quite

strong in the United States at this time. These religious prisons offer mass accommodation, at least for some believers, but especially
Christians.

There are two types of religious prisons. First, there is the Iowa model,
which has been tried in Texas, Kansas, and Minnesota as well, where,
Colson's Prison Fellowship Ministries, employing its "Christ-centered"
approach, takes over a wing of a prison at state cost. Second, there is the
Florida model, where the system designates certain prisons as religious,
gives inmates a choice to go and a choice to leave, and the religious activities are funded by private, religious entities. As a constitutional matter,
the former is on much shakier ground than the latter.

The Iowa experiment is Christian at its core. Prison Fellowship Ministries takes over a wing of a prison and sets up shop, hoping to convert as
many prisoners as possible. A report on National Public Radio indicated
that they call the cells the "God Pod," and the Warden describes them:
"The doors are wooden. One of the differences you notice, the doors are
unlocked as you come in. Cell doors are unlocked. They can come and
go by their schedule." The NPR Reporter then elaborated on the system:
"The men can stay up longer. They see more visitors. But they also have
a more disciplined regimen: no TV except for the news, up for prayer and
worship at 6 A.M., Bible study several hours a day, as well as vocational
training, workshops, mentoring programs, all by Christians. It is, in fact,
a virtual drenching in evangelical Christianity."[52] The cost of the extra
programming has been defrayed by the state revenue from all inmates'
phone calls.

Iowa is already fighting lawsuits brought by the ACLU and another by
Americans United for the Separation of Church and State.[53]

The Iowa system is reminiscent of the attempts to get Christian prayer
back into the public schools; a nostalgic attempt to create a Christian
country in the context of settled and contrary constitutional principles.
Those principles do not permit the government to single out any one
religious viewpoint for good or for bad, or to have the effect of advancing
religion, or of government endorsement of religion, or excessive entanglement of church and state. One could even say that in a prison context,
where privileges and open cell doors are rare, and therefore a tremendous incentive to do whatever it takes to get them, it is akin to coercion to
become Christian (or at least to participate in Christian activities). In an

interesting twist, the organization that fought for strict scrutiny of all prison regulations will have its sectarian program in the prisons subjected to strict scrutiny as well. The difference is that the prison regulations were neutral and generally applicable and therefore did not deserve searching judicial review, while there is every reason to assume that a state prison with a "God Pod" paid for by the state is probably unconstitutional. In the words of the Supreme Court, "when we are presented with a state law granting a denominational preference, our precedents demand that we treat the law as suspect and that we apply strict scrutiny in adjudging its constitutionality."[54]

Then there is the Florida model, which is being tried or considered in roughly a dozen states, where certain prisons have been designated as "faith based," and theoretically, all faiths are welcome. Inmates who have a certain level of good behavior within the system as a whole are eligible to go to the faith-based alternative for the last 36 months of their incarceration. While there, they are taught basic life skills, like writing a resumé and opening a checking account, by religious volunteers, and in the evenings, there is frequent religious programming. In addition, every morning, there are Christian devotions available to whoever desires to attend.

The Florida system is distinctive from the Iowa model in that the rehabilitative programming and staffing is supplied by religious groups from outside the prison. As one reporter noted, the Florida system has turned President George Bush's faith-based initiative "on its head."[55]

Instead of the government providing financial support for religious mission, the religious groups are giving money and services to a state system. This is an especially interesting phenomenon in light of University of Arizona sociology professor Mark Chaves's book, *Congregations in America*, which documents that religious groups spend relatively little on social services. In his words, "[F]or the vast majority of congregations, social services constitute a minor and peripheral aspect of their organizational activities, taking up only small amounts of their resources and involving only small numbers of people. We fundamentally misunderstand congregations if we imagine that this sort of activity is now, was ever, or will ever be central to their activities."[56] So the Florida experiment, with its intensive labor from church members and fairly significant costs, does seem to break new ground.

Like other religious phenomena in the United States, it is easy to be led down the path of thinking that the religious program is all to the good. There is an underbelly to the program, however, and that is that minority religions are not getting adequate attention. It is almost exclusively a Christian system, and in Florida, at least, it seems predestined to be a Christian system. It is at the mercy of the believers who live near the prison, and therefore any prisoner from outside the community who does not share its faith may well receive lesser religious instruction and worship than the others. The lopsided nature of the program in Florida has been accentuated by the fact that last year Florida slashed funds for chaplains and staff dramatically, making it ever more difficult to serve a wide variety of believers. The combination of the dependency on the local believers and the state's reduction in its professional chaplaincy make it all too likely that one prisoner has rightly assessed the situation: "You know, in the manual you would read that all religions are reverenced, but it's understood it's under Christian dictatorship."[57] The details are troubling: only one visit from a Muslim cleric in a year, while everyone is urged to participate in the Christian so-called "devotions" on a daily basis. Thus, the ACLU of Florida's executive director may well have a point: Governor Jeb Bush is "willing to improve conditions in prison facilities only for those inmates that are willing to accept religious proselytizing."[58] Like the Iowa model, though, the rational prisoner desires the placement, because there is more liberty, more education, and even more entertainment – so members of smaller faiths may be coerced – certainly induced – into signing up for a program that is predominantly Christian. Some of those from minority religions do not complain about the faith-based environment, though, because it is simply quieter than the average prison.[59]

With the seemingly intractable problems in most prisons, the temptation to treat the religious prisons as a cure-all is strong. Such wishful thinking probably accounts for the simultaneous reduction in the size of the chaplaincy at the same time the programs opened. But prison systems cannot suddenly dispose of sensible criminology principles, according to most experts. For example, as important as constructive religion may be in reducing the recidivism rate, religious programming should not replace other factors that are also known to help, including counseling, drug and alcohol abuse treatment, and job instruction. One critique of these plans is that they are jerry-rigged to make the religious effect look more powerful than it really is. Experts have said that recidivism will only be reduced when the most difficult criminals are included, while these programs are cherry-picking the believers who already have a good track record. Thus, the program's positive impact on recidivism may be a chimera. It may be that the success of the Florida program, at least, has more to do with its job training and life-skills courses than it does with religion, and those assessing these programs need to be hardheaded in making such determinations. If recidivism rates are reduced, that will save states many dollars while the general public is served by a reduction in criminal activity. If they do not, and the system has jettisoned the core criminological methods to rehabilitate prisoners, the people of the state of Florida will be in worse shape than they were when the program was introduced.

Like RLUIPA, these are experiments in accommodating and meeting religious prisoners' needs. Also like RLUIPA, there is good reason to worry whether the government is acting in a neutral and evenhanded manner toward particular religions or religion in general. If it strays from the path of neutrality, the Establishment Clause will raise barriers to the program, and prisons will either have to adjust or abandon these attempts. It is too early to tell how they will operate over the long term, but there is every reason to watch them with care, as their models have spread like wildfire through the state prison systems desperate to contain costs and reduce recidivism. The religious groups behind these programs have taken on some enormous social problems, and it is not just religious practice that is at stake, but also the general welfare of the society as a whole.

*The conflict between military requirements and religious dress requirements*

The military always has been given broad latitude to enforce the rules it believes are necessary for order, discipline, and defense of the country. The courts have not felt institutionally competent to take on the question whether this uniform or that practice is necessary to ensure a strong military. Those decisions belong in the hands of the executive, from the

Supreme Court's perspective. Thus, any accommodation by the military will have to come through Congress, and it has.

In the 1980s, the Air Force prohibited its officers from wearing headgear other than that which was officially authorized by Air Force rules. S. Simcha Goldman was an Orthodox Jew who was required by his religious beliefs to wear his yarmulke while on duty, as a clinical psychologist. He had worn it for several years with no disciplinary proceedings, but he was reported, and then told he could not wear the yarmulke with his uniform outside the hospital. Goldman rejected the order, saying that the free exercise of religion trumped the military regulation.

He won at the trial court, but the court of appeals reversed, and the Supreme Court agreed. Only two months and a few days after oral argument, in an opinion written by then-Justice William Rehnquist, and joined by Chief Justice Warren Burger and Justices Byron White, Lewis Powell, and John Paul Stevens (which was a politically diverse group), the court refused to second-guess the military's determinations regarding dress regulations. The regulation was reasonable and evenhanded, and accorded with the military's "perceived need for uniformity."[60] Despite the obvious burden on religious conduct, the court found no First Amendment guarantee to alter military uniform requirements. The court did not need to say it, but there was obviously no *obligation* for the Air Force to refuse to let Goldman wear the yarmulke, which left open legislative accommodation, upon due consideration of the need for uniformity in these circumstances.

In a telling dissent, Justice William Brennan, joined by Justice Thurgood Marshall, argued that the court had "abdicate[d] its role as principal expositor of the Constitution and protector of individual liberties in favor of credulous deference to unsupported assertions of military necessity."[61] The dissenters simply did not buy the claimed interest in uniformity, and would have penalized the Air Force, because it had yet to explain why a "neat and conservative yarmulke" was inconsistent with the uniform. Justice Harry Blackmun dissented separately to say that the Air Force had not convinced him that its interests were harmed by the yarmulke and he wanted to know why the service could not accommodate not only Goldman but also those with "indistinguishable requests for religious exemptions," so he would not have stopped with an exemption for yarmulkes, but would have used the Constitution to impose a uniform exemption policy in other circumstances as well.[62] Justice Sandra Day O'Connor, joined by Justice Marshall, also dissented, because she was not persuaded there was any threat at all to discipline or esprit de corps by an accommodation – she has always stood by judicial accommodation.[63] Every dissent was a quintessential example of legislative reasoning – carried out by unelected justices. The dangers of permitting courts to engage in such weighing is painfully evident, as each of the three dissents had a different accommodation in mind. A legislature would have been forced to examine all the choices, compromise, and find a single accommodation that was in the best interest of the public.

Now, the typical tale of the Free Exercise Clause in the United States would have many decrying the *Goldman v. Weinberger* decision as a sellout to the military, or an abdication of First Amendment principles, or an utterly unfair imposition of majority dress practices on a minority religion that could not protect itself in the political process. That is the standard story, and plenty were critical. According to one commentator, "in fact, there was no support offered by the government for its claims other than the bare assertion of military judgment and the abstract interest in military preparedness, duty, and discipline. . . . Yet for the *Goldman* Court, the abstract military interest and the military's judgment of reasonableness were constitutionally sufficient."[64]

But that is not the end of the story. When the Court refused to carve an accommodation out of a neutral and generally applicable regulation, the fight was taken to the halls of Congress. And guess what? Congress enacted an exemption for religious headgear,[65] and so Orthodox Jews (and other religious believers) may now wear religious headgear in many circumstances. The accommodation makes a lot of sense if one looks at the whole picture. What makes the most sense, though, is that the court declined to impose its limited knowledge of military uniform needs through a tortured reading of the Free Exercise Clause, and instead let the issue migrate to the political branch, where it was most appropriately addressed.

Such headgear accommodation, though, has its limits, as it must. A Sikh man insisted on wearing a turban, which is required by his religion, with his uniform – even when a helmet was required. The U.S. Court of Appeals for the Ninth Circuit held that the military had the right to court-martial someone who will only wear a turban in combat.[66] That is just plain common sense.

## Conclusion

Courts are institutionally incompetent to determine religious accommo-dation in the prisons beyond the Constitution's regime, which recognizes a right to be treated equally with similarly situated prisoners, a rule against singling out a particular religion for negative treatment, and a rule that the prison must at least show a "legitimate penological interest" to justify regulation. That is the right balance. Congress's decision with RLUIPA to alter the standard dramatically by making all prison regulations substan-tially burdening any religious inmate's religious conduct presumptively illegal is hard to defend. The record is too slim to justify the interference with the extraordinarily difficult job of running a prison. It is also telling that even though no members of Congress raised substantive concerns about any other regime governed by RFRA or RLUIPA, there was gen-uine concern on the part of Senators Reid, a Democrat, and Thurmond, a Republican.

As the yarmulke case makes clear, accommodation can be achieved in the legislative process, even when the group is a smaller religion and even when the Supreme Court has refused to craft a constitutional rule for the believer. Judicial deference to the military and to the prisons is not the end of religious liberty; it's just ordered liberty.

# DISCRIMINATION

There is little question that "discrimination" is a dirty word in the United States, and discrimination by religious entities is counterintuitive to the prevailing notion that religion is always a force for good. Religious groups do, though, clash with the antidiscrimination laws in two primary arenas: housing and employment. This is a context where legislative accommodation has played and should play an active role in measuring the conflicting rights claims. Legislative accommodation is needed, as opposed to judicial, because making a determination whether to accommodate the religious practice, for example, of excluding unmarried couples, or to favor a right to shelter requires broad-ranging and forward-thinking analysis. No court, deciding the issue in the context of a single case, is competent to take into account all of the interests that need to be considered. The final accommodation is a complicated equation that calls for legislative reasoning regarding what the law should be and not just an interpretation of a law.

This is not to say that the courts have not imposed their view of accommodation on these issues. In the employment context, the courts crafted the "ministerial exception," which has immunized religious employment decisions from judicial review in some circumstances. As I will discuss, there is reason to think that this accommodation is not consistent with current First Amendment doctrine. Equally, though, it is highly likely that legislatures would grant a rather similar legislative exemption for the cases involving a religious employer and religious employee.

There are two ends of the spectrum in these cases. Religious entities may always discriminate on the basis of religious belief. In other words, Presbyterians can decide only to hire Presbyterians to be a minister or elder. At the opposite end is race discrimination. Both ends of the spectrum appeared in *Hopkins v. Women's Div., Bd. of Global Ministries*, where a federal district court ruled that although Global Ministries could prevail on the *religious* discrimination claim under Title VII, the employee's claim regarding race-based discrimination was not covered by Title VII's exemption for religious entities and could not be the beneficiary of the "ministerial exception." Therefore, the race discrimination claim would go forward.[1] Thus, if a religious entity insists on discriminating according to race, it can be held liable under Title VII, or like Bob Jones University, it will find that it can be denied certain government privileges, like tax-exempt status.

The United States is still working out these issues, but if there is any movement, it is toward the enforcement of civil rights against religious entities and away from expansive immunity for them. Some will argue this proves the culture is being secularized by contemporary culture, whether it is from television, motion pictures, or music. I would posit, however, that the "secularization" card in the political context is, in fact, a red herring. The increasing inclination to hold religious entities to the mores of the general society is not a 20th- or 21st-century turn *against* religion, but rather a turn *toward* a shared sense of fundamental fairness, a concept that owes its origin in no small part to religious precepts. In the United States, religion has never been wholly separate from politics, and antidiscrimination principles have been derived as much from religious principles as secular.

Rather, Anglo-American culture has been working out a logic of justice vis-à-vis religious entities for centuries. As Chapter 9 demonstrates, the Catholic Church started in Britain as sovereign and above the state, but the internal logic of the common law and the now-overriding principle that one is not permitted to harm others have come together to deconstruct the arguments that at one time justified permitting religious entities latitude to harm others. Antidiscrimination is just the most recent iteration of the principle that one is not allowed to harm others. In this arena, a basic sense of fairness appears to be winning over libertarianism, and legislative accommodation fares better than judicial accommodation.

## Housing discrimination by religious individuals

In the United States, many religious home or apartment owners have dutiful scruples about letting their property be used by unmarried couples, gay couples, and/or unwed mothers. They have not fared terribly well under the fair housing laws, in no small part because the availability of shelter is one of the primary needs of humans.

The housing discrimination issue played a pivotal role during the passage of the Religious Freedom Restoration Act (RFRA), its invalidation, and then the Religious Land Use and Institutionalized Persons Act (RLUIPA). When RFRA was first proposed in 1990 and then passed in 1993, it was next to impossible to find anyone who objected to it, including initially myself. What could possibly have been wrong with more religious liberty? Indeed, those behind the law were on what seemed like a noble cause. Senators Orrin Hatch (R-Utah) and Edward Kennedy (D-Mass.), who frequently team up for religious entities, spoke in elegiac terms about what they were doing and others spoke in larger-than-life terms about their mission. They were the literal saviors of religious liberty, or so they said. Senator Kennedy, proclaimed, "Few issues are more fundamental to our country. America was founded as a land of religious freedom and a haven from religious persecution. Two centuries later, that founding principle has been endangered."[2]

Sen. Daniel K. Inouye (D-Hawaii) declared: "Today, we take a historic first step in assuring that the protections of the first amendment to the U.S. Constitution will not be diminished."[3] Senator Hatch certainly worked himself into a lather over the purported trivialization of religion:

> So, the time has come to put an end to the motivations blame game that seems to have become the fashion in this country. All too often, our society dismisses out-of-hand those who admit a religious motivation. The term "religious fanatic" is so overused – and misused – that anyone who seeks to translate religious belief into political action is demonized as a fanatic. . . . And that's what the Religious Freedom Restoration Act is all about – allowing people with sincere religious beliefs to act upon those beliefs, to participate in the public debate without having to run the gauntlet of unnecessarily large Government roadblocks.[4]

His statement makes RFRA sound a lot more reasonable than it was. In fact, RFRA did not merely remove the "unnecessarily large roadblocks" from religious conduct; it removed all legal roadblocks other than those deemed most necessary by the courts.

Hatch also failed to comprehend the irony of the entire RFRA process. According to him, and many others, RFRA was needed because the Supreme Court had thrown religious actors to the legislative process (translate, wolves), and one couldn't trust legislatures to do the right thing by religion.[5] Legislatures could not be trusted to protect religious liberty, but the federal legislature would enact the most far-reaching and beneficial statute for religious entities in United States history?

There is something so fundamentally wrong with this picture, it is hard to know where to start. Suffice it to say that Congress's willingness to pass a blind accommodation statute for dozens of religious groups – without asking whether disabling every law in the country might be a policy mistake – negates the theory that the Court had thrown believers off a cliff. It looks like a pretty soft landing.

While I do not question the sincerity or conviction of the members of Congress, I do have to question their common sense for two reasons. First, the scope of RFRA was mind-boggling. RFRA, by its terms, potentially disabled *every law in the country*, presumably including many the senators had fought to get enacted. Yet, they stayed within the religious advocate's bubble, where all that matters is making sure the believer is free, and the social context or the harm that might accrue lie outside their sphere of concern. As elected representatives, their job is to think outside the box of every legislative proposal, but it does not appear that it ever occurred to them that there was anything beyond the RFRA box. Part of the problem lay in the bill's modus operandi: It was a constitutional standard in form, and constitutional rules apply across the board. Moreover, the bill's breadth was so enormous that it drove analysis away from specific examples. If one is thinking of every law in the land, it is tough to come down to particular issues. There was no natural place to start criticizing it, so almost all of the analysis (with the exception of prisons at the end of the bill's history) resided at a very lofty and abstract level. None of this is to excuse the members for not asking any of the hard questions, but it is an explanation. And the members were not the only ones who didn't penetrate the surface of RFRA to its inherent problems.

Second, the variety of religious faiths in the United States is enormous, and some of them are downright scary. They had to have known that there were religious groups that engaged in conduct that is dangerous to others. What about the Ku Klux Klan, or the other white supremacists in the prisons, who almost always trace their racist beliefs back to the Bible? What about the religious militia in Montana and Idaho? Or the children who happen to die when their faith-healing parents do not take them to the doctor? RFRA was before September 11, so they get a quasi-pass on thinking about terrorists, although the first bombing of the World Trade Center was nine months before RFRA was signed into law on November 16, 1993,[6] and the ongoing religious wars between Israel and Palestinians, the Hindus and the Muslims in Kashmir, the ethnic and the Protestants and the Catholics in Ireland were at full tilt. In 1993, the Irish Republican Army bombed a fish shop in Belfast, killing 10.[7] Did they think that none of that religious fanaticism could reach the United States? The answer is that they simply did not think at all. One can imagine the members going to sleep the night RFRA passed the House, secure in the knowledge that they had done the "right thing." Unfortunately they had not.

In the members' defense, there were dozens of religious organizations behind RFRA as well as most of the major civil rights organizations. Even Americans United for Separation of Church and State loved it! It is typical in political action that the more groups that join the bandwagon, the more watered down the measure becomes. The members seemed to believe that the union of religious and civil rights groups ensured that the law would harm no one. This is only a partial list of those who were lobbying for the bill, which appeared in the Congressional Record:

Agudath Israel of America, American Association of Christian Schools, American Civil Liberties Union, American Conference of Religious Movements, American Humanist Association, American Jewish Committee, American Jewish Congress, American Muslim Council, Americans for Democratic Action, Americans for Religious Liberty, Americans United for Separation of Church & State, Anti-Defamation League, Association of Christian Schools International, Association of American Indian Affairs, Baptist Joint Committee, Coalitions for America, Concerned Women For America, Episcopal Church, Christian Legal Society, Church of Jesus Christ of Latter-day Saints, Church of Scientology, Evangelical Lutheran Church, Conference of Seventh-day Adventists, Jesuit Social Ministries, Mennonite Central Committee, National Association of Evangelicals, National Council of Churches, People for the American Way, Presbyterian Church, Southern Baptist Convention, Traditional Values Coalition, Union of American Hebrew Congregations, Union of Orthodox Jewish Congregations, United Methodist Church, United States Catholic Conference.[8]

The group dubbed itself the Coalition for the Free Exercise of Religion, and by the time the coalition filed an amicus brief in favor of RFRA in the *City of Boerne v. Flores* case, the list had expanded:

- American Association of Christian Schools
- Agudath Israel of America
- American Baptist Churches USA
- American Civil Liberties Union
- American Conference on Religious Movements
- American Ethical Union, Washington Ethical Action Office
- American Humanist Association
- American Jewish Committee
- American Jewish Congress
- American Muslim Council
- Americans for Democratic Action
- Americans for Religious Liberty
- Americans United for Separation of Church and State
- Anti-Defamation League
- Association of Christian Schools International

- Association on American Indian Affairs
- Baptist Joint Committee on Public Affairs
- B'nai B'rith
- Central Conference of American Rabbis
- Christian Church (Disciples of Christ)
- Christian Legal Society
- Christian Life Commission, Southern Baptist Convention
- Christian Science Committee on Publication
- Church of the Brethren
- Church of Scientology International
- Coalition for Christian Colleges and Universities
- Coalitions for America
- Concerned Women for America
- Council of Jewish Federations
- Council on Religious Freedom
- Council on Spiritual Practices
- Criminal Justice Policy Foundation
- Episcopal Church
- Friends Committee on National Legislation
- General Conference of Seventh-day Adventists
- Guru Gobind Singh Foundation
- Hadassah, the Women's Zionist Organization of America, Inc.
- Home School Legal Defense Association
- International Association of Jewish Lawyers and Jurists
- International Institute for Religious Freedom
- The Jewish Reconstructionist Federation
- Mennonite Central Committee U.S.
- Muslim Prison Foundation
- Mystic Temple of Light, Inc.
- National Association of Evangelicals
- National Campaign for a Peace Tax Fund
- National Committee for Public Education and Religious Liberty
- National Council of Churches of Christ in the USA
- National Council of Jewish Women
- National Council on Islamic Affairs
- National Jewish Commission on Law and Public Affairs
- National Jewish Community Relations Advisory Council

- National Sikh Center
- Native American Church of North America
- Native American Rights Fund
- North American Council for Muslim Women
- People For the American Way Action Fund
- Peyote Way Church of God
- Clifton Kirkpatrick, as Stated Clerk of the General Assembly of the Presbyterian Church (USA)
- Rabbinical Council of America
- Sacred Sites Inter-faith Alliance
- Soka-Gakkai International - USA
- Traditional Values Coalition
- Union of American Hebrew Congregations
- Union of Orthodox Jewish Congregations of America
- Unitarian Universalist Association of Congregations
- United Church of Christ, Office for Church in Society
- The United Methodist Church & The General Board of Church and Society and The General Council on Finance and Administration
- United Synagogue of Conservative Judaism
- Wisconsin Judicare
- Women of Reform Judaism, Federation of Temple Sisterhoods[9]

The dynamics of the group is worth more than one sociologist's or political scientist's career, as religious and civil rights groups that normally went head-to-head in the public sphere suddenly were sitting at the same table to empower each other.

The contrasts are stark. It is not often that the ACLU and the Traditional Values Coalition have policy goals in common. The Presbyterians and the Methodists were pro-choice, while the Southern Baptists and the Orthodox Jews (except in cases involving the life of the mother) surely were not. The Unitarian Church was behind equality for gays, but that has never been the agenda of the Church of Jesus Christ of Latter-day Saints. The Christian Scientists believed that the law should not interfere with their faith-based decision to refuse treatment for ill children, but a plethora of coalition members would require medical treatment in the same circumstances. The ACLU was officially opposed to housing discrimination against homosexuals and unmarried adults, while the

Christian Legal Society was pushing hard to obtain exemptions from the fair-housing laws so that their members could discriminate against those groups. Each group surely knew its public policy enemies, yet, the abstract quality of the "right to religious liberty" in the RFRA formulation led them to lay down their usual weapons. It was not politically rational, actually, but they were operating under false information about the Supreme Court's recent rulings on free exercise (as I discuss in Part Two), and partaking in the American myth that all religion is good religion.

In fact, each religious organization had certain public causes that they hoped would be furthered by RFRA. But that was not the topic of discussion at the table (at least that is what I am told). Rather, their attention was trained on making it difficult for the governments in the United States to enforce their laws, where the actor was religiously motivated. Until its invalidation at the Supreme Court in 1997, in *Boerne v. Flores*, the Coalition was able to operate relatively smoothly. One of the key issues that would cleave the organization, though, was housing discrimination.

The move for expansive religious liberty statutes did not stop in 1997, though. After RFRA was invalidated, groups like the Rutherford Institute, which is run and funded by attorney John W. Whitehead, fanned out to the 50 states to try to get state versions passed. At the same time, they asked Congress to pass another statute covering many, if not all, of the laws in the United States, and this time they called it the Religious Liberty Protection Act (RLPA). (One cannot fault them for their skill at choosing names that sound a lot like "apple pie, motherhood, and patriotism.") The problem for the coalition with this next iteration was that RFRA had awakened the slumbering secular groups whose interests were harmed by religious conduct: children's advocates, corrections officials, city planners, historical preservationists, and cities, among others. They had been caught off-guard, because a bill named the "Religious Freedom Restoration Act" gave out precious few clues that their objectives were about to be undermined. After all, they were in favor of religious liberty, too, just like every other American. As RFRA had been applied to individual laws over the course of its three-and-a-half year life, its power to undermine certain policies became increasingly apparent, and these groups slowly came to the realization that they needed to fight this law, even if it did sound like the ultimate all-American initiative. This realization literally took years, first because of the abstract quality of the statute and, second, because there were individual members even in these organizations so familiar with the harm religious entities could cause that were ardent defenders of the RFRA formulation.

Eventually, various groups lobbied against RLPA. In the beginning, the strategy was to push for wholesale defeat of not only RLPA, but the idea. The more effective tactic, though, turned out to be having each group specifically lobby to have their particular interest exempted from RLPA's reach. This posed a serious problem for the coalition, which was viable only so long as its members operated at an abstract level. With each request to have an area of law stripped from RLPA's reach, for example, children's issues, or land use, or prison administration, or housing discrimination, the dormant issues that normally would have divided the members came to the fore.

To keep RLPA (and the state RFRAs) from becoming a nullity through multiple exemptions, and to keep the coalition together, the group devised an interesting strategy: if there was any attempt to peel off a law or a category of law from RLPA or a state RFRA, the entire group would say, "no exemptions." They knew it was harder to kill the idea of religious liberty than it was to obtain a single exemption, so if the single exemption route was blocked, in all likelihood, the larger bill could stand. The strategy did not work at the federal level, though, because the members were becoming educated about RFRA/RLPA's likely impacts, and legitimate concerns were starting to arise that the pending legislation did have a downside. The members therefore resisted RLPA's one-size-fits-all religious conduct formula, which it had inherited from RFRA.

The coalition's strategies worked in some of the state RFRAs, like Connecticut, Florida, and Alabama, which have no exceptions. By the time Texas took the matter under consideration in 1999, though, private property advocates and cities were vocal, active, and effective. They succeeded in obtaining an exemption from the Texas RFRA for land-use laws.[10] The most recent one, Pennsylvania's Religious Freedom Protection Act of 2002 (RFPA), removed a number of categories from its reach, including criminal offenses; motor vehicles; licensing of health professionals, the health or safety of individuals in facilities operated under the public welfare code; the safe construction and operation of health-care facilities; health and safety in construction; and mandatory reporting of child abuse.[11] This is not to say that every entity that would have opposed the bill was heard; RFPA was passed quickly and without hearings, so by the time local government and land-use interests learned of the bill, it was too late to be relieved of its burdens. As a general trend, though, the more legislators have learned, the less likely they have been willing to operate at the abstract level that permitted RFRA to be enacted with minimal discussion of its actual impact.

The burgeoning understanding that this was not such a magical formula led to its defeat in states like Maryland and California in 1998, and is one of the reasons that only thirteen states have passed such a law. In Maryland, children's advocates led the opposition; and in California, it was a combination of children's advocates and local governments.

Perhaps the most interesting story about an interest group coming to understand what was really at stake in RFRA and then RLPA involves the ACLU and the fair housing laws. As most people know, the ACLU is often on the other side of religious groups and certainly goes against the social agenda of conservative Christians. For example, it has championed the rights of adults to have child pornography[12] and of unmarried couples or gay couples to be free from discrimination in the housing market.[13] Yet, its president in 1993, Professor Nadine Strossen, enthusiastically endorsed RFRA at hearings in the House, saying,

> The ACLU strongly supports [RFRA] because it restores religious liberty to its rightful place as a preferred value and a fundamental right within the American constitutional system. The First Amendment's guarantee of the 'free exercise of religion' has proven to be the boldest and most successful experiment in religious freedom the world has known.[14]

But there were conservative Christian and Orthodox groups at the table that were opposed to the ACLU's position on the fair-housing laws, and their interests were furthered by RFRA, while the ACLU's was not. It took more than five years for the ACLU to realize that it had made a colossal mistake in supporting RFRA's abstruse formula, and that it had, in fact, supported a law that was directly opposed to its primary agenda. When RLPA was considered in 1999, the ACLU testified against it, because of its impact on the antidiscrimination laws.

> [W]e are no longer part of the coalition supporting RLPA because we could not ignore the potentially severe consequences that RLPA may have on state and local civil rights laws. . . . We researched the issue and

found that landlords across the country were using state religious liberty claims to challenge the application of state and local civil rights laws protecting persons against marital status discrimination.[15]

It had taken years for them to see that their core interests were threatened by the RFRA formulation, and this is a savvy player in the political ballgame. Other organizations that were not monitoring Washington on a regular basis, or that failed to look beneath the surface of the law, took even longer. For example, it took the American Planning Association (APA) 11 years before it decided to weigh in on an RLUIPA land-use case, and these cases almost always involve arguments that are directly contrary to the APA's usual principles.

One of the reasons that RLPA never became law is that the ACLU, People for the American Way, and Americans United for Separation of Church and State ceased to be publicly vocal supporters. This is not to say that the ACLU got out of the business altogether; RLUIPA was drafted by someone in the ACLU, along with assistance from the Department of Justice. (The enthusiasm for this concept dies hard.)

*Two arenas for discrimination by religious entities:*
*Housing and employment*

Religious entities have had a prickly relationship with the antidiscrimination laws that have appeared since the 1960s. Many hold views or choose clergy according to criteria that contravene civil rights laws, and sometimes the religious entity wins, sometimes not. For example, Bob Jones University, which prohibited interracial dating, was notified by the Internal Revenue Service that its tax-exempt status was revoked because of its violation of the federal civil rights laws prohibiting racial discrimination.[16] The university argued vigorously that it was a private organization that should be able to believe anything, and that tax-exempt status should not turn on their views on racism. At the Supreme Court, it was supported by the American Baptist Churches, Center for Law and Religious Freedom of the Christian Legal Society, the National Association of Evangelicals, and Congressman Trent Lott (R-Miss.).[17]

The Supreme Court rejected their arguments, saying that "the Government has a fundamental, overriding interest in eradicating racial discrimination in education. . . . That governmental interest substantially outweighs whatever burden denial of tax benefits places on petitioners' exercise of their religious beliefs."[18] Taxation is not the only arena wherein religious institutions are forbidden to discriminate on the basis of race. A religious organization that is selling, renting, or limiting the occupancy of property (in a noncommercial context) may choose to deal only with those who share the same religion, unless "membership in such religion is restricted on account of race, color, or national origin."[19]

RLUIPA's language could have been stretched to cover the fair-housing laws, a result many conservative organizations would have hailed. Its legislative history, though, disavows any intent to reach that far.[20] Indeed, the ACLU may well have been at the helm of drafting RLUIPA in order to ensure that the new bill did not reach housing discrimination claims.

The fact that RLUIPA does not cover the fair-housing laws does not mean that the antidiscrimination laws apply in full force against religious entities. To the contrary, there are three ways such laws – whether applied in the housing or employment context – can be disabled by competing laws.

First, because many believe that applying RFRA to federal law is constitutional, the federal antidiscrimination laws (whether prohibiting housing, race, color, religion, sex, handicap, familial status,* or national origin discrimination) might be disabled by it.[21] RFRA has yet to be amended to reduce its scope, so it continues to have a breath taking sweep across every conceivable federal law.

Second, one of the 13 state RFRAs (Alabama, Arizona, Connecticut, Florida, Idaho, Illinois, Missouri, New Mexico, Oklahoma, Pennsylvania, Rhode Island, South Carolina, Texas) could disable any and all state antidiscrimination laws. While the RFRAs may be a threat to the antidiscrimination laws, there is not a large body of law yet.

Finally, a judicially crafted doctrine, called the "ministerial exception," and Title VII's exemption for discrimination on the basis of religious belief can mitigate the antidiscrimination laws as applied to religious employees, when they sue their religious institution for discrimination.[22]

---

*"Familial status" does not mean marital status, but rather whether the prospective tenant is a family with children. H. Rep. 100–711, 1988 U.S.C.C.A.N. 2173, 2184.

*Religious individuals and their objections to certain tenants*
*on religious grounds*

The first fair housing law was passed in California in 1959.[23] By 2005, 49 states and the District of Columbia had enacted laws prohibiting discrimination in the housing market. Most mirror the federal Fair Housing Act (FHA) and prohibit it on the basis of race, color, national origin, religion, sex, familial status, or handicap. Others are broader and encompass age, military status, sexual orientation, genetic disposition or carrier status, HIV status, gender identity, and source of income.[24] Approximately half of the states prohibit discrimination in housing based on marital status, but only a handful prohibit it based on sexual orientation.[25]

There are many interests at stake in these cases. Like the land-use cases discussed in Chapter 4, they implicate the right to determine how private property is to be used. In those lawsuits, the religious institutions are limited by the surrounding neighbors' rights in their private property. In these, they are limited by the government's strong interest in ensuring that all citizens are treated fairly in the housing market, where shelter is a human necessity. The courts also have tended to reject the religious landlord's religious defense, in part because they are not required by law to rent apartments or participate in the housing market. Thus, the law does not operate to place any burden on the landlord, who has chosen voluntarily to become a landlord.[26] They can avoid the burden.

One principle in this context, though, has tended to work in religious landlords' favor, and that is they have the right to choose to sell their noncommercial property to fellow believers, rather than outsiders. For example, St. Monica's Catholic parish near Milwaukee, Wisconsin, decided to sell a house it owned, and Michael and Barbara Bachman, who were Jewish, made an offer. In response, the parish pulled the house off the market and asked if any of its parishioners were interested. When none were, the parish sold it to a Catholic couple at a price higher than the Bachmans had offered, but with financing terms that may have made the Bachman deal the better offer. The Bachmans sued under the Fair Housing Act, claiming ancestral discrimination. St. Monica's prevailed. The U.S. Court of Appeals for the Seventh Circuit upheld the verdict, because the jury had been permitted to consider two mutually exclusive possibilities: either the refusal to sell rested solely on anti-Semitism or the congregation's decision had nothing to do with their ancestral heritage.[27]

In contrast, religious landlords have found it difficult to impose their religious criteria on prospective tenants for four reasons. First, even where the landlord succeeds in arguing that he or she has free-exercise right at issue, some courts have found that removing discrimination in this context is a compelling state interest.[28] This ground, though, is not entirely settled. With a RFRA in place (or strong state constitutional free-exercise guarantees), courts have had to consider whether preventing marital-status discrimination serves a compelling interest, and the results are not consistent across the board.[29]

Second, the harm that results from the exercise of these beliefs directly affects the victims of the discrimination. It is neither indirect nor insignificant.[30]

Third, there is no substantial burden on the religious entity's actual religious beliefs, because there is either no burden or only a de minimis burden.[31]

Finally, there is no other means of achieving the government's goal of eliminating discrimination on the basis of marital status, or sexual orientation, other than imposing the laws on all – even the religious – landlords.[32]

The Fair Housing Act was enacted to ensure that individuals were not excluded from the housing market on the basis of impermissible categories. It was not intended to make it possible for religious groups to force a neutral, generally applicable housing system to meet their beliefs. For example, four Orthodox Jewish students at Yale College brought an interesting lawsuit invoking the federal Fair Housing Act, though in the end it was not successful. They argued that Yale's coeducational dormitories, where all unmarried freshmen and sophomores were required to live, violated their religious belief in sexual modesty. The U.S. Court of Appeals for the Second Circuit held that the dormitory policies had been disclosed well before the students came to campus and, moreover, the FHA was not designed to accommodate the plaintiffs' unique religious beliefs. "Significantly, plaintiffs do not claim that defendants adopted their policy because of animus toward Orthodox Jews or that they grant exemptions to other religious groups or to students lacking a religious affiliation in a manner different from the exemption process for Orthodox Jews. Because plaintiffs seek exclusion from housing and not inclusion, they do not state an FHA claim. The purpose of the FHA is to promote integration and root out segregation, not to facilitate exclusion."[33]

There have been cases, though, where religious landlords have been able to engage in religiously motivated discrimination – by arguing that the governmental interest in the free exercise of religion trumps any state interest in protecting unmarried couples from discrimination. In Minnesota, Susan Parsons agreed to rent a house from landlord Layle French. Shortly thereafter, French learned that Parsons would be living with her fiancé. A member of the Evangelical Free Church, French believed that living together gives the "appearance of evil" and raised a religious defense to Parsons's action under the Minnesota Human Rights Act. The Supreme Court of Minnesota held that the state constitution's protection of religious beliefs exempted the landlord from compliance with the fair-housing provisions.[34] In California, a landlord turned down two prospective tenants as soon as she learned that they were unmarried and planned to cohabit. A devout Roman Catholic, the landlord believed that premarital sex was a sin and believed that renting the apartment to the couple would in itself be a sin. The Court of Appeal of California held that the landlord was entitled to an exemption from the fair-housing claim, because the constitutional interest in free exercise of religion was substantially greater than the state's lesser interest in eradicating discrimination against unmarried couples.[35]

This is an area of law in the United States that is not settled, at least with respect to discrimination involving marital status and sexual orientation. There is no consensus among state laws on these two categories, and the federal fair-housing laws do not address them. But the lack of uniformity is not necessarily a bad thing. Where the states have different regimes, it makes it possible to assess which rules work most effectively toward the public good, so one should expect the debate to continue. These rules are best crafted by legislatures, which can weigh the competing social interests implicated and learn from other states' experiments.

## Religious institutions and their employees

There are three means by which religious entities can avoid discrimination claims in hiring. First, Section 702(a) of Title VII, which was first enacted in 1964, grants religious organizations permission to discriminate on the basis of religion.[36] A more sensible accommodation one could not imagine. Jews should not be forced by law to hire Baptists as clergy and vice versa. When it is invoked, three issues tend to arise, and they all go to the question whether the relationship and the basis for the actions taken are in fact religious. The three include: (1) whether the defendant is a religious or really a secular organization,[37] (2) whether the individual suing works in a religious or secular capacity,[38] and (3) whether the reason for the employment action was based on religious belief, including whether Title VII imposed a substantial or a de minimis burden on that belief.[39] If any of these three criteria are not satisfied, the exemption does not apply. Once again, the doctrine makes a great deal of sense.

Second, the employment contract can impose binding antidiscrimination rules on the employer that the law does not.[40] Third, there is the "ministerial exception," the need for which is not quite as transparent. This judicially crafted exemption has been more elastic than Title VII's legislative exemption for belief though it has not given religious employers total autonomy from the law. The impetus for the doctrine is not hard to find: the identity of the religious leader lies at the heart of any religious identity, regardless of the required characteristics. There is a good question to ask, under the free-exercise doctrine, whether it was appropriate for the courts rather than the legislatures to have created such an exemption.

Beginning in 1972, courts started to recognize what would become known as the ministerial exception,[41] which recognized the principle that a religious organization's right to choose clergy is so important to the organization that it rises to the level of a constitutional right. Courts that recognize the ministerial exception refuse jurisdiction over employment disputes between clergy and their religious institutions, where the discrimination is religiously motivated, because, "[t]he relationship between an organized church and its ministers is its lifeblood. . . . Matters touching this relationship must necessarily be recognized as of prime ecclesiastical concern."[42] This principle has covered only the relationship between religious employer and ministerial employee, as opposed to other employees.

The religious institutions that have succeeded in these cases have done so in no small part because it is intuitive, given the history of religion, that they must be able to place restrictions on who their clergy will be. It is difficult to find a religion that does not place some kind of restriction on its clergy, which a secular employer could not. Catholics have only male priests; some conservative Christians do not permit divorced or unwed women in the pulpit; Orthodox Jews only permit men to become rabbis, though Reform, Conservative, and Reconstructionist Congregations also permit women; many denominations would not permit a homosexual to hold a clergy position, though this has been a source of deep division in denominations like the Presbyterians, Methodists, and Episcopalians. Thus, for the law to impose a rule that prohibits discrimination on the basis of a belief that requires a particular gender, race, or sexual orientation is to drastically alter the character of many religions. Conversely, if the characteristic is not required under the religion's set of beliefs, the antidiscrimination laws can apply full force. All of which is to say that the "ministerial exception" does not create a zone of "autonomy" around religion entities. It is only legitimately invoked where the otherwise prohibited discrimination is based in religious belief. An underlying rationale is that an adult who voluntarily works as a religious employee has voluntarily adopted the religious entity's religious beliefs.

The U.S. Supreme Court has never ruled that religious entities are immune from employment claims by their clergy, and it has never addressed the ministerial exception, which has been crafted by the lower courts. Those courts that have adopted the exception have been relying, and perhaps overreading, the Supreme Court's religious institution cases. Those cases say only that courts are not permitted to decide any solely ecclesiastical question between members from within the organization. That leaves a large universe of law to be applied to religious employers, which has been restricted legislatively only by Title VII's exemption for discrimination on the basis of religion.

Some of the formulations of the exception have been so broad that there have been attempts to expand it beyond the employment context. For example, one court stated, "the First Amendment barred civil courts from reviewing decisions of religious judicatory bodies relating to the employment of clergy."[43] Cases involving third-party harm, and not just employment disputes, have tried to build on this sort of formulation to argue that there is a general prohibition on courts taking jurisdiction over any case involving a religious entity and its employees. This a vast over-statement of the rule and its justification, however, which was crafted solely to deal with the employment relationship, not issues involving any other party. Moreover, it is an overstatement of the doctrine even within the employment context. An increasing number of courts apply the antidiscrimination principles to religious entities, where the discrimina-tion is not based on a religious motivation.

There is always a risk in any particular case (and this risk is magnified because this is a judicial creation never addressed by the Supreme Court, not a legislative rule limiting the courts to certain language, and there-fore the variations can be significant), that the religious entity will be permitted to engage in discrimination not actually required by its beliefs. In a way, it makes being a clergy member one of the least secure jobs in America. Many secular and religious employees have "at-will" contracts, which means that their employers can fire them for any reason and no reason. But the secular employer who fires the employee on the basis of race, gender, sexual orientation, religion, or marital status is inevitably bound by federal and state antidiscrimination laws. Thus, there is a legal deterrent that drives secular employers away from discrimination. In cir-cuits and states where the ministerial exception has been given a broad reading, the religious employee does not have the same degree of pro-tection from invidious or arbitrary employment decisions, and the results can be troubling.

For example, Sandy Williams, an ordained minister in the Episcopal Church, alleged that she was discriminated against on the basis of gender (a brand of discrimination not mandated by the Church's belief system). After she told the church that she believed she was receiving disparate treatment, she was constructively discharged – the hostile work environ-ment and gender discrimination and the diocese's unwillingness to do anything made her feel that she had no choice other than to resign.[44] Looking at the facts, the whole affair seems patently unfair. This woman pointed out an injustice, which is actually contrary to the church's beliefs, and then she appears to have been treated to the very treatment she had complained about! In a secular setting, that would be illegal. But in the religious setting, the court held that the ministerial exception shielded the church from any liability for retaliatory discharge.[45]

The award for the most despicable behavior by a religious entity toward one of its own should go to *Rosati v. Toledo, Ohio, Catholic Diocese*.[46] Mary Rosati, who desired to become a nun, was promoted from postulate to novice by the Contemplative Order of the Sisters of the Visitation. She then experienced severe health problems, including kidney problems, breast cancer, and a herniated disc that required surgery. Additional treatment was required, including the need for a lumpectomy or mastectomy, and "further cancer-related treatment." According to Rosati, after her diagnosis, Sister Bernard, her supervisor, told her, "Maybe God is trying to tell you something. Perhaps you don't have a vocation." She was let go after her diagnosis and lost her health insurance. When Rosati filed a claim under the Americans with Disabilities Act (which would have been effective against a secular entity), the order raised the ministerial exception, and won.[47]

Religious employers who receive expansive protection – under a broad reading of the "ministerial exception," and Title VII's exemption for discrimination from religious belief – have carte blanche to engage in discrimination, whether it is gender, or marital status, or sexual orientation, so long as the discriminatory decision can be explained at least tangentially by some religious belief. Narrower interpretations of the exception have led to a rule that where the conduct is unrelated to the religious belief or the employee does not perform a religious function, the church or religious institution can be subject to the discrimination rules.[48]

One of the dividing lines in Title VII cases is whether the employee is actually a religious employee or an employee of a religious institution performing secular duties. For example, the Southwestern Baptist Theological Seminary won and lost its attempt to avoid an investigation by the Equal Employment Opportunity Commission regarding its employees.[49] While those performing ministerial tasks were not able to take advantage of the antidiscrimination laws, the court found that at least four support personnel who performed nonministerial duties (yet were also ordained ministers) were "not entitled to ministerial status," and therefore their discrimination claims could go forward. In another case finding that accommodation was not required because the employee was not a religious employee for these purposes, the Pacific

Press Publishing Association, a nonprofit publishing house in California associated with the Seventh-day Adventist Church, was accused of engaging in gender and marital-status discrimination. Its policy was to pay employees according to sex and marital status, which led an unmarried secretary, Lorna Tobler, to bring charges of sexual discrimination (and retaliation) against the company. The U.S. Court of Appeals for the Ninth Circuit held the press liable for discrimination, because Tobler's duties did not go to the heart of the religious organization's operations, and the First Amendment was not implicated, because the impact of applying the antidiscrimination laws in this case on its religious belief was de minimis, especially when compared with the government's interest.[50]

The other criterion that can limit accommodation is whether the entity is a religious institution or not. In 1980, Mississippi College, a Southern Baptist-run school, sought a full-time faculty position in the department of educational psychology, and Dr. Patricia Summers, a part-time employee, applied. While Dr. Summers had extensive qualifications, she was a Presbyterian, and the school gave the position to another candidate who was Baptist (saying that he had more expertise in experimental psychology). Dr. Summers claimed religious and sex discrimination, and denied the college's argument its was exempt under Title VII, because it was not a church. The U.S. Court of Appeals for the Fifth Circuit agreed it was not a religious entity, and further that the First Amendment was not implicated, because the nondiscrimination law would only have a small impact on religious beliefs or conduct.[51]

The ministerial exception is not a unified doctrine, but has an accordion-like quality as it is interpreted by the various state courts and federal circuits. Like Sandy Williams's and Mary Rosati's cases, the following case involves disreputable behavior against a budding clergy member, but in this case, the ministerial exception was not permitted to bar all claims.

Christopher McKelvey planned to be a priest in the Camden, New Jersey, diocese, which offered to pay for his college and seminary education and, in its papers to him, emphasized the priestly requirement of celibacy. McKelvey made it through college and then headed for the St. Charles Borromeo Seminary near Philadelphia, where he lost enthusiasm for his career path when he allegedly was on the receiving end of repeated homosexual advances from other seminarians and priests,

including propositions to engage in homosexual acts, to discuss masturbation, and to accompany them to gay bars. According to McKelvey, he
was further demoralized when he reported the sexual harassment up the
chain of command, and expecting his supervisors to enforce the vow of
chastity, instead received hostile responses. When he did not return from
a leave of absence, the archdiocese terminated his candidacy and sent him
a bill for his education expenses in the amount of $69,002.57.[52] He sued.

The Diocese argued in response only one theory: the courts were
barred from taking the case at all on the ground that the First Amendment prohibited the courts from intervening in the dispute, because it
involved the relationship between a church and its clergy (or, in this
case, potential clergy). On its theory (and this tack is attempted in cases
across the country in any number of contexts, including clergy abuse),
the ministerial exception shielded the church from any claims brought by
a clergy member. The trial court agreed, and the intermediate appellate
court agreed. In a unanimous opinion, the New Jersey Supreme Court
did not agree, and ruled in favor of McKelvey. According to the court, the
problem with the lower courts' reasoning was that it was too clumsy. The
First Amendment might preclude the courts from settling internal disputes over the meaning of religious dogma, or might prohibit the courts
from getting involved in rendering interpretations of the church's beliefs.
But the First Amendment did not stand in the way of claims invoking
neutral principles of law where the analysis could be accomplished in
secular terms. Far from creating an impenetrable wall around religious
organizations' decisions regarding clergy, the court instructed the lower
New Jersey courts that they were required to examine each element of
each claim to determine whether the claim could be proved and analyzed using secular principles. The court quoted a decision by the U.S.
Court of Appeals for the Fifth Circuit that accurately characterizes the
law and explains why so many claims of ministerial privilege can be
adjudicated:

> The First Amendment does not categorically insulate religious rela-
> tionships from judicial scrutiny, for to do so would necessarily ex-
> tend constitutional protection to the secular components of these
> relationships.... The constitutional guarantee of religious freedom
> cannot be construed to protect secular beliefs and behavior, even when

they comprise part of an otherwise religious relationship. . . . To hold otherwise would impermissibly place a religious leader in a preferred position in our society.[53]

McKelvey, therefore, was permitted to go forward on theories of breach of contract and breach of fiduciary duty. The parties settled the case after it was remanded for a trial.

Whistleblowers within religious organizations have not fared terribly well. The Reverend Albert Dunn filed a RICO, or Racketeer Influence and Corrupt Organizations, suit against his church, the African Methodist Episcopal Church (AME), charging the leadership had a scheme to fraudulently collect funds that were then used to provide a lavish lifestyle and that it engaged in mail fraud, wire fraud, and money laundering. After he filed the suit, Dunn was not assigned to a church, and therefore he added a claim of breach of employment contract. He was barred from bringing the RICO claim, because he lacked standing; and his breach of contract claim was barred by the ministerial exception.[54]

In similar fashion, Darreyl N. Young, an African-American female who served as a probationary minister, was denied appointment as an elder after she was a vocal critic of the church on minority issues. The church argued that Title VII protected it from litigation involving any employee, an argument the court rejected. But the church still prevailed, because Title VII did immunize a church where the employment involved workers participating in the religious mission of the church.[55] There is an irony in this case, where the civil rights statute, Title VII, was employed to permit an employer to fire an employee speaking out for civil rights, but it is a prime example why the legislature is the appropriate body to deal with these issues. This is social policy, and the accountable legislature needs to weigh the many factors in the balance, something the courts are not equipped to do.

These cases focus the reader on a fascinating anomaly regarding overly expansive religious accommodation. The result of accommodation can be that religious entities are free – not to pursue their religious dictates so much as they are free to engage in immoral or antisocial behavior. It's the same principle seen in the behavior of the churches in the clergy-abuse cases. When a religious entity is sued for letting a known clergy pedophile have access to children, the argument often raised is that the First

Amendment shields it from any legal liability. In other words, its inde-fensible behavior is insulated because of its religious status – not because it was acting pursuant to religious beliefs. To grant First Amendment im-munity to the religious organizations in circumstances where its actions were not dictated by religious belief, but rather expediency or a desire for secrecy, is to invite misbehavior. Moreover, it seems unfair to deprive the poorly treated and now-estranged employee of any opportunity to bring the religious entity to account, when the institution's decision was not religiously motivated and violated widely accepted mores in the society. Every institution needs some checking of its worst urges, and the case has yet to be made that religious entities are exempt from this basic principle of human existence (indeed, the very purpose of this book is to show how apt it can be for religious entities).

It is not at all clear that the ministerial exception would be recognized by the Supreme Court, in light of its Religion Clause jurisprudence in the last couple of decades. The ministerial exception's process raises red flags. It is a court-created exemption from neutral, generally applicable laws, not the result of legislative consideration in light of the public good. The political theory behind the Court's current doctrine requires the legislature to make such an exemption, not the courts. This may be one of those academic points not worth much time, because it is highly likely that legislatures all over the country would quickly provide such an exemption. But it is worth noting that the judicial version flies in the face of the legislative exemption doctrine, and that it is not at all clear that Title VII's exemption for religious belief should not be the final word in this arena.

The cases seem to be moving in the direction of accountability for churches in most circumstances, but the movement is incremental. Following the Supreme Court's free-exercise decisions, the courts have been increasingly willing to find that the ministerial exception precludes jurisdiction over the religious reasons behind an employment decision, but they have then applied neutral, generally applicable laws to the en-tity's conduct. For example, a female minister, Monica L. McDowell Elvig, sued the Calvin Presbyterian Church of Shoreline, Washington, claiming that she had been subjected to a hostile work environment.[56] Elvig alleged that Will Ackles, the church's pastor, sexually harassed her. The church then retaliated by relieving her of certain duties, verbally abusing her, and engaging in intimidating conduct. After she filed a complaint with the EEOC, the church terminated her and refused to let her circulate her résumé, effectively preventing her from seeking other employment within the Presbyterian Church across the United States. The court held that if the claims implicated the church's right to hire ministers and determine their duties, the ministerial exception applied to deprive the court of jurisdiction *over that issue*. In other words, the church's religiously motivated conduct was protected, but the case was not disposed of by that finding. Rather, to the extent that she could allege facts that did not implicate the ministerial exception, her lawsuit could stand. The retaliatory harassment was not part of a protected employment decision and could therefore "be a valid basis for a retaliation claim." The Ninth Circuit's reasoning is a far cry from the theory (often espoused by religious organizations) that their hiring and firing decisions are completely secure from the force of the law. In effect, by allowing the case to go forward the opening for the antidiscrimination laws has been enlarged, so that the courts will not dismiss jurisdiction solely on the basis of the belief claim, even when the relationship between the church and the clergy member is implicated.

The rule is not brand new to the Ninth Circuit, either. Several years earlier, a federal district court in the same circuit dismissed a lawsuit where a Jesuit novice, John Bollard, claimed that he had been a victim of sexual harassment, invoking the ministerial exception.[57] Bollard alleged that his superiors, three Jesuit priests, sent him explicit pornographic materials through the mail, made unwanted sexual comments and gestures, and made unwanted solicitations and invitations for sexual acts.[58] The Ninth Circuit reversed, because the order's actions were neither part of an exercise of its prerogative to choose a pastor, nor motivated by any sincerely held religious beliefs.[59] Therefore, Bollard was permitted to pursue his sexual harassment claim, which he ultimately settled. In a 2004 case, a Kansas district court considered a case where a female minister, Sue Ann Dolquist, claimed to have been sexually harassed by one of the elders, and then when she complained, was criticized and disciplined.[60] She alleged that John Miller, the choir director and an elder, made offensive and inappropriate sexual comments and engaged in unwanted sexual conduct by kissing and touching her.

The court held that the church failed to prove that either the sexual harassment or the retaliatory harassment claim would impose on its religious beliefs or involve excessive entanglement. Therefore, the First Amendment was not even implicated, and the case was permitted to go forward.[61]

The placement of these parameters around the ministerial exception is reminiscent of the Anglo-American history of special privileges for religious entities that I describe in some detail in Chapter 9. In a nutshell, whereas the Catholic Church in England started as sovereign and the clergy were treated to a lax form of justice, as compared to laypeople, common law principles worked their way through the culture (and across the Atlantic), and the special privileges that permitted religious entities and their clergy to avoid liability lost their raison d'être. The reason for the privilege gives way to an emerging principle of fairness and accountability. That seems to be what is happening here as well. While courts are nowhere near forcing religious entities to hire, retain, or supervise clergy solely according to secular criteria, when the religious entity is acting outside its religious beliefs, and it actions are otherwise illegal, there is a marked trend to apply the law to it.

It must be noted, though, that the restrictions on the law's ability to make religious organizations accountable for their actions toward their religious employees, have no force when the case involves a harmed third party. The ministerial exception only applies, when it does apply, in an employment dispute brought by the religious employee. The language in the cases about the right of the organization to choose, hire, retain, and fire whomever it pleases on religious grounds does not immunize the churches from neutral, generally applicable laws that protect third parties. Therefore, tort and criminal laws retain their force in clergy sexual abuse cases brought by victims. The court is not being asked in such a case to determine religious criteria, but rather to assess whether the actions taken by the religious organization violate criminal or tort principles. An organization can use any religious criteria it desires to place clergy, but when it places anyone under its control it knows to be a pedophile within easy reach of children, it has endangered the welfare of children, among other crimes, and acted negligently on a number of theories. That distinction is crucial if religious institutions are to be deterred from putting their interests ahead of society's interests.

## Conclusion

Discrimination issues force accommodation analysis beyond the viewpoint of the believer or the institution into the arena of public concern. And where the public's interest is clear, as in eradicating racial discrimination or ensuring the availability of housing on an equal basis, the interest on the part of religious entities to discriminate can shrink in comparison.

Of all the arenas where religious groups are permitted to avoid the laws that apply to everyone else, the choice of clergy according to religious principles is the most appropriate. Similarly, the need for legislative accommodations to permit them to use their religious criteria in religious employee relationships should be self-evident. But where the religious entity is not acting according to its religious beliefs, but rather contravening public policy for less admirable motives, for example, engaging in sexual harassment or creating a hostile work environment, there is strong reason to apply the law. The attempts to stretch it to cover every conceivable context involving a religious employer and employee are difficult to defend.

**PART TWO**

# THE HISTORY AND DOCTRINE BEHIND THE RULE THAT SUBJECTS RELIGIOUS ENTITIES TO DULY ENACTED LAWS

# *BOERNE V. FLORES:* THE CASE THAT FULLY RESTORED THE RULE OF LAW FOR RELIGIOUS ENTITIES

From the 1960s into the 1990s, law schools taught two constitutional principles that were largely unquestioned; one might even say they were articles of faith. First, no government could enforce a law against a religious believer unless the government could prove that its law was passed for a compelling interest.[1] Second, Congress held the power to increase constitutional rights at will.[2] A generation of law students was taught that these principles were self-evident from the Constitution and Supreme Court cases.

In 1990, the U.S. Supreme Court rejected the first principle, and in 1997, it rejected the second. This chapter will explain the developments that led to what seemed to many like a revolution at the Court, but was less of a cataclysmic doctrinal shift than a conscious choice between internally inconsistent doctrines. In fact, in both categories, the four decades between 1960 and 2000 were a time when the Court straddled sometimes conflicting doctrinal approaches. Facing an either/or choice in each category, the Court in the 1990s did not so much invent new doctrines as it chose to excise doctrines that were causing friction. A 1997 Supreme Court case confirmed that the Court had made a definitive choice in each area. That case is *City of Boerne v. Flores, Archbishop of San Antonio*.[3]

The two issues – free exercise protection and the power of Congress – typically belong in separate constitutional domains. The first rests on interpretation of the Free Exercise Clause, while the latter requires interpretation of Section 5 of the 14th Amendment. Indeed, a conventional view would place the first under the heading of "individual rights," and the second under "congressional power," and therefore it is customary to teach them in separate constitutional law classes. This is a fault line in the law schools' approach, because it obscures the fact that every right is situated within a larger constitutional structure. Republican representative democracy – not to mention much theology and moral philosophy from John Locke to John Stuart Mill to Robert Nozick – rests on the assumption that no individual has the right to harm others, and therefore it limits rights a fortiori. When law schools, and their graduates, divorce rights from their structural context, they treat rights as a pure libertarian would: without reference to the rights holders' obligations to society. While the nation's law schools inculcated this mistake for decades, the Supreme Court has not made this mistake in the vast majority of its cases.

Free-exercise and even disestablishment theories too often have focused on religious entities by themselves, as though their well-being or their liberty is an adequate proxy for the general public good. That is certainly how the topic is taught in most law schools. This focus on religious entities and their corresponding interests and concerns is myopic and antidemocratic, and has led some legislatures to grant legislative exemptions for child neglect and physical abuse and some courts to refuse to hold churches accountable for their criminal and tortious actions, which are plainly in conflict with the public good. There is no simple equation between the needs of religious entities and the public good.

The two domains were unavoidably united – like the overlapping areas in a Venn diagram – in the *Boerne* case, because the congressional enactment at issue involved congressional deregulation of religious conduct.

The overlap required the Court, in a single opinion, to speak simultaneously to the scope of the rights under the Free Exercise Clause and the power of Congress to alter those rights. The result was a remarkably comprehensive theory of the role of religion in the polity, both as a private force and as a political actor.

*The free exercise cases before* Boerne v. Flores

There have been both dominant and dissenting themes within the historical sweep of the Supreme Court's free-exercise jurisprudence. The battle has been between republicanism and libertarianism, community and individualism, and isolation and obligation. The dominant approach has held that religious belief is absolutely protected, but religious conduct that can harm others is subject to duly enacted laws. Why not follow the logic of libertarianism and extend the absolute freedom of belief to conduct? While beliefs harm no one, conduct can. In the words of Thomas Jefferson, "The legitimate powers of government extend to such acts only as are injurious to others. But it does me no injury for my neighbor to say there are twenty gods, or no God. It neither picks my pocket nor breaks my leg."[4] This is a fundamental principle that unites the Free Speech and Free Exercise Clauses, and that rests on the republican form of government at the base of the constitutional order. John Stuart Mill explained it as follows: "The fact of living in society renders it indispensable that each should be bound to observe a certain line of conduct toward the rest."[5] Once one comes to understand the no-harm rule and its distinguished pedigree, autonomy, or immunity, of any institution – including a religious institution – from the rule of law becomes intolerable.

The alternative – libertarianism – was rejected by the framing generation as licentiousness. Liberty in the Constitution is couched in the larger concern about the public good and may legitimately be limited when the public good so demands. On this score, the First Amendment is no different than any other element of the Bill of Rights. Absolute, unqualified rights are the exception rather than the norm in the Constitution. The Second Amendment's right to "bear arms" does not mean that any criminal may own any gun he or she desires. Rather, the government has broad latitude to regulate gun ownership, especially when the owner has a criminal record. A homeowner's Fourth Amendment right of privacy, which prohibits searches and seizures without permission, is far from absolute. Where the police have "reasonable suspicion," they may enter even without the homeowner's permission. The Fifth Amendment right not to be "deprived of life [or] liberty" does not mean that the government may not take a traitor's life or impose a prison sentence on a criminal. When the government interest is strong enough, it can take both life and liberty. The "right to a speedy trial" in the Sixth Amendment does not mean the trial must take place the same day as the indictment, but rather at some reasonable time in the future.

One of the most difficult concepts to teach is that the "liberty" in the Bill of Rights is nowhere close to absolute, but rather must give way to a number of societal interests. Republicanism, which is the United States's representative form of government, is built on the belief that humans entering society must agree to (1) delegate their governing decision making to representatives and (2) create a system that is geared toward achieving the public good. Absolute freedom of religious conduct would give clergy carte blanche to abuse children; it would permit white supremacist prisoners to engage in race-based violence in the prisons; and the Church of Heroin to open on every street corner. For all but the most libertarian, such a culture is intolerable, and therefore liberty must be ordered liberty and that means the public good must be able to trump the demands of religious actors.[6] The rapist that attacks a child deserves lengthy time in prison, whether he is a priest or a layman. To paraphrase Gertrude Stein, a harm is a harm is a harm.

If a legislature finds an injury is significant enough to prohibit, religious entities that commit the same harm are as culpable as every other citizen. (The one exception would be where the legislature has made a considered decision that exempting the religious entity is consistent with the public good, an approach I will discuss in detail in Chapter 10.)

Beginning in 1963, the Supreme Court – in a select set of cases – turned away from republicanism and toward a more libertarian vision wherein religious entities could argue that a law was not permitted to affect religious conduct unless the government proved it was passed for a compelling interest. Under ordinary constitutional doctrine, the Court was treating every law that substantially burdened religious conduct as presumptively unconstitutional. This introduction of strict scrutiny for generally applicable, neutral laws did not displace the dominant view so much as it was awkwardly inserted into the jurisprudence in isolated cases. Despite the paucity of cases that followed this reasoning and its internal inconsistency with the Court's primary free-exercise principles, it became the favored approach among many academics and religious individuals and institutions. By the time the Court righted the jurisprudence in 1990, there was a widespread fallacy that religious entities should not be answerable to any law but the most necessary.

### The dominant doctrine

When the Court decided its first case interpreting the Free Exercise Clause in 1879, *Reynolds v. United States*,[7] which upheld the federal anti-polygamy laws, it articulated what would eventually become the dominant doctrine for the free exercise of religion: religious belief is absolutely protected, but religious conduct is subject to the rule of law. The Court quoted Thomas Jefferson: "The legislative powers of the government reach actions only, and not opinions."[8] The fact that the conduct arose from belief did not immunize the believer from the force of the law.

The Court's reasoning rested on a larger theory of the relationship between a citizen and the society. Individuals could not be given an unfettered right to act according to their own dictates, for otherwise the society would disintegrate into a collection of narcissistic individuals, and the sum would be decidedly smaller than the addition of its parts. In the Court's words:

> Can a man excuse his practices to the contrary because of his religious belief? To permit this would be to make the professed doctrines of religious belief superior to the law of the land, and in effect to permit every citizen to become a law unto himself. Government could exist only in name under such circumstances.[9]

The Court thereby relied on the long-recognized principle in representative democracies that individual rights are crucial, but they do not extend to harming another.[10] For Jefferson, as the *Reynolds* Court noted, there was a comfortable relationship between natural rights and the law, because he was "convinced [man] has no natural right in opposition to his social duties."[11] In other words, the rights of humans were never absolute, but rather were shaped to honor the necessity of social order and duty. Whether or not one believes in natural rights, once the social compact is in place and individuals must coexist with others, rights are to be measured against the backdrop of the public good.

Jefferson in turn had echoed the influential 17th century British political philosopher John Locke. As a starting point, Locke advocated a robust right of conscience, or belief.[12] He then argued that "God is the true proprietor" and therefore human beings could not "belong to one another, i.e., [they were] independently valuable."[13] From this precept, Locke derived a general "no-harm" principle: individuals were not to "take away, or impair the life, or what tends to the preservation of the life, the liberty, health, limb, or goods of another."[14] For Locke, then, individuals joining together in society had a general liberty of conscience, or belief, but the state legitimately restrained those actions that harmed others. The *Reynolds* Court formulated the Jeffersonian/Lockean theory of religion and government as follows: "Congress was deprived of all legislative power over mere opinion, but was left free to reach actions that were in violation of social duties or subversive of good order."[15]

The *Reynolds* Court was not only looking backward, however. Its holding also reflects the views of the most influential philosopher of the 19th century in the English-speaking world, John Stuart Mill, who died only a few years before *Reynolds* was decided. A defender of individual liberty, Mill set forth the following maxims:

> first, that the individual is not accountable to society for his actions, in so far as these concern the interests of no person but himself. . . . Secondly, that for such actions as are prejudicial to the interests of others, the individual is accountable, and may be subjected either to social or to legal punishments, if society is of opinion that the one or the other is requisite for its protection.[16]

This is a precise explanation of the Court's free exercise jurisprudence in the main.

Another way to approach the Court's free exercise jurisprudence is to examine the oft-repeated concept of "ordered liberty," which appears across the constitutional spectrum.[17] Liberty by itself was not valued at the time of the Constitution's framing, at the time of *Reynolds*, nor has it been the focus of the Supreme Court's subsequent rulings on religious liberty. The framing generation feared the licentiousness and the anarchy that arises from pure liberty, and thus did not institute libertarianism, but rather liberty anchored in the necessity of order. They believed that in the absence of order, there is no real liberty, but rather only a clash of individuals wills. The influential Rev. John Witherspoon, president of the College of New Jersey, who signed the Declaration of Independence, served in the Continental Congress, and trained James Madison and other Framers on governance principles,[18] put it this way: the "true notion of liberty is the prevalence of law and order, and the security of individuals," and therefore an "object of civil laws is, limiting citizens in the exercise of their rights, so that they may not be injurious to one another, but that the public good may be promoted."[19]

In cases involving religious conduct, the Court has kept in view the fact that religious individuals and institutions are firmly situated within the context of a society that entails mutual obligations.[20] Isolationism or pure libertarianism cannot be squared with this worldview.

The Court's approach, even with all of its distinguished support in history and philosophy, also has had lasting power, because it redounds in common sense. Even if the Court were inclined to recognize an individualistic right to do whatever one believes in doing, the practical result is anarchy. The strong libertarian position proposes what cannot be accomplished: the utter solitude of a single believer or the complete isolation of a religious group. In *Board of Education of Kiryas Joel Village School District v. Grumet,* [21] the Court addressed whether a religious organization could have a school district drawn according to the boundaries of its own community of believers. The Court refused to recognize the right of a religious organization to determine a political boundary, and in effect, held that religious organizations live in society, not out of it, and the constitutional order may not treat them as though they do not.

Some would point to *Wisconsin v. Yoder*[22] for the proposition that religious entities have a constitutional right to be isolated. In that case, the Court was willing to let the Amish operate independently of the public good by permitting them to take their children out of school after middle school in an opinion that was a paean to their way of life. *Yoder,* however, stands by itself, and is later explained by the Court as a case that is more easily explained in terms of parental rights than in terms of what religious entities owe to the public good.[23] In fact, as I will discuss, *Yoder* was wrongly decided. If religious children were to be excepted from the public school system, that decision belonged in the hands of the legislature, not the courts. In any event, if there was any question that the Court did not intend to shield the Amish in particular from the rule of law, 10 years later the Court held that they were required to pay into the social security system for their employees even though they did not believe in doing so.[24]

Once the religious individual or institution is understood to be shoulder-to-shoulder with fellow citizens (whether they are fellow believers or not) – and taking into account the fallibility of humans in every organization – it is irrational to conclude that the interests of the society and individuals directly affected are not necessarily relevant to the degree or scope of liberty the religious entity can enjoy. Religious conduct is a zero-sum game; the more liberty the religious actor has, the more at risk are those who could be hurt by his conduct. Even the arch-libertarian Robert Nozick has had to concede that there must be "side constraints" on the libertarian's behavior, because of the potential for harm to others.[25]

From the beginning of the U.S. experiment, the joinder of liberty and order meant that religious liberty was not irresponsible individualism, but rather a matter of the public good. Some liberty can and should be absolute and still consistent with the preservation of order – the liberty of belief. Other liberty cannot be absolute if the right level of order is to be preserved – the liberty of conduct.

### The two principles governing regulations affecting religious conduct

The Court has recognized two coordinate principles in its cases that address regulations affecting religious conduct and that turn on the concept of ordered liberty. The first is that religious entities, just as much as any other citizen, can be forestalled and prohibited from harming others and thus can be made to obey a myriad of laws, including narcotics laws, bureaucratic requirements, antipolygamy laws, property laws, and tax laws. The Court simply has not recognized in the vast majority of its cases a right to trump duly enacted laws for religious reasons.

By the same token, religious entities have not been subjected to laws that are hostile or motivated by animus toward religion in general or any sect in particular. "The fullest realization of true religious liberty [includes a rule that the government may] effect no favoritism among sects or between religion and nonreligion. . . . "[26] This is really a rule within the larger principle of the rule of law, which stands for the principle that laws should not be arbitrary. If a law applies to all those who are capable of the harm, the legislature has acted to ban a harm, not to single out any particular group or individual. The cases are legion that permit the religious entity to be subject to such laws. Where the law does not cover all those who engender the same harm, however, questions arise regarding whether the law was passed to prevent a particular harm or to burden certain, specific entities. Where the law targets a religious organization or religion in general – and animus or hostility can be discerned through the language of the law – the Court has been disinclined to uphold the law. If the law discriminates against a religious organization or religion in general, that law is constitutionally suspect, and therefore rightly subject to close judicial scrutiny.[27] Thus, the dominant approach has been to couple the application of the rule of law to religious entities, with a strong rule against discrimination aimed at particular religious sects or practices, or religion in general.

## The cases applying neutral laws to religious entities

In its dominant jurisprudence, the Court has been inclined to favor laws that, on their face, have been passed for the general public good, and without reference to religion. In *Reynolds*, the Court upheld the federal antipolygamy law that governed the Northwest Territory. The law was neutral on its face – it outlawed polygamy by anyone, regardless of belief.

*Reynolds* was more complicated than the run-of-the-mill case involving neutral, generally applicable law. While *Reynolds* involved a law that applied to everyone and that was written in neutral language, it was common knowledge that the motivation behind the law was to suppress the Mormon growth in the Northwest.[28] Some might think, then, that the antipolygamy law violated the antipersecution principle. They would be wrong. Under the dominant approach, had the law in its language singled out the Church of Jesus Christ of the Latter-day Saints, the law would have been unconstitutional under every principle the Court has laid down since that first free-exercise case. By singling out Mormons, the new law would have indicated Congress was not concerned about the harm engendered by polygamy, but rather by an intent to rid the country of that religious group holding that particular belief. Disparate impact, however, was not enough to scuttle the law, or even to subject it to close judicial scrutiny. Where the language was neutral, and the sweep of the law caught everyone now or in the future engaged in the same conduct generating the same harm, it was constitutional. In short, harm is harm, even when a religious entity is disproportionately responsible for inflicting that harm.

It is worth pausing for a moment to explain how the Court's decision in *Reynolds* fits in with its dominant free-exercise jurisprudence. The jurisprudence has rested on a judgment regarding institutional competence: one branch of government is best equipped to assess the public good, and that is the legislature, because it is the most capable of surveying and studying social issues – a legislature can call hearings, appoint expert commissions, and order extensive studies. Courts are incapable of examining the public good in any comprehensive way, because they are limited by the case and controversy requirement to the facts and arguments before them.[29] The executive, of course, lacks the multiple contact with the polity that makes for a more accurate assessment of the public's interest (even if the public's view is not always the equivalent of the public good) and is too capable of acting unilaterally to ensure that deliberation over the public good has taken place.

Because the legislature is superior to the courts and the executive in assessing the public good, where the legislature has spoken in language that is unambiguous, the Court has refused to look behind that language to ferret out improper motive. If the law identifies a harm, and it punishes everyone that engenders that harm, the Court has upheld the law. Indeed, the disparate impact argument that would have scuttled the antipolygamy law in *Reynolds* is a red herring. If an action is harmful to society without reference to the identity of the one who has acted, the fact that only a religious organization engages in that action does not change the calculus of harm. The touchstone throughout the free-exercise cases has been whether the legislature identified actions that led to unacceptable harm to society.

This reasoning has led the Court to sustain a wide variety of laws. The Amish lost their bid to avoid paying the Social Security taxes for their employees every other employer must pay.[30] Bob Jones University was not permitted to retain its tax-exempt status if it violated the racial anti-discrimination laws, a rule that applied to all who applied for tax-exempt status.[31] The Tony and Susan Alamo Foundation, a nonprofit religious foundation, was required to observe the Fair Labor Standards Act.[32] A United States Air Force captain who was also an Orthodox Jew and an ordained rabbi, could be prohibited from wearing his yarmulke indoors under a general regulation that banned all headgear not officially part of the uniform.[33] A welfare applicant who did not believe in assigning Social Security numbers to children was required to do so, along with all other applicants for benefits, in order to obtain the benefits.[34] The North-west Indian Cemetery Protective Association did not have a constitutional right to stop the federal government's neutral plans for federal lands even though it believed the land was sacred.[35] Members of the Church of Scientology were subjected to the tax rules regarding any and all charitable contributions and were not allowed to claim as a deduction contributions for which they received a quid pro quo.[36] Jimmy Swaggart Ministries was required to honor California's generally applicable sales and use taxes on the sale of its religious materials.[37] Religious prisoners could not avoid work detail on Friday afternoons.[38] And drug counselors could be denied unemployment compensation for violating the state's laws banning the use of the hallucinogen peyote, even though it was used as part of a religious ritual, which was the same treatment that would have been accorded any other employee within the state.[39]

Whatever one thinks of the outcome of any one these free-exercise cases, they are remarkably consistent in their theory and the application of that theory.* They show a dominant jurisprudence of republicanism and ordered liberty.

The last case – involving drug counselors who used hallucinogens during a religious ritual, were fired and then denied unemployment

*Under the Court's dominant jurisprudence, any disagreement with the outcome is an objection to be taken up with the legislature, not the courts. Thus, religious entities in these circumstances were not without options; the question was whether they were to approach the courts or the legislatures to obtain accommodation. See *Employment Div. v. Smith*, 494 U.S. 872 at 878–79. In the case of the peyote use and yarmulkes in the military, both were accommodated legislatively. See, e.g., William K. Kelley, *The Primacy of Political Actors in Accommodation of Religion*, 22 U. Haw. L. Rev. 403, 440 n. 174 and accompanying text.

compensation – is *Employment Division v. Smith*. It is a landmark case, in part because it generated tremendous resistance in the law schools and among intellectuals, and therefore a great deal of publicity, but more important, because it marked the Court's self-conscious decision to survey its free-exercise jurisprudence and to choose the dominant approach. According to the Court, the "vast majority" of its free-exercise cases had deferred to legislative judgments on public policy, where the law was "generally applicable" and "neutral."[40] The Court was positively correct in its assessment of its own jurisprudence. *Smith* was the first of two necessary steps to bring religious entities under the horizon of the rule of law and in harmony with the public good. Seven years later, in *Boerne v. Flores*, the Court would complete the project of returning religious entities to account for harm to others.

### The cases involving laws that treated religion with animus or hostility

Under the dominant free-exercise jurisprudence, strict scrutiny has been required in a small number of cases – those involving laws exhibiting animus or hostility toward religion. That is to say, where there is reason to suspect invidious discrimination, the government's actions are subject to close examination. The Court articulated the principle in 1997 as follows: "The Free Exercise Clause commits government itself to religious tolerance, and upon even slight suspicion that proposals for state intervention stem from animosity to religion or distrust of its practices, all officials must pause to remember their own high duty to the Constitution and to the rights it secures." In effect, the Court was describing "the fundamental" principle of the First Amendment: the "nonpersecution principle."[41]

In point of fact, the Court has not been faced with a large number of laws that discriminated against religious interests in the United States. That is because the United States and its legislatures have been generous toward religious entities. As the Court noted in *Smith*, "a society that believes in the negative protection accorded to religious belief can be expected to be solicitous of that value in its legislation."[42]

The leading case addressing animus toward religion is the 1993 decision in *Church of Lukumi Babalu Aye v. City of Hialeah*,[43] where the city passed an ordinance outlawing the "sacrifice" of animals. The choice of the language made it clear to the Court that the city was not engaged in a neutral lawmaking effort, but rather was targeting the one group in its jurisdiction that believed in the sacrifice of animals as part of its religious ritual – the Santerians. Moreover, the law was crafted to apply to Santerians and Santerians only. The animus was patent, and the Court mandated not only a strict scrutiny that required close judicial inspection of the law, but also seemed to say that such animus was per se unconstitutional.

In another case, the Court found animus where the law singled out ministers by prohibiting them from being candidates for the state legislature;[44] when a believer was forced to choose between his beliefs and a government benefit;[45] or the government applied its law to some religions, but not others.[46] Beyond these examples, there has been a paucity of religious persecution, at least in those cases that made their way up to the U.S. Supreme Court.

In 2004, the Court further explained its dominant free-exercise jurisprudence in *Locke v. Davey*, a Washington state case asking whether a state scholarship fund could exclude those studying for ministry. There were some that had read *Smith* to stand for the proposition that if a law was not completely generally applicable, that is, if it had a single exception, it was presumptively unconstitutional, and therefore subject to strict scrutiny. They took this from language in *Smith* and *Lukumi*, where the Court first identified "generally applicable, neutral" laws and then distinguished the "generally applicable" from the "neutral." Religious groups focused on the former term and seized the theory that the Court must have meant that any law creating an exception for one class of beneficiaries and not for religious individuals, or any law that singled out religious individuals, would be presumptively unconstitutional. In other words, any legislative distinction was sufficient to make a law constitutionally suspicious under the Free Exercise Clause, even without government hostility or animus toward religion, and therefore the Court would defer to the legislative judgment.

On their reasoning, the fact that the Washington scholarship excluded ministry majors made it presumptively unconstitutional.[47] The Supreme Court would have none of it, saying, "We reject [the petitioner's] claim of presumptive unconstitutionality, however; to do otherwise would extend the *Lukumi* line of cases well beyond not only their facts but their reasoning."[48] The Court went on to explain, repeatedly, that the gold standard for presumptive unconstitutionality (and therefore the necessity of strict scrutiny) was governmental "hostility" or "animus" toward religion. A law, like the Washington scholarship program, exhibited a respect for the state's disestablishment clause, not hostility toward religion.

Of course, the exclusion of religious individuals or institutions from legal benefits *could* trigger strict scrutiny in later cases, but only when the government was demonstrably (through the legislative language or the operation of the law) hostile toward the religious group or religion in general.

When read together, *Smith, Lukumi,* and *Locke* identified pivotal principles: (1) the courts are to apply a default rule in favor of applying duly enacted, neutral, and generally applicable laws to religious conduct and (2) that default rule is only overcome in the face of evidence of persecution of religion.

### The competing doctrine: Strict scrutiny for generally applicable, neutral laws affecting religious conduct

Between 1963 and 1990, in a small number of cases, the Court departed from its dominant approach to the Free Exercise Clause. The Warren Court and then the Burger Court did not so much abandon the dominant doctrine, as it engrafted a new doctrine onto it, introducing internal contradictions into the doctrine. The new approach mandated that neutral and generally applicable laws could be subjected to strict scrutiny.[49] Thus, there were now three rules: the default position of the rule of law, the rule against religious persecution, and a competing default rule that required strict scrutiny of neutral, generally applicable laws. This latter rule was first introduced by Justice William Brennan and steadfastly defended by him throughout his tenure on the Court.[50] Only at the very end of his tenure on the Court, did the new analysis he introduced completely lose traction.[51]

A literal handful of cases followed this new reasoning; they include four unemployment compensation cases[52] and one involving a state compulsory education law, *Yoder.*[53]

The Court made its first foray from its dominant free exercise jurisprudence in the 1963 decision in *Sherbert v. Verner,* which was written by Justice Brennan and which addressed the question whether a Sabbatarian could obtain unemployment compensation after refusing to work on her Sabbath, Saturday. The South Carolina Unemployment Compensation

Act "provide[d] that, to be eligible for benefits, a claimant must be 'able to work and . . . available for work'; and, further, that a claimant is ineligible for benefits 'if . . . [s]he has failed, without good cause . . . to accept available suitable work when offered [her] by the employment office or the employer. . . . '" It appears that the "good cause" requirement is what bothered the Court. "Good cause" was used to permit exceptions to the law for valid secular reasons but not for religious reasons. While some could avoid Saturday work if needed, the Sabbatarian was forced "to choose between following the precepts of her religion and forfeiting benefits, on the one hand, and abandoning one of the precepts of her religion in order to accept work, on the other hand."[54] The states' willingness to let some avoid the law, but not others, led the Court to apply strict scrutiny and hold the statute unconstitutional.

*Sherbert* controlled the next three unemployment compensation cases. *Thomas v. Review Bd. of Ind. Employment Sec. Div.* involved a man who quit his job at a foundry after being transferred to a division that manufactured armaments, claiming "his religious beliefs prevented him from participating in the production of war materials." The state denied his unemployment claim "by applying disqualifying provisions of the Indiana Employment Security Act," which prohibited any "individual who has voluntarily left his employment without good cause" from receiving benefits.[55] The Supreme Court reversed. *Hobbie v. Unemployment Appeals Com. of Fla.* involved a woman whose "employer discharged her when she refused to work certain scheduled hours because of sincerely held religious convictions adopted after beginning employment." Florida's unemployment compensation scheme provided benefits only "to persons who become 'unemployed through no fault of their own.'"[56] The Supreme Court invalidated the law. *Frazee v. Ill. Dep't of Employment Sec.* involved a man who turned down a temporary position "because the job would have required him to work on Sunday" and he told the employer that "as a Christian, he could not work on 'the Lord's day.'" Unlike the appellant in *Sherbert*, "Frazee was not a member of an established religious sect or church, nor did he claim that his refusal to work resulted from a 'tenet, belief or teaching of an established religious body.'" Even so, the Court found that "Frazee's refusal was based on a sincerely held religious belief" and therefore he was entitled to "invoke First Amendment protection."[57]

*Sherbert* was widely criticized after it was first announced,[58] because it was such a departure from bedrock constitutional principles, but by the late 1970s, a chorus of approval began.[59] Once the academy began to embrace the concept of treating neutral, generally applicable laws as presumptively unconstitutional, the way was open for the later arguments – not wholly supported by the reasoning of the opinion – that strict scrutiny should apply in most free-exercise cases.[60] This notion that all neutral, generally applicable laws were presumptively unconstitutional when applied to religious entities opened the door for the most extreme libertarian arguments, including the argument that churches should be immune from criminal liability. They raised such arguments in the cases involving the sexual abuse of children by their clergy, even when they knew about the abuse, permitted the abuse to continue, transferred the perpetrator to other parishes where he could have access to further children, and never reported the pedophile clergy member to the police. It even led prosecutors to stand down from prosecuting clergy pedophiles, even though they knew about the abuse. The Supreme Court, however, only extended *Sherbert*-type analysis to one other scenario – compulsory school laws in *Wisconsin v. Yoder*.[61]

In *Yoder*, the religious claimants were Amish and Mennonite parents, who argued that the compulsory education laws that required children to attend school through the 12th grade violated their religious principles, which required students to cease their education in eighth grade. They also argued that the state law was a threat to their religious way of life, which required them to be "aloof from the world" and had been in place for 300 years. Even though the Wisconsin law was neutral on its face, the Court held that it violated the Free Exercise Clause, because the state had failed to prove a compelling interest in having Amish children go to school through high school:

> Wisconsin's interest in compelling the school attendance of Amish children to age 16 emerges as somewhat less substantial than requiring such attendance for children generally.... There is no intimation that the Amish employment of their children on family farms is in any way deleterious to their health or that Amish parents exploit children at tender years.[62]

In effect, the Court weighed public policy and carved out an exemption from Wisconsin's generally applicable, neutral law solely for the Amish.

The new doctrine that invalidated neutral, generally applicable laws in favor of religious conduct found enthusiastic support in the academy. Professors Ellis West and William Marshall stood alone for a significant period of time in their defense of the rule of law.[63] In 1990, just after the Court had chosen between the two competing approaches in its free-exercise cases in the *Smith* decision, University of Chicago Law School professor Michael McConnell published an article in the *Harvard Law Review*, which set forth a historical justification for the notion of "mandatory exemption" from legislative enactments.[64] To be fair to Professor McConnell, I will let him describe his conclusions:

> The conclusions of this [article] are (1) that exemptions were seen as a constitutionally permissible means for protecting religious freedom, (2) that constitutionally compelled exemptions were within the contemplation of the framers and ratifiers as a possible interpretation of the free exercise clause, and (3) that exemptions were consonant with the popular American understanding of the interrelation between the claims of a limited government and a sovereign God. While the historical evidence may not be unequivocal (it seldom is), it does, on balance, support *Sherbert*'s interpretation of the free exercise clause.[65]

McConnell's assessment of the historical record has been soundly rejected by prominent scholars who have examined the record with his conclusions in mind.[66] Though I will not retread their potent criticisms, it is important to note that McConnell's thesis was deeply at odds with the reigning theological views during the historical era he examined. Calvinism dominated the culture at the time of the framing, and its tenets required obedience to duly enacted laws unless the law dictated that religious entities abandon their religious beliefs.[67] Many preachers at the time repeatedly urged their believers to obey the rule of law, to such an extent that one can make a case that the rule of law in the United States was instituted in large part from the pulpit.[68]

For the 18th-century preachers, the horizon under which legislatures were to make legitimate law was the public good, as opposed to individual freedom at the expense of the common good. For example, in 1747, Charles Chauncy declared that civil "rulers... have an undoubted right to make and execute laws, for the public good."[69]

A separate problem with McConnell's suggestion of mandatory accommodation was that it had not been applied in so many contexts for so many years; his thesis could not explain why his approach had been rejected (or forgotten) until 1963. If the history supported mandatory exemption, even if weakly, as he suggested, then what had the Court been thinking in the raft of cases straightforwardly applying the rule of law? Before and after 1963, the Court did not apply strict scrutiny to neutral, generally applicable laws. The assumption in most of the cases that the rule of law controlled was evident in each case, with the result that religious entities were straightforwardly subject to the vast majority of laws.

McConnell's article was the last gasp of the minority mandatory exemption approach. The Court definitively chose between its two competing rationales in the same year in *Employment Div. v. Smith*, and the rule of law prevailed.[70] This is the case that involved the question whether two private drug counselors in Oregon, Alfred Smith and Galen Black, who used peyote – an illegal drug – in a religious ritual, could obtain unemployment compensation after they were fired for work-related "misconduct." This case forced the Court to choose between its two competing threads. The enthusiastic reading of the *Sherbert* line of cases and *Yoder* would have applied strict scrutiny to Oregon's unemployment law, which incorporated by reference Oregon's narcotics laws. That is precisely what the counselors' lawyers argued.[71] In other words, the Oregon law was presumptively unconstitutional. But the case was more in sync with the Court's other free-exercise cases, where the rule of law had been applied to the religious entity, and that argument was pressed heavily by Oregon's attorney general, David Frohnmayer.[72] It was inconceivable to think that the drug laws could be gainsaid by a claim to religious motivation. In the end, the Court could not countenance the by-then overinflated reading of *Sherbert* and *Yoder* as repudiations of the rule of law as applied to religious entities. The Court declared: "We have never held that an individual's religious beliefs excuse him from compliance with an otherwise valid law prohibiting conduct that the State is free to regulate." Thus, neutral and generally applicable laws with the "incidental effect" of burdening religious conduct did not offend the First Amendment.[73]

The Court did not close its decision with a simple rejection of the *Yoder* approach, but rather also fit its religion clause jurisprudence into the larger structure of the Constitution and society. The message of the opinion was that Galen and Black had come to the wrong institution. Religious entities were not required to abandon their desire to engage in particular religious conduct; they could not, however, find their solution in the courts. They were directed to the legislature, where they would have to justify their request for exemption to the body charged with assessing and choosing public policy. The Court explained that discourse would not necessarily disfavor religious entities in this society:

> Values that are protected against government interference through enshrinement in the Bill of Rights are not thereby banished from the political process. Just as a society that believes in the negative protection accorded to the press by the First Amendment is likely to enact laws that affirmatively foster the dissemination of the printed word, so also a society that believes in the negative protection accorded to religious belief can be expected to be solicitous of that value in its legislation as well.[74]

Some decried the notion that religious entities could be thrown into the political process,[75] but the purpose of this book is to illustrate how deeply entrenched religious entities have been in the political sphere and especially the legislative process before and after *Smith*. There have been a significant number of conflicts between religious entities and the general laws enacted for the public good, and religious entities have not stood on the political sidelines. For the Court, that conflict was better debated under the horizon of the public good in the legislature than in the rarified atmosphere of a courtroom. The Free Exercise Clause would not be permitted to absolve religious entities of social and legal obligations: "[T]he right of free exercise does not relieve an individual of the obligation to comply with a 'valid and neutral law of general applicability on the ground that the law proscribes (or prescribes) conduct that his religion prescribes (or proscribes).'"[76]

While the *Smith* Court repositioned the Court's free-exercise reasoning, and firmly rejected the by-then entrenched assumption that religious entities had a constitutional right to avoid the obligations of generally applicable, neutral laws, it did not overrule any particular case. Rather, it cast the preceding cases that had seemed to rest on a principle at odds with the dominant approach, in a different light to show that they were not inconsistent with the long-established principles the Court was reaffirming. *Sherbert* (along with its unemployment case progeny) was recast as a discrimination case wherein the government had offered exemptions from the law for secular reasons, but had not offered them for religious reasons. In effect, the Court saw the difference in treatment to be a governmental retreat from any sincere devotion to deterring the harm. Indeed, the government was demonstrating that it was willing to tolerate the harm in some circumstances, and thus there was reason to closely scrutinize the government's action in failing to permit religious individuals to avoid the law.

With respect to *Yoder*, the Court's attempt to incorporate the decision into its overarching jurisprudence was less convincing. The Court labeled it a "hybrid rights" case where the rights of parents were being combined with the potential for free exercise rights against otherwise neutral laws, giving rise to presumptive unconstitutionality. The reasoning of *Yoder* was directly at odds with the reasoning in *Smith*, however, and a more straightforward assessment would have overruled *Yoder* which seems to have been driven by admiration or nostalgia for certain religious beliefs, including their biblical basis, as much as any neutral legal principles:

> [W]e see that the record in this case abundantly supports the claim that the traditional way of life of the Amish is not merely a matter of personal preference, but one of deep religious conviction, shared by an organized group, and intimately related to daily living. That the Old Order Amish daily life and religious practice stem from their faith is shown by the fact that it is in response to their literal interpretation of the Biblical injunction from the Epistle of Paul to the Romans, 'be not conformed to this world. . . .' [T]he respondents' religious beliefs and attitude toward life, family, and home have remained constant – perhaps some would say static – in a period of unparalleled progress in human knowledge generally and great changes in education. The respondents freely concede, and indeed assert as an article of faith, that their religious beliefs and what we would today call "life style" have not altered in fundamentals for centuries. Their way of life in a church-oriented community, separated from the outside world and "worldly" influences, their attachment to nature and the soil, is a way inherently simple and uncomplicated, albeit difficult to preserve against the pressure to conform. Their rejection of telephones, automobiles, radios, and television, their mode of dress, of speech, their habits of manual work do indeed set them apart from much of contemporary society; these customs are both symbolic and practical.[77]

For very good reason, the Court's preservation of the reasoning in *Yoder* and its introduction of a "hybrid rights" approach has been rejected as unworkable in the lower courts.[78] If a law does not deserve strict scrutiny under any single constitutional provision, it makes little sense to impose strict scrutiny simply because two constitutional claims are invoked. Two weak rights do not amount to a strong constitutional right.

Had the Court overruled *Yoder*, the Amish would have had to approach their state legislatures to avoid upper-level compulsory education for their children. Instead of the courts imposing their views of public policy on the people, the legislature could have considered and weighed the many competing interests, including the value of religious liberty, the best interests of children, and society's need for a well-educated citizenry. The Burger Court was prone to placing religion and religious reasons on a pedestal, with little regard for society's interests. The Court's decision preempted such a debate, and permitted the Amish to make their arguments divorced from any serious consideration of the public good. If one reads *Yoder* with some care, it becomes quite obvious that the Court took it upon itself to preserve a religious way of life regardless of the society's assessment of the public good, that is, to prefer the religious to the legislative. That in itself should have been reason to revisit *Yoder*. But this was also the Court, after all, that decided *Bowers v. Hardwick*, where it used Anglo-American religious reasons to uphold laws against sodomy. The Rehnquist Court reversed *Bowers*, in *Lawrence v. Texas*. It should have explicitly reversed *Yoder* as well.

After *Smith* was decided, a chorus argued that the Court had overturned a long-settled doctrine that required strict scrutiny of any law, no matter how neutral, that substantially burdened religious conduct.[79] That was the belief in the law schools, to be sure. The well-known church/state scholar, Professor Douglas Laycock, declared that *Smith* was "inconsistent with the original intent, inconsistent with the constitutional text, inconsistent with doctrine under other constitutional clauses, and inconsistent with precedent."[80] McConnell wrote that the *Smith* Court's "use of precedent is troubling, bordering on the shocking."[81] Professor Steven D. Smith of the University of Colorado said the *Smith* Court "chose . . . to promote an advocacy of intolerance."[82] Professor Harry F. Tepker, Jr., of the University of Oklahoma said that *Smith* illustrated "judicial willingness to distort precedents to destroy traditional concepts of individual liberty."[83] Professor James D. Gordon III of BYU said that "[T]he Court wanted to reach its result in the worst way, and it succeeded" and in so doing "'depublished' the free exercise clause."[84] It is not hyperbole to say they were all wrong. *Smith* was no tsunami in free exercise law; it was simply a reaffirmation of cornerstone constitutional principles.

The fault for the intense response to the *Smith* decision does not rest entirely on those who misread the previous cases. To the contrary, the Court invited the heated response to *Smith*, by reaching an issue that was neither briefed nor argued. The petitioners Black and Smith and their supporters in the academy believed the case only addressed how *Sherbert's* strict scrutiny applied, not whether. After all, *Smith* was an unemployment case and the four preceding unemployment cases starting with *Sherbert* had applied strict scrutiny to the benefit of the religious entity. In the pigeonhole mentality that frequently infects constitutional thinking, most expected the Court to reach for the prior unemployment cases and those cases alone, and then to dispose of the case with little effort. That the Court would look beyond the unemployment compensation aspect of the case to its free-exercise cases in other contexts and ultimately to the larger question of whether a generally applicable, neutral law is binding on religious entities was wholly unexpected.

In hindsight, the Court should have laid the groundwork for the decision by asking for rebriefing and reargument, which is the usual procedure when the Justices perceive a new and potentially dispositive issue in a case already under consideration.[85] There was no emergency that blocked the Court from holding the case over for the next term. Instead, the Court moved forward without warning. There was not even any intimation from the bench at oral argument that the members were preparing to realign, or right, the entirety of its free-exercise jurisprudence.[86] Even those like Professor William Marshall, who had defended the rule of law approach before *Smith*, castigated the Court: "The opinion is...a paradigmatic example of judicial overreaching. The holding extends beyond the facts of the case, the lower court's decision on the issue, and even the briefs of the parties. In fact, it appears that the Court framed the free exercise issue in virtually the broadest terms possible in order to allow it to reach its landmark result."[87]

It would have been far better had the members in the majority in *Smith* – Justices Antonin Scalia, Byron White, John Paul Stevens,

Anthony Kennedy, and Chief Justice William Rehnquist – let the parties and those watching know that they were ready to repudiate the under-stood approach in *Sherbert* and *Yoder* in favor of a more robust dedication to the rule of law as applied to religious entities. If there ever were a need for the venting function of the First Amendment's Free Speech Clause, this was it. In the end, though, these procedural objections did not render its substantive analysis wrong.

The problem with the hyperbolic substantive arguments against *Smith* was that the Court had followed two paths of reasoning that were inter-nally inconsistent in the free-exercise cases between 1963 and 1990, not one. The preceding jurisprudence had employed what the critics saw as the *only* approach in free-exercise cases in just a few cases – while the jurisprudence they found so shocking in *Smith* was in fact the domi-nant rule throughout the Court's free-exercise jurisprudence. The *Smith* Court retired the anomaly first introduced in *Sherbert*, and little more. Despite the inflamed declarations by law professors and religious organi-zations, the Court had not produced a doctrine out of whole cloth. It had done no more than affirm its dominant doctrine and reject a bad rule that had been applied in a bare handful of cases.

Even so, Congress listened to the religious entities and the law pro-fessors and within four months of the *Smith* decision, held hearings to castigate the Supreme Court.[88] Religious groups, believing they had lost more than they actually had, turned to Congress to deliver what they claimed was their constitutional right: a "return" to strict scrutiny of every law in every free-exercise case. Starting with a small number of religious organizations in Washington, D.C. who gathered soon after *Smith* was de-cided, and following the advice of Professor Douglas Laycock, the group that would later call itself the Coalition for the Free Exercise of Religion drafted a statute that laid the analysis of *Sherbert* and *Yoder* across all legal domains. They named it the Religious Freedom Restoration Act (RFRA, pronounced riff-rah), and no member of Congress found it within him or herself to block a statute so named.[89]

The hearings were filled with vitriol aimed at the Court, and with members of Congress castigating the author of *Smith*, Justice Scalia, in particular. The same tactic was used among academics. It was as though Scalia had singlehandedly destroyed religious liberty. To this day, those who despise *Smith* talk about it in terms of, "Scalia wrote," or "Scalia said." In fact, the justices that joined Scalia – Chief Justice Rehnquist, and Justices Kennedy, White, and Stevens – had sided with the rule of law approach even before *Smith*, but castigating Justice Scalia was part of the public relations attack on *Smith*.

After three years of hearings in which the members of the House and Senate denounced the Court (in over 450 pages of the Congressional Record) for abandoning a doctrine that had never been applied across the board, Congress passed RFRA, which established what *Smith's* detractors claimed (incorrectly) the preceding doctrine had required. It would be too much to say that some of the United States's most prominent church/state scholars deceived Congress, but it is not an exaggeration to say that their inaccurate assessment of the prior case law led Congress down the wrong path. Congress was persuaded that it was standard free-exercise doctrine to subject every single law to strict scrutiny, an approach the Supreme Court had never even broached, let along reached. Under RFRA, every law was to be subject to strict scrutiny, whether neutral and generally applicable or not. RFRA provided that:

(a) In General. – Government shall not substantially burden a person's exercise of religion even if the burden results from a rule of general applicability, except as provided in subsection (b).

(b) Exception. – Government may substantially burden a person's exercise of religion only if it demonstrates that application of the burden to the person –

1. is in furtherance of a compelling governmental interest; and
2. is the least restrictive means of furthering that compelling governmental interest.[90]

In *Smith*, the Court had reinstituted the rule of law as applied to religious entities, but it encouraged them to go to the legislatures for relief from particular laws imposing particular burdens on religious practice. For example, the Court pointed approvingly to state law exemptions for the use of peyote from generally applicable drug laws.[91] And, in fact, a number of states and the federal government would follow suit after *Smith*, in effect proving the efficacy of the Court's approach for religious entities. But those positive developments for religious liberty after *Smith* were lost in the maelstrom of invective against it. In a move that was fueled by the endemic misinterpretations of the Court's pre-*Smith*

jurisprudence and, to be frank, political opportunism, the religious entities looked to Congress to reverse the Court's doctrine altogether. Ironically, the religious organizations did precisely what *Smith's* detractors
seemed to believe they either could not or should not: they petitioned a
legislature, Congress, and they obtained what they sought. In effect, they
proved the political feasibility of the *Smith* Court's political theory.

With *Smith*, the Court had articulated the relationship between religious entities, the government, and society. Its constitutional vision was
based on fundamental principles of republican democracy, the public
good, and the rule that no one may harm another. The statute that was
generated in the wake of *Smith* – RFRA – raised the corollary question
whether Congress could unilaterally rearrange the relationship between
religious entities, the law, and the public good. If so, then the larger republican and democratic principles at the base of *Smith* could be abandoned
in favor of permitting religious entities to avoid most generally applicable, neutral laws. It would take the decision addressing RFRA – *Boerne
v. Flores* – to vindicate the bedrock republican principles that justify and
require subjecting religious entities to the generally applicable, neutral
laws that govern everyone else.

*The congressional power cases before* Boerne v. Flores

From the 1930s until 1995, the Supreme Court systematically deferred
to congressional exercises of power. The result was an unaccountable,
headstrong Congress that sincerely believed it held plenary power over
all issues, despite the plain meaning of the Constitution's structure and
language limiting its powers. The federalism component of the Constitution disappeared through inattention, and Congress's power subsumed
the states'. By 1995, the Court began to see the problems attendant upon
an unaccountable Congress, and gingerly began to draw some boundaries around what had become an arena with no limits. The Court's
reinstitution of federalism brought to the foreground the inherent limits of Congress's power, vis-à-vis the states. Congress was supposed to be
an institution of enumerated powers, not plenary power. Initially, the
Court was accused of being insular, harsh, and unsympathetic to civil
rights.[92] For others, the Court was simply power hungry,[93] but in fact
the cases have been moderate in trend, with the Court striking the most

outrageous reaches for federal power, including the Religious Freedom Restoration Act, as it has upheld the Family Medical Leave Act[94] and Title II of the Americans with Disability Act.[95] The RFRA and *Boerne v. Flores* arrived at the Court in this era of revived federalism. Thus, the Court was predisposed to ask whether Congress constitutionally held the power it exercised. The Court's attention in the late 1990s was trained on two congressional powers: the Commerce Clause and Section 5 of the 14th Amendment. The latter power was a focus of *Boerne*.

### *The background behind the Section 5 cases leading up to* Boerne

Beginning in the late 1950s and the 1960s, the United States witnessed an explosive growth in federal civil rights law. Congress passed increasingly expansive civil rights acts.[96] The attorney general enforced these new laws in the face of strong opposition in the states.[97] And the Supreme Court dramatically expanded the protections afforded under the Equal Protection Clause in the wake of its landmark 1954 case, *Brown v. Board of Education*.[98] The Court struck down laws forbidding interracial marriage[99] and interracial cohabitation,[100] and requiring ballots to indicate the race of candidates.[101] It overturned convictions for disturbing the peace by sitting at race-reserved lunch counters,[102] for refusing to sit in a courtroom's segregated section,[103] and for murder where there was prima facie evidence of discrimination in grand and petit jury selection.[104] The Court also expanded the power of Congress under the Commerce Clause to prohibit racial discrimination in motels,[105] expanded the definition of state action by defining a private restaurant as a state actor where the restaurant leased public space and was maintained with public funds,[106] and by including in the definition of state action any agency of the state taking action.[107] Finally, the Court refused to permit private discrimination in housing.[108]

It was a time of cataclysmic but positive social change for the rights of minorities. As between the states and the federal government, there was no question that the federal government was *the* protector of liberty. When the federal government freed minorities from the oppressive discrimination under which they had labored for two centuries in the United States, it was a noble enterprise. The federal government was liberating an oppressed people, and in the process unmasking the depth of the entrenched racial discrimination in the country. While the United States deserves plenty of criticism for its Constitution's early acquiescence in slavery and then its failure to end discrimination for decades following the civil war and the Reconstruction era, the 1960s civil rights era was impressive.

Inevitably, the reasoning of expanding rights found its way into other doctrines. It certainly influenced Justice Brennan's push to expand the rights of religious entities starting with *Sherbert* in 1963. The equal protection issues and the free-exercise issues, though, were on completely different planes. Minorities were demanding, and obtaining at least from the federal government, equal rights with all others under the law. They were asking for a level playing field, but the religious entities were starting from equality under the law and then asking for privileges beyond equal treatment.

The religious entities did not request equality, but rather the right to trump the law, to be treated better than others who were similarly situated and governed by the same law. Thus, while the Court's work for minorities was heroic, its decision to abandon the rule of law for religious entities was a serious mistake, for which the United States continues to pay in terms of harm to children, the inculcation of terrorism in the prisons, and the dilution of private property rights. Like the free-exercise cases, the congressional power cases beginning in the 1960s sprang from an environment conducive to altering the law and veered off the right course until the 1990s. The deference to the federal government – which was earned by its valiant and successful fight for civil rights for minorities – was transformed into a dogmatic belief in the unassailability of whatever Congress attempted. The result was an engraved invitation to congressional overreaching.

The Religious Freedom Restoration Act was invalidated in *Boerne v. Flores* on the ground that Congress lacked the power to enact it. Thus, the case posed the raw question: What precise power did Congress have over constitutional rights? The Court's answer shocked the academy and, more important, Congress: Congress could enforce the guarantees of the 14th Amendment, including the incorporated bill of rights, but it could not unilaterally create and expand upon constitutional rights. In other words, for the Constitution to change, it had to be amended via Article V and its onerous requirement[109] of a two-thirds vote in Congress followed by ratification by three-fourths of the states – not by a simple majority vote in both houses of Congress. As four members of the Court had explained in dissent in *EEOC v. Wyoming*,[110] at the apex of Congress's power, "[a]llowing Congress to protect constitutional rights statutorily that it has independently defined fundamentally alters our scheme of government."[111]

The academy was so entrenched in its belief that Congress could set the level of constitutional rights at will, that it had coined a phrase to explain it: Congress had the power, they said, to "ratchet" up rights.[112] This novel power was defended on the ground that it was a "one-way ratchet,"[113] so no rights could be diminished by Congress, but they could be increased at will. If that was Congress's proper role, then RFRA was a no-brainer. It dramatically expanded the rights of religious entities, and certainly did not diminish them.

For that reason, RFRA's legislative history includes precious little discussion of Congress's power to enact it. If the prominent law professors were not concerned about congressional power, one can be certain that the members of Congress were even less so. The basic justification for RFRA was provided by Professor Laycock, who described it as "[a]n attempt to create a statutory right to the free exercise of religion, pursuant to Congress' power under Section 5 of the Fourteenth Amendment to enforce the Fourteenth Amendment and therefore presumably to enforce all the rights incorporated in the Fourteenth Amendment."[114]

In Professor Laycock's defense, this is what the vast majority of the academy assumed to be the doctrine.[115] As with most dogmas, it was not open to much question, which is why *Boerne*, which would limit Congress's power under § 5, was a shock that generated the same sort of hyperbole that dogged *Smith* in the free-exercise context.

Those who had invested in the ratchet theory, argued that the argument against RFRA rested only on dissents addressing congressional power.[116] To be fair, they are right, but only to a limited extent. In fact, there were different and even conflicting themes running through the cases, and in particular, the leading case regarding Congress's power under Section 5 of the 14th Amendment, *Katzenbach v. Morgan*.[117]

Like *Sherbert*, which took the Free Exercise Clause astray, the controversial *Katzenbach v. Morgan*, was written by Justice Brennan, who was appointed by a Republican administration, but who became one of the most libertarian Justices. He was not an ideologue, but rather pursued his libertarian agenda pragmatically. He typically altered the Court's direction not by overruling previous precedents, but rather by doing what he did in both *Sherbert* and *Katzenbach*: engrafting onto the existing doctrine a new branch that sent the doctrine in a wholly new direction. He was very good at crafting a change in emphasis that would then alter doctrine, outcomes, and eventually the theory.

In *Katzenbach*, the Court addressed the constitutionality of the Voting Rights Act of 1965, § 4, which prohibited the states from excluding any voter on the ground that he or she could not speak or write English. The law affected several hundred thousand immigrants from Puerto Rico in New York. Registered voters in New York City brought suit, arguing that Section 4 was unconstitutional, because Congress lacked the power to override their voting laws, which required English proficiency. The question was plain, even if the answer was somewhat complicated: what power did Congress have to pass Section 4 of the Voting Rights Act of 1965?

Justice Brennan provided two rationales to uphold the act. First, Congress was simply enforcing constitutional guarantees against the states pursuant to Section 5 of the 14th Amendment, which states: "Congress shall have power to enforce, by appropriate legislation, the provisions of this article."[118] The Constitution forbade discrimination on the basis of race or origin, and therefore Congress was enforcing the guarantee to equal treatment. The problem with that analysis, however, was that the Court previously had held that there was no constitutional right that forbade English proficiency requirements.[119] Therefore, Congress was requiring the states to do more than the Constitution required, and the states argued that such an expansive requirement violated the reserved rights of the states in the Constitution.

Justice Brennan explained this expansion as Congress exercising its "prophylactic" power.[120] Where the states had engaged in persistent constitutional violations, Congress was given broad latitude to force the states to toe a more difficult line than the Constitution required. There was no question that the discrimination at issue was widespread, intransigent, and persistent. In an earlier case, the Court had characterized the congressional record for the Voting Rights Act as follows:

> Two points emerge vividly from the voluminous legislative history of the [Voting Rights] Act contained in the committee hearings and floor debates. First: Congress felt itself confronted by an insidious and pervasive evil which had been perpetrated in certain parts of our country through unremitting and ingenious defiance of the Constitution. Second: Congress concluded that the unsuccessful remedies which it had prescribed in the past would have to be replaced by sterner and more elaborate measures in order to satisfy the clear commands of the Fifteenth Amendment.[121]

The prophylactic power made sense in the face of the studied recalcitrance to equal protection guarantees in the South and parts of the North during the 1950s. If state governments decided to flout the Constitution's requirements over and over again, Congress had the power to hold them to even stricter conduct than the Constitution required in order to get them to obey the Constitution. This reading of Congress's power under Section 5 was not controversial.

More controversial was the second *Morgan* rationale. Justice Brennan introduced a new element to assess congressional power – the so-called "ratchet theory," which would have permitted Congress to expand the constitutional right itself by simple majority vote. The theory was criticized by Justice John Marshall Harlan, in dissent, who accused Justice Brennan of expanding congressional power too far: "In effect the Court reads § 5 of the Fourteenth Amendment as giving Congress the power to define the *substantive* scope of the Amendment."[122] Harlan reasoned that if Congress had unilateral power to alter the scope of constitutional rights that it could decrease as well as increase them. Brennan dismissed in a footnote Harlan's logical deduction that the power to set rights included the power to diminish them.[123]

From 1966 to 1990 (only three years shy of *Sherbert*'s reign), the Court had available a theory that would provide Congress considerable new power.

As indicated earlier, the ratchet-up theory became quite popular in the law schools, and many legal scholars came to accept that Congress did indeed have such a power. Professor Archibald Cox explained the force of the ratchet theory as follows:

> The etymological meaning of section 5 may favor the narrower reading. Literally, "to enforce" means to compel performance of the obligations imposed; but the linguistic argument lost much of its force once the *South Carolina* and *Morgan* cases decided that the power to enforce embraces any measure appropriate to effectuating the performance of the state's constitutional duty.[124]

There was not universal acceptance, however. Professor William Cohen of Stanford Law School criticized the theory in 1977 in the *Stanford Law Review* as follows:

> Justice Brennan's "ratchet" interpretation of section 5 presents two problems. First, it does not satisfactorily explain why Congress may move the due process or equal protection handle in only one direction.... The second and more significant problem with the ratchet theory is the difficulty in determining the direction in which the handle is turning.[125]

But it also suffered from an ivory tower assessment of liberty. Increasing the liberty to act for one almost always means a diminution of liberty for someone else. This is a zero-sum game.

In the free-exercise context, Brennan had been able to insert the novel reasoning of *Sherbert* into a small number of cases involving virtually identical facts. While this was not a striking accomplishment, he was less successful in propagating the ratchet theory in the Court's cases. Unlike *Sherbert's* new rule in the free-exercise context, this new congressional power theory was never the dispositive basis for any Supreme Court decision.[126] Even in *Morgan*, it was only an alternative basis for decision. During the same term as *Morgan*, and a few months before it was decided, the Court held that Congress could not "attack evils not comprehended by the Fifteenth Amendment," and therefore devalued the currency of the ratchet theory – at least with respect to a similar amendment – several months before it appeared. Five members of the Court rejected the theory in 1970 in *Oregon v. Mitchell*,[127] which then-Justice Rehnquist pointed out in *City of Rome v. United States*.[128]

In *Oregon v. Mitchell*,[129] for which admittedly one needs a scorecard to know precisely what was held and who on the Court reached the holding, five justices agreed to some limits on congressional power under Section 5; as was stated in the dissent to *EEOC v. Wyoming*, there was a "limitation on the extent to which Congress may substitute its own judgment for that of the states and assume this Court's 'role of final arbiter.'"[130] Thus, by the time *Boerne* arrived at the Court in 1996, there were two competing theories in § 5 cases in circumstances where Congress forced states to toe a line more restrictive than the Constitution.

While the ratchet theory was never as widely accepted in the academy as the *Sherbert* approach to free-exercise cases,[131] the bulk of law professors assumed, like Laycock, that the Religious Freedom Restoration Act would be upheld on the theory. And it did not appear to be wishful thinking, but rather a conviction that the ratchet theory was impregnable. Nor is there any indication that the members of Congress read their power any more narrowly than the ratchet theory would have afforded.

When Congress passed the Religious Freedom Restoration Act, it forced the Court's hand on the § 5 issue. The petitioner's certiorari petition specifically asked the Court to answer the question whether Justice Brennan's prophylactic power theory explained Congress's power under § 5, or whether the ratchet theory did. Once the question was posed, academics became more circumspect than they had previously been, and a number argued against the ratchet theory. For example, Professors Eugene Gressman and Angela Carmella argued as follows:

> [O]ne can imagine other RFRA-like statutes [justified under the ratchet theory] that would (1) ratchet obscenity and pornography up to the status of free speech, which the Court has refused to do, (2) ratchet up the personal interest in reputation to the level of a constitutionally protected liberty interest, (3) ratchet up the right to an education to the status of a constitutionally protected right, subject to strict scrutiny, (4) ratchet up gender and sexual orientation to the highest levels of scrutiny, (5) define and ratchet up additional unenumerated privacy rights as yet unrecognized by the Court, or (6) restore and ratchet up those privileges and immunities of citizens of the United States that were destroyed by the Slaughterhouse Cases. In short, the RFRA model can be used by Congress to reform, destroy or restore a wide variety of the Court's constitutional interpretations, thus putting Congress into the heart of the judicial function.[132]

The ratchet theory thus was an opportunity for tremendous mischief by a Congress that could alter constitutional rights on a sliding scale through simple majority vote. Indeed, in light of the practice in both Houses of Congress of using "unanimous consent," which permits the leaders to bring a bill to the floor with virtually no other members present and with no recorded vote, rights could be altered by a mere handful of the leadership in either House. The Court simply could not sign on to such a theory, because it was too far removed from the accepted constitutional practices surrounding rights. Moreover, it sidelined the Court in constitutional determinations. Accordingly, not a single member of the Court wrote approvingly of the ratchet theory in the landmark congressional power case, *Boerne v. Flores.*

## Boerne v. Flores

After the sharp and even bitter criticism of *Smith*, the Supreme Court might well have thought better of its reasoning and recrafted it. That did not happen. Three years after *Smith*, the *Church of Lukumi Babalyu Aye* case was decided, and the Court explained its approach to the plainly discriminatory ordinance against the backdrop of *Smith*. With RFRA, the Court had another opportunity to alter its free-exercise doctrine or to cast it in a different light, but the Court held firm on the rule requiring courts to apply neutral, generally applicable laws to religious entities and judged RFRA in light of that constitutional standard. The Court took neither the opportunity provided by the *Babalu Aye* case nor the *Boerne* case to adjust its free-exercise jurisprudence.

Congress's action in passing RFRA, however, reopened the door to religious entities that had sought to trump generally applicable, neutral laws. Indeed, it covered far more instances than Justice Brennan's theory had been permitted to: It applied strict scrutiny to every law in the country, state or federal, executive, legislative, or judicial, and past or present. It was, as the petitioner's brief stated, "breathtaking." Thus, while *Smith* might have reinstated with clarity the principle that religious entities are properly subject to neutral, generally applicable laws, RFRA threatened to alter the regime altogether and to place religious entities above a vast portion of the law.

236 / GOD VS. THE GAVEL

This is not a book on congressional power so much as it is about religious accommodation, so I will not describe the Court's reasoning in *Boerne* at length, but suffice it to say that the Court plainly rejected Justice Brennan's ratchet theory:

> Congress' power under § 5, however, extends only to "enforcing" the provisions of the Fourteenth Amendment. . . . The design of the Amendment and the text of § 5 are inconsistent with the suggestion that Congress has the power to decree the substance of the Fourteenth Amendment's restrictions on the States. Legislation which alters the meaning of the Free Exercise Clause cannot be said to be enforcing the Clause. Congress does not enforce a constitutional right by changing what the right is. It has been given the power "to enforce," not the power to determine what constitutes a constitutional violation. Were it not so, what Congress would be enforcing would no longer be, in any meaningful sense, the "provisions of [the Fourteenth Amendment]."[133]

The prophylactic theory was embraced, by itself. Congress could not hold the states to standards more stringent than the Constitution required unless there was proof of widespread and persisting constitutional violations in the states and the federal law was "congruent and proportional" to the degree of constitutional overstepping by the states. Thus, entrenched and invidious discrimination in the vast majority of circumstances across the states against religious entities might have justified RFRA's draconian requirements, but the Court saw no such set of facts, either through judicial notice or the congressional record supporting RFRA: "While preventive rules are sometimes appropriate remedial measures, there must be a congruence between the means used and the ends to be achieved. . . . A comparison between RFRA and the Voting Rights Act is instructive. In contrast to the record which confronted Congress and the judiciary in the voting rights cases, RFRA's legislative record lacks examples of modern instances of generally applicable laws passed because of religious bigotry."[134] But the record by itself was not dispositive. The central inquiry was whether Congress had acted in a way that was proportional to the constitutional harm identified. "Regardless of the state of the legislative record, RFRA cannot be considered remedial, preventive legislation, if those terms are to have any meaning. RFRA is so out of proportion to a supposed remedial or preventive object that it cannot be understood as responsive to, or designed to prevent, unconstitutional behavior."[135]

The case simultaneously rejected discordant subdoctrines in both the free-exercise and Section 5 contexts. First, the Court upheld *Smith* and refused to hold that strict scrutiny was mandated in free-exercise cases, which meant religious entities could not go to the courts to trump generally applicable, neutral laws.

Second, the *Boerne* Court chose *Morgan's* prophylactic theory and held that Congress could not give religious entities the right to across-the-board strict scrutiny in the absence of proof of widespread and persisting discrimination against religious entities – proof that the religious entities will never be able to accumulate, because of their significant though often underestimated power in the political sphere and because of the sheer numbers in the United States who are religious. (One of the purposes of this book is to bring to light the remarkable power of religious entities to obtain special treatment in the legislatures.)

The net result of the *Boerne* decision was to foreclose religious entities' arguments that religious motivation should absolve religious actors of neutral laws governing their conduct.

It would be a mistake to think that *Boerne* was only a culmination of U.S. legal principles, because it was also the endpoint of the larger Anglo-American struggle between religious entities and secular authorities, a struggle that that had proceeded for hundreds of years. Seemingly unbeknownst to those lobbying for a religious liberty that undercut neutral, generally applicable laws and permitted religious entities to be above the law, the British government had long experience in the field, and had rejected the rule they advocated. The next chapter will explain the centuries of history that put *Smith* and *Boerne* in proper perspective.

# THE DECLINE OF THE SPECIAL
# TREATMENT OF RELIGIOUS
# ENTITIES AND THE RISE OF THE
# NO-HARM RULE

There has been an ongoing dialectic between religious entities, the law, and the public good for centuries, and it has tended from strong privileges for religious entities toward the application of the rule of law to them. This play of power has yielded a construct that incorporates lessons learned. As Justice Oliver Wendell Holmes said, "the life of the law has not been logic: it has been experience."

There was a time in Anglo-American history when established religious entities were sovereign and the clergy enjoyed special treatment under the law. It would have come as no surprise to anyone that the established religious institution was immune to the requirements of the law or that clergy were relieved of its requirements while all other citizens were not. A citizen could be put to death for raping a child, while a clergy member could commit the same crime and be sentenced to a year at a monastery.

That era, however, was centuries ago. Today, the rule in the United States is that every entity – including a religious entity – is subject to the law.

This chapter places the United States' religious liberty principles in historical context. The contemporary system – reaffirmed in *Employment Div. v. Smith* and *Boerne v. Flores* – is not a 20th-century concoction, but rather the result of centuries of development.

There are, of course, many reasons to invoke history; the purpose here is two-fold. First, this chapter is intended to show that there are two British antecedents that informed the U.S. system: (1) the robust – and then dwindling – special treatment of clergy and religious institutions in Britain, and (2) the burgeoning development of the common law there, followed by the growth of republicanism and the rule of law here. Both are critical to understanding today's rules for religious entities. Too often the Supreme Court's decision in *Employment Division v. Smith* holding that religious entities are subject to generally applicable and neutral laws is treated as though *Smith* came out of the blue. Chapter 8 argues to the contrary that it represented the dominant trend in the Supreme Court's jurisprudence; this chapter shows that it is the culmination of centuries of legal and social development. The decision was neither ad hoc nor accidental.

Second, this chapter is intended to put to rest the pervasive – but misguided – belief that religious liberty at the time of the framing meant that religious entities were to be superior to the law. The developments in the colonies and then the states picked up where Britain left off. This is not an originalist argument that the views of the framers are binding today, or that intellectual history moves in a single straightforward progression. In the Anglo-American tradition, though, there is a value set on experimenting with different approaches to see what works best; that experimentation has led both Britain and the United States to reject special privileges for religious entities and to embrace the rule of law. The United States thus has the benefit of centuries of experimentation and the capacity to learn from past mistakes, which is the essence of the common law. The plainest lesson to be taken from these hundreds of years of development is that even religious reasons are inadequate to justify harming others.

Since the 12th century, when Henry II took the first steps toward a common law by resisting a separate sphere of justice for clergy, the justifications for special treatment of religious entities have become increasingly hollow. Although it took centuries for Henry II's intended reforms to be fully effected, the logic of Henry's attempts to place clergy under the same justice system as all others was ineluctable: the victim of rape or murder by a clergy member is just as injured as the victim of an ordinary citizen. The injury demands proportional punishment, which is determined according to the harm, not the identity of the actor. Thus, the drive to avoid the law by contemporary religious entities is not a new development, but it is an anachronistic one.

The internal logic of Anglo-American common law has drawn the United States to the conclusion that the public good requires the deterrence and punishment of harmful actions, regardless of the identity of the actor. I will call this the no-harm principle.

Before the common law and its equalizing principles were entrenched and before the creation of the United States, churches did have autonomy from the law. The rights of religious institutions and their clergy were above those of ordinary citizens. From the 3rd to the 16th centuries in Britain, church autonomy was in fact the order of the day. The Roman Catholic Church was permitted to harbor fugitives from the law under the practice of "sanctuary." The church was co-sovereign with the state, and it instituted ecclesiastical courts that provided separate (and far more lenient) justice for the criminal acts of clergy, which came to be called the benefit of clergy. In more recent times, a judicial doctrine was crafted that shielded religious institutions from civil lawsuits demanding monetary damages for harm done by the institution or its employees. Each of these tacks provided meaningful autonomy for religious institutions, each permitted such institutions to be unaccountable to the public good, and each has been repealed or overruled or, in the case of charitable immunity, significantly weakened in Britain and the United States.

*An introduction to the historical evolution of the no-harm rule*

The modern-day claims to religious autonomy and privilege in cases involving tortious or criminal behavior are in fact remnants of the long history of the British and then the U.S. trial of various regimes whereby religious entities were protected from the law. At the outset, going back at least to the 12th century, the church was a co-sovereign with the Crown, so institutional liability was not an issue. Two privileges – sanctuary and the benefit of the clergy – ensured that clergy (at least the clergy of the established church) were either beyond the reach of the law or held to lesser punishments than others. Experience with these immunities and the rise of the common law led to the abolition of these two privileges by the mid-16th century. In the 17th century, most civil and criminal matters were transferred from the ecclesiastical courts to the common law courts and the newly created courts of chancery. This triumph of the common law coincided with the rise of Puritanism, the interregnum, and the Restoration. During the 19th century, Parliament statutorily abolished most of the jurisdiction of the ecclesiastical courts. They retained jurisdiction only over discipline of clergy, certain types of sexual offenses committed by laypersons, and minor matters concerning worship services.[1]

There has been an almost instinctual drive in the United States to treat religious entities as though they can do no harm and as though they need protection in the political sphere, but each privilege has been rolled back when the harm caused became an obvious and incontrovertible fact. By the mid-19th century, two forces came together. First, the logic of the common law that all similarly situated individuals should be governed by the same laws overtook the earlier claims to privilege.[2] Second was the concept of "ordered liberty," and its corollary, the no-harm rule,[3] each of which opened the door to those who had been harmed to sue religious institutions for their tortious behavior.[4] In response to this development, the courts introduced the doctrine of charitable immunity, which protected the coffers of charitable institutions – including religious institutions – from such lawsuits.[5] Charitable immunity was abandoned in England before it was ever entrenched and was honored in the United States only for a limited time.[6] It is now defunct in most jurisdictions in the United States, with some trying caps on liability, which is a movement that extends beyond charitable immunity.[7] In sum, the fundamental fairness that is at the foundation of the common law and the rule of law combined to exert an inexorable logic that has led to the rejection of the notion that religious institutions and their volunteers need not be held accountable for the harm they cause.[8]

At the same time that these principles joined forces, the status of whose who were most likely to be harmed by religious entities – children, women, and minorities – improved. As women, children, and minorities were shifted from being the property of white men to inherently valuable beings, the harm done to them became increasingly intolerable. It took both the legal developments and this sociological movement to reach the full flowering of the no-harm rule in the United States.

*Historical privileges that placed clergy and religious institutions above the law*

In Britain, there have been three historical privileges that benefited religious individuals and entities: sanctuary, the benefit of clergy, and charitable immunity. All three privileges have been discarded or discredited in Britain. Analyzing this history provides crucial background for understanding that church autonomy today is a throwback, not a step forward.

The spirit of these three principles has been repudiated by the U.S. Supreme Court, but they still haunt religious institution theories[9] and the legal tactics of religious institutions themselves.[10] It is important to learn and understand this history, because it formed the background for the Framers and for the early formation of the law governing religious institutions and individuals in the United States. It is also important because it uncovers past experiences with church autonomy that did not, and could not, withstand the growth of republicanism and the rule of law in Britain and then in the United States.

*The sanctuary privilege and the geographical sovereignty of the Roman Catholic Church*

As early as the third century A.D., secular authority recognized the ecclesiastical right to provide sanctuary, or protection, for those threatened by "private vengeance for alleged wrongdoing."[11] Sanctuary was intended to forestall blood feuds and the vigilantism of the times. Although secular governments tried to retain the rights of control over some categories of wrongdoers, the ecclesiastical authorities held full sway to determine whether and what kind of sanctuary would be made available. The church further refused to deliver anyone who was within its sanctuary unless promises were made that the wrongdoer would not be harmed.[12]

Seven centuries after the practice first appeared, the Crown created the chartered sanctuary, a form of asylum that was backed by the king.[13] Chartered sanctuaries provided greater protection than church sanctuary, including a broader geographic and temporal scope, and a greater range of protected offenses. Fugitives hidden in chartered sanctuaries were governed by the church, and lived in a fugitive community, apart from the rest of the world.[14] Such sanctuaries could be quite large geographically. Secular authorities recognized this practice well into Tudor times. The sanctuary privilege shielded both laity and clergy, but clergy were often given special dispensation. The power of sanctuary was fortified by "fear of Divine vengeance," thus "when the Church said that those who sought her protection must be treated with leniency and mercy, and their lives and persons spared, no state or individual was strong enough or bold enough to refuse to comply."[15] As the Crown sought to enlarge its jurisdiction and attitudes about the proper role of the church changed, so too did secular deference to the practice of sanctuary. Beginning in 1467, the Crown began to reduce the types and locations of offenses covered by sanctuary and, by 1540, chartered sanctuary was abolished.[16] Sanctuary was completely repealed in 1623 by act of Parliament during the reign of James I, though the practice persisted unofficially with regard to service of process until the end of the 17th century.[17] By that time, the Crown found the separate justice system insupportable, because it made criminal punishment nonuniform.[18]

Sanctuary is a good means to come to terms with the enormous power of the Roman Catholic Church at the time. It was sovereign in the sanctuary territories, which it ran as separate universes from the Crown's territory. The church created a quasi-citizenship for fugitives, determined if and what punishment it would permit, and answered to no one.

The end of sanctuary marked the end of the church's geographical control in Britain. But it did not signal the end of special treatment for the clergy, but rather was only one stage in the movement away from church autonomy toward the rule of law under the common law. "Despite its formal demise, the spirit of sanctuary lived on in the practice known as 'benefit of clergy,' which did not offer outright immunity, but served, when available, to mitigate the severity of secular law."[19]

*The benefit of the clergy privilege and the juridical sovereignty of the Roman Catholic Church over its clergy*

To understand the benefit of clergy principle, one must go back to 12th-century Britain. In that era, King Henry II (1154–1189) succeeded the lax reign of King Stephen (1135–1154), who had permitted the barons and the Roman Catholic Church to exercise overweening power. Henry II, who is known as the father of the common law, took on both the barons and the church, but ultimately failed to make the church and its clergy accountable to the general public good.[20]

From 1076, when William the Conqueror established the dual court system, until 1576, during the reign of Elizabeth I, the royal courts and the ecclesiastical courts shared jurisdiction over criminal law,[21] which brought conflict and dissension. Henry II saw the need to standardize criminal justice, and sought to bring clergy under the jurisdiction of the civil courts. But the succeeding scandal with Archbishop Thomas Becket derailed his plans and led to a system of special treatment of clergy criminals that lasted several centuries.

Under Stephen, the clergy had become accustomed to unaccountability to the civil, or royal, courts.[22] Henry II thought their privilege to be above the law was dangerous, and in 1164, he called a meeting with the bishops to require them to agree to observe the customary powers of the king in the area of criminal law.[23] Specifically, he demanded that criminal clerics be defrocked by the church and handed over to the civil courts:

> Henry II was too astute a ruler not to perceive the immense evils arising from [the special treatment for the church], and the limitation which it imposed upon the royal power by emancipating so large a class of his subjects from obedience to the laws of the realm. When in 1164 he endeavored, in the Constitutions of Clarendon, to set bounds to the privileges of the church, he therefore especially attacked the benefit of clergy, and declared that ecclesiastics were amenable to the royal jurisdiction.[24]

At first, the archbishop of Canterbury, Thomas Becket, agreed. Becket's approval was a victory for Henry, because the Canterbury bishopric was the most powerful prelate in Britain, second only to the pope.[25] As archbishop, Becket had the power to excommunicate and was the cleric empowered to perform coronations in the event of a new king.[26] Thus, Becket's approval was crucial for the king's plans to unify the criminal justice system. To Henry's dismay, Becket reversed his position under pressure from other bishops.[27] As a result of the disagreement, Henry halted Becket's income and exiled him to France in 1164.[28]

Six years later, and anxious to secure succession, Henry sought to have his eldest surviving son crowned. Because Becket was in exile and therefore unavailable, Henry had Canterbury's ancient rival, the archbishop of York, preside over young Henry's coronation. Becket was enraged at the affront and, with papal backing, threatened to lay England under the ban of interdict.[29] He and Henry reached a truce, which allowed Becket to return to England in the autumn of 1170. The Sheriff of Kent accused Becket of returning to unseat Young Henry. Becket replied, "I have not the slightest intention of undoing the king's coronation. . . . But I have punished those who defied God and the prerogative of the church of Canterbury by usurping the right to consecrate him."[30] Despite the truce, just before returning to England, Becket raised Henry's ire by excommunicating all of the bishops who had participated in young Henry's coronation. It was after this incident that Henry declared in frustration to his assembled court, "Will no one rid me of this turbulent prelate?"[31]

In response to this furious statement, four of Henry's barons murdered Becket in Canterbury Cathedral on December 29, 1170. Although he publicly disavowed involvement with the murder, Henry was subsequently overcome with remorse and from his weakened position, acquiesced in the ecclesiastical courts' jurisdiction over clerics accused of crimes.[32] From the aftermath of this feud, the practice known as benefit of clergy became entrenched.[33]

The benefit of clergy, or *privilegium clericale*, was often the difference between life and death.[34] In the king's courts, capital punishment was mandated for all felonies.[35] In contrast, capital punishment was beyond the power of the ecclesiastical courts. Hence, clergy and laypeople could commit the same illegal actions, and the layperson's sentence would be death while the cleric's sentence would be defrocking, incarceration in a monastery, or forfeiture of belongings other than land.[36]

There were also procedural advantages for clergy members. Ecclesiastical trials of criminal matters were conducted by compurgation – the accused would take a formal oath that he was innocent of the crime and bring into court an "arbitrary" number of compurgators who would swear to their belief in his oath.[37] Acquittal was typical, because evidence was only adduced from the defense, and perjury by the defendant and compurgators was routine.[38] In addition, the clergy were exonerated from all prior criminal acts upon conviction of a single crime.[39] Thus, the rape of a girl and the murder of her father – both perpetrated by a single cleric – could be reduced to a single crime and a single punishment of suspension from ministry for two years.[40] The same crimes by any other citizen would have been tried as individual crimes and death would have been the likely sentence for either or both. From this history, one can draw many interesting conclusions, but "the remarkable point is that the clergy should have been able to maintain for centuries a special privilege in crime. This is a corollary to the magnitude and power of the church."[41]

Many laypeople, as well as Henry II, viewed the privilege for clergy as grossly unfair.[42] If clergy could avoid the death penalty, why couldn't laymen who had committed the identical crimes? This sense of fundamental unfairness did not abolish the privilege, but rather caused it to be eventually extended beyond clergy to cover all first-time offenders.[43] The extension of the privilege operated out of the same principle that would abolish special privileges for religion: Identical actions should yield similar punishments, the measure of which must be degree of harm, not the identity or status of the offender.

The power of the religious institutions during the British monarchy was also evidenced by the existence of the "high courts" of the royal and ecclesiastical courts: the Star Chamber and its ecclesiastical counterpart, the High Commission, the beginnings of which appeared during the reign of Henry VIII and came to full flower under Elizabeth I. These were the "prerogative courts."[44] "The court of High Commission stood to the church and to the ordinary ecclesiastical courts somewhat in the same relation as the Council and Star Chamber stood to the state and the ordinary courts of the state, central and local."[45] Upon declaring himself the head of the church in England, Henry VIII used both courts to enforce spiritual uniformity on the people, a tradition followed by his successors (whether Catholic or Protestant), until the courts were abolished in 1641.[46]

By 1576, under Elizabeth I, the benefit of clergy privilege had been extended beyond clergy to all those who were literate (there was a time when only the clergy were literate), and therefore the benefit of the clergy was not only a means for the clergy to move their trials to the friendlier ecclesiastical courts, but it also became a tool for laypeople to reduce the likely sentence for a crime, even though they were being tried in secular courts.[47] It was assumed that a felony was "clergyable," that is, capable of preventing capital punishment, unless the Parliament explicitly stated otherwise. Eventually, during the latter half of the 16th century and the beginning of the 17th, the benefit became inapplicable to murder, rape, abduction, thefts of the person exceeding a shilling, burglary, highway robbery, stealing horses, and stealing from churches.[48]

Also in 1576, Parliament abolished the ecclesiastical courts' jurisdiction over crimes committed by clergy, roughly 400 years after Henry tried and failed to do so.[49] At the same time, the "benefit of clergy" became a gambit to be invoked at sentencing for laypeople and clergy alike – that is, it was not merely a guarantee of a particular court, with special procedural rules, for clergy.[50] Parliament removed the criminal jurisdiction of the ecclesiastical courts because it perceived that the church had taken over a large portion of its criminal jurisdiction.[51] Moreover, the Crown was appalled at the level of perjury and corruption in the ecclesiastical courts:

> This scandalous prostitution of oaths, and the forms of justice, in the almost constant acquittal of felonious clerks by purgation, was the occasion, that, upon very heinous and notorious circumstances of guilt, the temporal courts would not trust the ordinary with the trial of an offender. . . . As, therefore, these mock trials took their rise from factious and popish tenets, tending to exempt one part of the nation from the general municipal law; it became high time, when the reformation was thoroughly established, to abolish so vain and impious a ceremony.[52]

As a result, Blackstone writes, the 1576 statute abolished the practice of purgation (and with it, the ecclesiastical courts' jurisdiction over clergy members who committed crimes), by directing that an offender who pled the benefit of clergy "was not to be delivered to the [ecclesiastic courts], as formerly," but instead was to be burned on the hand to show that he had used the privilege for a first-time felony, (a practice that became ceremonial in some cases) and, at the judge's discretion, could be sentenced to up to a year in prison.[53] The 1576 statute served two purposes: Parliament did away with the corrupt practice of trial by compurgation while it effectively enlarged the Crown's criminal jurisdiction at the expense of the ecclesiastical courts. The loss of ecclesiastical jurisdiction over crimes committed by clergy was significant, though not nearly as divisive as it had been in Henry II's and Becket's day.

In England and in the colonies, the benefit of clergy eventually became a tool for all defendants to avoid the death penalty. It was replaced by "transportation" away from the jurisdiction during the 18th century and ultimately abolished in the 19th century.[54] Moreover, early America did not recognize special, ecclesiastical courts for clergy that substituted for secular courts in criminal matters. Rather, clergy members were subject to the law of the secular courts as were all citizens.[55] The "benefit of clergy," therefore, did not confer any special benefit on clergy *qua* clergy in the colonies or later, the states. Instead, it was a tool for juries and judges to avoid the death penalty as applied to first-time felonies.[56]

The end of sanctuary, the end of benefit of clergy, and the end of a politically sovereign church signaled the demise of the structural mechanisms that had protected religious individuals or institutions from criminal liability in Britain. When the colonies were first established in the early 17th century, the settlers were part of a generation that had been ruled by Queen Elizabeth I, during whose reign the ecclesiastical courts were definitively removed from criminal jurisdiction. Neither the privileges nor the ecclesiastical courts made it across the Atlantic. Once the United States was established, the states did not reinvigorate the rejected British privileges. Instead, they picked up where Britain had left off and permitted the government to bring clergy under civil court authority[57] and religious institutions to account.[58] Current attempts by religious organizations to avoid criminal liability by invoking alleged privileges do have their roots in history, but they lost their moral and legal underpinnings long ago.[59]

### The charitable immunity experiment

Charitable immunity was a rule that protected the coffers of charitable organizations from actions in tort. Unlike sanctuary and the benefit of clergy, it was not a privilege limited to churches or clergy. Rather, it was intended to shield volunteer or charitable associations in general.[60] The doctrine of charitable immunity protected charitable organizations from tort lawsuits, which meant that victims could not bring successful tort claims against the employees of those organizations.[61]

It appears to have developed based on a variety of justifications. The doctrine, originally developed in England in 1846, was based on a trust theory "that the funds of the charity are not to be diverted from the purposes intended by their donors and applied to the payment of liabilities in tort."[62] Another theory offered was that since charities do not gain or benefit from the services they offer, they could not be held liable under the doctrine of respondeat superior for works done on their behalf. A third justification was that the recipients of charity assume the risk of negligence when they accept the benefit, thereby waiving their right to sue. It has also been put forward that the acts of charitable organizations are analogous to municipalities and therefore, charities deserve the protection that governmental immunity offers. Finally, public policy – fueled by a fear that people and institutions working to better society would no longer contribute if they were liable for actions associated with that work – justified charitable immunity.[63]

The public policy argument was especially forceful in late 19th-century America. When public charities first emerged in the United States, they were foundering institutions run only on an experimental basis. Any substantial judgment against them would have led to their demise, or at the very least, discouraged contributions. In an effort to foster their growth and thus benefit the public, most state courts adopted the policy of shielding charities from tort liability.[64]

In England, the charitable immunity rule did not involve religious institutions specifically. In the United States, the definition of a charitable organization eventually reached beyond the traditional nonprofit groups that aided the poor to include hospitals, schools, and churches. At its height, the immunity provided complete protection against any damage awards and therefore made charitable organization's coffers autonomous from any countervailing social responsibility. In the minority of jurisdictions, immunity extended only to certain persons or certain sources of the organization's income (trust funds and donations).[65]

The now disfavored doctrine entered the common law in 1846, as dictum in the House of Lords' decision in *The Feoffees of Heriot's Hospital v. Ross*: "To give damages out of a trust fund would not be to apply it to those objects whom the author of the fund had in view, but would be to divert it to a completely different purpose." The case was an action for damages for wrongful exclusion from the benefits of the charity, not for any personal injury inflicted in its operation.[66] Thirty years later, Massachusetts was the first state to adopt the doctrine of charitable immunity in *McDonald v. Mass. Gen. Hosp.*,[67] with many other state courts following suit. By 1900, seven state supreme courts followed suit, with another 33 joining the charitable immunity movement by 1938.[68] Ironically, by the time the doctrine became entrenched in the American courts, it was no longer good law in England.[69] By 1871, after only 25 years experience with the doctrine, the English courts rejected it on the ground that it made no sense to hold charities blameless for the harm they caused. As a 1909 case characterized it: "It is now well settled that a public body is liable for the negligence of its servants in the same way as private individuals would be liable in similar circumstances."[70]

By the early 20th century, American scholars considered charitable immunity a faulty doctrine based on a weak foundation.[71] In *Georgetown College v. Hughes*, one of the first American cases rejecting charitable immunity, the court characterized it as an "anomaly," stating that "[t]he doctrine of immunity of charitable corporations found its way into the law . . . through misconception or misapplication of previously established principles."[72] Even defenders of limited liability for charitable organizations recognize that the "traditional rationales for denying *all* tort recovery against charitable organizations cannot withstand close scrutiny."[73] The reasoning is obvious: When the law is intended to redress harm, and charitable institutions are intended to assist those in need, permitting them to avoid liability for the harm they cause is perverse. As with sanctuary and especially the benefit of clergy, the driving logic of the common law and the rule of law and the no-harm principle cannot be squared with a special dispensation for charitable organizations when they engender harm.

Still, some vestiges of the doctrine remain.[74] While it has been thought appropriate to hold charitable organizations accountable for the actions of their employees, their liability for volunteers has been contested.[75] Additionally, a minority of states has imposed monetary caps on damage awards against charitable organizations.[76] Both iterations are under attack, because they cannot be made consistent with the no-harm rule.

Like the benefit of clergy and sanctuary, charitable immunity was vulnerable to the rule of law and its fundamental presupposition that all citizens who act in the same way should be subject to the same law. As in Britain, in the United States, charitable immunity was nullified by the larger legal system within which religious and charitable organizations, their clergy, and their employees are accountable to those they harm. The three benefits could not withstand modern beliefs in fairness, deterrence, and accountability.

*The Reformation's influence on the rejection of special privileges for religion*

The Reformation also bolstered the arguments against special legal treatment for religious entities. As co-sovereigns, the Church and the Crown continuously came into conflict throughout the medieval period over questions of jurisdiction.[77] In the 13th century, the gap between them widened when secular lawyers replaced ecclesiastics on the benches of the common law courts.[78] Yet, they rested on similar grounds. The rival courts were separate systems of law, differed in many of their rules and derived their force from different sovereigns,[79] but they were based on the same philosophical foundation – "the will of God expressed through authority" – whether ecclesiastical or royal.[80] So long as the one ground existed to justify each, there was little question of separate identities between Church and Crown. There was a single whole under God, though its elements were often in tension.

All this changed with the Reformation in the 16th century. The attack on the authority of the church was in effect an attack on the whole medieval system of law. Thus, religion was no longer universally considered the basis of civil government, and the premises of the common law firmly gained ascendancy over ecclesiastical law.[81]

The scope of ecclesiastical jurisdiction began to decline at the outset of the Reformation, reflecting a "basic shift in attitude towards the proper role of the Church in men's lives."[82] The end of benefit of clergy, which shifted power away from ecclesiastical courts to civil courts, led to a corresponding decline in the sovereign authority of the established church in Britain.[83] It became clear that a "shift in the balance of power" to secular authority at the expense of the ecclesiastical "had to be carried out in the context of legal competition and compromise."[84] The ecclesiastical courts continued to exercise jurisdiction over some matters that had been in their purview since the medieval period, such as tithing, probate, marriage, defamation, and cases involving "mortal sins" such as fornication and adultery.[85] The increasing entrenchment of the common law,[86] the Roman Catholic Church's loss of moral authority during the Reformation,[87] and the subsequent growth of Protestantism with its emphasis on accountability[88] reduced the ecclesiastical courts' power and

undermined whatever argument the Church once had to be sovereign
or to have its clergy immune from the criminal law.

### The Star Chamber and the High Commission

During the Tudor and Stuart years, 1485–1714,[89] the Crown engaged in
a systematic suppression of religious dissent and the persecution of those
whose beliefs differed from those of the established church. In 1526,
Henry VIII divided his king's council into two branches: a privy council
to consider domestic and foreign policy issues, which came to be known
as the Star Chamber, and the court of High Commission, to address
ecclesiastical issues. When Henry VIII officially became the head of the
church eight years later in 1534,[90] he was able to use both commissions, or
prerogative courts, to exercise control over religious belief and practice.
The unification of church and state made "any deviation from the new
religious order a threat to royal supremacy." Thus, heresy and treason became indistinguishable as the Star Chamber cases involving "sedition" or
"subversion" and the High Commission cases involving "heresy" worked
in tandem to rid Britain of religious dissenters. "Those who continued to
support the authority of the pope, Henry VIII sent to the executioner's
chopping block; those who preached new doctrines he sent to the fires
at Smithfield."[91]

Henry VIII's successors carried on his practices. His son, Edward VI,
was only 10 years old when he ascended to the throne on Henry's death
in 1547, but the dukes of Somerset and Northumberland ruled in his
name, and both promoted Protestantism as the established and sole religion of the realm.[92] The Catholic Queen Mary (1553–58) ruled in a
country dominated by Protestants,[93] whom she believed invited divine
retribution on her reign for their heresy.[94] She atoned by burning hundreds of Protestants at the stake, including Bishops Cranmer, Ridley, and
Latimer, during her short reign.[95]

Protestant Elizabeth I (1558–1603) gained control of a country divided
by religion. To reunite the country, she ruthlessly suppressed Catholicism
(she was excommunicated by the pope in 1570[96]) through her enforcement of the Acts of Supremacy and Uniformity, which she employed
the High Commission to institute, and through her use of the Tower

of London to execute heretics.[97] After centuries of sovereign control in Britain, the Catholic Church found itself in the 1570s instructing Catholics to avoid Anglican worship services and to attend their own "despite the penalties for doing so."[98] James I (1603–1625) and Charles I (1625–1649) avidly suppressed religious opposition. Only five years before the end of James I's reign, in 1620, the Mayflower pilgrims sailed for America.[99] Throughout his reign, Charles I aggressively suppressed Puritans.[100] Abuses by the Star Chamber and the High Commission were legion, and thousands of British citizens left for the American colonies (and the Netherlands), bringing with them certain knowledge of the consequences that result when a government joined forces with a single religion. After refusing to convene Parliament from 1629 until 1640, Charles I finally did so, then the Puritans seized power and soon thereafter abolished the prerogative courts (the Star Chamber and High Commission) and their abusive practices.[101]

The jurisdiction of the prerogative courts – the Star Chamber and the High Commission – was repealed, because "so large a prerogative," as was manifested in the courts' inquisitorial form and their arbitrary procedures, was "no longer compatible with liberty."[102] In addition, in a dramatic move forward for the common law, the ecclesiastical courts were deprived of *all* criminal jurisdiction, the entirety of which was placed in common law courts.[103]

The Crown did not respond to the Reformation by embracing religious pluralism. Rather, each British monarch, no longer bound to share power with one church, chose between Roman Catholicism and Protestantism, and forced her subjects to follow suit.

The Tower of London was an essential tool for the inculcation of the established religion of the realm. It was employed by Catholic Queen Mary to imprison and execute Protestants, after she revived the heresy laws at the end of 1554. The first Protestant martyr was publicly burned in 1555.[104] Between 250 and 300 were burned alive, while hundreds more were imprisoned.[105] Her successor, Protestant Queen Elizabeth I, used similar techniques to ward off Catholic Europe and those who refused to attend Church of England services by incarcerating bishops, archbishops, and others for years.[106] "There were as many executions of Catholics under Elizabeth as there were Protestants under Mary, though over a reign nine times as long."[107] James I continued to use the Tower as a prison, as the Tudors had done.[108] This was the era of the United States' first colonization.

In 1643, Parliamentarians seized control of the Tower during the Civil War in 1643. Throughout the Restoration, the Tower's function as a state prison declined and it became a military headquarters and munitions storehouse. The last execution was in 1747, long after the first wave of emigrants left for the New World in the late 16th and early 17th centuries. Indeed, the first permanently established settlement in the United States, in Jamestown Virginia, was established a mere four years after the end of Queen Elizabeth's reign.[109]

The Bloody Tower, as it is often called, is a monument to the British history of religious dominance and intolerance. It was unquestionably stamped on the mind-set of any British subject at the time, and scores of them emigrated to the New World. The founding generation and the Framers thought about organized religion in this British context and did not have to leap to reach the conclusions that granting governing power to religion could be dangerous and that religious individuals and entities needed to be curbed by just laws. The signal innovation in the United States was religious pluralism, with each state, or smaller jurisdiction, establishing its own church or establishing multiple churches. The resulting variety of religious sects was an important step on the way to the privatization of religion in the United States, which in turn contributed to the treatment of religious entities as accountable citizens rather than sovereigns.

*Influences on the Framers that informed the First Amendment*

No one was more aware of the capacity of religious institutions to harm the public good than the framing generation, many of whom escaped England and its entrenched religious authorities that had suppressed their particular faith with the aid and acquiescence of the monarchy.[110] The Reformation, which spawned a multiplicity of sects in tension with the established church, ended only 20 years before the first emigrants started across the Atlantic.[111] Thus "[w]hen English settlers first sailed for America in 1584, they carried with them a faith worked out over fifty years of religious turbulence."[112] This turbulence continued well into the next century. Religious persecution in Britain only abated when the Puritans rose to power and disbanded the Star Chamber and the High Commission in 1641.[113] To be sure, the colonists did not swear off of established churches or persecution of nonbelievers or false believers immediately, but such principles were neither instituted nor praised in the federal Constitution. Rather, the federal Constitution, including the Bill of Rights, weighed heavily against both, in some measure because of the framing generation's knowledge of the abuses that had gone before.

### The influence of the Inquisition on the framers

While drafting the Constitution, Madison – and the Framers in general – had the despotic practices of the Catholic Inquisitors stamped on their political consciousness, a fact proven by Madison's direct reference to the Inquisition in his *Memorial and Remonstrance*, where he argued against state payment of certain Christian educators as follows:

> Because the proposed establishment is a departure from the generous policy, which, offering an Asylum to the persecuted and oppressed of every Nation and Religion, promised a lustre to our country, and an accession to the number of its citizens. What a melancholy mark is the Bill of sudden degeneracy? Instead of holding forth an Asylum to the persecuted, it is itself a signal of persecution. It degrades from the equal rank of Citizens all those whose opinions in Religion do not bend to those of the Legislative authority. Distant as it may be in its present form from the Inquisition, it differs from it only in degree. The one is the first step, the other the last in the career of intolerance. The magnanimous sufferer under this cruel scourge in foreign Regions, must view the Bill as a Beacon on our Coast, warning him to seek some other haven, where liberty and philanthrophy in their due extent, may offer a more certain respose from his Troubles.[114]

There can be no question that the excesses of the Inquisition (1184–1834), which encompassed the Spanish Inquisition (1474–1834), as well as the public executions of those whose faith differed from the Crown in England (1531–1689) and the excesses generated by the unity of power between the monarchies and organized religion, were part of the calculus the framing generation used to calibrate the need for government, the reach of religious liberty, and the need to make religious institutions accountable to the public good. Nor can there be any question that they believed in placing legal limitations on the religious institutions, because the Framers believed at a visceral level that religious institutions were not worthy of blind trust. These are complex institutions that are run and staffed by humans, who are inherently imperfect. That is, after all, the worldview on which the constitutional scheme is based. According to the Framers, humans are inherently likely to abuse whatever power they hold. They hoped that a structured society based on the rule of law, and a structured Constitution pitting various power centers against each other, could forestall the inevitable temptations to abuse power.[115]

Indeed, Madison's mentor, the Rev. John Witherspoon, president of the College of New Jersey, which later became Princeton University, explained the history of the United States in the context of the Inquisition:

> [A]t the time of the Reformation when religion began to revive, nothing contributed more to facilitate its reception and increase its progress than the violence of its persecutors. Their cruelty and the patience of the sufferers naturally disposed men to examine and weigh the cause to which they adhered with so much constancy and resolution. At the same time also, when they were persecuted in one city, they fled to another and carried the discoveries of Popish fraud to every part of the world. It was by some of those who were persecuted in Germany that the light of the Reformation was brought so early into Britain.

> [T]he violent persecution which many eminent Christians met with in England from their brethren, who called themselves Protestants, drove them in great numbers to a distant part of the New World where the light of the gospel and true religion were unknown.[116]

Under the reign of Pope Gregory IX, in response to the spread of "heretic" beliefs, Roman Catholic bishops conducted medieval "inquisitions" designed to rid France, Germany, and Italy of non-Catholics. Because these events influenced the framing generation's perception of the qualities of religious organizations, it is important to understand their history. Investigation of heresy was traditionally the duty of the bishops.[117] The Inquisition, then known as the Holy Office, is perhaps best known for convicting Galileo at trial in 1633 for his "dangerous" scientific beliefs.[118] Most Inquisition trials resulted in a guilty verdict, and those convicted faced a myriad of horrific punishments as well as fines, imprisonment, and death.[119]

The Spanish Inquisition was independent of the medieval Inquisition, but it was also part of that history the framing generation would have known and used to judge contemporary ideas. The purpose of the Spanish Inquisition was to discover and punish converted Jews (and later Muslims) who were insincere.[120] It was established in 1478 by King Ferdinand and Queen Isabella with the reluctant approval of Pope Sixtus IV.[121] The institution was entirely controlled by the Spanish crown – the pope's only check on the Inquisition was in naming and appointing the nominees to be inquisitors.[122] In 1483, the Crown created a new royal council of the Supreme and General Inquisition to expand the operation of the Inquisition throughout Spain. The notorious Tomas de Torquemada was named inquisitor general, who was the head of the council, responsible for creating branches of the Inquisition in various cities by establishing local tribunals.[123] The Spanish Inquisition was not finally abolished until 1834, nearly 60 years after the Declaration of Independence was signed.[124]

### The early move toward religious pluralism

In Britain in 1662, during the Restoration, Anglicans and Presbyterians attempted to form a national British church, but the effort failed. Parliament passed a new Act of Uniformity, and Presbyterian ministers who refused to conform were expelled from their congregations.[125] Dissenting Protestant worship became legal in 1689, but the dissenters were not allowed to hold property to construct churches unless they were subject to the oversight of the Court of Chancery. Not until 1791 were Catholics given parity with other Protestant dissenters. The inability of the established Anglican Church to answer to the public good when dealing with issues involving taxation, tithing, local government, marriage, education, and charity led to the assumption of civil jurisdiction over those issues. It was the measuring stick of the public good that transformed Britain from a country with only one recognized religion to one of religious liberty. "English pluralism was the result of a gradual wearing away of a unitary system through concessions made because it seemed right to make them."[126]

Like Britain, the United States did not begin as a fully pluralistic and tolerant society. The early colonies and then some of the states, with the exception of Pennsylvania, had established churches with corresponding privileges for members and disabilities for dissenters. Notably though, there was no Tower of London or Star Chamber and High Commission to force the established church's beliefs on others. Moreover, the establishments, such as they were, gave way not long after the Constitution and then the Bill of Rights were ratified.

The Establishment Clause is testimony to the founding generation's rational fear of overweening religious power and of the mischief that can be fostered by religious institutions, particularly when they are sovereign. It cannot be, as Professor Carl Esbeck argues, a rule solely intended to protect religious entities.[127] The history leading up to the founding of United States and the Protestant cast of governance theories at the time undermine such attempts to treat religion as though it is not a dangerous and potent social force that must be limited, just as the state must be.

### The Protestant influence on the framing generation

The dominant mind-set of the early Americans was Protestant.[128] At its most fundamental level, all Protestantism incorporates the view that religious individuals and institutions have the capacity to stray from a holy path into the path of evil.[129] For Protestants, individuals are locked into original sin. According to John Calvin, who, along with Martin Luther, sparked the Reformation and Protestantism, there was never a moment in history when humans could be blindly trusted to be, or do, good:

> [L]et us hold this as an undoubted truth which no siege engines can shake: the mind of man has been so completely estranged from God's righteousness that it conceives, desires, and undertakes, only that which is impious, perverted, foul, impure, and infamous. The heart is so steeped in the poison of sin, that it can breathe out nothing but a loathsome stench. But if some men occasionally make a show of good, their minds nevertheless ever remain enveloped in hypocrisy and deceitful craft, and their hearts bound by inner perversity.[130]

Thus, Calvin counseled in favor of a diligent surveillance of one's own actions and the actions of others at the same time he endorsed the value of the law (both biblical and secular) to guide human behavior away from its propensity to do wrong.[131] Granted, no human could ever live up to all of the law's demands, but laws were valuable as a checking measure nonetheless.

Protestantism equally discounted the likelihood that a religious institution could be trusted on its own to serve the public good. "[Protestantism] is essentially an attempt to check the tendency to corruption and degradation which attacks every institutional religion."[132] The early Protestants, after all, were the Catholic dissenters who eventually rejected the 16th-century Roman Catholic Church for its malignant ways.[133] The belief that the Catholic Church had led the Christian Church down evil paths was a fervently held belief at the time of the framing as well, with John Adams identifying the "worst tyranny ever invented" as "the Romish superstition."[134]

The attitude of the framing generation on this subject differed little from Calvin's description of the 16th-century Roman Church's hubris and unaccountability:

> Because of the primacy of the Roman Church, they say, no one has the right to review the judgments of this See. Likewise: as judge it will be judged neither by emperor, nor by kings, nor by all the clergy, nor by the people. This is the very height of imperiousness for one man to set himself up as judge of all, and suffer himself to obey the judgment of none. But what if he exercise tyranny over God's people? If he scatter and lay waste Christ's Kingdom? If he throw the whole church into confusion? If he turn the pastoral office into robbery? Nay, though he be utterly wicked, he denies he is bound to give an accounting.[135]

The solution for the wayward path of the Catholic Church, at least according to Calvin, was proper government, a need the early Presbyterians (and Calvinists), identified both in the society and the Church:

> Man's depraved apostate Condition renders Government needful. Needful both in the State and the Church. In the former without Government Anarchy wou'd soon take place with all its wild and dire Effects and Men wou'd be like the Fishes of the Sea where the greater devour the less. Nor is Govern[ment] in the Church less needful than in the State and this for the same Reason.[136]

*The framing generation and the development of the*
*no-harm principle*

There is nearly universal agreement that a no-harm rule undergirds and justifies criminal, tort, and regulatory laws (at least those laws that prohibit harm to others).[137] The no-harm rule was a notion articulated by John Locke in the 17th century, widely shared by the framing generation in the 18th century, and entrenched in modern philosophy and law by John Stuart Mill,[138] who was the most influential philosopher in the 19th-century English-speaking world. He set forth the following maxims, which came to be known collectively as the Harm Principle:

> first, that the individual is not accountable to society for his actions, in so far as these concern the interests of no person but himself. . . . Secondly, that for such actions as are prejudicial to the interests of others, the individual is accountable, and may be subjected either to social or to legal punishments, if society is of opinion that the one or the other is requisite for its protection.[139]

Mill thereby restated the Lockean principle in a way that honed it down to a no-harm rule itself. It is a firm rejection of individual (or institutional) autonomy from the laws that protect others from harm.

He also advocated absolute dominion over one's mind, which entailed tolerance of conflicting beliefs: "If all mankind minus one, were of one opinion, and only one person were of the contrary opinion, mankind would be no more justified in silencing that one person, than he, if he had the power, would be justified in silencing mankind."[140] The universe of actions was divided into two categories: those that will not harm others and those that will. The former should not be regulated, and the latter should.

In the 20th century, the no-harm principle was further elaborated by H. L. A. Hart and Joel Feinberg. H. L. A. Hart stated in the 1960s that the line to be drawn between legitimate laws and illegitimate laws rested on the Harm Principle.[141] Joel Feinberg further developed the theory.[142] By the latter half of the 20th century, the no-harm rule was widely accepted as the best justification for criminal, tort, and regulatory laws. It remains the dominant approach.

As discussed in Chapter 8, Locke believed in a robust right of conscience, but also that belief must be coupled with the obligation not to harm others through one's actions. The no-harm principle is part and parcel of the core principle of ordered liberty embedded in republicanism: the maximal amount of liberty is calibrated to achieve the minimal amount of harm.[143] Order must be fitted with liberty.

Locke's no-harm principle was taken as a commonplace during the era of the framing. Thomas Jefferson famously explained, "the legitimate powers of government extend to such acts only as are injurious to others. But it does me no injury for my neighbour to say there are twenty gods, or no God. It neither picks my pocket nor breaks my leg."[144] Freedom of belief and "free argument and debate" were essential human rights, but when those "principles break out into overt acts against peace and good order" it is the "rightful purpose[] of civil government, for its officers to interfere."[145] Jefferson articulated the same principle when he wrote to James Madison in 1788 to outline the rights he thought necessary to include in a bill of rights. He backed a bill of rights, but he was also conscious that rights had the capacity to "do evil." Thus, he explained what the "freedom of religion" in the bill of rights would (and would not) accomplish: "The declaration that religious faith shall be unpunished, does not give impunity to criminal acts dictated by religious error."[146]

James Madison – drafter of the First Amendment – equally recognized the right to complete freedom of belief: "Religious bondage shackles and debilitates the mind and unfits it for every noble enterprise, every expanded project."[147] He admired the tolerance of religious beliefs in Pennsylvania, which exhibited a "liberal, catholic, and equitable way of thinking as to the rights of Conscience."[148] His discussions of "conscience" were discussions about belief, and not conduct.

Madison was particularly harsh regarding the potential abuses of power by religious institutions and especially their clergy. When backed by state authority, he declared, the clergy "tend to great ignorance and corruption, all of which facilitate the execution of mischievous projects." He castigated some believers at the time: "Poverty and luxury prevail among all sorts: pride, ignorance, and knavery among the priesthood, and vice and wickedness among the laity. . . . That diabolical, Hell-conceived principle of persecution rages among some, and to their eternal infamy, the clergy can furnish their quota of imps for such business."[149] Obviously, Jefferson and Madison envisioned the potential for great harm to the public good when a religious entity abuses power.[150] For this reason, absolute liberty for religious organizations was never contemplated by them, or their fellow citizens. In fact, the primary assumption at the Constitutional Convention – and it is the most important principle that has contributed to the Constitution's success – was that every individual and every institution holding power was likely to abuse that power and therefore must be checked.[151]

Many in the framing era were also distrustful of religious organizations and clerics. The Deists at the time, like Jefferson, believed in Christ, but were unwilling to align themselves with the theology of any particular organized religion because, in their eyes, most theologies were a corruption of Christianity.[152] Jefferson famously excised portions of the Bible he found unacceptable to create his own creed.[153] Thus, Jefferson declared, "To the corruptions of Christianity, I am indeed opposed; but not to the genuine precepts of Jesus himself."[154] The Deists dominated the universities, and had a disproportionate effect on the culture compared to their numbers. Among Christians other than the Deists, anticlericalism also was an entrenched viewpoint.[155]

The Protestant mind-set, and its interpretation of the violent history of religion in Europe, holds relevance for understanding the legal system that emerged in early America. It is no accident that the rise of Protestantism, its elemental rejection of the Roman Catholic Church, and its affirmation of the sinfulness of all humans – including and especially those who were clerics – coincided with the demise of the ecclesiastical courts and the benefit of clergy.[156]

Protestant theology, the reformed branch in particular, has long rested on a deep mistrust of human nature rooted in original sin, which has led to the necessity of government and a no-harm rule.[157] In fact, the Calvinist-Presbyterian branch of reformed theology contributed to the construction of the U.S. Constitution's emphasis on checks and balances, separation of power, and the necessary division of power between state and federal governments.[158] This starting point is shared by the Framers, Catholic Social Thought, and reformed theology. All three equally value the rule of no harm, that is, the necessity of deterring all citizens and institutions from harming others. For Protestant theology, government rightly exists to serve the common good, and that good is served best when the potential to do harm is restrained through duly enacted laws.

One particularly relevant idea in Protestant theology is the theory of "sphere sovereignty" introduced by a reformed theologian, Abraham Kuyper, in the late 19th century.[159] Under sphere sovereignty (or authority as some have suggested), church and state (and the arts and business, among other social organizations) each have their own sovereign base, but each also has a distinctive role. "[T]he *telos* of the state is the common good." Thus, the distinctive role of the state is to "prevent the spheres from infringing upon one another, and it may use compulsion when necessary to maintain order."[160] He further explained:

> The cogwheels of all these spheres engage each other, and precisely through that interaction emerges the rich, multifaceted multiformity of human life. Hence also rises the danger that one sphere in life may encroach on its neighbour like a sticky wheel that shears off one cog after another until the whole operation is disrupted. Hence also the raison d'être for the special sphere of authority that emerged in the State. It must provide for sound mutual interaction among the various spheres, insofar as they are externally manifest, and keep them within just limits.[161]

This oversight role includes the power to protect the powerless in every sphere.[162] Thus, no sphere is considered immune from the sovereignty or power of another, but rather each sphere is to exercise its authority according to its own *telos*. Moreover, the state holds the authority to "intervene when the authorities in other spheres *are manifestly abusing their power.*"[163]

The just criticism of the sphere sovereignty theory is that it is fuzzy at the boundaries, and it does not fully articulate the specific role of either the state or the religious institution.[164] Its value, however, lies in its articulation of the *role* of government vis-à-vis the church. It is not at all a stretch to claim that the powers identified are those undergirding the no-harm doctrine: the state is a neutral arbiter that ensures peace and protects the powerless. The state that chooses church autonomy is at odds with this notion.

*Religious attitudes toward obedience to the rule of law in the framing generation*

The dominant view at the time of the framing was that the rule of law was to be applied to religious individuals and institutions.[165] As the experiments with democracy around the world in the last 30 years have taught, the rule of law cannot operate without the widespread acceptance of this principle among the people.[166] During the latter half of the 18th century, such acceptance in this country was significantly furthered by sermons in a wide range of Protestant churches – Baptist, Presbyterian, Congregational, and Episcopalian.[167]

Whether religious believers would be subject to the general laws of the new country was a topic that was frequently on the minds of preachers in the latter half of the 18th century. Their sermons, as well as governing documents of their churches, show the religious leaders of 18th-century society articulating a fairly cohesive vision for the coexistence of God's law and civil law. I do not intend to overstate the consistency of their claims, because there are dissenting, minority views and not every preacher adopts every tenet discussed here. Nevertheless, there is a generally accepted view that is sufficiently repeated to justify the claim that it was an important and formative element in the social mix.

To be sure, the ideas that the various sermons set forth are consistent with and can even plausibly be traced to not only theology but also to political philosophy of the time. In particular, many of the sermons reference the work of John Locke. In any event, religious leaders at the time of the formation of the Constitution conveyed a vision to their members: Congregants were urged by their religious leaders to follow the rule of law on a number of grounds.

The discussion of religion and the rule of law in the pulpit usually proceeded by an acknowledgment of the existence of two concurrent realms, one civil, one religious, each with a rightful pull on the citizen. While the argument for the superiority of God's obligations is made, a number of ministers assert that the civil law is, in fact, a form of God's law. Believers were not to focus solely on their private understanding of what God asks of them individually, but rather, as part of their Christian practice, to take into account the good of the whole in their obedience to the law. Preachers also argued, in the larger picture, that obedience to the civil law is necessary for the realization of true liberty and that the freedom of religion does not extend to conduct beyond worship. Far from the overly simplified assumption that conflicting laws automatically should give way to religious claims, 18th-century religious leaders cautioned their members of the perils to the broader society of failing to follow the law.

Respected clergymen tended to be well-educated, and were the political and social leaders of their day. There was no national government or identity, so elected officials were limited geographically to a particular state or city. But many of the clergy were itinerant, often crossing state boundaries and delivering political and social news from state to state. The two elements – travel across state lines and high regard – made them formidable influences immediately before, during, and after the Revolution up till the Constitutional Convention. Thus, it is well worth one's time to examine what they had to say about the law and religious entities at the time.

In 18th-century sermons, there was a repeated emphasis on the existence of two concurrent and distinguishable realms of power: church and state. Each was to have its rightful, limited claim on human conduct and mutual boundaries.[168]

Civil law made legitimate claims on religious believers when civil law operated in the proper realm. For example, Elisha Williams in 1744 stated that "obedience is due to civil rulers in those cases wherein they have power to command, and does not call for it any farther." In other words, according to Williams, "[t]he ground of obedience cannot be extended beyond the ground of that authority to which obedience is required."[169] The proper ground included the preservation of "life, liberty, money, lands, houses, family, and the like."[170] Three years later, Charles Chauncy echoed that civil "rulers . . . have an undoubted right to make and execute laws, for the publick good."[171] The horizon under which legislatures were to make law was the public good. According to John Lathrop, "[I]f the essential parts of any system of civil government are found to be inconsistent with the general good, the end of government requires that such bad systems should be demolished, and a new one formed, by which the public weal shall be more effectually secured."[172]

The two domains were coterminous and mutually exclusive. Thus, civil government's proper realm ended when it attempted to "establish any religion" by instituting or requiring "articles of faith, creeds, forms of worship or church government [in part because] . . . these things have no relation to the ends of civil society."[173]

To be sure, the clergy did not intend to rubber stamp the rule of any civil government per se, but rather only that government that flows directly or indirectly from the people and that is obligated to the public good. The law that binds is the law derived as follows:

> [R]eason teaches men to join in society, to unite together into a commonwealth under some form or other, to make a body of laws agreeable to the law of nature, and institute one common power to see them observed. It is they who thus united together, *viz.* the people, who make and alone have right to make the laws that are to take place among them; or which comes to the same thing, appoint those who shall make them, and who shall see them executed. For every man has an equal right to the preservation of his person and property; and so an equal right to establish a law, or to nominate the makers and executors of the laws which are the guardians both of person and property.[174]

For at least one preacher in 1784, the fact that citizens legitimized the government by choosing their rulers led to the conclusion that such rulers were to be obeyed.[175]

Part of this shared vision depends on a notion of differentiation between church and state. But it is not a total separation that forces the believer to choose one sphere over the other, but rather a distinction of spheres, each with a legitimate, concurrent, and strong pull on the believer's allegiance. Thus, the free exercise of religion was to be pursued not in isolation but rather in "so far as may be consistent with the civil rights of society."[176] Taking the image of concurrent but distinguishable realms to its logical end, Isaac Backus reasoned that when each is functioning properly within its own realm, "the effects are happy, and they do not at all interfere with each other." The key to such happiness lies in their separate spheres, with "mischiefs" ensuing whenever "these two kinds of government . . . have been confounded together."[177]

The one realm reinforced allegiance to the other, and thus the obligation to obey the civil law was treated as part of the Christian's obligation. Peace was to be achieved when men lived under these two authoritative regimes, because Christians "are taught to obey [civil] magistracy."[178] Thus, the allegiance to the Christian Church carried with it an allegiance to laws duly enacted by those who were appointed by the people and entrusted with serving the public good.[179]

*The 18th-century preachers' reasons to obey the civil law*

Far from urging civil disobedience, many 18th-century sermons exhorted believers to obey the civil law. There are three reasons offered by the clergy to obey the law. First, the law is given by God and therefore the believer must obey. Second, the rule of law serves the good of the whole. Third, which is a subset of the second justification, true or real liberty cannot be achieved in the absence of the rule of law functioning in a system appointed by the people.

First, for many of the preachers in the 18th century, God was present in both types of government – civil and ecclesiastical – in the sense that God has instituted government and that reason is founded in God. In a strong challenge to the notion that church and state are completely separate, Charles Chauncy in 1747 rejected the notion that civil government is purely a "humane constitution." Rather, civil government arises out of reason and therefore is "essentially founded on the will of God. For the voice of reason is the voice of God." Indeed, God's hand is in the very institution of civil government.[180]

Applying these grounding principles, Elizur Goodrich preached in 1787 that "transgress[ing] the laws of society . . . [will] expose ourselves to the high displeasure of Almighty God."[181] In other words, the obligation to obey the law is not merely based on principles of reason, but rather is a directive from God.

Second, in contemporary debate, the argument is oft raised that churches and their believers have a right to be left alone by the law, to isolate themselves from the community, in effect. Indeed, one of the most common justifications used to defend mandatory judicial exemptions is that the law should leave religious believers alone. In other words, no regulation affecting religion should be the baseline.[182] That was not the framing generation's vision.

This is a world view that would have been alien to the religious leaders of the latter half of the 18th-century. It is as though history is being read through the anachronistic prism of Brandeis's famous 20th-century argument for the "right to be let alone."[183] By contrast, in the 18th-century sermons, there was a strong focus on the importance of believers contributing to the greater good and the community at large. In Nathaniel Eells's words in 1743, "We are not made for our selves alone, but we are made to help in making the World better."[184] Parishioners were exhorted to "promot[e] the public peace and happiness," not just their private salvation. The failure to submit to the "just commands of the civil authority" was contrary to God's will and worked "an injury . . . to the community."[185]

On these terms, there would be no true liberty, but rather only anarchy, in the isolationist Brandeis-like vision. Thus, "[p]ublic good is not a term opposed to the good of individuals; on the contrary, it is the good of every individual collected." The Protestant preachers rejected the notion that Christians can live apart from society, isolated and not responsible for the common good. "'Let regard be had only to the good of the whole' was the constant exhortation by publicists and clergy."[186]

To secure true liberty, Christians were to be part of the tapestry of the society, contributing to its highest ends: peace, welfare, and security. "True liberty was 'natural liberty restrained in such manner, as to render society one great family; where every one must consult his neighbour's happiness, as well as his own.'"[187] Isaac Backus further explained the principle as follows: "Each rational soul, as he is a part of the whole system of rational beings, so it was and is, both his duty and his liberty to regard the good of the whole in all his actions."[188]

As parts of the fabric of society, Christians had obligations to ensure that the greater good was secured to the society as a whole in many categories. In Jonas Clarke's words,

> In a word, as by the social compact, the whole is engaged for the protection and defense of the life, liberty and property of each individual; so each individual owes all that he hath, even life itself, to the support, protection and defence of the whole, when the exigencies of the state require it. And no man, whether in authority or subordination, can justly excuse himself from any duty, service or exertions, in peace or war, that may be necessary for the publick peace, liberty, safety or defense, when lawfully and constitutionally called thereto.[189]

The alternative to this vision was anarchy, division, and war. Thus, God's directive to seek peace was to be achieved by the body of Christians operating as a community together pursuing the common good.

Late in the 18th century, Jonathan Edwards reaffirmed this view of Christian community with an obligation to the common good: "it especially becomes this [Christian family], visibly to unite, and expressly to agree together in prayer to God for the common prosperity."[190] Under this understanding, believers were obliged not simply to look after their own interests and to follow duly enacted law, but rather to embrace the needs of the polity as a whole as part of the Christian mission here on earth.

Third, real liberty was to be achieved through obedience to law as well as the good of the whole. John Witherspoon taught his students, a number of whom later became Framers, including James Madison, at the Presbyterian College of New Jersey, now Princeton University, that the "true notion of liberty is the prevalence of law and order, and the security of individuals."[191] The various 18th-century sermons state that liberty from the law of a legitimate government is no liberty at all. Government is necessary and obedience to just laws is necessary for there to be "real liberty." Indeed, "it is so far from being necessary for any man to give up any part of his real liberty in order to submit to government, that all nations have found it necessary to submit to some government in order to enjoy any liberty and security at all."[192]

The peace and good order imposed by a just government, that is, one chosen by the people, was not to be undermined by the religious believer. "[W]hen a man adopts such notions as, in their practice, counteract the peace and good order of society, he then perverts and abuses the original liberty of man, and were he to suffer for thus disturbing the peace of the community, and injuring his fellow-citizens, his punishment would be inflicted not for the exercise of a virtuous principle of conscience, but for violating that universal law of rectitude and benevolence which was intended to prevent one man from injuring another."[193]

Thus, the laws ensuring peace, tranquility, and order obligated the believer and trumped counterinstincts for the purpose of achieving the fullest liberty. "It is true, the interests of society require subordination, but this deprives none of liberty, but helps all to enjoy it better."[194]

Finally, the framing generation believed that conduct, even when religiously motivated, was regulable by the state in the interest of others. One of the most interesting aspects of the sermons, taken as a whole, is that they are consistent in naming the arenas over which the church has complete control as they leave the achievement of peace and order to the civil government. The churches' domain included the "power to make or ordain articles of faith, creeds, forms of worship or church government."[195] Conversely, "[t]he duty of magistrates is not to judge of the divinity or tendency of doctrines"[196] but rather to constrain actions that harm others and the public good. "[D]isturbers . . . ought to be punished."[197]

The ecclesiastical domain ended and the civil domain appropriately held sway when the beliefs, faith, worship, and church governance turned into "overt acts of violence [or effect]."[198] So even when overt acts involved the subject areas of ecclesiastical government, the civil authority permissibly dominated. Thus, religious defenses to a wide range of antisocial conduct, such as "murder, theft, adultery, false witness, and injuring our neighbor, either in person, name, or estate" were immoral or irreligious or both.[199] One sermon explained as follows:

> A Shaking-Quaker, in a violent manner, cast his wife into a mill-pond in cold weather; his plea was, that God ordered him so to do. Now the question is, Ought he not to be punished as much as if he had done the deed in anger? Was not the abuse to the woman as great? Could the magistrate perfectly know whether it was God, Satan, or ill-will, that prompted him to do the deed? The answers to these questions are easy.

> In the year of 1784, Matthew Womble, of Virginia, killed his wife and four sons, in obedience to the Shining One . . . to merit heaven by the action. . . . Neither his motive, which was obedience, nor his object, which was the salvation of his soul had any weight on the jury.[200]

In other words, actions taken in contravention of public peace and safety, under a civil government chosen by the people, left the perpetrator, even if a religious believer, vulnerable to civil action.[201] "The subjects of the kingdom of Christ, claim no exemption from the just authority of the magistrate, by virtue of their relation to it. Rather they yield a ready and cheerful obedience, not only for wrath, but also for conscience sake. And should any of them violate the laws of the state, they are to be punished as other men."[202]

The portrait of society painted by the sermons of the 18th century brought Christians from a wide sweep of denominations under a shared horizon of working toward the public good in concert with the government, a task that required obedience to duly enacted law governing actions. Backus captured this worldview when he explained that religious believers had "an unalienable right to act in all religious affairs according to the full persuasion of his own mind, where others are not injured thereby."[203]

In sum, the no-harm principle was widely accepted, especially among religious believers, clergy, and political leaders at the time of the framing. The arguments[204] that have been made for a mandatory constitutional right to avoid the application of the law to religious conduct simply cannot be supported.[205] Religious autonomy – in the sense of an independent power to act outside the law – was not part of the Framers' intent or of the framing generation's understanding, not to mention the vast majority – and the best – of the Supreme Court's free-exercise jurisprudence.[206]

As Justice Scalia reasoned in *Boerne*, the most plausible reading of early free-exercise enactments is a "virtual restatement of *Smith*:"[207] He correctly pointed to the many state constitutional provisos that imposed the public interest in safety, health, and welfare on religious conduct. These important public safeguards transcended absolute liberty from the beginning in the United States:

> Religious exercise shall be permitted *so long as it does not violate general laws governing conduct.* The "provisos" in the enactments negate a license to act in a manner "unfaithful to the Lord Proprietary" (Maryland Act Concerning Religion of 1649), or "behave" in other than a "peaceable and quiet" manner (Rhode Island Charter of 1663), or "disturb the public peace" (New Hampshire Constitution), or interfere with the "peace [and] safety of the State" (New York, Maryland, and Georgia Constitutions), or "demean" oneself in other than a "peaceable and orderly manner" (Northwest Ordinance of 1787). See *post*, at 8–12. At the time these provisos were enacted, keeping "peace" and "order" seems to have meant, precisely, obeying the laws.[208]

In fact, "[e]very breach of law is against the peace."[209]

*Conclusion*

The notion of religious autonomy starts at the wrong end when it begins – and certainly when it ends – with only a discussion of what the church or religious individual needs or demands.[210] That was the focus in Britain between the 12th and 16th centuries, but it has long been rejected, except by those few who would return the United States to a system of preferences for religious entities.

The elimination of religious sovereign power by definition made religious institutions private, and therefore on a more equal footing with other private entities. As such, they must be checked by the law. The constitutionally relevant question is not what is best for any church – indeed that question is forbidden by the neutrality principle underlying the Establishment Clause.[211] The proper question instead is whether the liberty accorded is consonant with the no-harm principle. If so, the public good has been properly served, because both liberty and order have been taken into account. If not, the public good – and therefore the constitutional order – has been subverted. As the no-harm principle has developed over the centuries, it has become an insuperable barrier for the claim that the Constitution can or should place religious entities above the law.

The current revelations of worldwide childhood sexual abuse by clergy, when combined with the concomitant secret knowledge of their individual religious institutions, reinforces what the founders of this country knew in the 17th and 18th centuries: religious entities often will abuse what power they have. To set aside the law for them without consideration of the public good is to choose liberty at the expense of order and to make society responsible for the harm they can cause. The right free exercise doctrine gives a wide berth to religious belief, but follows the rule that no American may act in ways that harm others without consequence.

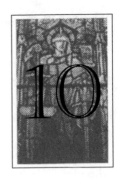

# THE PATH TO THE PUBLIC GOOD

Were all religious institutions and individuals always beneficial to the public, this book would not be needed. The rule would be plain: Religious liberty is absolute. Religious entities would not need to be deterred from criminal or tortious behavior. The purpose of this book has been to explain why even religious individuals and institutions must be governed by duly enacted laws.

The logistics of the landmark *Boerne v. Flores*[1] case, discussed in chapter 8, brought me into contact with the many groups in this society that lobby against damaging religious conduct, like the American Academy of Pediatrics, Children's Healthcare Is a Legal Duty (CHILD), district attorneys, and state regulatory agencies. Getting to know them educated me in two ways. First, I learned that my original theory of free exercise that would have excused religious entities from the vast majority of laws was patently absurd. It was a product of the ivory tower – a theory based on ignorance of religious conduct. As I soon came to recognize, I (like many Americans) was a Pollyanna when it came to religion.

Second, I came to see what I could not see before. Religious conduct in the United States (and around the world) had an underbelly few knew about, fewer discussed, and even fewer discussed publicly. It was Aristotle who said: "We have to learn before we can do . . . we learn by doing."[2] My experience with RFRA – which covered every law in the United States and therefore affected every possible victim of religious entities – forced my eyes open and led me to comprehend that the widespread cultural presupposition that religion is inherently and always good for society is baseless. The "religion" that should be freed from legal constraints was a chimera: beautiful and comforting, but distinct from reality. In the final analysis, a theory of religious liberty cannot sustain itself unless it factors in the possibility of heinous harms by religious individuals and institutions, some of which are detailed in Part One.

It is a simple fact that religious entities are not invariably beneficial. As Part One shows, religious entities can be responsible for lethal medical neglect of children, childhood sexual abuse, the takeover of neighboring property owners' rights under the zoning laws, and the undermining of civil rights laws, among other conduct. Unfortunately, religion is often used (or misused) to harm others. These behaviors are intolerable in a civil and civilized society, and the state must have the power to deter and punish them. The proper default rule subjects the religious to general constraints on harmful behavior.

In essence, I am arguing for the application of the rule of law to religious entities as it is applied to all others. The governing law should not be one that any one individual decides according to his or her own perspective, but rather a set of laws created by duly enacted legislatures charged with consideration of the public good. It is a simple and a profound principle, but in this context it has been muddied by legal battles and special interests.

The hard question that has been at the heart of the religious debate since the 1960s is when, if ever, a religious individual or institution should be given freedom from the general law. As explained in chapter 8, the typical rule at the Supreme Court has been that neutral, general laws apply to everyone, religious or not. And that is the right default rule.

Many, however, have argued that the law should not encumber religious conduct unless it is an extremely important law. For them, *Wisconsin v. Yoder*[3] was rightly decided, and the courts should scrutinize the legislature's enactments to determine whether they are important enough to trump religious conduct. The net result is unacceptable: religious entities have broad sway to violate the vast majority of laws and the courts determine which legislation is important and which is not, according to their own lights. For those who understand the capacity of religious individuals and institutions to hurt others, the notion that religious entities ought to trump all but the most necessary laws is unacceptable. Moreover, the courts are not equipped to make relative determinations about social policy regulating conduct.

Even so, it is the rare individual who would jettison religious liberty altogether. Some modern scholars have tried, by reducing religious liberty to equality. Nonetheless, that approach fails to take into account the potent and distinctive drive of religious belief in every human society and its distinctive value for society. While the courts should not have the power to pick and choose between the laws that affect religious conduct, there should be some mechanism where the government can take into account the inherent value of religious liberty and weigh that value against the impact on the public good of letting the religious entity avoid the law. If an exemption will not harm others, it should be provided – by a legislature.

This final chapter lays out the three necessary conditions for legitimate religious accommodation. Exempting religious conduct from neutral, general laws must be (1) duly enacted by a legislature, not decreed by a court; (2) must be debated under the harsh glare of public scrutiny; and (3) must be consistent with the larger public good. Where the burden on religious conduct can be lifted by the legislature with only de minimis harm to the public, there is good reason to accommodate the religious conduct. But where the religious conduct harms others, accommodation is not consistent with the public good, and the exemption is likely a legislative sellout that shortchanges important interests in society and that violates the Establishment Clause. This is the permissive accommodation rule that fits with the larger constitutional scheme and honors both religious liberty and the obligation of the government to protect citizens from harm.

*Religious conduct in the context of the Constitution's structure*

Freedom of religion is an integral part of the Constitution, not a principle somehow divorced from the rest of the document. The same underlying principles that drove the Framers' other choices also set in motion their placement of religion within American society. Any theory of the First Amendment that fails to take into account the Constitution's larger structure is not complete.

One principle infused throughout the Constitution is distrust of the powerful. The Framers believed that every individual and every institution holding power was likely to abuse that power.[4] They did not trust the King, the executive, the legislatures, and even the people, and therefore no single entity could be trusted to govern. Distrust led the Framers to the checks and balances that are now so familiar. The three branches – legislative, executive, and judicial – were to check each other, and the federal and state governments were mutual checks.[5]

It should come as no surprise that the Framers started from a position of distrust. The years between the Declaration of Independence and the Constitutional Convention were years of disillusionment. The Declaration was an ebullient Enlightenment document that reflected the freed colonists' optimism about the future after breaking ties with the British monarchy and Parliament. There was widespread hope and expectation that they would institute the first truly successful republican form of government the world had seen. The Articles of Confederation established 13 separate states, asserting "Each state retains its sovereignty, freedom, and independence, and every power, jurisdiction, and right, which is not by this Confederation expressly delegated to the United States, in Congress assembled."[6] Because the Continental Congress had no power to force states to do other than they desired, the Articles recognized 13 wholly independent sovereigns. To say that the state governments that followed did not deliver on the Declaration's hopes is to severely understate the matter. Because of their distrust of the king, the newly formed states disabled their governors and therefore placed virtually all governing authority into the hands of the state legislatures.

That move would teach them the hard lesson that unchecked power is abused power. In the face of crushing trade and monetary problems, the states were incapable of acting in the interest of the public and even more incapable of coordinating themselves, thus provoking the ineffectual Continental Congress to eventually disband in the mid-1780s.[7] The result was that the unchecked state legislatures descended into vortices of corruption that rendered laws for individuals but failed abysmally to address the pressing needs of the times, from mass forfeitures to a lack of stable currency to a failure of trade or military coordination.[8] The result was a descent into discord between the states, as the new citizens came to distrust the governing structures they had built. The fall from high hopes to failure led to desperate measures. The famous Shays' Rebellion (where distinguished Revolutionary veterans took up arms against their own relatively new state governments) was just one symptom of the severe failure of governance.[9] The Framers gathered at the Constitutional Convention because a more suitable government was necessary, and the focus of the debate was on how to stem the human impulse to abuse power in ways that harm the public interest.[10] The Constitution's republican, or representative, structure was chosen and crafted for the purpose of making representatives accountable to the public good.[11]

As if the post-Revolutionary disappointments would not have been enough, the framing generation was predisposed to distrust the exercise of power by humans, because so many were Protestant and a significant percentage of those were Calvinist. Protestantism rested on the premise that governing institutions, even the Church, were capable of being corrupted. The Calvinists, whose theological worldview was dominant at the time,[12] held the paradoxical belief that all men were corrupt but that their inclinations to abuse power could be deterred by well-crafted governing structures. Calvin himself suggested fixing the corrupt Catholic Church in the 16th century by transforming it from an absolute monarchy into a representative structure, where the people would have some say over their ministers.[13]

When the First Amendment was amended to the Constitution, the same principle of distrust found its way into the document. The First Amendment's Establishment Clause, which states: "Congress shall make no law respecting an establishment of religion . . ."[14] is an explicit check on the power of religion in the political sphere. At a very minimum, it means no religious institution will hold governing power.

Following the historical developments detailed in chapter 9, the Framers made a conscious decision that religion and the state could not be co-sovereigns.[15] The combination of their power was the definition of tyranny.[16] This principle has crossed national boundaries and become a bellwether for freedom. Leading Middle East scholar Bernard Lewis explained it as follows: "Separation [of church and state] . . . was designed to prevent two things: the use of religion by the state to reinforce and extend its authority and the use of state power by the clergy to impose their doctrines and rules on others."[17]

By denying religion the constitutional authority to rule, the Constitution privatized religion. There would be two sovereigns, but they were secular governments: the state and the federal. That does not mean that religion lost social power. It could and would still occupy the bully pulpit and use its influence among the people and in the legislatures to shape public policy, but it could not be government itself.

The Establishment Clause's prohibition of religious sovereignty is inadequate by itself to ensure that religious entities do not undermine the public good. By privatizing religion and protecting the right of conscience, the First Amendment instigated a teeming marketplace of belief. Religious views compete with other religious views in the public square, and influence not only the people but also government and public policy. The privatization of religion also raised an important issue. If they were not sovereign and therefore could not be checked by the Constitution's internal structures (like the three branches and the two sovereigns – state and federal – established), what would keep any one or any group of religions from harming others? The answer is that religious entities must be checked as are all other private entities – by the rule of law.

The end, perhaps the inexorable, result of the privatization of religion in the United States is the rule that religious conduct is properly subject to "neutral principles of law."[18] The Supreme Court in 1971 explained the principle as follows: "Our cases do not at their farthest reach support the proposition that a stance of conscientious opposition relieves an objector from any colliding duty fixed by a democratic government."[19] In other words, when a democratic government passes a law, that law is as binding on religious conduct as it is on secular conduct.

Some will persist in asking: If religious freedom is a precious right in the United States, why force religious believers to be governed by laws that conflict with their beliefs? The answer is that the duties created by a democratic government – the law – are created for the purpose of furthering the public good, which is served when bad actors are deterred from harming others and punished if they do. When religious believers avoid laws enacted in light of the public good, they undermine the public policy that led to the law. Every civilized society recognizes the rule of no harm, and none can afford to give individuals the right to harm others just because they are religiously motivated.

Those who would place religious believers above or outside the law start at the wrong end when they begin their analysis – and certainly when they end it – with only a discussion of what the religious entity needs or demands.[20] The constitutionally relevant question is not what is best for any church. Indeed that question is forbidden by the neutrality principle underlying the Establishment Clause.[21] Instead, representatives must consider whether the liberty accorded is consonant with the no-harm rule. If so, the public good has been properly served. If not, the public good, and therefore the constitutional order, has been subverted. Both values – liberty and no harm to others – are absolutely necessary elements of any First Amendment calculus. The no-harm rule is a restatement of the Supreme Court's rule – from *Reynolds v. United States* to *Gillette v. United States* to *Employment Division v. Smith, Boerne v. Flores,* and *Locke v. Davey* – that religious entities are subject to neutral, generally applicable laws.

The typical answer to this analysis is that legislatures often pass laws that are nonsensical, unnecessary, and just plain political, so why should religious entities have to subvert their religious conduct in the face of such laws? Moreover, the explosive growth in regulation since the time of the framing surely argues against applying the law to religious believers, because there is a lot more law now than there was then. Therefore religious believers are far more burdened by laws today than they were in the past, or so the argument goes.

The questions are fair and deserve a response, but they do not undermine the argument for applying duly enacted laws to religious entities. In a perfect world, with legislatures operating as the Framers intended them to, legislatures are focused only on the public good and only enact laws to serve the public good. In that perfect world, legislators make independent judgments in the interest of the public good. Moreover, they only enact laws that actually serve a public interest. Were the world and legislators perfect, the application of neutral laws to religious entities would be justified in every instance.

This is far from a perfect world, however, and legislatures have passed laws that are ill-conceived. Moreover, the impact of a law often cannot be assessed until the law is in place, so a well-intentioned law may generate effects that were not considered when it was passed. For these reasons, religious believers who find their religiously motivated conduct substantially burdened by a law should be able to ask for relief. That is not to say they have a constitutional right to relief. Most laws are intended to prevent or deter some harm, so letting a religious entity violate the law may well harm others. It is up to the discretion of the legislature, which has the tools – including the power to commission studies, investigate issues, and hold public hearings – to consider the accommodation request in light of the public interest.

When approached by the religious believer or institution, the legislature can consider anew the need for the law, including what harm it was intended to prevent, and then assess the impact a religious believer's exemption would have on others and society as a whole. It is a matter of line drawing. When the harm to others is de minimis with the exemption, religious believers should be granted the exemption.

There are numerous exemptions that pass this test. The peyote exemptions are an excellent example of well-crafted relief. State and federal exemptions lift the drug laws to permit individuals to use peyote for religious purposes. Peyote is used during Native American Church ceremonies, and was the conduct at stake in *Smith*. The *Smith* Court condoned peyote exemptions as it made clear they were not constitutionally required.[22] The Drug Enforcement Agency's dossier on the drug notes that, "While peyote produced rich visual hallucinations that were important to the native peyote cults, the full spectrum of effects served as a chemically induced model of mental illness."[23] If used recreationally, users could be a danger to others if they operated machinery, or drove a car, or cared for children. Therefore, both the federal and state governments are well within their power to prohibit it, and therefore it can be applied to religious entities. That was in fact the holding of *Smith*.

At the same time, peyote is a drug that is not widely abused, because it frequently fails to produce the desired effect and not infrequently leaves its users with a headache or nausea. Nor do small amounts trigger addiction. The difficulty involved in peyote cultivation makes it highly unlikely that its use could become widespread. Unlike heroin, cocaine, or crack, an exemption for peyote is unlikely to increase the number of addicts or to foster an illegal drug trade independent of the religious purpose. Moreover, it is used for religious purposes in overnight ceremonies, and therefore it is unlikely religious users will drive while impaired. By permitting religious believers to use it for their ceremonies, the state is still adequately protecting others from harm.

A second example of a praiseworthy exemption is the exemption for the sacred use of communion wine during the United States' doomed-to-failure attempt to prohibit alcohol use during Prohibition.[24] The small amounts of wine used during communion did not introduce the harm to society that Prohibition was designed to prevent. Proponents of the 18th Amendment such as Carry Nation and East Coast industrialists pointed to improved worker reliability, morals, and family life to justify the total prohibition on alcohol.[25] The religious use of wine was no threat to those principles.

A third example involves the armed services. There was a time when no member of the military could wear any headgear other than that prescribed by the government. Orthodox Jewish men found that it substantially burdened their belief in wearing a yarmulke. When the Supreme Court was asked to invalidate the law under the Free Exercise Clause, it refused to do so, saying "The desirability of dress regulations in the military is decided by the appropriate military officials, and they are under no constitutional mandate to abandon their considered professional judgment. . . . [T]he First Amendment does not require the military to accommodate such practices in the face of its view that they would detract from the uniformity sought by the dress regulations."[26] The Orthodox Jews turned to Congress and asked for an exemption. Clearly, the addition of a yarmulke to a serviceman's uniform, conceivably the most unobtrusive headgear available, would not severely impact on the operation of the military. Congress weighed the necessity of the rule against the potential harm to the public if an exemption was created for religious headgear, and quite rationally chose the exemption and enacted a nuanced response that accommodated religious liberty to maximum extent while serving the public good as much as possible. It was a solution to the problem that would have been beyond the courts' ability. Members of the armed forces were permitted to wear "religious apparel" with exceptions where there was a determination that the item interfered "with the performance of the member's military duties" or if it is not "neat and conservative."[27] Today, Orthodox Jewish males in the military routinely wear yarmulkes. Where the headgear interferes with combat uniforms, however, as in the case of a Sikh turban, the Navy was permitted to ban it.[28]

With Title VII in 1964, Congress crafted an exemption for religious personnel engaged in "religious activities" from the antidiscrimination laws.[29] The law prevents ridiculous results. For example, Orthodox Jews can not be forced to hire Baptists to be rabbis nor can Pentecostalists be forced to hire Islamicists as pastors, etc. Without the exemption, religious institutions' very belief systems are at risk of the anti-discrimination laws. Nor does the exemption breach the public good, because there is a small likelihood that a Baptist would even want to be a rabbi, let alone be interested in taking legal action if not hired.[30]

The exemption was expanded beyond clergy in 1972, raising closer questions of constitutionality and the public interest.[31] A building engineer at a facility run by the Church of Jesus Christ of Latter-Day Saints challenged the exemption as the lead plaintiff in a class action. He claimed discrimination when the Mormons fired him because he could not qualify as a member in good standing of the Church. The intuitive point was that janitors are not clergy. The Supreme Court, though, upheld the exemption, finding that it did not violate the Establishment Clause, because there was more danger of violating the separation of church and state if the state imposed such laws on religious entities than if it did not.[32] On this ground, the decision made sense, especially in light of the huge variety of religious practices. Hierarchical churches were well-protected under the first exemption, but religious entities that recognize all or some of their members as clergy, (e.g., the Quakers, the Jehovah's Witnesses, or the Mormons) could force the courts to determine whether the employee was "really" a clergy member, which is an inquiry into solely ecclesiastical belief, and that is forbidden under settled Supreme Court precedent.[33]

Finally, the federal government has provided an exemption from the military draft since the earliest years of the republic, for those who have a conscientious objection to war.[34] Quakers during the earliest conflicts dissented from military duty.[35] The exemption has been upheld for religious as well as nonreligious objectors.[36] Such objectors are not relieved of government service during wartime altogether, but rather are required "to perform . . . such civilian work contributing to the maintenance of the national health, safety, or interest as the local board pursuant to Presidential regulations may deem appropriate."[37] Congress's determination is respectful of religious beliefs that have long been a part of U.S. culture, but more importantly it is also a conclusion that is consistent with the larger public good. Religious entities are not permitted to use their religious beliefs to avoid their obligation to serve the war effort, but rather are moved to other positions that will accomplish the same end through different work. That is good for the religious believer, but it also is good for the country.

*Contrary to popular belief, in the United States, the legislature is not a majoritarian institution*

The most common objection to the scheme I am advocating is that the legislature will do nothing for minority religions. That objection, though, stems from a pervasive, but false understanding of representative democracy in the United States and from an underestimation of the power religious entities have wielded. So-called minority religions are not necessarily or even usually consigned to a life of belief divorced from action under a republican form of government. To understand why, it is necessary to explain the main features of the U.S. representative form of government.

At the Constitutional Convention, Pennsylvania's James Wilson, perhaps the most brilliant man there, opined that he could not abandon "his judgment to any supposed objections that might arise among the people" because he had been charged with doing what was in their interest. His frame of reference in crafting the Constitution was the public good, not public sentiment. He wondered aloud, "what he should say to his constituents in case they should call upon him to tell them why he sacrificed his own judgment in a case where they authorized him to exercise it?" If he told them he was simply "flatter[ing] their prejudices" he expected them to "retort: did you suppose the people of Penn[sylvania] had not good sense enough to receive a good Government?"[38] In short, he was sent to the Convention to reach a result in the public's interest, not according to the public's predilections at the time.

The system simultaneously frees the representatives to do what is best for the country – even if the people do not fully comprehend the issues or agree on the course taken – but it also imposes the difficult burden on elected representatives to make independent decisions in the larger public interest. For the representative, it would be far simpler to follow the dictates of his or her constituents. Because representatives are the trustees of the people's interest, and are supposed to take into account far more than the majority's preferences, history – not numbers – is the ultimate judge of any elected official in the United States.

Majorities elect representatives, but after the election, those representatives have substantial latitude to listen to minority interests, and in fact do.[39] The legislature is constructed so that legislators are not subject to the unfettered will of the people, but rather free to do what they believe is right, even when the majority disagree. "Republican liberty signifies government in pursuit of the common good, where no citizen is subjected to the unfettered will of another. The central meaning of republican government since Cicero has been legislation for the 'res publica' or common good of the people."[40]

As proof that U.S. citizens continue to believe in republicanism, one of the most common complaints about Congress is that it is "captured" by special interests, which are not representative of the people and which operate within their own narrow self-interest. This objection is commonly raised by those who believe their representatives have a duty to consider a larger public good than any one entity's entreaties.

For example, a significant majority of the American public in the 1960s was prejudiced against racial minorities. The South practiced an entrenched racism that is shocking to our children. Blacks were relegated to particular restaurants, restrooms, and occupations. Numerous states imposed "poll taxes," "grandfather clauses," or literacy requirements for the very purpose of excluding racial minorities from the voting booth.[41] In the wake of *Brown v. Board of Education*,[42] in which the Supreme Court required the desegregation of public schools, public officials and townspeople took extreme measures, including closing down public schools, to avoid the Court's mandate.[43] The racial war was played out on the television every night. Racism was not limited to the South, of course. Desegregation had to be court-ordered in Boston,[44] Denver,[45] and Detroit,[46] and Hispanics found themselves blocked from the voting booth in New York, because they did not speak English.[47] Many states had bans on interracial marriage until these laws were declared unconstitutional in 1967.[48] Race-based housing discrimination was given a judicial imprimatur in 1948,[49] and was not declared unconstitutional for nearly two decades.[50] The majority was prejudiced, but the federal government still fought discrimination, as discussed in chapter 8.

There is a form of democracy where legislation is driven by majorities, but it is not the constitutional order in the United States. It is called direct or pure democracy. The most familiar example is the town-meeting style government of some New England towns, for example, Marshfield, Massachusetts.[51] The Framers were certainly familiar with such a brand of democracy, in New England as well as Greece. But this form of government was definitively rejected by them, because they deeply distrusted what they considered "mob rule," a view that was informed by the experiences under the Articles of Confederation and the state constitutions that gave the people the right to instruct their representatives. Instead, they opted for representative democracy, wherein the people choose representatives, but do not control their public policy decisions during the term of office.[52]

To be a representative in the U.S. system requires courage and vision, because it is the representative who is responsible for the quality of the common good, and who will be judged accordingly. They have to choose between popularity and good results, which is a real choice, because good results will make them popular even if in the short term they are not. In fact, the work of the brilliant political scientist Mancur Olson showed that cohesive minorities with a clear message fare significantly better in the legislature than do amorphous majorities – a political fact that is now widely accepted.[53] This political fact is why lobbyists representing the disabled, and homosexuals, and racial minorities have done as well as they have at both the state and federal level. If majorities of citizens drove legislative results, none of those reforms would have been likely, because each places a burden on some powerful element in the majority. "The purpose of popular sovereignty is not to subject individuals to the will of the nation, but to protect all citizens from subjection to anyone's will, by coordinating the whole in pursuit of the common good."[54]

*Why representative democracy opens the door for small*
*as well as powerful religions*

For the following reasons, the oppressed minority religion argument is a red herring. First, the use of the term "minority," which conjures up invidious discrimination, is somewhat misleading. In the United States, there is no majority religion. Protestantism, taken as a whole, which would encompass a vast number of faiths, is a dwindling majority, and will not be the majority religion in the very near future.[55]

Second, as Part One illustrated, smaller religions have done quite well in obtaining exemptions in the legislatures – sometimes too well – which would seem to weaken the argument significantly.[56] The often-stated concern that the courts are the better institution to secure religious liberty because they are better than legislatures at protecting minorities has not been proven as an empirical matter.

Third, as discussed above, it is a misconception of the U.S. republican form of government to think of it as a majoritarian system. A majority of the people chooses their rulers, but those rulers are then set free from the majority to rule in the public good.[57] There is communication throughout the term of service to be sure, but citizens only directly affect government when they choose their representatives.

During the term of representation, majority views do not necessarily prevail, and small groups do quite well. Political scientists now accept as fact that minorities with a coherent message even tend to fare better in the legislative process than unorganized majorities.[58]

Fourth, the argument seems to be that small religions will be subject to covert and inevitable discrimination, but that is already redressed by the Religion Clauses, which discourage legislatures from acting on such motives. For example, any law specifically singling out a particular religious organization for detrimental treatment is unconstitutional. Besides, as a matter of fact, in the legislative process, the scale has definitely been weighted on the side favoring smaller religions, who have obtained the various exemptions and special treatment detailed in Part One. In addition, there is some insurance against discrimination under the *Smith* formulation favoring neutral, generally applicable laws, which drives legislatures toward general prohibitions. Where the legislature has decided that particular actions are unacceptable, because they generate certain harm, and issued a blanket prohibition on the action, there is some insurance that the legislature has not acted out of discriminatory motive. The willingness to burden all actors with the law means that the legislature is concerned about the harm, not the identity of the actor.

Fifth, the constitutional culture weighs against such discrimination, at least as compared to other Western democracies. The most entrenched constitutional right in the United States is the absolute right to believe anything at all. The result is the most pluralistic religious culture in history, with new faiths appearing all the time.[59] In that context, unusual faiths are a commonplace in the American experience, and hardly an automatic target for negative treatment by the legislature. Add to that a history that never recognized a national established religion and such discrimination seems even less likely. In the United States, no particular religion has ever been able to obtain singular privileges for itself, and therefore all religions are "outside" the government. The same cannot be said for Europe, where new or upstart religions have experienced difficulties. "Although many European constitutions ostensibly grant rights to religious minorities, the existence of dominant religions in the European States forces the remaining confessions into a hierarchy, the bottom tier of which may only legally exercise those rights by engaging in practices that conform to the doctrines of the dominant religions."[60]

Even then, perhaps there is a risk that some small, politically powerless religions that are incapable of putting together a coherent message for the legislature or incapable of enlisting the support of mainstream religions may well have problems obtaining exemptions. The system does not generate perfect results, no matter how exemptions are handled. In the end, the *Smith* Court correctly weighed the alternatives in this scenario as follows:

> It may fairly be said that leaving accommodation to the political process will place at a relative disadvantage those religious practices that are not widely engaged in; but that unavoidable consequence of democratic government must be preferred to a system in which each conscience is a law unto itself or in which judges weigh the social importance of all laws against the centrality of all religious beliefs.[61]

The legislature is institutionally competent to hear the concerns of the burdened religious entities and to make the determination whether relieving them of an obligation to a particular law is consistent with the public good. Thus, the route for those individuals and institutions that find their religious conduct at odds with the prevailing law lies beyond the courts. The Supreme Court in *Smith* made it clear that religious entities may ask for legislative exemptions narrowly tailored to their religious practices.[62] If a religious entity can persuade a legislature (that is doing its job and serving the public good) that exempting it from the law will not harm the public good, then an exemption is consistent with ordered democracy.[63] If not, then the religious entity is rightly prevented from doing the harm proscribed by the legislature.

*The arguments raised in the wake of* Employment Division v. Smith

Many scholars and religious organizations roundly criticized the *Smith* Court's reaffirmation of the rule of law for religious entities. *Smith* said "Our decisions reveal that the [correct] reading [of the Free Exercise Clause] is... [that] [w]e have never held that an individual's religious beliefs excuse him from compliance with an otherwise valid law prohibiting conduct that the State is free to regulate."[64] For Professor Douglas Laycock, the architect of RFRA, replies:

> The most important religious conflict in the United States is not the conflict of one religion against another, but of the secular against the religious. On one side are all those people who take religion quite seriously, for whom religion still makes a substantial difference in their lives. On the other side are all those people who do not take religion seriously, who cannot imagine why these superstitions persist, and who cannot understand why religious minorities are demanding special treatment from the secular administrative state.[65]

Laycock, however, has manufactured religion's enemies. Everyone in this culture takes religion seriously, because they must. There is no denying it – religious belief led to 9/11; was the force behind Alabama Justice Roy Moore, who, at his own expense, placed a granite monument to the Ten Commandments in a public courthouse; and is the basis for the most important rites of passage – baptisms, weddings, and funerals.

Eighty-five percent of the country professes some sort of religious belief.[66] Even atheists, agnostics, and humanists have to take it very seriously, because it affects so many elements of their lives.

Laycock is also fundamentally wrong about the conflict between religions. On the one hand, this society has done a remarkable job of welcoming an ever-growing and enormous collection of religions – literally tens if not hundreds of thousands. But on the other hand, because of the nature of religious faith and its truth claims, there is always the potential for conflict between religious believers. In fact, those conflicts are heightened as religious entities are given more power to trump the laws that govern everyone else. For example, the Religious Land Use and Institutionalized Persons Act (RLUIPA) has led to the sort of religious tension Professor Laycock, and probably many others, believes has been stilled. When a religious landowner in a residential neighborhood decides to install a homeless shelter, a large day-care center, or an additional story that will block the homeowner's views, frequently the religious landowner takes one or both of the following tacks during the zoning process: (1) the project must take priority over its neighbors' interests, because it has been directed by higher forces, that is, the project's purposes are superior to the concerns of the average homeowners; or (2) the neighbors objecting are simply anti-fundamentalist Christian, -Semitic, -Muslim, and so forth. The claims lead to deep divisions between neighbors, because the odds are overwhelming that the neighbors objecting are religious in their own right and resent being told that their values are necessarily in conflict with "higher principles" or that they are opposed to any particular religion simply because they value their neighborhood's relative peace, safety, and aesthetics – all elements of the American dream. The bad feelings do not disappear once the case has been concluded, and too often, the religious division that was not there before the religious landowner invoked RLUIPA to trump his neighbor's property rights becomes a marked characteristic of the neighborhood. The likelihood in these scenarios – given the depth of the feeling on both sides – is that the neighborhood will become mono-religious or that an invisible divide between one religion and every other will make itself visible in times of political upheaval.

Professor (now federal appellate Judge) Michael McConnell responded to *Smith* with a full-dress parade of horribles, which are worth repeating here, because they bring into focus the Chicken Little quality of the post-*Smith* criticism:

> Consider the fact that employment discrimination laws could force the Roman Catholic Church to hire female priests, if there are no free exercise exemptions from generally applicable laws. Or that historic preservation laws could prevent churches from making theologically significant alterations to their structures. Or that prisons will not have to serve kosher or hallel food to Jewish or Moslem prisoners. Or that Jewish high school athletes may be forbidden to wear yarmulkes and thus excluded from inter-scholastic sports. Or that churches with a religious objection to unrepentant homosexuality will be required to retain an openly gay individual as church organist, parochial school teacher, or even a pastor. Or that public school students will be forced to attend sex education classes contrary to their faith. Or that religious sermons on issues of political significance could lead to revocation of tax exemptions. Or that Catholic doctors in public hospitals could be fired if they refuse to perform abortions. Or that Orthodox Jews could be required to cease and desist from sexual segregation of their places of worship.[67]

Fifteen years into *Smith's* reintroduction of the rule of law for religious entities, his list is more imagination than fact. Not only that, but it is based on a false assumption that this culture is hostile to religion. It is not, and the sky has not fallen. To my knowledge, no conservative church has been required to hire an organist or music director who was openly gay, and religious institutions have been permitted to deny employment to homosexuals.[68] Nor has the government entered orthodox temples and required the men to sit with the women. Churches have avoided land-marking laws that affect liturgy.[69] State legislatures have permitted children to opt out of sex education courses.[70] Courts have held that prison officials' refusal to provide kosher or Muslim diets was unreasonable.[71] No yarmulke-wearing athletes have been barred from the field. And since 2000, federal law exempts doctors with religious objections from being required to perform abortions.[72]

The issue regarding whether churches should be able to support particular political candidates and retain their tax-exempt status does not involve the impact of *Smith*. Rather, there is a federal law that does deny tax-exempt status when churches support political candidates.[73] The purpose of the law was to ensure that political action committees could not avoid taxes under the ruse of being a nonprofit, charitable organization. While the purpose made some sense, the impact on the political speech of religious institutions is not good for them or for society. U.S. citizens are better off knowing which candidates are being backed by particular religious powers, because religious entities are extremely active in the political process, and the people deserve to know which interests in the society are pressuring which representatives and on which issues. If nothing else, this book should make clear why backroom deals for religious institutions are just as inconsistent with the public good as backroom deals that favor businesses or interest groups.

In 1990, Stephen Carter published *The Culture of Disbelief: How American Law and Politics Trivialize Religious Devotion*, which argued that religious interests were being sidelined in the United States. He stated: "there is much depressing evidence that the religious voice is required to stay out of the public square."[74] The book was an influential bestseller, and even appears in the hand of President William Jefferson Clinton in Yale University's portrait of him. The problem with Professor Carter's thesis was that religious institutions were not politically powerless, but his thesis permitted them to exercise political power while appearing to be socially weak. Carter, of course, is not the only person who has argued that U.S. culture has been "secularized."[75] It's a dominant theme in contemporary culture, and one that fosters religious entities' political agendas rather nicely. In the midst of the rhetoric regarding secularization, it is easy to assume that religious institutions are either politically dormant or that they are politically ineffective, and therefore to think they need exemptions from the law, or for representatives to think they deserve special treatment. Neither is accurate. Jerry Falwell's Moral Majority in the 1970s was just one example of the many efforts by religious entities to influence the process. More recently, Catholics have formed Catholic Citizenship, which is intended to mobilize Catholic citizens. In the words of their executive director:

> Utilizing the Internet, the Catholic Citizenship network will be able to interact more effectively with our public officials. Thus, when vital issues arise, our network will be prepared to provide an immediate response to legislators – on the state or national level – and thereby more effectively strengthen the Catholic influence on the political process.[76]

In light of the political realities, I would back a Sunshine Law that would repeal the prohibition and encourage religious institutions to make their political agendas as public as possible, for reasons that should be apparent from Part One.[77]

The basic problem with McConnell's analysis is that it assumes that legislatures are inclined to suppress religious liberty, that religious lobbyists are weak in the legislative process, and that there are strong lobbies to achieve the anti-religion ends he cites. In fact, the contrary is true. Religious entities are uncannily able to obtain what they seek in the legislative context. As the *Smith* Court stated, "a society that believes in the negative protection accorded to religious belief can be expected to be solicitous of that value in its legislation as well."[78] Thus, the assumption among those opposing *Smith* that legislative accommodation would result in no accommodation was simply inaccurate. That is why Senator Hatch's declaration that without RFRA there would be no "basis to challenge Government regulations which infringe on the rights to the free exercise of religion" cannot be taken seriously.[79] It is hyperbole, and no more.

Also in response to *Smith*, McConnell further argued that the legislative process would be inimical to religious interests. According to McConnell, the Free Exercise Clause provides protection for those who lack "the ability to protect themselves in the political sphere" and for anyone who might find him or herself "caught in conflict with our secular political culture." The religious entity as weakling in the legislative process is simply not persuasive for all the reasons presented in this chapter, but McConnell makes a further mistake. In a claim typical of those who argue for expansive rights for the religious to avoid legal obligations, he talks about "our secular political culture."[80] What exactly is that? In the United States, the culture is not divorced from religion. Religion informs the beliefs of the vast majority of citizens and their leaders; the history of ideas that fed the culture's political institutions are rooted in no small part in theological constructs; and there is a healthy and vital public debate about religion and its role in society. Major newspapers have religion pages and religion news reporters, the radio air waves and cable television are filled with religious messages, and the war on terror has trained our attention – whether we like it or not – on the radical Islamicists' fanaticism and their theological worldview. Religion is quite literally inescapable. Some – the most prominent being Columbia's Professor Kent

Greenawalt – have argued that religious reasons should not be part of the debate over public policy.[81] It's an interesting theory, but utterly impossible. Religion cannot be avoided. There is no community without a house of worship, and typically there are many in any one town. There are approximately 325,000 houses of worship in the United States,[82] and just over 280 million people.[83] That is roughly one house of worship for every 860 people. Religion is everywhere, and any atheist will tell you that it is impossible to inhabit a "secular" political environment in the United States.

For Professor Steven Smith, "*Smith* reaches a low point in modern constitutional protection under the Free Exercise Clause" and results in the "withdrawal of constitutional protection for the free exercise of religion."[84] This is an exaggeration that underestimates the critical value of the anti-persecution principle and the existing legislative drive to provide for religious entities.

In sum, the passionate objections to *Smith* have turned out to be more passion than persuasion. Fifteen years later, there has been no decline in religious liberty or in religion's political power.

*Religious liberty is not simple (or even complex) equality*

Permissive legislative accommodation has not been the only theory that has led to a rejection of the special privileges for religion. With their typical eloquence, Professors Christopher Eisgruber and Lawrence Sager argue that religious liberty cannot mean privilege:

> At its core, religious liberty is about the toleration – the celebration – of the divergent ways that members of our society come to understand the foundational coordinates of a well-formed life. To single out one of the ways that persons come to understand what is important in life, and grant those who choose that way a license to disregard legal norms that the rest of us are obliged to obey, is to defeat rather than fulfill our commitment to toleration. Yet that favoritism is precisely what the privileging view of religious liberty requires. ... The problem lies not with religious liberty but with the paradigm of constitutional privilege and with the principle of unimpaired flourishing that paradigm sponsors.[85]

To this point, we are in complete agreement. They turn from this approach, however, to a concept of equality that is inadequate to the task of guiding legislatures and courts on the parameters of religious liberty. They advocate "equal regard," which requires "that government treat the deep, religiously inspired concerns of minority religious believers with the same regard as that enjoyed by the deep concerns of citizens generally."[86] At some level, their theory sounds like the Golden Rule: Do unto others as you would have them do unto you. The principle is strong in Western culture, but it does not provide adequate guidance to legislatures and courts faced with the question whether the right balance between religious liberty and order has been preserved.

For them, "[g]overnment betrays the ideal of equal regard when it treats religious interests less favorably than secular ones, when it treats some religious interests better than others, and when it treats religious interests more favorably than secular ones."[87] The first two principles are essential to the Religion Clauses, but the third brings legislative accommodation into question.

Equality fails on two grounds. First, as a matter of cultural description, religion is simply different from other deeply held convictions, because it is an illogical belief that defines an individual's entire worldview. Religion is about the search for the meaning of existence itself. History and fact show that it is capable of engendering the most passionate and the most violent positions. For this reason, it is accorded specific attention in the First Amendment, and needs to be addressed specifically.

Second, equality is a principle that is capable of taking the law to the lowest common denominator. For example, each of the Eisgruber/Sager principles stated above is satisfied by a law that throws all believers in jail, because they are all treated equally, but that surely is not the system of liberty envisioned by the Framers, current culture, or the authors. Equality simply is not enough. There must be a further principle, and I believe that principle is the republican form of government, which entails maximal liberty in light of the public good and the no-harm rule.

The equality position is more likely to result in less religious liberty, because the law must stay at the level of general applicability and cannot take into account the religious practices that are substantially burdened by the law. Religious exemptions from generally applicable, neutral laws do not treat religious and nonreligious reasons equally, because they only exempt the religious conduct, and therefore they violate the equal-regard principle. In the end, the Eisgruber/Sager thesis is in fact an argument for giving secular entities the same exemptions as the religious, and vice versa, and they have followed that tack in suggested legislation. In contrast, the public good analysis in this chapter leaves room for the religious entity to be free, as it ensures that that freedom is not had at the expense of others.

Because of religion's authoritarian force in so many people's lives, religion deserves separate treatment, and legislatures should be able to take that into account. Religious liberty needs to be a balance between liberty and the public good. Equality loses a great deal in translation, because it tends toward rote application of a single principle in a context where complex legislative judgment is necessary and the public good must be the polestar.

*The best path for religious liberty that preserves the public good: Permissive legislative accommodation*

There are three principles that make permissive legislative accommodation legitimate and worthy of the Constitution's system of ordered liberty.

**(1)** *Religious accommodation is a legislative, not a judicial, function.* There are some who see little functional difference between law made by a court and law made by a legislature. That is particularly true in the religious liberty context. For example, Judge Michael McConnell, when he was a law professor, papered over the constitutional distinctions between the legitimacy of legislative decisions and judicial decisions. For him, there was no meaningful distinction between an exemption granted by a court and one granted by a legislature: "If there is nothing wrong with statutory commands of the sovereign that make exceptions from generally applicable laws in cases of conflict with religious conscience, then there should be nothing wrong with constitutional commands of the same sort."[88] McConnell makes one of the cardinal errors of those who argue for religious liberty beyond legislative accommodation: his touchstone is what the religious believer requires. In effect, the only relevant question is whether the religious believer gets the accommodation. The right process, though, is just as important, especially in this context.

Under the Constitution's structure, the legislative process is definitively different from a court's, and legislative statutory commands are dramatically different from a judicial decree. The judicial process is a packaged affair with strict limitations on the latitude of the judge to make policy determinations. In contrast, the legislative process is at its very best when it engages in wide-ranging debate and investigation that can determine social policy out of a universe of options.

Courts may only consider the claims of the parties before them, and only their arguments. To a significant degree, the parties control the court's (and especially the less experienced clerk's) worldview. Their facts – and only their facts – are relevant in the case. That is why activists look for "test cases," that is, those cases that present the facts as they would like the court to think they are usually. It is true that in some cases, outside interests can expand the judge's understanding of the underlying social issues by filing amicus, or friend of the court, briefs, but that is rarely done at the trial level, and the practice does not give the amicus standing to engage in briefing on the merits or oral argument.

Nor does the court have the prerogative to choose the law it is to apply. It is constrained in its examination of the law by the issues raised by the parties and prudential issues, such as standing or jurisdiction. A judge is not supposed to decide legal issues that are not presented in that particular case (as much as he might like to do so).

Judges are also in a fundamentally different position than are legislators. A judge is required to be open-minded, to be evenhanded, and to read the law as the legislator intended. The symbol of the judicial system, seen in courtrooms throughout the United States, is blindfolded Lady Justice. According to the ABA Model Rules of Professional Conduct and Code of Judicial Conduct, "A judge shall perform judicial duties without bias or prejudice. A judge shall not, in the performance of judicial duties, by words or conduct manifest bias or prejudice, including but not limited to bias or prejudice based upon race, sex, religion, national origin, disability, age, sexual orientation or socioeconomic status, and shall not permit staff, court officials and others subject to the judge's direction and control to do so."[89] Thus, "[e]ach justice or judge of the United States shall take the following oath or affirmation before performing the duties of his office: 'I, __, do solemnly swear (or affirm) that I will administer justice without respect to persons, and do equal right to the poor and to the rich, and that I will faithfully and impartially discharge and perform all the duties incumbent upon me as__under the Constitution and laws of the

United States. So help me God.'"[90] And where there is a particular case raising the specter of a judge's bias, there are rules that demand recusal: "Any justice, judge, or magistrate [magistrate judge] of the United States shall disqualify himself in any proceeding in which his impartiality might reasonably be questioned."[91] By comparison, the legislature has unlimited latitude to frame the issues over which it has power, to determine the extent of its investigation, and to take a position. Both fact-finding *and* lawmaking are at the prerogative of the legislator.

Assuming it is making law within its constitutional powers, Congress can consider laws already in place, laws enacted by other legislatures, and laws never before imagined by anyone else. Indeed, members may even decide to investigate a social problem in depth before deciding whether any law is needed. They have at their disposal the power to subpoena witnesses, to hold extensive hearings, to commission studies, and to elicit the views of any expert. The legislative power to study the social welfare is so large that members also have the power to reject the facts and theories presented to them. In contrast, no court can ignore the facts of a case, if only to determine whether the party has standing, but a legislature sets its own parameters for consideration.

When the public good must be considered, the only legitimate branch is the legislature. It is not that the courts are somewhat less qualified to make determinations of the public good, but rather that they are incompetent to do so. The courts may not make law by "judicially decreeing what accords with 'common sense and the public weal.' Our Constitution vests such responsibility in the political branches."[92] Because religious liberty must be determined in the context of the public good, it is the legislature that is in the best position to decide on exemptions. The legislator's task is one of balancing the value of religious liberty over and against the harm to others if a religious individual or institution is permitted to act contrary to the law. No court has the tools to make the determination.[93]

The legislator bears the burden of assessing the public good in light of all the circumstances and facts, and weighing social goods and harms. In this context, the task is no different. When considering whether to relieve a religious entity of a legal duty, the legislature should weigh, on the one hand, the importance of respect and tolerance for a wide panoply of religious faiths, and on the other hand, whether the harm that the law was intended to prevent can be tolerated in a just society.

A further value of enlisting legislative judgment here (as opposed to judicial judgment) is that the legislature has tremendous power to repeal the laws that it finds are noxious in practice. Precedent has not nearly the pull that it has in the judicial arena. Thus, judgments about relative harm can be revisited and reweighed. The power to repeal legislation reflects the human nature of regulation – it is always based on imperfect understanding and always capable of being viewed through different lenses at a later time.[94] After a generally applicable law is passed, those burdened by it in practice can still request an exemption, and can show how the law operated in fact. Conversely, when an exemption renders more harm than originally understood, it can be rescinded.

**(2) *The accommodation must be consistent with the public good.*** Having shown that the legislature is the branch most fit to consider exemptions leaves open the question whether legislators will in fact consider the public good. An exemption is not legitimate unless it is the product of balancing religious liberty and the public interest. Yet, the very latitude that permits legislators to make judgments about the public good also creates the conditions for them to act without taking into account the public good. Representation is an enormous power and responsibility. The legislator receives the power from the people to make laws without popular veto and without mindless deference to the majority, so that he can consider the public good. The question is whether he will. We know he will listen to the religious entity.

This is the typical image of the legislator: captured by special interests and incapable of acting in the public's interest. It is a caricature, to be sure, but it is also too often true. As discussed above, legislatures are engineered to hear messages from cohesive groups even if they are small. The lobbyist for a minority, therefore, is not necessarily at the disadvantage of large majorities. This quality in the legislative process in fact supports permissive legislative accommodation, because there is no reason to assume minority religions will not be heard. As discussed above, plenty have been heard and accommodated.

Their implicit argument, however, is that other, and possibly less savory, interests will drown out the religious lobbyist. This rests on an assumption that religious liberty is not valued by elected representatives. That cannot be supported. The very existence of RFRA and its progeny – which affect every law and therefore a vast majority of the interests in the United

States – disproves the point, as do many of the exemptions examined in Part One. As Justice Antonin Scalia said in *Smith*, "a society that believes in the negative protection accorded to religious belief can be expected to be solicitous of that value in its legislation."[95] Such a large percentage of Americans attest to religious belief – nearly 85 percent – the objection of weakness in the political process is based more on social myth than reality.[96]

In part, that myth is constructed by indefensible presuppositions about religious entities in the political sphere. There is a widespread, though often undeveloped, assumption that religious entities are above the dirtiness of the legislative, political process. They supposedly operate at a higher and purer level. In point of fact, religious entities are a potent and vocal presence in the legislative and political process, and know how to operate the levers as well as any other lobbyist. Their success in obtaining exemptions, e.g., that immunize from prosecution those faith-healing parents who let their children die of treatable medical ailments, speak for themselves. They pressure legislators on abortion, the death penalty, welfare, tax issues, foreign affairs, and the environment, to name only a few. Moreover, many religious leaders wield the kind of social power that makes them just as desirable A-list invitees as any member of Congress or a state legislature, meaning that politicians and religious leaders associate outside the legislative arena. That familiarity greases the way for them to request and obtain exemptions. But, even those without A-list status have the capacity to influence the legislative process.

Representatives hear the religious entities' requests (sometimes because they share the same religion), and they respond eagerly. The phenomenon deserves further study. It is difficult to fully explain their eagerness to grant requests for exemptions from general laws that they would never entertain had the request come from a secular source. What legislator would even grant a meeting with a group asking for the right to avoid prosecution if they let children die or for the right to avoid liability for putting children within reach of known pedophiles? Is there a legislator in the country that would entertain a proposal to permit secular motion picture theaters to avoid land use laws? There is an element of recklessness to these legislative decisions, as the results I described in Part One illustrated.

The real question is whether they will consider the larger public interest. To reach a legitimate exemption, the legislature may not merely hear the religious entities' request and grant it. That would be the essence of the establishment of religion – the government ceding its responsibility to the people to religious interests. Instead, the legitimate exemption should be a product of the legislature exercising its power and responsibility to consider the effect on the public if the religious entity is permitted to avoid the law.

All legislative judgments should include consideration of the public interest in order to achieve the ideals of a republican form of government. But such consideration is essential for exemptions, because it proves that the exemption is not a handout to religion that sells out the public's interest. The Establishment Clause forbids blind exemptions – those that are granted because the recipient is religious and not because the larger public good is benefited by it.

**(3) The legislative determination must be debated under the harsh glare of public scrutiny.** The mechanics for legislative religious exemptions are in place. Legislatures are competent to grant them and many religious entities are well-schooled in the legislative process. But the public good is often sacrificed in favor of religious entities, as can be seen in the over thirty states that provide religious exemptions to excuse the death of a child from the failure to obtain medical treatment. Too often, the determination is made in the back halls of the legislative rotunda, rather than in the harsh glare of public scrutiny. This is what I will call silent accommodation.

As I discussed in Chapter Two, the Followers of Christ Church in Oregon allowed three infants to die of medical neglect in 1998. When authorities investigated and they discovered a large cemetery of children, both prosecutors and the public became concerned.[97] When prosecutors sought to bring them to justice, only then did they learn about the religious defenses to felonies in their state.[98] The original exemption had been granted without publicity. Once the consequences were made real and in the newspapers (consequences that could have been easily imagined had legislators done their job and considered the larger public good in the course of granting the exemption in the first place) and children were dead, the public discussion that should have taken place in the first instance began.

The result, however, was astounding. The power of the religious interests – even in the face of the numerous deaths of children – prevailed, and spiritual exemptions still stand in the way of children's interests in life in Oregon. The proposed amendment would have repealed religious defenses in homicide and child abuse cases, so that every parent shared equal responsibility to ensure that their child did not suffer and die from a treatable medical ailment.[99] Initially, the Oregon State Senate and House of Representatives bills were popular among representatives, regardless of party lines, but that did not last for long. When it appeared that a single bill, combined from the original bills, had a fighting chance, the faith-healing lobbyists went into action. What was their argument? That the Constitution guaranteed their right to religious freedom, and that freedom entailed a right to choose prayer over medical treatment for their ill children. They confused constitutionally ill-informed legislators who were already predisposed to follow the requests of religious organizations. Thus, legislative incompetence is why Oregon's faith-healing exemptions for murder and first-degree manslaughter remain in place.[100] The silver lining, however, is that the issue was brought to light, and those concerned about children at risk can now pay close attention.

The states have required professionals to report child abuse to civil authorities. Many states, unbeknownst to the public at large, also granted clergy an exemption from the requirement – even though clergy are often in a good position to know whether a child is in trouble. Subsequently, those who had the most knowledge about childhood sexual abuse at the hands of trusted clergy were under no obligation to report it, and the abuse continued with further abuse and new victims. It is an issue that was not a part of the public debate until thousands of Catholic Church victims were revealed between 2002 and 2004. Once again, had legislatures asked what best served the public good under the public spotlight rather than provide a silent exemption, some of this harm might have been prevented.

The Religious Freedom Restoration Act (RFRA) is probably the best example of the phenomenon of silent (as well as blind) exemption. A bill that disabled the vast majority of laws in the United States as they applied to religious entities prompted next to no concern in the House or the Senate. Late in the process, there was some passing concern about its impact on prisons, but no investigation was initiated to determine the likely actual impact on prison order. There was no debate about children who died from religiously motivated medical neglect, or from physical abuse in fundamentalist work camps, or in unlicensed child care centers. Or, about fair housing laws, or schools. Because Congress did not ask the hard questions about the public good, it and the public did not understand that so many potential victims were in harm's way.

RFRA's progeny also spawned numerous silent exemptions. The Pennsylvania Religious Freedom Protection Act of 2002, for example, was passed without hearings and as quickly as possible so as to avoid opposition. Holding a single hearing would have prompted a public debate, because by the time it was passed, a great deal was known about the negative impact of RFRA and its progeny.

The legitimate exemption has three characteristics: it is enacted by a politically accountable legislature charged with consideration of the public good; it is not a blind exemption, but rather one that takes into account the public's interest; and it is not a silent exemption, but occurs in the crucible of public debate.

## Conclusion

Some might respond to this book by asking why the entire system of religious liberty should be built on a presumption that religious organizations and individuals will harm the public good. That's just perverse, they would say. And they might add, while the examples in the first part of this book are disturbing, to be sure, they are the exceptions that prove the rule. A few bad apples are no reason to burden every religious group with the vast number of laws in the United States, or so the argument would go. The instinct is understandable. Because if religion is capable of enough immoral or evil acts that it deserves only limited liberty, then it may seem like there is little hope for society.

The instinct is too dangerous to the helpless to be the basis of the law. When self-deception leads the United States to give religious conduct a berth that results in intolerable harm were it perpetrated by any other entity, this country proves that religion can be the "opiate of the masses."[101] The Marxist wholesale jettisoning of religion was a doomed social experiment, but Marx was indisputably correct that religion is too often an excuse for sloppy thinking and delusional optimism. Such blind trust is an abdication of social responsibility that will in the end undermine the culture altogether.

Others might not take such an extreme position in defense of religion. Even if they conceded my factual claims, they would argue that I have gotten the default rule wrong. Instead of placing the default rule at the rule of law, and then permitting exceptions in extraordinary circumstances, they would place the default rule at religious liberty but with ample room for government regulation. That is, in fact, the approach taken by Justice Sandra Day O'Connor. She has favored strict scrutiny of laws that burden religious conduct, but she has identified a broad range of government interests that are sufficient to trump the claim to religious liberty. In *Smith*, she concurred in the majority's upholding of Oregon's narcotics and unemployment compensation laws, on the theory that they were of sufficient government importance to justify the regulation. Truth be told, there is not a large difference between Justice O'Connor's approach and the one advocated in this book in terms of results. Our main disagreement is on institutional competence. While she would have the courts weigh the public interest, I believe the legislatures are better suited to the inquiry.

Still others – like the *Smith* dissenters – will argue for a more robust version of Justice O'Connor's approach, and demand that the government interests that can trump the religious conduct be narrowly circumscribed. They are the supporters of *Sherbert* and *Yoder*, the detractors of *Smith*, and the believers in the RFRA laws – federal and/or state. Like O'Connor, they would have the courts determine what is in the public's interest, but they also weigh the interests of religious believers so heavily that the scale naturally tips toward religious interests. Instead of using the public good as the governing principle, religious interests would be presumed to trump duly enacted laws. That is not a neutral treatment of religion, but rather a biased perspective that guarantees the public good will not be served in many instances. It creates too much space for the mischief of religious conduct in too many circumstances.

The rule of law is a canopy of mutual protection reached through legitimate legislative processes, under which all members of the society must abide by the same rules and observe the rule of no harm to others. The rule of law is diminished when individuals may use their personal beliefs to avoid the law and to harm others. That is a system wherein individuals are permitted to be laws unto themselves, the very anathema to a rule of law regime, and the approach that was rejected more than

125 years ago by the Supreme Court in *Reynolds v. United States*. The methodology advocated in this book is the only approach that is consistent with the high ideal of republicanism – to yield the greatest good possible for the people. Unlike the narcissism that has become an integral part of American morality, the rule of law recognizes the dignity of the "other." Those who sacrifice the interests of women and children in the name of religion, or the rights of homeowners to religious landowners have imposed a system that demotes the public good to a secondary value. They have subverted the rule of law.

The burden rests on the religious believer demanding exemption from a law to prove that his conduct is not harmful to the society and individuals within it. To date, the primary obstacles to the proper function of these principles have been judicial activism and overly deferential legislatures. Too many ill-considered exemptions have been granted, solely because the one demanding the exemption was religious and the legislator abdicated his or her responsibility to ask whether the exemption might in turn harm others. The result has been all manner of harm to women and children and property interests – and to the public good in general.

When most Americans learn the details of the exemptions that have been granted, for example, to protect parents who medically neglect their children, they are shocked, because the core instinct in the United States is not to harm others and there is an assumption that the legislatures are doing their appointed job of ensuring there is as little harm as possible.

The United States' system, though it started on the right track, has been derailed in recent decades into a system of possessive individualism – the "conception of the individual as essentially the proprietor of his own person or capacities, owing nothing to society for them."[102] Religious entities have argued either that the laws are too onerous *for them* or that the default rule should be complete deregulation. They have coined a phrase to describe their view of religion and the society within which it resides: Church Autonomy.[103] This libertine agenda has persuaded legislatures to permit religious entities to trump the public good by permitting them to avoid accountability. It is a triumph of the urge to power, in Nietzsche's sense, not a sacred right.[104]

Professor Ira Lupu has described the phenomenon beautifully:

> Recognizing ... claims of autonomy will, by definition, insulate from regulation behavior that the political branches have decided needs

regulating. As the autonomy cloak spreads, the quantity of such other-wise illegal behavior, and the harms it causes, will presumably increase. And as the scope of autonomy moves farther away from the special activities that legitimate the autonomy claim, tolerance of those harms becomes increasingly difficult to justify.

Moreover, assertions of autonomy may be as likely to cloak economically self-interested behavior as they are to protect ideological purity. Because institutional autonomy claims will provide this cloak for behavior that is self-interested and otherwise unlawful behavior, their availability will create incentives for organizations to hide a variety of non-religious or non-speech activity behind the cloak. This, in turn, will tend to debase activities which we have come to respect as constitutionally special, turning them into easily accessible havens for economic and social outlaws.[105]

The mindset in the United States regarding religion must change if there is ever to be true liberty as the framing generation rightly understood it. The culprits in the cases that I described in Part One are not only the religious entities lobbying for privileges without regard to their victims, but, more importantly, the legislatures that have failed to ask whether a religious exemption might hurt anyone, or, worse, when they knew of the harm, still enacted the exemption. Indeed, in the U.S. scheme of government, the latter are the more culpable. There is an expectation that lobbyists pursue their own narrow interests, regardless of public good or the needs of others. Part One of this book demonstrated that this principle applies emphatically to religious entities. Legislators are supposed to stand between lobbyists and individual self-interest. Elected representatives make the law that mediates those interests, and they owe the people the duty of investigating who will be harmed by *any* lobbyist's demand.

The point of this book is to show that a vigorous legislative investigation is just as crucial, and sometimes more crucial, in the context of religious demands, as it is in any secular context. The United States must abandon its adolescent belief in the inevitable goodness of every religious entity and instead demand an accounting when religious entities seek to avoid the laws that govern everyone else. This is not so much a matter of distrusting religious entities as it is an invitation for the public good to re-enter the religious liberty calculus.

# EPILOGUE

After the late 2004 Asian tsunami took more than 150,000 lives and brought devastation to the survivors, many religious relief organizations sprang into action and provided necessary assistance to the suffering. It was a reminder of the great good that religious entities regularly and frequently contribute to the global community. No one and no theory, least of all this book, can take that away from them. *God vs. the Gavel*, however, brings balance to the assessment of religion in society by acknowledging the great contributions of religion as it reveals religion's capacity in some instances to harm individuals and the public good. The truth is that religious organizations are staffed by humans, who are by nature imperfect and too often driven by the pursuit of power, prestige, and personal pleasure rather than the good of their neighbors and fellow citizens. The correct legal system takes into account both sides. The Religion Clauses prohibit any law that is hostile to religion, but they do not mandate naivete on the part of legislators and the citizens they serve.

That is why duly enacted criminal and civil laws must be enforced against conduct even when it is religiously motivated.

The 2004 Presidential election brought home the fact that religion, politics, and power are intimately connected in the United States. Religious entities are not above the political fray at all, but rather delivering potent blows within it. Anyone who believes that religion has been marginalized or trivialized in the United States has not been paying close attention.

Before the election, the U.S. Conference of Catholic Bishops distributed a flyer to Catholics declaring that

> [a]s we approach the elections of 2004, . . . some Catholics may feel politically homeless, sensing that no political party and too few candidates share a consistent concern for human life and dignity. However, this is not a time for retreat or discouragement. We need more, not less engagement in political life.[1]

And its urgings may well have benefited Republicans, with 52 percent of Catholics choosing President Bush. The flyer was silent on the clergy abuse scandal – as one might have expected given that the scandal has been a nearly lethal blow to the Church's public and moral authority – but it urged believers to focus primarily on opposing abortion and euthanasia, and then the destruction of human embryos, and human cloning, just to name a few of the 26 political issues prescribed. Even in the face of the widely publicized, ongoing lawsuits and criminal investigations into the Church's role in the childhood sexual abuse of thousands of children, the Conference soldiered on as though its power over its believers could not be questioned.

After the election, when conservative Christians were credited (rightly or wrongly) with delivering the election to President Bush, they wasted no time flexing their political muscle. The Rev. Richard Land of the Southern Baptist Convention said it best, "As we say in Texas, [President Bush] is going to dance with the one who brung him. We haven't come to this place to go home and not push our values and our beliefs."[2] Their ambitious agenda included overturning *Roe v. Wade*, legalizing absolute bans on partial-birth abortion, blocking same-sex marriage, increasing the federal government's faith-based spending, and "the welcoming of faith perspectives in public policy," to quote Land again.

The silence of the conservative Christians on the extraordinary harm done to children by trusted clergy in the Catholic Church, the Jehovah's Witnesses, and others, reinforced the Catholic Church's silence. Both groups have placed the abolition of abortion at the top of their policy lists, and they therefore expended considerable political capital on the unborn child, but the real-life suffering of living children within U.S. borders elicited no position in the political fray.

At the same time the election was dominated by political viewpoints, the Rev. Jerry Falwell (who established the Moral Majority in 1979) opened a law school at his Liberty University, where students were to be educated as "Christian lawyers" with the goal of increasing the political influence of conservative Christians in the courts and the legislatures. In Falwell's own words, the mission of the school is to produce "Christian activists" who "understand the Bible is the infallible word of God, that the American Constitution is a sacred document and that the Christian worldview is their matrix of service."[3] There is hardly a more succinct summary of any religious group's drive to political power.

Further evidence that conservative Christians currently feel entitled to control the culture from their religious perches appeared in December when Judge Ashley McKathan entered his chambers in judicial robes on which the Ten Commandments were embroidered. According to him, he would use the Commandments for the purpose of deciding cases, which should trouble every freedom-loving American. The first four are religious mandates, and one can only wonder how the mandate to believe in only one God will play out in a courtroom where he may well have defendants who believe in multiple gods or no God.

In this climate, it is rather hard to take seriously the prevalent complaints about secularization or the purported removal of religion from the public square. Instead, the facts dictate a fresh appraisal of who is operating the levers of power, what the political process has produced for religious entities, and how the courts have interpreted these enactments. It is just as important to divine what is flying under the radar. And that will require the media to swear off of its squeamishness on religion. Well-known commentator Andy Rooney clearly articulated the problem (without acknowledging it requires a solution) when he said that there were many topics not reported in the United States because the people did not want to hear about them. "Religion is the best example of that. People don't want to talk about religion if it's negative."[4] That is quite an indictment of the media, which must share responsibility for the suffering of many of the victims detailed in this book, especially the children.

The Religious Freedom Restoration Act (as applied to federal law) showed its true colors when the U.S. Court of Appeals for the Tenth Circuit enjoined the federal government from enforcing the Controlled

Substances Act against the O Centro Espirita Beneficiente Uniao Do Vegetal, which uses the illegal substance hoasca in its religious ceremonies. RFRA's strict scrutiny standard meant that the court overtook Congress's role in crafting religious accommodation and decided that the group had to be permitted to use the drug. Without hearings or studies on the short or long-term effect of this drug, the court found itself competent under RFRA's power to carve hoasca out of the Controlled Substances Act. The case may well create an opportunity for the Supreme Court to rule on RFRA's constitutionality as applied to federal law. In the same legal fold, the Supreme Court will decide in 2005 whether the prison side of the Religious Land Use and Institutionalized Persons Act is unconstitutional.

While one cannot say that clergy abuse has been flying under the media radar, it has not received the sort of concentrated attention from the state or federal legislatures it deserves. The need becomes more apparent everyday, and the victims are not just children, but also emotionally disabled adults. Religious organizations obviously need the law's guiding hand on these issues. New York Orthodox rabbi, Mordecai Tendler, was accused of sexual harassment by a number of women who had turned to him for help with their failing marriages. The Rabbinical Council of America, the most important organization of Modern Orthodox rabbis, hired an outside firm to investigate the charges, and then without contacting the victims, the RCA immediately shared the report, which included the names of the victims, with the alleged perpetrator and his attorney.[5] The investigation is ongoing, but without clearer legal guidelines regarding a religious organization's obligations, the pattern of assisting the perpetrator and re-victimizing the victim is going to perpetuate itself.

Despite the desperate attempts by conservative Christians to exercise a quit-claim deed on United States culture, pluralism cannot be wished away. NonChristian citizens are here for the long haul; indeed, many have been here for generations. Peter Gilmore, High Priest of the Church of Satan, has said that "[i]t's a very good time for Satanism these days."[6] The U.S. Armed Services has recognized Satanist believers, and now the British Royal Navy has followed suit. While Gilmore asserted that Satanists were forbidden from illegal activities, the focus is on dark magic. According to him, "Halloween is amateur night, because people are trying to reach down and see the dark side of themselves and Satanists do that 365 days of the year."[7] The mix of religions is not going to homogenize anytime soon.

The case against fundamentalist polygamy from a woman's rights perspective has been strengthened. A former polygamist, John R. Llewellyn, has revealed that in some sects, not only do the men take multiple wives, but their belief that only a church-sanctioned marriage is legitimate has led them to pursue women in marriages from other faiths. According to him, "it is considered an act of righteousness for a fundamentalist man to indoctrinate and seduce the wife of another man. By taking her as a plural wife, he is saving her, exalting her, and he will be the one who resurrects her into the celestial kingdom."[8] The inherently abusive quality of the many polygamous marriages he witnessed has led him to urge legislation that would make criminal "coerced sexual exploitation by a person of trust, power, and authority." Given the utter inability of the existing legal system to save children from being sexually abused by clergy who had their trust or to protect the girls who have been lured into polygamous marriages, this is a worthwhile and interesting path for state legislatures to consider – once they come to understand that a legal system that holds religious entities unaccountable can be neither just nor safe.

Finally, there is the recently published story of the Family International, a cult initiated in the 60s, which practiced routine incest, rape, and physical child abuse. Ricky Rodriguez, 29, who was designated by his parents as the group's messiah when he was a child, and publicly seduced, raped, and abused, recently murdered a former nanny in the context of searching for his biological mother to avenge the crimes against him. In 1986, the group instituted a new rule threatening excommunication for members who engaged in childhood sexual abuse, but that did not redress the harm already done, which had not been forestalled by either the law or the media. If one has any lingering doubt that the United States prescribes rose-colored glasses for religious conduct – the group's musicians, the Family Singers, have performed at the White House.[9]

Each day there are more reasons to embrace the Supreme Court's reasoning in *Employment Division v. Smith* and the principle that religious conduct must be governed by the same laws that govern the rest of us. At the same time, the argument for permissive accommodation remains strong – so long as the legislature takes into account the larger public good. Forbidding religious exemptions altogether would be tyranny, but granting them as of right is anarchy.

# NOTES

## 1. The Problem

1. Winnifred Fallers Sullivan, *Religious Freedom and the Rule of Law: Exporting Modernity in a Postmodern World*, 22 MISS. L. REV. 173, 174 (2004).

2. *See* American Association of Fundraising Council, 2003 *Contributions: $240.72 Billion by Type of Organization, in* GIVING USA 2004, *also available at* http://www.aafrc.org/bytypeof67.html (last visited Aug. 5, 2004).

3. *See generally* HAROLD KOENIG, M.D., THE HEALING POWER OF FAITH (1999).

4. *See* U.S. DEPARTMENT OF STATE, COUNTRY REPORTS ON HUMAN RIGHTS PRACTICES – 2001: CHINA (INCLUDES HONG KONG AND MACAU) (Mar. 4, 2004), *available at* http://www.state.gov/g/drl/rls/hrrpt/2001/eap/8289pf.htm (last visited Aug. 5, 2004).

5. ANNUAL REPORT OF THE UNITED STATES COMMISSION ON INTERNATIONAL RELIGIOUS FREEDOM (May 2004), *available at* http://www.uscirf.gov/reports/ 12May04/finalReport.php3#_china (last visited Oct. 15, 2004).

6. Friends of Falun Gong U.S.A., *What Is Falun Gong?, at* http://www.fofg.org/ about/about_what_is_fg.php (last visited Aug. 5, 2004).

7. *See* Freedom House Center for Religious Freedom, *China Moves to Crush Millions-Strong Christian House Church*, May 19, 2004, *at* http://www. freedomhouse.org/religion/news/bn2004/bn-2004-05-19.htm (last visited Aug. 20, 2004).

China's crackdown on Falun Gong has affected U.S. interests regarding international religious freedom, human rights, trade relations, and the treatment of U.S. permanent residents and citizens. P.L. 105–292, the *Freedom from Religious Persecution Act of 1998*, created a U.S. Commission on International Religious Freedom and authorizes the President to impose sanctions upon countries that violate religious freedom. On the basis of the Commission's findings, the Department of State has identified China as a "country of particular concern." P.L.

106–286 (H.R. 4444) extends permanent normal trade relations (PNTR) status to the PRC but criticizes China's denial of religious, spiritual, and other freedoms, including the government's persecution of Falun Gong adherents, and establishes a special commission to monitor human rights in China.

8. Thomas Lum, China and "Falun Gong" 6 (Cong. Research Serv. 2001), *available at* http://www.globalsecurity.org/military/library/report/crs/RS20333.pdf (last visited Aug. 23, 2004).

> In 2002, the commission reviewed a second report on Falun Gong, which included updates on events in China including the self-immolation of six practitioners in Tiannanmen Square, new tactics of practitioners to bolster recognition of their cause, and the continuing crackdown by the Chinese Government. These events led Congress to institute two resolutions "condemning China for its poor human rights record, and . . . calling upon the PRC to cease its persecution of Falun Gong practitioners.

*Id.* at 4–6. In 2003, the Congressional Report noted that, "Government authorities continue to repress spiritual groups, including the Falun Gong spiritual movement, chiefly through the use of anti-cult laws." Congressional-Executive Comm. On China, 108th Cong., Annual Report 2003 1 (Comm. Print 2003).

9. *See* Anatoly Andreevich Krasikov, *Church State Relationships in Russia: Yesterday, Today, and Tomorrow*, in The Law of Religious Identity 168 (Andras Sajo & Shlomo Avineri, eds. 1999); *Cf.* Dr. Slavi Pachovski, *The Real Reason for the Fall of Communism*, in Global Voice (May 2000), *available at* http://www. advocatesinternational.org/site/gv3.htm (last visited Aug. 5, 2004) (Pachovski was the ambassador of Bulgaria to the United Nations from 1992 to 1997).

10. *See* Ivan Andreyev, *The Catacomb Church in the Soviet Union*, Orthodox Life, Mar.-Apr. 1951, *available at* http://www.holycross-hermitage.com/ pages/Orthodox_Life/CatacombChurch.htm (last visited Aug. 20, 2004); *see also* Anatoly Andreevich Krasikov, *supra* note 9, at 161–68.

11. *See generally* Ronald A. Christaldi, *The Shamrock and the Crown: A Historic Analysis of the Framework Document and Prospects for Peace in Ireland*, 5 J. Transnat'l L. & Pol'y 123, 124–52 (1995).

12. W. Ward et al., The Cambridge Modern History 650 (1934); Charles H. Lea, A History of the Inquisition of Spain 173–74 (1907), *also available at* http://libro.uca.edu/lea1/1lea.htm (last visited Sept. 13, 2004).

13. *See* J. H. Hexter, Parliament and Liberty from the Reign of Elizabeth to the English Civil War 4–5 (1992) ("During the century long rule of [the Tudors] a few hundred martyrs or zealots lost their lives by hanging, burning, or beheading. More numerous were the victims who had taken up arms on religious grounds against their Tudor rulers of whatever religious persuasion.").

14. Amit Gupta & Kaia Leather, Kashmir: Recent Developments and U.S. Concerns 2 (Cong. Research Svc. 2002), *also available at* http://www.fas.org/ man/crs/RL31481.pdf (last visited Aug. 23, 2003).

15. Unlike similar trials in Europe that were run by the Church itself, the Salem witch trials were handled in ostensibly secular courts. *See* Richard Weisman,

WITCHCRAFT, MAGIC, AND RELIGION IN SEVENTEENTH-CENTURY MASSACHUSETTS 12–14 (1984). Nevertheless, Puritan beliefs and colonial clergy played an important role in the witchcraft statutes, trials, and subsequent executions. *Id.* at 23–29.

16. The Muslim Brotherhood was founded in Egypt in 1928 by Hassan al-Bana. *See* Stephen Kinzer, *Muslim Scholar Loses U.S. Visa as Query is Raised*, N.Y. TIMES, Aug. 26, 2004, at A14.

17. *See generally* ANDREA MOORE-EMMETT, GOD'S BROTHEL (2004).

18. *See* Janna C. Merrick, Symposium, *Spiritual Healing, Sick Kids and the Law: Inequities in the American Healthcare System*, 29 AM. J. L. & MED. 269, 273 (2003) ("Christian Science deaths from diabetes and malignancy were twice the national average.").

19. STEPHEN CARTER, THE CULTURE OF DISBELIEF: HOW AMERICAN LAW AND POLITICS TRIVIALIZE RELIGIOUS DEVOTION (1994).

20. Religious Freedom Restoration Act of 1993, 139 Cong. Rec. S 14461, 103rd Cong., 1st Sess. (statement of Sen. Hatch).

21. *See* Marci A. Hamilton, *The Belief/Conduct Paradigm in the Supreme Court's Free Exercise Jurisprudence: A Theological Account of the Failure to Protect Religious Conduct*, 54 OHIO ST. L.J. 713, 794 (1993).

## 2. Children

1. Kathleen Alaimo, *Historical Roots of Children's Rights in Europe and the United States, in* CHILDREN AS EQUALS: EXPLORING THE RIGHTS OF THE CHILD 3 (Kathleen Alaimo & Brian Klug eds., 2002) ("If adults take responsibility for the protection of children, doesn't that potentially limit their freedom?").

2. For purposes of this book, I will use "pedophile" as a term encompassing both pedophiles and ephebophiles. Technically, a pedophile is defined as "[a] person who over at least a 6 month period has recurrent, intense sexually arousing fantasies, sexual urges, or behaviors involving sexual activity with a prepubescent child or children (age 13 years or younger)." AMERICAN PSYCHIATRIC ASSOCIATION, DIAGNOSTIC AND STATISTICAL MANUAL OF MENTAL DISORDERS (4th ed. 1994). "Adults who sexually interact with adolescents are called ephebophiles. However, there is neither a medical definition nor a medical diagnosis for this group." Gene G. Abel, M.D., & Nora Harlow, *The Abel and Harlow Child Molestation Prevention Study* 4 (updated 2002), *in* THE STOP CHILD MOLESTATION BOOK (2001), *also available at* http://www.stopchildmolestation.org/pages/about.html (last visited October 2, 2004).

3. *See* Bill Bowen, *Is There a Problem?, at* http://www.silentlambs.org/answers/Isthereaproblem.htm (last visited Oct. 2, 2004) (hereinafter *Is There a Problem?*).

4. Rev. Michael Peterson, F. Ray Mouton, & Rev. Thomas P. Doyle, *The Problem of Sexual Molestation by Roman Catholic Clergy: Meeting the Problem in a Comprehensive and Responsible Manner* 2, 10 (1984) (confidential report on Catholic clergy abuse directed to bishops) (on file with author), *also available*

*at* http://natcath.org/NCR_Online/archives2/2002b/051702/051702a.htm (last visited Sept. 30, 2004) (hereinafter *Problem of Sexual Molestation by Roman Catholic Clergy*).

5. *Id.* at 3, 4, 11, 88.

6. Estimates range from 10,000 to 100,000. Sociologist and Catholic priest Andrew Greeley predicted that there are probably 100,000 clergy-abuse victims in the United States. *See* Andrew M. Greeley, *How Serious Is the Problem of Sexual Abuse by Clergy?*, AMERICA, Mar. 20, 1993, at 6, *also available at* http://www.bishop-accountability.org/resources/resource-files/timeline/1993-03-20-Greeley-HowSerious-1.htm (last visited October 2, 2004) (hereinafter Greeley) ("A not unreasonable estimate of the victim population would then be well in excess of 100,000, each one a human being who has suffered a terrible personal tragedy."); NATIONAL REVIEW BOARD FOR THE PROTECTION OF CHILDREN AND YOUNG PEOPLE, A REPORT ON THE CRISIS IN THE CATHOLIC CHURCH IN THE UNITED STATES 23 (2004) (hereinafter REPORT ON THE CRISIS IN THE CATHOLIC CHURCH), *also available at* http://www.usccb.org/nrb/nrbstudy/nrbreport.pdf (last visited Sept. 30, 1994).

7. Mark Donald, *Judging Amy?; Jehovah's Witnesses Sued for Allegedly Protecting Members Who Abuse*, 20 TEXAS LAWYER 1 (May 3, 2004) (quoting Fort Worth lawyer Kimberlee Norris, who said she "talked to my 1,500th alleged victim in March 28, 2003 . . . After I reached 2000, I stopped counting.") (hereinafter *Judging Amy?*); *see also* www.silentlambs.org (website that assists survivors of Jehovah Witness abuse, run by a former church elder, Bill Bowen).

8. In 1980, two news organizations won Pulitzer Prizes for their reporting about the financial misdealings of religious institutions. Bette Swenson Orsini and Charles Stafford of the St. Petersburg (Fla.) *Times* won the Pulitzer for National Reporting "for their investigation of the Church of Scientology," which is *available at* http://www.lermanet.com/scientologynews/sptimes/spt-series-index.htm (last visited Sept. 29, 2004). The same year, the Gannett News Service won the Pulitzer for Public Service for "its series on financial contributions to the Pauline Fathers." The Pulitzer Board Presents, *The Pulitzer Prize Winners of 1980, available at* http://www.pulitzer.org/cgi-bin/year.pl?type=w&year=1980&FormsButton2=Retrieve (last visited Sept. 29, 2004). In 1988, The Charlotte (N.C.) *Observer* won the Public Service Pulitzer "for revealing misuse of funds by the PTL television ministry through persistent coverage conducted in the face of a massive campaign by PTL to discredit the newspaper." The Pulitzer Board Presents, *The Pulitzer Prize Winners of 1988, available at* http://www.pulitzer.org/cgi-bin/year.pl?type=w&year=1988&FormsButton2=Retrieve (last visited Sept. 29, 2004).

9. *See* JASON BERRY, LEAD US NOT INTO TEMPTATION: CATHOLIC PRIESTS AND THE SEXUAL ABUSE OF CHILDREN (1992); JASON BERRY & GERALD RENNER, VOWS OF SILENCE : THE ABUSE OF POWER IN THE PAPACY OF JOHN PAUL II (2004).

10. *See* Susan Hogan-Albach, *Years of Conflict*, DALLAS MORNING NEWS, June 10, 2002, at 10A.

11. FRANK BRUNI & ELINOR BURKETT, A GOSPEL OF SHAME: CHILDREN, SEXUAL ABUSE, AND THE CATHOLIC CHURCH 98–101 (1993).

12. *Problem of Sexual Molestation by Roman Catholic Clergy, supra* note 4, at 7 (detailing press outlets actively pursuing the issue at the time).

13. *See generally* BILL WRIGHT DZIECH & JUDGE CHARLES B. SCHUDSON, ON TRIAL: AMERICA'S COURTS AND THEIR TREATMENT OF SEXUALLY ABUSED CHILDREN 10–11 (1989).

14. *Federal Assistance to States to Prevent the Abuse of Children in Child Care Facilities: Hearings on S. 521 and S. 1924 before the Senate Judiciary Committee,* 98th Cong. 30 (Apr. 11 and Sept. 18, 1984) (statement of Melvin D. Mercer and Kenneth V. Lanning).

15. Melinda Beck & Tessa Namuth, *An Epidemic of Child Abuse,* NEWSWEEK, Aug. 20, 1984, at 44.

16. Russell Watson, et al., *A Hidden Epidemic,* NEWSWEEK, May 14, 1984, at 32.

17. Glen Martin & Delfin Vigil, *Study Reveals Clergy Abuse Figures,* S. F. CHRON., Feb. 2, 2004, at A1.

18. Greeley, *supra* note 6.

19. REPORT ON THE CRISIS IN THE CATHOLIC CHURCH, *supra* note 6, at 23.

20. The American Academy of Pediatrics (AAP) has been a staunch advocate for children at risk of medical neglect. *See* American Academy of Pediatrics, *Religious Exemptions from Child Abuse Statutes,* 81 PEDIATRICS 169 (1988). The AAP has a Child Abuse and Neglect home page, *available at* http://www.aap.org/sections/scan/ (last visited Oct. 18, 2004). AAP also filed an amicus brief, along with other health organizations, opposing Medicare and Medicaid reimbursement for institutions run primarily by Christian Scientists (because the practice encourages faith healers to deny children appropriate medical care). *See* Brief Amicus Curiae of the American Academy of Pediatrics, the American Medical Association, the Iowa Medical Society, and the American Nurses Association in Support of Petitioners, Children's Healthcare Is a Legal Duty, Inc. v. Min De Parle, 212 F.3d 1084 (8th Cir. 2000). AAP is also on the record opposing state exemptions for parents who have denied medical care to their children for religious reasons. *See* Press Release, American Academy of Pediatrics, *Pediatricians File Brief in Prayer vs. Medical Care Case* (Dec. 29, 1998) (on file with author), *also available at* http://www.aap.org/advocacy/washing/prayer.htm (last visited Oct. 18, 2004).

21. *See* Memorandum in Support of Plaintiffs Motion for Summary Judgment, Bronson v. Swenson, No. 02:04-CV-0021 (TS) (D. Utah filed Apr. 27, 2004).

22. *Federal Assistance to States to Prevent the Abuse of Children in Child Care Facilities: Hearings on S. 521 and S.1924 Before the Senate Judiciary Committee,* 98th Cong. 29 (Apr. 11 and Sept. 18, 1984) (statement of Melvin D. Mercer and Kenneth V. Lanning); *Federal Assistance to States to Prevent the Abuse of Children in Child Care Facilities: Hearings on S. 521 and S.1924 Before the Senate Judiciary Committee,* 98th Cong. 29 (Apr. 11 & Sept. 18, 1984) (statement of Melvin D. Mercer and Kenneth V. Lanning); *see also id.* at 26 (oral testimony).

23. *Id.* at 31.

24. *Id.* at 30 (according to Dr. Ann Burgess). *See also* KENNETH V. LANNING, CHILD MOLESTERS: A BEHAVIORAL ANALYSIS 18–19 (3d ed. 1992), *also available at* http://www.skeptictank.org/nc70.pdf (last visited Sept. 26, 2004).

25. Ralph Ranalli, *A Curious Twist in Geoghan Case*, BOSTON GLOBE, Oct. 25, 2003, at B3.

26. Ralph Ranalli, *Priests in Church Scandal Barred*, BOSTON GLOBE, May 7, 2004, at B1.

27. Leary v. Geoghan, No. 2001-J-0688, 2001 WL 1902391, at *1 (Mass. App. Ct. Dec. 21, 2001) (affirming trial court decision that First Amendment did not bar discovery of Church files).

28. Videotape: "Jennifer Chapin Detailing Childhood Sexual Abuse by Monsignor Francis" (on file with author).

29. *See* William Lobdell & Jean Guccione, *Church to Pay $3 Million in Rape*, L.A. TIMES, Jan. 24, 2004, at B1.

30. Glen Martin & Delfin Vigil, *Study Reveals Clergy Abuse Figures*, S.F. CHRON., Feb. 2, 2004, at A1.

31. Charles Burress, *CA Woman Makes Plea to Victims of Clergy Abuse*, S.F. CHRON., Jan. 26, 2004, at B2.

32. *Id.*

33. Ralph Ranalli, *Reardon Victims Still Wait for Help: Diocese Yet to Pay for Sex Abuse Care*, BOSTON GLOBE, June 16, 2003, at B1.

34. Eric Convey, *Reardon Victim Settles YMCA Claim for $35G*, BOSTON HERALD, July 19, 2003, at 10.

35. Kevin Cullen & Stephen Kurkjian, *Church in an $85 Million Accord*, BOSTON GLOBE, Sept. 10, 2003, at A1.

36. Fernanda Santos, *Parishioners: Priest Heard about Abuse*, EAGLE-TRIBUNE (Haverhill, Mass.), Feb. 1, 2002, at 1; Tom Mashberg, *Records: Molesters Advised other Abusers*, BOSTON HERALD, June 6, 2002, at 28.

37. Parks v. Kownacki, 193 Ill. 2d 164, 168–70, 181 (2000).

38. WIS. STAT. ANN. § 990.06 (2003) provides:

> In any case when a limitation or period of time prescribed in any act which shall be repealed for the acquiring of any right, or barring of any remedy, or for any other purpose shall have begun to run before such repeal and the repealing act shall provide any limitation or period of time for such purpose, such latter limitation or period shall apply only to such rights or remedies as shall accrue subsequently to the time when the repealing act shall take effect, and the act repealed shall be held to continue in force and be operative to determine all such limitations and periods of time which shall have previously begun to run unless such repealing act shall otherwise expressly provide.

39. Laurie Goodstein & Jodi Wilgoren, *2 Paths, No Easy Solution on Abusive Priests*, N.Y. TIMES, Mar. 3, 2002, at 1 (hereinafter 2 Paths, No Easy Solution).

40. Robert Goodrich, *Retired Priest Named in New Sex Abuse Case*, ST. LOUIS POST-DISPATCH, Sept. 26, 2003, at B1.

41. SARAH BARRINGER GORDON, THE MORMON QUESTION 1 (2002). The federal law banning polygamy, 12 Stat. 501, passed by Congress in 1862, was upheld against attack by a Mormon man in Reynolds v. United States, 98 U.S. 145, 167 (1879).

42. See The Doctrine and Covenants: Section 132, in THE CHURCH OF JESUS CHRIST OF LATTER-DAY SAINTS, THE SCRIPTURES (Internet Edition), available at http://scriptures.lds.org/dc/132 (last visited Oct. 1, 2004). See also JOHN KRAKAUER, UNDER THE BANNER OF HEAVEN 255 (2003) [hereinafter UNDER THE BANNER OF HEAVEN] (Fundamentalist Mormons "pointed out that D&C 132 was still an accepted part of the Mormon scripture (and indeed still is today).").

43. Complaint, Jeffs v. Jeffs, et al., at ¶ 22, ¶ 2, 23–24 (Utah 3d Jud. Dist. Ct. 2004) (on file with author).

44. Karen Brooks, Polygamists Accused of Rape, DALLAS MORNING NEWS, July 31, 2004, at 5A.

45. Complaint, Jeffs v. Jeffs, at ¶¶ 25–28.

46. ANDREA MOORE-EMMETT, GOD'S BROTHEL 33 (2004) (hereinafter GOD'S BROTHEL); Lucinda Dillon, Graham Deputy is Seeking to Suceed Her, DESERET NEWS (Salt Lake City), Oct. 12, 1999, at B1.

47. See Fabian Dawson, 13 Year Old Sent to B.C. for Husband, PROVINCE (Vancouver, B.C.), Dec. 16, 2000, available at http://www.rickross.com/reference/polygamy/polygamy50.html (last visited Sept. 26, 2004); The Canadian Home of Polygamy, CBC NEWS, Jan. 15, 2003, transcript available at http://www.rickross.com/reference/polygamy/polygamy99.html (last visited Sept. 26, 2004).

48. 18 U.S.C. § 2423 (2003); Complaint to BC Human Rights Tribunal, Regarding Polygamous Practices in Bountiful, British Columbia (May 19, 2004) (filed by Jancis M. Andrews) (referring to Ruth Chatwin, who at 13 was "traded into Bountiful from the States").

49. Id.; see also GOD'S BROTHEL, supra note 46, at 125–27.

50. Referred to in Estimates: Ministry of Families and Children: Official Report of Debates of the Legislative Assembly 36th Parl., 4th Sess. 16,937–38 (B. C. Hansard) (June 28, 2000) (statement of Hon. G. Mann Brewin, questioned by B. McKinnon), available at http://www.legis.gov.bc.ca/2000/hansard/h00628p.htm#16937 (last visited Oct. 1, 2004).

51. Id. at 16,938.

52. See Ending a Half Century of Exploitation, ECONOMIST (London), July 8, 2004, also available at http://www.economist.com/displayStory.cfm?story_id=2907136 (last visited Oct. 1, 2004) ("[I]nertia stems from a case in 1992 when police recommended that two Bountiful men be charged with polygamy. But the crown attorney's office declined to do so, following legal advice that conviction was impossible because the guarantee of religious freedom in Canada's Charter of Rights and Freedoms renders the law against polygamy unconstitutional."); see also Complaint to BC Human Rights Tribunal (May 19, 2004) (describing Canadian government officials' failure to enforce the law against polygamy, because it "may be unconstitutional").

53. Letter from Seven Complainants, former wives or concubines at Bountiful commune, to Tribunal Members, B.C. Human Rights Tribunal 1 (May 19,

2004) (on file with author). The complainants request anonymity as a condition of participation in tribunal proceedings. For that reason, I will not publish their names.

54. *Id.*

55. GOD'S BROTHEL, *supra* note 46, at 172; *see also* UNDER THE BANNER OF HEAVEN, *supra* note 42, at 25 (quoting the polygamous police chief of Colorado City).

56. Allison Hanes, *I Married 10-year-old, Says Man, 52*, GAZETTE (Montreal), Aug. 19, 2004, at A1.

57. *Connie Chung Tonight: Witnesses Abused? Church Accused of Failing Children* (CNN television broadcast, Aug. 24, 2002), *transcript available at* http://www.watchtowerinformationservice.org/chung.htm (last visited Sept. 29, 2004).

58. *See, e.g., Judging Amy?, supra* note 7 ("According to scripture [Deuteronomy 19:15], for a person to be disciplined, there needs to be at least two witnesses to substantiate the charge or an admission of sin."); Dennis O'Brien, *Another Church Facing Charges of Sexual Abuse: Former Jehovah's Witness Leader to Be Tried on Sex Offenses, Attempted Rape*, BALT. SUN, May 21, 2002, at B1 (hereinafter *Another Church Facing Charges of Sexual Abuse*).

59. CAL. CODE CIV. P. § 340.1 (1999). In fact, the window was opened for civil and criminal statutes alike, but the Supreme Court held the retroactive effect of the revival of the criminal charges was unconstitutional in Stogner v. California, 539 U.S. 607 (2003). California opened a second year-long window for victims who had pressed criminal charges before *Stogner* forced their cases to be dismissed, so that they can file civil claims against those who caused and aided and abetted childhood sexual abuse. CAL. CODE CIV. P. § 340.1(c) (2003).

60. Complaint, West v. Watchtower Bible & Tract Society of New York, Inc., at ¶ 30 (filed Cal. Sup. Ct. Yolo County), *also available at* http://www.silentlambs.org/Novemberlawsuit.htm (last visited Oct. 1, 2004).

61. *Connie Chung Tonight: Witnesses Abused? supra* note 57.

62. Meyer v. Lindala, 675 N.W.2d 635, 641 (Minn. Ct. App. 2004), *review denied*, 2004 Minn. LEXIS 308 (Minn., May 26, 2004) (quoting Lundman v. McKown, 530 N.W.2d 807, 826 (Minn. App. 1995)).

63. *See* Bowen, *Is There a Problem?, supra* note 3.

64. *Another Church Facing Charges of Sexual Abuse, supra* note 58.

65. *See* Bowen, *Is There a Problem?, supra* note 3.

66. *See* Bryan R. v. Watchtower Bible & Tract Soc'y of New York, 738 A.2d 839 (Me. 1999); Rees v. Watchtower Bible & Tract Soc'y of New York, No. CV-98-60, 1998 Me. Super. LEXIS 211 (Me. Super. Ct. Aug. 18, 1998); *see also* Swanson v. Roman Catholic Bishop, 692 A.2d 441 (Me. 1997) (involving sexual activity between a priest and an adult woman).

67. Decorso v. Watchtower Bible & Tract Soc'y of New York, 829 A.2d 38 (Conn. App. Ct. 2003).

68. Abrams v. Watchtower Bible and Tract Soc. of New York, Inc., 715 N.E.2d 798 (Ill. App. Ct. 1999), *appeal denied*, 186 Ill.2d 565 (1999) (holding that the court was

deprived of jurisdiction to adjudicate a complaint involving ecclesiastical principles and doctrines).

69. *Bryan R.*, 738 A.2d at 848.

70. Gibson v. Brewer, 952 S.W.2d 239, 243–44 (Mo. 1997).

71. *Id.* at 247.

72. Michael Wilson, *Judge Orders Mormons to Provide Sex-Abuse Records*, OREGONIAN, Feb. 9, 2001, at D1.

73. Gustav Niehbur, *Mormons Paying $3 Million to Settle Sex Abuse Case*, N.Y. TIMES, Sept. 5, 2001, at A14.

74. Andrea Albright, *Minister Pleads Guilty in Second County*, TOPEKA CAPITAL J. (Kan.), Dec. 11, 2001.

75. Chris Grenz, *Minister Sentenced to Five Years*, TOPEKA CAPITAL J. (Kan.), Dec. 6, 2001.

76. Franco v. The Church of Jesus Christ of Latter-day Saints, 21 P.3d 198 (Utah 2001).

77. *Man Jailed on Internet Sex Charges*, PITTSBURGH POST-GAZETTE, Aug. 28, 1995, at D2.

78. *Sentence in Molestation*, WASH. POST, Feb. 1, 1996, at B3.

79. MISS. CODE ANN. § 41-23-27 (1972) (upheld as constitutional in the face of free exercise challenge in Brown v. Stone, 378 So. 2d 218 (Miss. 1979), *cert. denied*, 449 U.S. 887 (1980)); W. VA. CODE § 16-3-4 (2004); *see also* State v. Riddle, 168 W. Va. 429, 439) (1981) (upholding conviction of parents for failing to send children to school in face of free exercise challenge, and citing for support the mandatory immunization statute as an "urgent public policy.").

80. *See* CHILD, Inc., *Religious Exemptions from Healthcare for Children*, at http://www.childrenshealthcare.org/ (last visited Oct. 1, 2004).

81. P.L. 93–247 (Jan. 31, 1974) did not, on its face, require an exemption. However, it was interpreted to mean that by the Department of Health and Human Services. This was corrected when Congress subsequently amended the Bill in 1983. *See* 48 Fed. Reg. 3698 (Jan. 26, 1983) (codified at 45 CFR § 1340.2). 42 U.S.C. § 5106i(a)(2) (2004), enacted in 1983, provides: "Nothing in this Act . . . shall be construed . . . to require that a State find, or to prohibit a State from finding, abuse or neglect in cases in which a parent or legal guardian relies solely or partially upon spiritual means rather than medical treatment, in accordance with the religious beliefs of the parent or legal guardian."

82. *See, e.g.*, In re Green, 448 Pa. 338 (1972) (refusing to appointment a guardian for a boy suffering from paralytic scolios, whose Jehovah's Witness mother refused to consent to corrective surgery that would require a blood transfusion and holding that "as between a parent and the state, the state does not have an interest of sufficient magnitude outweighing a parent's religious beliefs when the child's life is *not immediately imperiled* by his physical condition.") (emphasis in original).

83. Prince v. Massachusetts, 321 U.S. 158, 170 (1944).

84. *Religious Exemptions for felonies*: ARIZ. REV. STAT. ANN. §§ 8-201.01, 8-531.01 (1974) (exemption from child or vulnerable adult abuse); COLO. REV. STAT.

§ 19-3-103 (2003) (from child neglect, but not an absolute defense to child abuse charges, People v. Lybarger, 790 P.2d 855 (Colo. App. 1989)); CONN. GEN. STAT. ANN. § 17a-104 (1992) (exemption from Endangering the Welfare of a Child ("EWOC")); DEL. CODE ANN. TIT. 11, § 1104 (1987) (EWOC); FLA. STAT. ANN. §§ 39.01(30)(f), (45), 984.03(37) (Abuse, aggravated abuse, and neglect of a child); GA. CODE ANN. § 15-11-2(8) (2004) (neglect); IDAHO CODE § 16-1602(24)(a) (2004) (neglect); IOWA CODE ANN. § 726.6(1)(d) (2004) (child endangerment); IND. CODE §§ 35-46-1-4(c), -5(c) (2000) (neglect); LA. REV. STAT. ANN. tit. 14, § 93(B) (cruelty); ME. REV. STAT. ANN. tit. 22, § 4010(1) (abuse or neglect), tit. 17-A, § 557 (2004) (EWOC); MICH. COMP. LAWS ANN. § 722.634 (2004) (abuse); MINN. STAT. ANN. § 609.378(a)(1) (2004) (neglect and endangerment); MISS. CODE ANN. § 43-21-105(l)(i) (2004) (neglect); MO. ANN. STAT. § 210.115(3) (2003) (EWOC); NEV. REV. STAT. ANN. § 200.5085 (abuse or neglect); N.M. STAT. ANN. 1978, § 32A-4-2(E)(5) (2004) (same); N.D. CENT. CODE § 50-25.1-05.1(2) (2003) (same); OHIO REV. CODE ANN. § 2919.22(A) (EWOC); OKLA. STAT. ANN. tit. 21, §§ 852(C), 852.1(B), (2002) (omission to provide for a child); 23 PA. CONS. STAT. ANN. § 6303 (1991) (EWOC); R.I. GEN. LAWS § 40-11-15 (2004) (cruelty or neglect); S.C. CODE ANN. § 20-7-490(2)(c) (2003) (unlawful conduct toward a child); TEX. PENAL CODE ANN. § 22.04(k)(2) (Vernon 2003) (injury to a child); UTAH CODE ANN. 1953 §§ 62A-4a-101(18)(c), 76-5-110(3)(a), 78-3a-103(1)(s)(iii) (2004) (abuse and neglect); VA. CODE ANN. § 18.2-371.1(C) (2004) (abuse and neglect); WASH. REV. CODE ANN. §§ 9A.42.005, 26.44.020(3) (2004) (criminal mistreatment); WIS. STAT. ANN. §§ 48.981(3)(c)(4), 948.03(6) (2003) (abuse and neglect).

Many of the statutes listed above can also be a defense for misdemeanors. The grading of the crime will often depend on the degree of harm. *See, e.g.,* MINN. STAT. ANN. § 609.378(b)(2) (2004) (endangerment is normally a misdemeanor, however, if "the endangerment results in substantial harm to the child's physical, mental, or emotional health, the person may be sentenced to imprisonment for not more than five years . . . " In such cases, the crime would be a felony.).

*Exemptions for misdemeanors* (usually Class A): ALA. CODE § 13A-13-6(b) (1975); ALASKA STAT. § 11.51.120(b) (1983); CAL. PENAL CODE § 270 (1988); KAN. STAT. ANN. § 21-3608(1)(b) (1995); WYO. STAT. § 14-3-202(a)(vii); 6-4-403(c) (2004) (Abandoning or endangering children is a misdemeanor for the first violation, a felony for the second). *See also* NATIONAL CLEARINGHOUSE ON CHILD ABUSE AND NEGLECT INFORMATION, 2003 CHILD ABUSE AND NEGLECT STATE STATUTE SERIES STATUTES-AT-A-GLANCE (Dept. Health & Human Services 2003), *also available at* http://nccanch.acf.hhs.gov/general/legal/statutes/define.pdf (last visited Oct. 3, 2004).

85. *Compare* Hermanson v. State, 604 So. 2d 775, 782 (Fla. 1992) ("In this instance, we conclude that the legislature has failed to clearly indicate the point at which a parent's reliance on his or her religious beliefs in the treatment of his or her children becomes criminal conduct."); *and* State v. McKown, 475 N.W.2d 63, 68-69 (Minn. 1991), *cert. denied,* 502 U.S. 1036 (1992); *with* Walker v. Superior

Court, 47 Cal. 3d 112, 142 (1988) ("The 'matter of degree' that persons relying on prayer treatment must estimate rightly is the point at which their course of conduct becomes criminally negligent. In terms of notice, due process requires no more."); *and* Hall v. State, 493 N.E.2d 433, 435 (Ind. 1986).

86. *See, e.g., Walker*, 47 Cal. 3d at 131 n. 11 (describing lobbying activities of Christian Scientists in California); CAROLINE FRASER, GOD'S PERFECT CHILD: LIVING AND DYING IN THE CHRISTIAN SCIENCE CHURCH 282 (1999) (hereinafter GOD'S PERFECT CHILD).

87. Most religious exemptions are worded in general terms that would extend to any religious believer relying on faith rather than medicine, but there are statutes that have been crafted solely with the Christian Scientists in mind. *See* Children's Healthcare Is a Legal Duty, Inc. v. Vladeck, 938 F. Supp. 1466 (D. Minn. 1996) (holding 42 U.S.C. § 1395x(e) and 42 U.S.C. § 1395x(y)(1), which explicitly referred to Christian Science practices as unconstitutional). After the church-specific law was found unconstitutional, Congress responded by passing a broader regulation, that was not sect specific, although virtually no other religious organization would satisfy the description. The new regulations, 42 U.S.C.S. § 1395x(ss)(1) and 42 U.S.C.S. § 1395i-5(a)(2), have been held constitutional since they are not facially discriminatory and a permissible accommodation of religion. Children's Healthcare Is a Legal Duty, Inc. v. De Parle, 212 F.3d 1084 (8th Cir. 2000), *cert. denied*, 532 U.S. 957 (2001).

88. MARY BAKER EDDY, SCIENCE AND HEALTH 120, 1 (1994), *also available at* http://www.spirituality.com/dt/toc_sh.jhtml (last visited Oct. 1, 2004) (hereinafter SCIENCE AND HEALTH).

89. GOD'S PERFECT CHILD, *supra* note 86, at 337.

90. *Spiritual Healing – A Family Affair*, CHRISTIAN SCIENCE SENTINEL, July 23, 2001, at 7.

91. *See, e.g.*, Lundman v. McKown, 530 N.W.2d 807, 819 (Minn. Ct. App. 1995), *cert. denied*, 516 U.S. 1099 (1996) ("Appellants [including Christian Science Church] challenge the existence of a duty of care and a breach of that duty.").

92. *See id.* at 814–15 (When child was not admitted to Christian Science Nursing Home because he was under 16, his mother considered taking him to the hospital. She dismissed this idea after the nursing home "proposed hiring a private Christian Science nurse to come to the McKown home."); *see also What Is a Christian Science Practitioner?*, CHRISTIAN SCIENCE SENTINEL, Aug. 30, 2004, at 13 (Answer of Jon Benzon, practitioner, to the question "Have you ever refused to give someone treatment?" Benson responded: "Yes, though rarely.... I realized that Christian Science treatment was being asked for to 'hedge their bets,' so to speak, while the patient was also relying on medical treatment."); *Id.* at 18 ("What should the patient's role be when you are praying for him or her?" Practitioner Leide Lessa responded: "A patient needs to be sincere. And I can feel it clearly when this is not the case."); ROBERT PEEL, SPIRITUAL HEALING IN A SCIENTIFIC AGE 34 (1987) (hereinafter SPIRITUAL HEALING IN A SCIENTIFIC AGE) ("Christian Science treatment and medicine do not mix well.").

93. Mary Trammell, *A Prayer-First Approach to Healthcare,* CHRISTIAN SCIENCE SENTINEL, July 23, 2001, at 1.

94. SCIENCE AND HEALTH, *supra* note 88, at 4.

95. *Spiritual Healing – A Family Affair,* CHRISTIAN SCIENCE SENTINEL, July 23, 2001, at 7 (quoting Christian Science practitioner Richard Biever).

96. GOD'S PERFECT CHILD, *supra* note 86, at 329. Practitioners pray for the sick, while nurses tend to their physical needs.

97. SPIRITUAL HEALING IN A SCIENTIFIC AGE, *supra* note 92, at 151.

98. *See* Janna C. Merrick, *Christian Science Healing of Minor Children: Spiritual Exemption Statutes, First Amendment Rights, and Fair Notice,* 10 ISSUES IN L. & MED. 321 (1994).

99. Some have asserted that the Christian Scientists were the only organization that asked for the rule. They did not testify, but that is no indication of whether they sought the rule behind the scenes. *See id.* at 330 (between 1967 and 1974 "the church began a widespread lobbying effort to enact laws that would protect its members from future prosecutions.").

100. *See, e.g.,* Michael Higgins, *Boy's Death Puts Religious Exemption in Spotlight,* CHI. TRIB., Sept. 5, 2003, at C18 ("Forty-one states, including Illinois, have exemptions in their civil laws, such as those governing when child welfare officials can remove a child from a home. . . . Some of the laws stem from lobbying by Christian Science Church members, many of whom use prayer instead of science-based medicine."); *see also* Gayle White, *Variety of Faiths Make Views Known at Capitol,* ATLANTA J.-CONST., February 16, 2002, at 2B.

101. Seth M. Asser, M.D., & Rita Swan, *Child Fatalities from Religion-motivated Medical Neglect,* 101 PEDIATRICS 625 (1998).

102. *See* 1995 Or. Laws 657 (H.B. 2492). Other states have similar statutes. *See* ARK. CODE ANN. § 5-10-101(a)(9) (1997) (affirmative defense for capital murder); W. VA. CODE § 61-8D-2(d) (2004) (same).

103. The investigation, by Oregon's medical examiner, showed that at least 21 of the 78 children who died since 1955 probably would have survived with medical treatment. Mark Larabee & Peter D. Sleeth, *Followers Children Needed Medical Care, Experts Say,* CLEVELAND PLAIN DEALER, June 28, 1998, at 21A.

104. Mark Larabee, *Bill Aims to Lift All Oregon Religious Shields,* OREGONIAN, Jan. 22, 1999, at C6.

105. OR. REV. STAT. § 163.115(4) (2003).

106. *See* OR. REV. STAT. §§ 163.115(1); 163.125(2003).

107. *Walker,* 47 Cal. 3d at 118–19, 138–39, 141.

108. Lawrence J. Goodrich, *Christian Scientist's Case Settled in California,* CHRISTIAN SCIENCE MONITOR, June 25, 1990, at 8.

109. *See generally* MANSLAUGHTER WORKING GROUP, REPORT TO THE (U.S. SENTENCING GUIDELINE) COMMISSION (Dec. 15, 1997), *also available at* http://www.ussc.gov/publicat/MANSLAUG.PDF (last visited Oct. 2, 2004) (discussing median sentences for involuntary manslaughter).

110. *Lundman,* 530 N.W.2d at 813–14, 815. The Minnesota Supreme Court reversed the punitive damage award, but allowed the compensatory damages (reduced by the trial court to $1.5 million) to stand. *Id.* at 832.

111. *Id.* at 817, 819, 825.

112. *Id.* at 816, 832.

113. "Today, many LDS women and men are involved in health care practice and research. Church members, who are advised to seek medical assistance from competent licensed physicians, generally believe that advances in medical science and health care have come though the inspiration of the Lord." Cecil O. Samuelson, Jr., *Medical Practices, in* 2 ENCYCLOPEDIA OF MORMONISM (1992), *also available at* http://www.lightplanet.com/mormons/daily/health/Medical_Practices_EOM.htm (last visited Oct. 6, 2004). The faith does prescribe a health regimen: "Among its provisions: no alcoholic drinks, no smoking or chewing of tobacco, and no 'hot drinks' – believed to refer specifically to tea and coffee. 'Wholesome herbs,' along with fruits and grains, are specifically recommended. Meat is to be used sparingly. Church of Jesus Christ of Latter-day Saints, *Health Professionals See Sense in Latter-day Saints' 170-Year-Old Health Code, at* http://www.lds.org/ newsroom/ showpackage/0,15367,3899-1 – 44-2-513,00.html (last visited Oct. 6, 2004).

114. Katy Kelly, *A Dangerous Parent Trap,* U.S. NEWS & WORLD REP., Oct. 13, 2003, at 12.

115. *MRI Abnormal in Boy Whose Parents Reject Chemotherapy,* CHI. TRIB., Sept. 28, 2003, at 20.

116. *Couple Missing after Fleeing with Sick Son,* CHI. TRIB., Aug. 21, 2003, at 20.

117. *Utah Won't Force Parents to Treat Son,* MILWAUKEE J. SENTINEL, Sept. 30, 2003, at 4A; Amy Joi Bryson, *Parental Rights Gain Momentum in Senate,* DESERET MORNING NEWS (Salt Lake City), Feb. 1, 2005.

118. Dave Wedge, *Cult Mom Acquitted in Baby's Starving Death,* BOSTON HERALD, Feb. 4, 2004, at 8.

119. Marie Szaniszlo, *Cultist's Guilty Plea Expected for Vision That Starved Baby,* BOSTON HERALD, Feb. 10, 2004, at 12.

120. Dave Wedge, *Jury Finds Cult Dad Guilty of Killing Son,* BOSTON HERALD, June 15, 2002, at 1.

121. Ted McDonough, *Lost Boys Found: How the Plight of Several Young Men Became a Legal battle to Bring Down a Polygamous Sect,* SALT LAKE WEEKLY, Sept. 23, 2004, *also available at* http://www.slweekly.com/editorial/2004/feat_2004-09-23.cfm (last visited Oct. 3, 2004).

122. *Id.; see also* Pamela Manson, *"Lost Boys" File Suit Against FLDS Church,* SALT LAKE TRIB., Aug. 28, 2004, at B1.

123. Brooke Adams, *Polygamy's "Lost Boys" Need Not Walk Alone,* SALT LAKE TRIB., Aug. 1, 2004, at B1.

124. *See* Derrick Nunnally, *Minister Gets 30 Months in Boy's Death,* MILWAUKEE J. SENTINEL, Aug. 18, 2004, at 1B.

125. Commonwealth v. McBurrows, 2001 PA Super. 164, 779 A.2d 509 (2001), *appeal denied*, 815 A.2d 632 (Pa. 2002), *cert. denied*, 124 S.Ct. 60 (2003).

126. Keith Herbert, *Pastor Is Sentenced In Beating*, PHILA. INQUIRER, Aug. 28, 2004.

127. Jim Vertuno, *Two on Trial in Bible Studies Beating*, ASSOC. PRESS, Dec. 3, 2003.

128. Claire Osborn, *Brothers Get Prison Terms for Beating*, AUSTIN AMERICAN-STATESMAN (Tex.), Dec. 13, 2003, at B1.

129. Associated Press, *Church Members Sentenced on Abuse Charges*, LAWRENCE J.-WORLD (Kan.), Jan. 7, 2004.

130. Associated Press, *Case Involved Restraining Kids with Belts, Cords*, TOPEKA CAPITAL-J. (Kan.), Feb. 8, 2004.

131. Associated Press, *Church Members Sentenced*, *supra* note 129.

132. *See* Richard Greer, *Preacher Convicted in Whipping Faces Jail for Directing DeKalb Church Beating*, ATLANTA J.-CONST., June 5, 1993, at 1B.

133. Steve Visser & Jill Young Miller, *Strong Words End Church Trial*, ATLANTA J.-CONST., Oct. 15, 2002 at 1B.

134. Jill Young Miller, *House of Prayer's Preacher Leaves Jail*, ATLANTA J.-CONST., Jan. 26, 2003, at 7C.

135. Steve Visser, *Minister Sentenced to 2 Years*, ATLANTA J.-CONST., Aug. 26, 2003, at 3B.

136. Michael Ferraresi, *Teen Reach Founder Fires Back at State*, ARIZ. REPUBLIC, Apr. 3, 2004, at 1B.

137. The bill has not yet been passed into law.

138. Cara Connelly, *Former Students, Prosecutors Question Methods of Some 'Tough Love' Schools*, KY3 NEWS (Springfield, Mo.), Apr. 30, 2004, *available at* http://www.ky3.com/newsdetailed.asp?id=6189 (last visited Oct. 24, 2004).

139. MO. REV. STAT. § 210.254 (2004).

140. Paul Pinkham, *Is Camp Salvation or Ruin? Children's Home Again Defends Itself against Abuse Complaints*, FLORIDA TIMES-UNION, July 13, 2003, at B1.

141. Paul Pinkham, *Second Lawsuit Alleges Abuse at Camp: Harvest Baptist Church Runs Camp for Troubled Youths*, FLORIDA TIMES-UNION, June 7, 2003, at B1; *see also* Pinkham, *Is Camp Salvation or Ruin?*, *supra* note 140.

142. Jessie-Lynne Kerr, *Law & Disorder: Church Settles Abuse Suit*, FLORIDA TIMES-UNION, Nov. 8, 2003, at B3.

143. Pinkham, *Is Camp Salvation or Ruin?*, *supra* note 140.

144. Pinkham, *Second Lawsuit Alleges Abuse at Camp*, *supra* note 141.

145. Pinkham, *Is Camp Salvation or Ruin?*, *supra* note 140.

146. *See generally* NATIONAL ASSOC. FOR REGULATORY ADMIN. & THE CHILDREN'S FOUNDATION, 2004 FAMILY CHILD CARE LICENSING STUDY (2004).

147. *See* Christian Bottorff, *Judge Rules Church Is in Contempt*, TENNESSEAN, Sept. 8, 2004, at 1B.

148. *See, e.g.*, Health Serv. Div., Health & Env't Dep't v. Temple Baptist Church, 814 P.2d 130 (N.M. 1991); North Valley Baptist Church v. McMahon, 696 F. Supp. 518 (E.D. Cal. 1988), *aff'd.* 893 F.2d 1139 (9th Cir. 1990), *cert. denied*, 496 U.S. 937 (1990); Michigan Dep't of Soc. Serv. v. Emmanuel Baptist Preschool, 455 N.W.2d 1 (Mich. 1990); State v. Corpus Christi People's Baptist Church, Inc., 683 S.W.2d 692 (Tex. 1984), *appeal dismissed*, 474 U.S. 801 (1985); State ex rel. O'Sullivan v. Heart Ministries, Inc., 607 P.2d 1102 (Kan. 1980); North Carolina v. Fayetteville Street Christian School, 258 S.E.2d 459 (N.C. App. Ct. 1979), *vacated and remanded on other grounds*, 261 S.E.2d 908 (N.C. 1980), *vacated and remanded on other grounds following reh'g*, 265 S.E.2d 387 (N.C. 1980), *appeal dismissed*, 449 U.S. 807 (1980).

149. Mo. Rev. Stat. § 210.211(1)(5), (2) (2004). The other states with complete exemptions are: Alabama (Code of Ala.§ 38-7-3 (2004)); Arkansas (Ark. Code Ann. §§ 20-78-206, 209(a), 9-28-402 (2004)); Florida (Fla. Stat. § 402.316); Indiana (Ind. Code Ann. § 2-17.2-2-8(5) (2004)); Maryland (Md. Code Ann. § 5-574(b) (2004)); North Carolina (N.C. Gen. Stat. § 131D-10.4(1) (2004)); Vermont (Vt. Stat. Ann. tit. 33, § 3502(b)(3) (2004)). Some states exclude religiously operated child care from the definition of "child care" and provide the exemption that way. *See, e.g.*, Michigan (Mich. Comp. Laws § 722.111(1)(e) (2004)); New Hampshire (N.H. Rev. Stat. Ann. §170-E:3(I)(d) (2004)); New Jersey (N.J. Stat. Ann. §30:5B-3(b)(3) (2004)). Ohio is slightly different, because the exemption only applies where the parent, guardian, or custodian are participating in religious services on the same premises. *See*Ohio Rev. Code Ann. § 5104.02(b) (2004)).

150. *See* Indiana Family and Social Services Administration, et al., The ABC's of a Child Care Business 3-4 (3d ed. 2002) (contrasting the requirements of licensed facilities with those of facilities registered by ministries to illustrate this point), *available at* http://www.in.gov/fssa/carefinder/become/abc.pdf (last visited Oct. 18, 2004); *see also* Vermont State Auditor, Review of Child Care Licensing and Registration by the Child Care Services Division of the Department of Social and Rehabilitation Services (December 18, 1997), *available at* http://www.state.vt.us/sao/reviews/ch_final.htm (last visited Oct. 18, 2004) (explaining the distinction in Vermont's dual system).

151. The states are: Delaware (Del. Code Ann. tit. 31, § 343 (2004)); Kansas (Kan. Stat. Ann. § 65-501 (2003)); Maryland (Md. Code Ann., Fam. Law § 5-509 (2003)); Massachusetts (Mass. Ann. Laws ch. 28A, § 11 (2004)); Michigan (Mich. Comp. Laws § 722.111 (2004) which only exempts from licensing "A facility operated by a religious organization where children are cared for not more than 3 hours while persons responsible for the children are attending religious services."); Oklahoma (Okla. Stat. tit. 10, § 403 (2004)); Washington (Wash. Rev. Code § 74.15.090 (2004) with an exception only for Native American tribes).

152. Ala. Const. Amend. No. 622 (1999); Ariz. Rev. Stat. §§ 41-1493 to -1493.02 (1999); Conn. Gen. Stat. Ann. § 52-571b (1993); Fla. Stat. Ann. §§ 761.01-.05 (1998); Idaho Code §§ 73-401 to 404 (2000); 775 Ill. Comp. Stat. Ann. 35 (1998);

N.M. Stat. Ann. §§ 28-22-1 to -5 (2000); Okla. Stat. Ann. tit. 51, §§ 251-258 (2000); Pa. Stat. tit. 71, §§ 2401-2407 (2002); R.I. Gen. Laws §§ 42-80.1-1 to .1-4 (1993); S.C. Code §§ 1-32-10 to -60 (1999); Texas Civ. Prac. & Rem. Code§§ 110.001 to .012 (1999).

153. Employment Div. v. Smith, 494 U.S. 872 (1990).

154. Attorney General v. Desilets, 636 N.E.2d 233, 236 (Mass. 1994) ("In interpreting [the state constitution], we prefer to adhere to the standards of earlier First Amendment jurisprudence.").

155. Rourke v. New York State Dep't of Correctional Serv, 603 N.Y.S.2d 647, 650 (N.Y. Sup. Ct. 1993), aff'd, 201 A.D.2d 179 (N.Y. App. Div. 1994) ("[I]t is hard to imagine that New York would not continue to apply a 'strict scrutiny' standard of review, and a balancing of the state's competing interests and the fundamental rights of the individual.").

156. State v. Hershberger, 462 N.W.2d 393, 397 (Minn. 1990) ("Minnesotans are afforded greater protection for religious liberties against governmental action under the state constitution than under the first amendment of the federal constitution").

157. Swanner v. Anchorage Equal Rights Comm'n 874 P.2d 274, 281 (Alaska 1994), cert. denied, 513 U.S. 979 (1994) ("[E]ven though the Free Exercise Clause of the Alaska Constitution is identical to the Free Exercise Clause of the United States Constitution, we are not required to adopt and apply the Smith test to religious exemption cases involving the Alaska Constitution merely because the United States Supreme Court adopted that test to determine the applicability of religious exemptions under the United States Constitution. We will apply [the Sherbert standard], to determine whether the anti-discrimination laws violate Swanner's right to free exercise under the Alaska Constitution.").

158. State v. Miller, 549 N.W.2d 235 (Wis. 1996) ("We hold that our state constitution provides an independent basis on which to decide this case. . . . We will apply the compelling state interest/least restrictive alternative test.").

159. First Covenant Church of Seattle v. City of Seattle, 840 P.2d 174, 187 (Wash. 1992) ("State action is constitutional under the free exercise clause of [the state constitution] if the action results in no infringement of a citizen's right or if a compelling state interest justifies any burden on the free exercise of religion.").

160. Humphrey v. Lane, 728 N.E.2d 1039, 1045 (Ohio 2000) ("[T]he Ohio Constitution's free exercise protection is broader, and we therefore vary from the federal test for religiously neutral, evenly applied government actions. We apply a different standard to a different constitutional protection. We adhere to the standard long held in Ohio regarding free exercise claims – that the state enactment must serve a compelling state interest and must be the least restrictive means of furthering that interest.").

161. Rupert v. City of Portland, 605 A.2d 63 (Me. 1992) (quoting and reaffirming Blount v. Department of Educational & Cultural Services, 551 A.2d 1377 (Me. 1988), utilizing the Supreme Court's pre-Smith free exercise test.

162. *See* In re Browning, 476 S.E.2d 465, 467 (N.C. App. 1996) (applying strict scrutiny).

163. State v. Evans, 796 P.2d 178, 180 (Kan. Ct. App. 1990) ("The Kansas Constitution contains a strong prohibition against religious coercion. We are persuaded that . . . 'only those interests of the highest order' ought to override the free exercise of religion.'") (quoting Wright v. Raines, 571 P.2d 26, *rev. denied*, 222 Kan. 749 (1977), *cert. denied* 435 U.S. 933 (1978)).

164. Barbara Baird, *Youth Groups Fear Specter of Sexual Abuse*, L.A. TIMES, Sept. 25, 1988, at 4 (quoting psychiatrist and sexual abuse expert, "most of those identified [accused] as molesters are never booked; most of those who are booked are dismissed without charges. And any charges are often negotiated down so that they are not recognizable as a sexual crime. The effective child molester will be active all his life without attracting accusations. Only the inept losers get caught.").

165. *See supra* note 8 (describing coverage).

166. *2 Paths, No Easy Solution*, *supra* note 39.

## 3. Marriage

1. Goodridge v. Dep't of Pub. Health, 440 Mass. 309, 313–14 (2003).

2. *Id.* at 320–21.

3. Opinions of the Justices to the Senate, 440 Mass. 1201, 1205–1206 (2004).

4. *See* Terence Neilan, *High Court in Massachusetts Rules Gays Have Right to Marry*, N.Y. TIMES, Nov. 18, 2003, *available at* http://www.nytimes.com/2003/11/18/national/18CND-GAYS.html?ex=1097640000&en=cb3367646f6d6b61&ei=5070&hp (last visited Oct. 11, 2004); *see also* Pam Belluck, *Same-sex Marriage: The Overview*, N.Y. TIMES, Nov. 19, 2003, at A1 (quoting Tony Perkins of the Family Research Council: "[I]t is inexcusable for this court to force the state Legislature to 'fix' its state constitution to make it comport with the pro-homosexual agenda of four court justices.").

5. Beliefnet, *Reactions to the Massachusetts Supreme Court Ruling*, at http://www.beliefnet.com/story/136/story_13603_1.html (last visited Oct. 12, 2004) (quoting Brian Fahling, Senior Trial Attorney, AFA [American Family Association] Center for Law & Policy).

6. Elizabeth Mehren, *Mass. High Court Backs Gay Marriage*, L.A. TIMES, Nov. 19, 2003, at A1 (quoting Roberta Combs, Pres, Christian Coalition of America).

7. *See* Pam Belluck, *Same-sex Marriage: The Overview*, *supra* note 4 (quoting President George W. Bush).

8. Rose Arce, *Massachusetts Court Upholds Same-sex Marriage*, CNN, Feb. 6, 2004, *available at* http://www.cnn.com/2004/LAW/02/04/gay.marriage/ (last visited October 11, 2004) (quoting President George W. Bush).

9. *See* Marriage Protection Amendment, H.R.J. Res. 106, 108th Cong. (Sept. 23, 2004), *also available at* http://thomas.loc.gov/cgi-bin/query/z?c108:H.J.res.106: (last visited Oct. 12, 2004); H.R.J. Res. 56, 108th Cong. (May 21, 2003). Marriage Protection Act of 2004, H. R. 3313, 108th Cong. (passed in the House of Representatives on July 22, 2004).

10. *"The Musgrave Federal Marriage Amendment"*: *Hearing Before the Subcomm. on the Constitution of the House Comm. On the Judiciary,* 108th Cong. (May 13, 2003) (statement of U.S. Rep. Marilyn Musgrave), *also available at* http://www. house.gov/judiciary/musgrave051304.htm (last visited Oct. 13, 2004). The proposed Federal Marriage Amendment resolution stated: "Marriage in the United States shall consist only of the union of a man and a woman. Neither this Constitution or the constitution of any State, nor state or federal law, shall be construed to require that marital status or the legal incidents thereof be conferred upon unmarried couples or groups." H.R.J. Res. 56, 108th Cong. (May 21, 2003).

11. *"Limiting Federal Court Jurisdiction to Protect Marriage for the States"*: *Hearing Before the Subcomm. on the Constitution of the House Comm. On the Judiciary,* 108th Cong. (June 24, 2004) (statement of Former U.S. Rep. William E. Dannemeyer), *also available at* http://www.house.gov/judiciary/ dannemeyer062404.pdf (last visited Oct. 13, 2004). There were 19 Senator co-sponsors to the joint resolution to amend the Constitution to forbid gay marriage (S.J.RES.40), and 131 Representatives (H.J.RES.56).

12. *Editorial: Call Congress Now; Urge Support for Marriage Amendment During Sept. 30 Vote,* Sept. 24, 2004, BAPTIST PRESS, *available at* http://www.bpnews. net/bpnews.asp?ID=19174 (last visited Oct. 15, 2004).

13. Jerry Falwell Ministries, Petition for Support of the Federal Marriage Amendment, *available at* http://www.onemanonewoman.com/ (last visited Oct. 15, 2004).

14. Robert P. George, *One Man and One Woman,* WALL STREET J., Nov. 28, 2003 at A8.

15. Matthew D. Staver, *Why Do We Need a Federal Marriage Amendment?,* in SAME-SEX MARRIAGE: PUTTING EVERY HOUSEHOLD AT RISK (2004), *available at* http://www.lc.org/ProFamily/FMA_why_we_need04.htm (last visited Oct. 15, 2004).

16. *See National Briefs: Polygamist's Appeal Based on Gay Sex Ruling,* HOUSTON CHRON., Dec. 2, 2003, at A17; Complaint, Bronson v. Swenson, No. 04-CV-0021 (D. Utah filed Jan 12, 2004), *also available at* http://marriagelaw.cua.edu/Law/ cases/ut/Complaint.pdf (last visited Oct. 12, 2004).

17. *See* Angie Welling, *Green's Conviction Is Upheld by Ruling,* DESERET MORNING NEWS (Salt Lake City), Sept. 4, 2004, *also available at* http://deseretnews. com/dn/view/0,1249,595089043,00.html (last visited Oct. 12, 2004).

18. *See* Complaint, Bronson v. Swenson, No. 04-CV-0021 (D. Utah filed Jan 12, 2004), *also available at* http://marriagelaw.cua.edu/Law/cases/ut/Complaint.pdf (last visited Oct. 12, 2004).

19. *Id.*

20. Press Release, Alliance for Marriage, *Introduction of the Federal Marriage Amendment in Congress,* (May 15, 2002) (on file with author), *also available at* www.allianceformarriage.org/site/PageServer?pagename=mac_coalition_statement (last visited Oct. 15, 2004).

21. Vatican Offices of the Congregation for the Doctrine of the Faith, *Considerations Regarding Proposals to Give Legal Recognition to Unions Between Homosexual*

*Persons,* June 23, 2003, at ¶ 4 (approved by Pope John Paul II on Mar. 28, 2003), *also available at* http://www.vatican.va/roman_curia/congregations/cfaith/documents/rc_con_cfaith_doc_20030731_homosexual-unions_en.html (last visited Oct. 15, 2004).

22. Dennis M. Mahoney, *Is Homosexuality a Sin?,* COLUMBUS DISPATCH (Ohio), Sept. 12, 2003, at F1.

23. *See id.*

24. Bill Graves, *Faiths Clash on Gay Marriage,* OREGONIAN, Sept. 19, 2004, at B1.

25. Don Lattin, *Black Clergy Gathering to Fight Gay Matrimony,* S.F. CHRON., May 15, 2004, at A4.

26. Alliance Defense Fund, What We Believe: Faith Mission, *available at* http://www.alliancedefensefund.org/about/whatwebelieve.php# (last visited Oct. 13, 2004).

27. Alliance Defense Fund, *Protecting Family Values,* at http://www.alliancedefensefund.org/issues/familyvalues.php (last visited Oct. 15, 2004).

28. *See* Alan Cooperman, *Opponents Of Gay Marriage Divided,* WASH. POST, Nov. 29, 2003, at A1 (interviewing Matt Daniels, President of Alliance for Marriage); *see also* Mathew D. Staver, Esq. et al., Letter on behalf of The Liberty Counsel, *The Federal Marriage Amendment Preserves Marriage as the Union of One Man and One Woman and is Consistent with Constitutional Jurisprudence and Federalism,* Jul. 10, 2004, *available at* http://www.lc.org/marriage/fma_memo_senate_071004.pdf (last visited Oct. 12, 2004); *Editorial: Call Congress Now; Urge Support for Marriage Amendment During Sept. 30 Vote,* BAPTIST PRESS, Sept. 24, 2004, *available at* http://www.bpnews.net/bpnews.asp?ID=19174 (last visited Oct. 12, 2004).

29. *See* Press Release, Cardinal Adam Maida, Archbishop of Detroit, An Open Letter to Michigan's United States Senators [Levin and Stabenow], July 2, 2004 (on file with author), *also available at* http://www.aodonline.org/aodonline-sqlimages/ PressReleaseStatements/Maida/040702letter_senators.pdf (last visited Oct. 12, 2004). Orthodox Jews also support the Amendment. *See* Press Release, Union of Orthodox Jewish Congregations of America, Union Of Orthodox Jewish Congregations Supports Constitutional Marriage Amendment, July 13, 2004 (on file with author), *also available at* http://www.ou.org/public/statements/2001/nate31.htm (last visited Oct. 24, 2004).

30. Todd Hertz, *Christian Conservatives Split on Federal Marriage Amendment,* CHRISTIANITY TODAY.COM, June 20, 2004, *available at* http://www.christianitytoday.com/ct/2002/123/43.0.html (last visited Oct. 12, 2004) (discussing divide among Christian conservatives whether FMA was adequate to ensure there would be no marriages in the United States other than heterosexual).

31. *See, e.g.,* Human Rights Campaign, Organizations Opposed to a Federal Anti-Marriage Rights Constitutional Amendment (as of May 13, 2004), *at* http://www.hrc.org/Template.cfm?Section=Center&CONTENTID=17630& TEMPLATE=/ContentManagement/ContentDisplay.cfm (last visited Oct. 12, 2004).

32. *See* James D. Besser, *Gay Marriage Debate Now Embroiling Jews*, JEW-ISH WEEK, Mar. 12, 2004, *available at* http://www.thejewishweek.com/news/newscontent.php3?artid=9179 (last visited Oct. 11, 2004).

33. Lawrence v. Texas, 539 U.S. 558 (2003).

34. Harold O. J. Brown, *A Decisive Turn to Paganism*, 48 CHRISTIANITY TODAY 39 (Aug. 2004), *also available at* http://www.christianitytoday.com/ct/2004/008/24.39.html (last visited Oct. 15, 2004).

35. DIANA L. ECK, A NEW RELIGIOUS AMERICA: HOW A "CHRISTIAN COUNTRY" HAS BECOME THE WORLD'S MOST RELIGIOUSLY DIVERSE NATION (2001).

36. *Id. at* 1.

37. Lee Duigon, *Why Is This Happening? "Gay Marriage" as a Scourge*, CHALCEDON FOUNDATION, Mar. 6, 2004, *available at* http://www.chalcedon.edu/articles/ 0403/040306duigon.php (last visited Oct. 12, 2004).

38. *See* Michael Paulsen, *Protestants Weigh Same-Sex Marriage*, BOSTON GLOBE, Nov. 30, 2003, at B10; Don Lattin, *Rabbinical Group Backs Gay Marriage*, S. F. CHRON., Mar. 20, 2004, at A2.

39. Sharon Sheridan, *New Same-sex Rites Resolution Emerges*, EPISCOPAL NEWS SERVICE, Aug. 3, 2003, *available at* http://www.episcopalchurch.org/3577-17813_ENG_HTM.htm (last visited Oct. 13, 2004); Lydia Polgreen, *Episcopalians Ponder New Gay Bishop*, N.Y. TIMES, Aug. 11, 2003, at A4.

40. THE LAMBETH COMMISSION ON COMMUNION, THE WINDSOR REPORT 2004, at ¶¶ 3, 157 (Anglican Communion Office, London 2004), *also available at* http://windsor2004.anglicancommunion.org/windsor2004/downloads/windsor2004full.pdf (last visited Oct. 25, 2004).

41. *Proceeding with Gay Unions – Same-sex Marriages*, CHRISTIAN CENTURY, Aug. 16, 2000, *also available at* http://www.findarticles.com/p/articles/mi_m1058/is_23_117/ai_65014567 (last visited Oct. 13, 2004).

42. *Id.*

43. *Id.*

44. *Id.*

45. *Id.*

46. *See* Richard Cameron Blake & Lonn Litchfield, *Religious Freedom in Southern Africa: The Developing Jurisprudence*, 1998 B.Y.U.L. REV. 515, 521 (1998) ("The Dutch Reformed Church (known in Afrikaans as Nederduitse Gereformeerde Kerk (NGK)) provided the moral and philosophical underpinnings for Nationalist apartheid policies. It also gave support to particular laws and made statements supporting the government's actions.").

47. DUNBAR ROWLAND, 1 JEFFERSON DAVIS 286 (1923).

48. *Ephesians* 6:5–9 (Jerusalem Bible).

49. *See* WILLIAM H. SEIBERT, THE UNDERGROUND RAILROAD FROM SLAVERY TO FREEDOM 93–99 (1968) (discussing the role of Quakers and Methodists in the crusade against slavery).

50. For example, the Christian Legal Society was part of a coalition supporting the Freedom from Religious Persecution Act of 1998, *see* H.R. 2431, 105th Cong.

H3,267–69 (May 14, 1998), during the same year they supported the Religious Liberty and Charitable Donation Protection Act of 1998, *see* H.R. 2604, 105th Cong. H4,001 (June 03, 1998).

51. *Policy Responses to the Denial and Restriction of Religious Liberty in the People's Republic of China: Hearing Before the United States Commission on International Religious Freedom* (Mar. 16, 2002) (Prepared Statement of Rev. Drew Christiansen, S.J., Woodstock Theological Center [Georgetown University] Washington, D.C.), *also available at* http://www.uscirf.gov/hearings/16mar00/christiansenPT.php3 (last visited Oct. 15, 2004).

52. *See* HAROLD J. BERMAN, LAW AND REVOLUTION II: THE IMPACT OF THE PROTESTANT REFORMATIONS ON THE WESTERN LEGAL TRADITION 209–10, 215–16 (2003) (Between 1630 and 1640, an estimated twenty thousand religious dissenters fled to the Massachusetts Bay Colony, and a similar number emigrated to the Netherlands); *see also* ROBERT E. RODES, JR., LAW AND MODERNIZATION IN THE CHURCH OF ENGLAND: CHARLES II TO THE WELFARE STATE 81 (1991); 1 WILLIAM S. HOLDSWORTH, A HISTORY OF ENGLISH LAW (7th ed. 1956).

53. 539 U.S. 558 (2003).

54. *Id.* at 578.

55. *Id.*

56. *Id.* at 590 (Scalia, J. dissenting).

57. Harold O.J. Brown, *A Decisive Turn to Paganism, supra* note 34.

58. *Id.*

59. *In re* Kandu, No. 03-51312, 2004 WL 1854112, at *9–10 (Bankr. W.D. Wash. Aug. 17, 2004) (distinguishing *Goodridge* on the basis of the more protective Massachusetts Constitution and holding that "there is no basis for this Court to unilaterally determine at this time that there is a fundamental right to marry someone of the same sex"). In similar cases, an appeals court in Oregon held that the state deprived same-sex couples of fundamental rights by not allowing same-sex marriage and found the statute unconstitutional. Li v. State, No. 0403-03057, 2004 WL 1258167, slip. op. at *10, (Or. Cir. Apr. 20, 2004), and a trial court in New Jersey decided two weeks before *Goodridge* that "[t]here is nothing in the New Jersey Constitution or the judicial decisions in this State to support the conclusion that same-sex marriage is a fundamental right." Lewis v. Harris, No. MER-L-15-03, 2003 WL 23191114, at *16 (N.J. Super. Ct. Nov. 5, 2003).

60. Kate Zernike, *Groups Vow Not to Let Losses Dash Gay Rights,* N.Y. TIMES, Nov. 14, 2004, at 30.

61. Anti-Polygamy Acts (the Morrill Act), ch. 126, 12 Stat. 501 (1862) (repealed 1910). The only reference to polygamy in the current U.S. Code deals with immigration law (Inadmissible aliens include "Practicing polygamists. Any immigrant who is coming to the United States to practice polygamy is inadmissible." 8 U.S.C.S. § 1182 (a)(10)(A) (2004)).

62. AMERICAN HERITAGE DICTIONARY OF THE ENGLISH LANGUAGE (4th ed. 2000), *also available at* http://www.bartleby.com/61/41/P0424100.html (last visited Oct. 17, 2004).

63. AMERICAN HERITAGE DICTIONARY OF THE ENGLISH LANGUAGE (4th ed. 2000), *also available at* http://www.bartleby.com/61/48/P0424800.html (last visited Oct. 17, 2004).

64. *Lawrence,* 539 U.S. at 578.

65. Reynolds v. United States, 98 U.S. 145, 166 (1879) ("Laws are made for the government of actions, and while they cannot interfere with mere religious belief and opinions, they may with practices.").

66. *Id.* at 166–76.

67. State v. Barlow, 153 P.2d 647, 653 (Utah 1944).

68. *Hunting Bountiful: Ending Half a Century of Exploitation,* ECONOMIST (London), July 8, 2004.

69. Daphne Bramham, *Editorial: See No Evil, Hear No Evil, Speak No Evil: Local People and Politicians Are Uncomfortable That Police and State Are Opening the Closed Doors at Bountiful,* VANCOUVER SUN (B.C.), Aug. 21, 2004 at C7.

70. *Opinion: B.C. Must Confront Polygamy Abuse,* EDMONTON JOURNAL (Alta.), Sept. 13, 2004, at A14 (despite doubts in the B.C. government whether the anti-polygamy law would survive free exercise scrutiny, "Canada's Justice Minister Irwin Cotler, however, is confident the law would stand.").

71. 401 U.S. 437 (1971).

72. *Id.* at 461.

73. *See* Angie Welling, *Green's Conviction Is Upheld by Ruling,* DESERET MORNING NEWS (Salt Lake City), Sept. 4, 2004 (quoting Green's attorney John Bucher on his plans to appeal to the Supreme Court because "It's got to be appealed. It can't stand. . . . "); *see also* Complaint, Bronson v. Swenson, No. 04-CV-0021 (D. Utah filed Jan 12, 2004).

74. *See, e.g.,* Davis v. Beason, 133 U.S. 333, 348 (1890); *Reynolds,* 98 U.S. at 166; White v. United States, No. 01-4225, 41 Fed. Appx. 325, 326 (10th Cir. May 23, 2002); Potter v. Murray City, 760 F.2d 1065, 1070 (10th Cir 1985); *In re* State in Interest of Black, 283 P.2d 887, 903–904 (Utah 1955); State v. Barlow, 153 P.2d 647, 653 (Utah 1944); United States v. Snow, 9 P. 697, 700–701 (Utah 1886).

75. *In re* State in Interest of Black, 283 P.2d at 904 (emphasis in original).

76. Republican Platform of 1856, *in* 1 NATIONAL PARTY PLATFORMS 1840–1972, at 27, 27 (Donald B. Johnson & Kirk H. Porter eds., 5th ed. 1975).

77. *See* Sarah Barringer Gordon, Symposium, *A War of Words: Revelation and Storytelling in the Campaign Against Mormon Polygamy,* 78 CHI.-KENT. L. REV. 739, 747–57 (2003).

78. *See* Susan Mazur, *Seven Brides for One Brother: Plural Marriage Is Rife in the Western United States,* FINANCIAL TIMES (London), Oct. 28, 2000, at 1; Fabian Dawson, *13 Year Old Sent to B.C. for Husband,* PROVINCE (Vancouver, B.C.), Dec. 16, 2000, *available at* http://www.rickross.com/reference/polygamy/polygamy50.html (last visited Sept. 26, 2004); *The Canadian Home of Polygamy,* CBC NEWS (Canada), Jan. 15, 2003, *transcript available at* http://www.rickross.

com/reference/polygamy/polygamy99.html (last visited Sept. 26, 2004). The Mann Act provides, in pertinent part: "A person who knowingly transports an individual who has not attained the age of 18 years in interstate or foreign commerce. . . with intent that the individual engage in prostitution, or in any sexual activity for which any person can be charged with a criminal offense. . . . " 18 U.S.C. § 2423 (a) (2003).

79. Cleveland v. United States, 329 U.S. 14, 20 (1946).

80. *Grants for Outreach To Target Populations under the Trafficking in Persons Program*, U.S. Department of Health and Human Services, Administration for Children and Families (ACF), Office of Refugee Resettlement, Funding Opportunity No. HHS-2004-ACF-ORR-ZV-0006 (filed Jul. 29, 2004), *available at* http://www2.acf.hhs.gov/grants/open/HHS-2004-ACF-ORR-ZV-0006.html (last visited Oct. 16, 2004).

81. *See, e.g.*, United States v. Cole, 262 F.3d 704 (8th Cir. 2001); United States v. Draper, No. 98-10082, 1999 U.S. App. LEXIS 10990 (9th Cir. May 25, 1999); United States v. Niece, No. 93-5011, 1993 U.S. App. LEXIS 27327 (6th Cir. Oct. 19, 1993).

82. John Dougherty, *Janet's Missed Opportunity: Governor Napolitano Went to Utah, and All We Got Was Some Lousy Ring Kissing*, PHOENIX NEW TIMES, Oct. 7, 2004, *also available at* http://www.phoenixnewtimes.com/issues/2004-10-07/news/dougherty.html (last visited Oct. 16, 2004).

83. Joseph A. Reaves, *Troubles Dogging Polygamy Prophet*, ARIZONA REPUBLIC, Aug. 1, 2004, at 1A (listing "key dates" for FLDS).

84. Amanda J. Crawford, *Polygamy Town Gets Outside Aid*, ARIZONA REPUBLIC, Aug. 10, 2004, at 3B.

85. *See, e.g.*, Brooke Adams, *Polygamy's "Lost Boys" Need Not Walk Alone*, SALT LAKE TRIB., Aug. 1, 2004, at B1; Patty Henetz, *Krakauer Still Vexed by FLDS*, DESERETNEWS.COM (Salt Lake City), July 31, 2004, *available at* http://deseretnews.com/dn/print/1,1442,595081003,00.html (last visited Oct. 16, 2004); Nancy Perkins, *FLDS Church, Leaders Sued by 6 "Lost Boys"*, DESERET MORNING NEWS (Salt Lake City), Aug. 28, 2004.

86. Travis Reed, *Group Calls Utah Soft on Polygamy*, FLORENCE NEWS (Ariz.), July 15, 2004, *available at* http://www.zwire.com/site/news.cfm?newsid=12354937& BRD=1817&PAG=461&dept_id=222076&rfi=8 (last visited Oct. 16, 2004).

87. Patrice St. Germain, *Utah Gets Grant for Rural Communities: Money Will Be Used to Help Domestic Violence Victims in Polygamous Colonies*, SPECTRUM (St. George, Utah), Aug. 31, 2004.

88. Mindelle Jacobs, *Blind Eye Turned to Forced Polygamy*, EDMONTON SUN (Alta.), June 12, 2004, at 11.

89. Kevin Martin, *Editorial: Leave Bountiful to Courts*, CALGARY SUN (Alta.), July 29, 2004, at 15.

90. Melissa Ridgen, *Commune Cop Probe Welcomed*, CALGARY SUN (Alta.), July 24, 2004, at 2.

91. Letter from Seven Complainants, former wives or concubines at Bountiful commune, to Tribunal Members, B.C. Human Rights Tribunal 1 (May 19, 2004) (on file with author); *see also* Ethan Baron, *British Columbia Failed Commune's Women, Girls, Complaint Alleges*, NATIONAL POST (Vancouver B.C.), Sept. 1, 2004, at A6.

92. Bill Laye, *Caution Urged in Cult Case*, CALGARY SUN (Alta.), July 30, 2004, at 2.

93. *Editorial: More Perfect Unions*, SALT LAKE TRIB., Aug. 15, 2004.

94. Brian Barnard, *Public Forum Letters*, SALT LAKE TRIB., Aug. 22, 2004.

95. Andrea Moore-Emmett, *Inherently Destructive*, SALT LAKE TRIB., Aug. 31, 2004, at A12.

96. Jonathan Turley, *Polygamy Laws Expose Our Own Hypocrisy; Rights Should Be Based on Principle, Not Popularity*, USA TODAY, Oct. 4, 2004, at A13.

97. *Id.*

98. Associated Press, *Judge Upholds Charges Against Wesson*, L.A. TIMES, Apr. 13, 2004 at B7 ("Police said Wesson engaged in a lifestyle of incest and polygamy, fathering children with his own daughters and nieces. They allege that he held total control over his family and likened himself to God.").

99. *See, e.g.,* In re Conduct of Kirkman, 830 P.2d 206, 207 (Or. 1992) (disbarring a judge accused of bigamy and saying "These were not 'victimless' crimes. The accused's duplicity existed over a period of years, causing injury and humiliation to both of his families."); Lateef Mungin, *Alleged Bigamist May Have Fled to Tennessee*, ATLANTA J.-CONST., Nov. 5, 2003, at 4J (describing allegations against Anthony Glenn Owens, "who may have been married to at least nine women at the same time" and married the "women to steal money from them."); John Ellement, *Bigamist Sentenced for Theft of Funds*, BOSTON GLOBE, February 27, 2003, at B2.

100. Press Release, Tapestry Against Polygamy, June 18, 2004, (on file with author), *also available at* http://www.polygamy.org/releases.shtml (last visited Oct. 14, 2004).

101. ANDREA MOORE-EMMETT, GOD'S BROTHEL: THE EXTORTION OF SEX FOR SALVATION IN CONTEMPORARY MORMON AND CHRISTIAN FUNDAMENTALIST POLYGAMY AND THE STORIES OF 18 WOMEN WHO ESCAPED (2004) [hereinafter GOD'S BROTHEL].

102. Email from Nancy Mereska, Coordinator, Stop Polygamy in Canada, to Marci A. Hamilton, Oct. 18, 2004 (on file with author).

103. *See, e.g.,* GOD'S BROTHEL, *supra* note 101, at 38; TODD COMPTON, IN SACRED LONELINESS: THE PLURAL WIVES OF JOSEPH SMITH 199 (1997).

104. No Child Left Behind Act of 2001, 20 U.S.C. §§ 6301 et seq. (2004). "The purpose of this title is to ensure that all children have a fair, equal, and significant opportunity to obtain a high-quality education and reach, at a minimum, proficiency on challenging State academic achievement standards and state academic assessments." 20 U.S.C. § 6301.

105. Mike D'Amour, *Sect Wives Defend Lives: Women Say Polygamy Choice Is Theirs*, CALGARY SUN (Alta.), July 29, 2004, at 4.

106. *See* Brooke Adams, *Plural Wives Defend Lifestyle*, SALT LAKE TRIB., Feb. 13, 2004, at C1. *See also* MARY BATCHELOR, ET AL., VOICES IN HARMONY: CONTEMPORARY WOMEN CELEBRATE PLURAL MARRIAGE (2000) (a collection of essays by women who are living in polygamous marriages supporting their lifestyle); *see also* Catherine Elsworth, *Investigation Launched into Polygamous Sect Dubbed "Canada's Dirty Little Secret,"* DAILY TELEGRAPH (London), Aug. 5, 2004, at 14.

107. Rasheed Oluwa, *In Marriage, Three's a Crowd – And a Crime*, POUGHKEEP-SIE JOURNAL (N.Y.), Apr. 28, 2003, at 1A.

108. Naomi Schaefer Riley, *Yes, Polygamy Is Everybody's Business*, L.A. TIMES, Feb. 9, 2004, at 11.

109. *See* Nicholas Bala and Rebecca Jaremko Bromwich, *Context and Inclusivity in Canada's Evolving Definition of the Family*, 16 INT'L J. L. POL'Y & FAM. 145, 169 (2002) (quoting Flanagan: "'the historical record shows that monogamy, like private property, is indispensible to constitutional democracy... Constitutional government has emerged only in societies where monogamy was the legally enforced, or at least the commonly observed, social norm... The modern adoption of constitutional democracy in non-Western societies such as Japan and India has been accompanied by the parallel acceptance of monogamy. Those regions of the world where polygamy is still practiced... are precisely the areas where constitutional democracy has made the least progress.'").

110. *See* John Dougherty, *Double Exposure: Arizona's Finally Followed Utah's Lead and Launched Serious Action to Stop Abuses by Polygamists*, PHOENIX NEW TIMES (Ariz.), Dec. 25, 2003; *see also* Mark Havnes, *Hildale Polygamist Guilty of Unlawful Sex, Bigamy*, SALT LAKE TRIB., Aug. 15, 2003, at A1 ("FLDS members believe taking plural wives is a direct commandment from God, to be followed even if it means violating civil law.").

111. John Dougherty, *Blasphemous Backlash*, PHOENIX NEW TIMES (Ariz.), Jan. 29, 2004.

112. John Dougherty, *Bound by Fear: Polygamy in Arizona*, PHOENIX NEW TIMES (Ariz.), Mar. 13, 2003 (reporting what Ruth Stubbs says Jeffs told her when she considered leaving the sect).

113. Reuters, *Taliban Ally Urges Afghans to Boycott Elections*, NAVHIND TIMES (India), Sep. 3, 2004, *available at* http://www.navhindtimes.com/stories.php?part=news&Story_ID=090362 (last visited Oct. 16, 2004).

114. *Polygamy Law Streamlined*, DAILY EXPRESS (East Malaysia), Aug. 12, 2004.

115. Dorothy L. Hodgson, *Women's Rights as Human Rights: Women in Law and Development in Africa (WiLDAF)*, 49 AFRICA TODAY 3 (2002), *also available at* http://iupjournals.org/africatoday/aft49-2.html (last visited Oct. 26, 2004).

116. Campaign Against Polygamy & Women Oppression In Nigeria and Africa, *available at* http://www.tk-one.com/ (last visited Oct. 24, 2004) (explaining the beliefs of the organization).

117. Traci Mayette, Interview, *A Conversation with Dr. Mojubaolu Olufunke Okome, reprinted in* 10:2 AFRICA UPDATE NEWLETTER (2003), *also available at* http://www.ccsu.edu/Afstudy/upd10-2.html (last visited Oct. 26, 2004).

118. Phillip Bobbitt, *Africa's Plight – The 2050 Scenario*, THE GLOBALIST (Online Magazine), Jan. 10, 2004, *available at* http://www.theglobalist.com/DBWeb/StoryId.aspx?StoryId=3681 (last visited Oct. 26, 2004).

119. *General Recommendation 21 on Equality in Marriage and Family Relations*, Comm. on the Elimination of Discrimination Against Women, 13th Sess., at 14, U.N. Doc. A/49/38 (1994). President Jimmy Carter signed it on July 17, 1980, but the Senate never ratified it. "Both last fall and for years beforehand, the vigilance of Sen. Jesse Helms (R-NC), a longtime opponent of measures that compromise U.S. sovereignty, was the dominant reason why CEDAW never came up for ratification." Melana Zyla Vickers, *The Convention on the Elimination of All Forms of Discrimination Against Women: A Leading Example of What's Wrong With International Law* 2, FEDERALIST SOCIETY FOR LAW AND PUBLIC POLICY STUDIES, *available at* www.fed-soc.org/Intllaw& AmerSov/CEDAWvic.pdf (last visited Oct. 17, 2004).

## 4. Religious Land Use and Residential Neighborhoods

1. ZONING AND LAND USE CONTROLS § 40.03 (Matthew Bender 2002) (hereinafter ZONING AND LAND USE CONTROLS).

2. Allison B. Cohen, *Neighbors Divided*, L.A. TIMES, April 25, 2004, at K1 (hereinafter *Neighbors Divided*).

3. ZONING AND LAND USE CONTROLS, *supra* note 1.

4. *See generally* Scott Thumma, *Exploring the Megachurch Phenomena: Their Characteristics and Cultural Context* (Hartford Inst. for Relig. Research 2000), *available at* http://hirr.hartsem.edu/bookshelf/thumma_article2.html (last visited Oct. 29, 2004); *see also* Gustav Niebuhr, *Where Religion Gets a Big Dose of Shopping-Mall Culture*, N.Y. TIMES, Apr. 16, 1995, at A1; Patricia Leigh Brown, *Megachurches as Minitowns*, N.Y. TIMES, May 9, 2002, at F1; Lisa Shafer & Jack Brown, *Church Center's Profile Brings Fears: Bensalem's Christian Life Complex Goes Far Beyond Sunday Services*, PHILA. INQ., May 14, 1999, at B1 (hereinafter *Church Center's Profile Brings Fears*).

5. Haya El Nasser, *Megachurches Clash with Critics Next Door*, USA TODAY, Sept. 23, 2002, at 1A (discussing Brentwood Baptist Church in Houston, Texas).

6. Daniel B. Wood, *Cathedral Reflects a New Vision of Church*, CHRISTIAN SCIENCE MONITOR, Sept. 9, 2002, at 3 (quoting religious architecture expert Jeanne Kilde of Macalester College in St. Paul, Minn.).

7. *See* David A. Roozen, *Denominations Grow as Individuals Join Congregations*, *in* CHURCH AND DENOMINATIONAL GROWTH 20–28 (1993), *also available*

*at* http://hirr.hartsem.edu/bookshelf/Church&Denomgrowth/ch&dngrw-ch1.pdf (last visited Oct. 30, 2004); C. Kirk Hadaway, *Is Evangelistic Activity Related to Church Growth?, in* CHURCH AND DENOMINATIONAL GROWTH 178–80 (1993), *also available at* http://hirr.hartsem.edu/bookshelf/Church&Denomgrowth/ch&dngrw-ch8.pdf (last visited Oct. 30, 2004).

8. *Church Center's Profile Brings Fears, supra* note 4 (quoting John Vaughan, Church Growth Today, which studies growth and decline of new and established churches).

9. Mark Chaves & William Tsitsos, *Are Congregations Constrained by Government? Empirical Results from the National Congregations Study,* 42 J. CHURCH & STATE 335, 342, Apr. 1, 2000, *available at* 2000 WL 20257776 (hereinafter Chaves & Tsitsos); MARK CHAVES, CONGREGATIONS IN AMERICA (2004) (hereinafter CONGREGATIONS IN AMERICA).

10. Quoted in Plaintiffs' Second Amended Complaint, LRNA v. Los Angeles, Case No. CV-03-4890-HLH (C.D. Cal. Filed May 6, 2004) (appeal pending).

11. *See* Complaint, LRNA v. Los Angeles, Case No. CV-03-4890-HLH, AT ¶ 13 (C.D. Cal. Filed July 10, 2003), *also available at* http://www.thelrna.org/pdfs/hancockparklawsuit.pdf (last visited Oct. 30, 2004) (quoting Congregation Etz Chaim v. City of Los Angeles, No. BC192517 (L.A. Sup. Ct.)).

12. *Id.*

13. *Id.* at ¶14.

14. Congregation Etz Chaim v. City of Los Angeles, 371 F.3d 1122, 1129 (2004) (Aldisert, J., dissenting).

15. I represent the neighbors in that litigation. *See* Order Granting Motion to Dismiss Second Amended Complaint League of Residential Neighborhood Advocates v. City of Los Angeles, No. CV 03-4890 (CAS) (C.D. Cal. Jul. 15, 2004) (appeal pending), *also available at* http://www.thelrna.org/pdfs/071404.pdf (last visited Oct. 26, 2004).

16. *The Religious Liberty Protection Act of 1998, Hearing before the House Judiciary Committee,* 105th Cong. (Feb. 26, 1998) (statement of Rabbi Chaim Baruch Rubin), *also available at* http://www.house.gov/judiciary/22382.htm (last visited Oct. 26, 2004).

17. *Id.*

18. *Religious Land Use and Institutionalized Persons Act,* 105th Con. Rec. S7, 774–75 (Jul. 27, 2000) (joint statement of Sen. Kennedy & Sen. Hatch), *available at* http://thomas.loc.gov/cgi-bin/query/F?r106:3:./temp/~r106KoUUeD:bo: (last visited Oct. 29, 2004).

19. Douglas Laycock, *State RFRAs and Land Use Regulation,* 32 U.C. DAVIS L. REV. 755, 779 (1999).

20. Belle Terre v. Boraas, 416 U.S. 1, 9 (1974).

21. *Neighbors Divided, supra* note 2 ("There is such greater emphasis on land in California," Storzer said. "You don't see these kinds of cases in North Dakota. Most of the time this is about neighbors' NIMBYism and churches' abilities to worship.") (quoting Roman Storzer, attorney for the Becket Fund).

22. Anthony R. Picarello, Jr., *RLUIPA is Constitutional*, 56 PLAN. & ENVTL L. 3 (2004), *also available at* http://www.becketfund.org/other/RLUIPA%20Is%20 Constitutional.pdf (last visited Oct. 31, 2004).

23. *See* Chaves & Tsitsos, *supra* note 9; CONGREGATIONS IN AMERICA, *supra* note 9.

24. *See generally*, Marci A. Hamilton, *Federalism and the Public Good: The True Story behind the Religious Land use and Institutionalized Persons Act*, 78 IND. L.J. 311 (2003).

25. Freedom Baptist Church v. Township of Middletown, 204 F. Supp. 2d 857, 862 (E.D. Pa. 2002).

26. Haya El Nasser, *Megachurches Clash with Critics Next Door*, *supra* note 5.

27. Vanessa Ho, *Mainline Religions Dwindle as Megachurches Gain Ground*, SEATTLE POST-INTELLIGENCER, Mar. 18, 2002, at A1.

28. *Neighbors Divided*, *supra* note 2.

29. Justin Catanos, *What Form Faith?*, NEWS & RECORD (Greensboro, NC), May 14, 1995, at A1.

30. Laycock, *State RFRAs and Land use Regulation*, *supra* note 19, at 755, 776–80.

31. *Id.* at 760.

32. *Id.* at 758.

33. *See* John I. Gilderbloom & John P. Markham, *The Impact of Homeownership on Political Beliefs*, 73 SOCIAL FORCES 1589, 1592 (1995) ("Research has also shown that homeowners are more likely to be involved in community political activities, to be more neighborly, to be members of church or community organizations, and to be more aware of local affairs.") (internal citations omitted).

34. Grosz v. Miami Beach, 721 F.2d 729, 730 (11th Cir. 1983).

35. *Id.* at 732.

36. *Id.* at 739.

37. *Neighbors Divided*, *supra* note 2.

38. Juan Otero & Veronique Pluviose-Fenton, *City of Cheyenne, Wyo., Wins Religious Land use Case*, NATION'S CITIES WEEKLY, June 23, 2003, at 3.

39. Terry Sheridan, *Federal Law Invoked as Pastor in Broward Fights County Zoning*, BROWARD DAILY BUS. REV. (Fla.), Apr. 15, 2003 at A1.

40. ZONING AND LAND USE CONTROLS, *supra* note 1, at § 5.01; *see also id.* at § 34.02 ("Two additional valid objectives of zoning enabling legislation are prevention of overcrowding of land and ensuring against undue concentration of population.").

41. Euclid v. Ambler Realty Co., 272 U.S. 365, 367–68 (1926).

42. Lemon v. Kurtzman, 403 U.S. 602, 612 (1971).

43. *See* Locke v. Davey, 124 S. Ct. 1307, 1312–13 (2004); Church of Lukumi Babalu Aye v. City of Hialeah, 508 U.S. 520, 532–33 (1993); Employment Div. v. Smith, 494 U.S. 872, 877 (1990).

44. Chaves & Tsitsos, *supra* note 9.

45. Employment Div. v. Smith, 494 U.S. 872, 890 (1990).

46. Walz v. Tax Comm'n of New York, 397 U.S. 664 (1970).

47. St. Bartholomew's Church v. City of New York, 914 F.2d 348 (2d Cir. 1990).

48. Keeler v. Mayor & City Council of Cumberland, 940 F. Supp. 879, 886 (1996).

49. *See* East Bay Asian Local Dev. Corp. v. California, 24 Cal. 4th 693 (2000), *cert. denied*, 532 U.S. 1008 (2001) (upholding Cal. Gov't Code §§ 25373, 37361 "which have the effect of granting an exemption from landmark preservation laws to noncommercial property owned by a religious organization that objects to landmark designation and determines in a public forum that the organization would suffer a substantial hardship if the property were designated a historic landmark.").

50. Tom Barnes, *Council Shelters Religious Building*, PITTSBURGH POST-GAZETTE, Feb. 26, 2003, at B3.

51. Judy Evans, *District Approved, Minus Churches*, DALLAS MORNING NEWS, May 8, 2002, at 1R.

52. First Covenant Church v. City of Seattle, 840 P.2d 174 (Wash. 1992).

53. Oregon City v. Hartke, 400 P.2d 255, 261 (1965).

54. *First Covenant Church*, 840 P.2d at 185.

55. Editorial, *So Glorious, Yet So Vulnerable*, OPELIKA-AUBURN NEWS (Ala.), Aug. 23, 2000.

56. Paul Davis, *Auburn Shows Its Prowess in Handling a Real Emergency*, OPELIKA-AUBURN NEWS (Ala.), Aug. 20, 2000.

57. 42 U.S.C.S. § 2000bb et seq. (2004) (Nov. 16, 1993, P.L. 103–41, § 2, 107 Stat. 1488). The law currently only applies to the federal government. It was held unconstitutional as applied to state and local governments.

58. City of Boerne v. Flores, 521 U.S. 507 (1997).

59. Amy Dorsett, *1997 Year in Review: Trees, Traffic among Top Issues*, SAN ANTONIO EXPRESS-NEWS (Tex.), Jan. 1, 1998, at 1S.

60. 42 U.S.C. 2000cc et seq. (2004).

61. *See generally* Marci A. Hamilton, *Religion and the Law in the Clinton Era: An Anti-Madisonian Legacy*, 63 LAW & CONTEMP. PROBS. 359 (2000).

62. Statement on Signing the Religious Land use and Institutionalized Persons Act of 2000, 36 WEEKLY COMP. PRES. DOC. 2168 (Sept. 22, 2000).

63. 42 U.S.C. 2000cc(b) (2004) provides:

(1) Equal terms. No government shall impose or implement a land-use regulation in a manner that treats a religious assembly or institution on less than equal terms with a nonreligious assembly or institution.

(2) Nondiscrimination. No government shall impose or implement a land-use regulation that discriminates against any assembly or institution on the basis of religion or religious denomination.

(3) Exclusions and limits. No government shall impose or implement a land-use regulation that –

(A) totally excludes religious assemblies from a jurisdiction; or
(B) unreasonably limits religious assemblies, institutions, or structures within a jurisdiction.

64. 42 U.S.C. 2000cc(a) (2004).

65. American Religious Identification Survey of 2001, conducted by City University of New York, *available at* http://www.gc.cuny.edu/studies/key_findings.htm (lasted visited October 22, 2004).

66. *Boerne*, 521 U.S. at 537 (Stevens, J., concurring).

67. 42 USC § 1988(b) (2004) provides, in pertinent part: "In any action or proceeding to enforce a provision of . . . the Religious Land Use and Institutionalized Persons Act of 2000 . . . the court, in its discretion, may allow the prevailing party, other than the United States, a reasonable attorney's fee as part of the costs."

68. Cohen v. City of Des Plaines, 8 F.3d 484 (7th 1993); Congregation Beth Yitzchok v. Ramapo, 593 F. Supp. 655 (S.D.N.Y. 1984); Abram v. Fayetteville, 661 S.W.2d 371 (Ark. 1983); State v. Maxwell, 617 P.2d 816 (Haw. 1980); Medford Assembly of God v. Medford, 695 P.2d 1379 (Ore. Ct. App. 1985); Yusuf v. Villa Park, 458 N.E.2d 575 (Ill. App. Ct. 1983); Rose Lees Hardy Home & School Assoc. v. District of Columbia Bd. of Zoning Adjustment, 324 A.2d 701 (D.C. Ct. App. 1974); Heard v. Dallas, 456 S.W.2d 440 (Tex. Ct. Civ . App. 1970).

69. Love Church v. City of Evanston, 671 F. Supp. 508, 513 (N.D. Ill. 1987).

70. *See* Roman Catholic Welfare Corp. v. Piedmont, 45 Cal. 2d 325 (Cal. 1955).

71. Harvest Christian Ctr. v. Zoning Appeals Bd., 55 Va. Cir. 279, 284 (Va. Cir. Ct. 2001) (quoting Trustees v. Guthrie, 86 Va. 125, 140–41 (1889)).

72. Grace United Methodist Church v. City of Cheyenne, 235 F. Supp. 2d 1186 (D. Wyo. 2002).

73. *Id.* at 1190.

74. *Neighbors Divided, supra* note 2.

75. See Order, Missionaries of Charity, Brothers v. City of Los Angeles, No. CV 01-08115-SVW (C.D. Cal. Jul. 11, 2003), *also available at* http://www.rluipa.com/cases/MOC-Order7-11-03.pdf (last visited Oct. 31, 2004).

76. The Becket Fund, RLUIPA Court Cases, Missionaries of Charity, Brothers v. City of Los Angeles, *available at* http://www.rluipa.com/cases/MissionariesOfCharity.html (last visited Oct. 31, 2004) (The Becket Fund represents the plaintiffs in the case.).

77. Along with local counsel, I represent the township in this case. Congregation Kol Ami v. Abington Twp., No. 01-1919, 2004 U.S. Dist. LEXIS 16397, at *9 (E.D. Pa. Aug. 12, 2004); Congregation Kol Ami v. Abington Twp., 309 F.3d 120 (3d Cir. 2002).

78. Congregation Kol Ami v. Abington Twp., 161 F.Supp.2d 432, 435 (E.D. Pa. 2001).

79. *Id.* at 437.

80. Civil Liberties for Urban Believers v. City of Chicago, 342 F.3d 752, 766 (7th Cir. 2003); Bethel Baptist Church v. United States, 822 F.2d 1334, 1339 (3d Cir. 1987).

81. *See* Braunfeld v. Brown, 366 U.S. 599, 605 (1961); *Civil Liberties for Urban Believers*, 342 F.3d at 762; *Grosz*, 721 F.2d at 736 (citing *Braunfeld*).

82. Congregation Kol Ami v. Abington Twp., No. 01-1919, 2004 U.S. Dist. LEXIS 16397, at *28 (E.D. Pa. Aug. 12, 2004).

83. *Id.* at *29.

84. Patrick Korten, Vice President, Becket Fund for Religious Liberty, *Churches Don't Stand a Prayer*, WALL STREET J., Jan. 22, 2003, at A14.

85. Castle Hills Baptist Church v. City of Castle Hills, No. SA-01-CA-1149-RF, 2004 WL 546792, at *4, *13, *14 (W. D. Tex. Mar. 17, 2004).

86. Guru Nanak Sikh Soc'y v. County of Sutter, 326 F. Supp. 2d 1140, 1142 (E.D. Cal. 2003).

87. *Id.* at 1152 (quoting Cottonwood Christian Center v. Cypress Redevelopment Agency, 218 F. Supp.2d 1203, 1226 (C.D. Cal. 2002)).

88. 146 Cong. Rec. S7,776 (daily ed. July 27, 2000) (joint statement of Senator Hatch and Senator Kennedy).

89. Westchester Day Sch. v. Village of Mamaroneck, No. 03-9042, 2004 U.S. App. LEXIS 20327, at *6–7 (2d Cir. Sept. 27, 2004):

90. *Id.* at *15.

91. Westchester Day Sch. v. Village of Mamaroneck, 280 F. Supp. 2d 230, 243–44 (S.D.N.Y. 2003).

92. Westchester Day Sch., No. 03-9042, 2004 U.S. App. LEXIS 20327, at *16.

93. San Jose Christian College v. City of Morgan Hill, 360 F.3d 1024, 1035 (9th Cir. 2004).

94. Murphy v. Zoning Comm'n, 289 F. Supp. 2d 87 (D. Conn. 2003).

95. Locke v. Davey, 124 S. Ct. 1307, 1312 (2004).

96. 42 U.S.C. § 2000cc(a)(2)(C) provides:

This subsection applies in any case in which . . . the substantial burden is imposed in the implementation of a land use regulation or system of land use regulations, under which a government makes, or has in place formal or informal procedures or practices that permit the government to make, individualized assessments of the proposed uses for the property involved.

97. The lead case employing this reasoning is Sherbert v. Verner, 374 U.S. 398, 404 (1963).

98. *See* F.O.P. Newark Lodge No. 12 v. City of Newark, 170 F.3d 359 (3d Cir. 1999).

99. *See* Sherbert v. Verner, 374 U.S. 398 (1963).

100. Freedom Baptist Church v. Twp. of Middletown, 204 F. Supp. 2d 857, 868 (E.D. Pa. 2002).

101. *Murphy*, 289 F. Supp. 2d at 119 (quoting *Freedom Baptist Church*, 204 F. Supp. 2d at 869). *See also Guru Nanak Sikh Soc'y*, 326 F. Supp. 2d at 1155 ("Relying on RLUIPA's legislative history, several courts have concluded that 'these

provisions codify existing Equal Protection Clause and Free Exercise Clause jurisprudence.'" quoting Petra Presbyterian Church v. Village of Northbrook, 2003 WL 22048089, at *11 (N.D. Ill. Aug, 29, 2003); *see also Freedom Baptist Church of Delaware County*, 204 F. Supp.2d at 869 (Sections (b)(1) and (b)(3) of RLUIPA "codify existing Supreme Court decisions under the Free Exercise and Establishment Clauses of the First Amendment as well as under the Equal Protection Clause of the Fourteenth Amendment.").

102. *See* ALA. CONST. AMEND. 622 (2004) (enacted 1999), ARIZ. REV. STAT. § 41-1493.01 (2004) (enacted 1999), CONN. GEN. STAT. § 52–571b (2003) (enacted 1993), FLA. STAT. ch. 761.03 (2004) (enacted 1998), IDAHO CODE § 73–402 (2004) (enacted 2000), 775 ILL. COMP. STAT. 35/1 et seq. (2004) (enacted 1998), N.M. STAT. ANN. § 28-22-3 (2004) (enacted 2000), 71 PA. CONS. STAT. § 2401 et seq. (2004) (enacted 2002), R.I. GEN. LAWS § 42-80.1-3 (2004) (enacted 1993), S.C. CODE ANN. § 1-32-40 (2003) (enacted 1999), respectively.

103. *See* OKLA. STAT. tit. 51, § 258 (2004) (enacted 2000); TEX. CIV. PRAC. & REM. CODE § 110.010 (2003) (enacted 1999).

## 5. Schools

1. PHILLIP HAMBURGER, SEPARATION OF CHURCH AND STATE 219–20, 222, 283, 310 (2002).

2. Rev. Jerry Falwell, Commentary, *Defending Prayer in School*, WORLD-NETDAILY (online), Oct. 27, 2001, *at* http://www.worldnetdaily.com/news/article.asp?ARTICLE_ID=25107 (last visited Nov. 2, 2004).

3. Christopher John Farley, *Without a Prayer*, TIME, Dec. 20, 1993, at 41.

4. *Id.*

5. The Hon. Minister Louis Farrakhan, *Atonement: The Road to Peace*, THE FINAL CALL (online), Oct. 29, 2001, *at* http://www.finalcall.com/columns/mlf/mlf-atonement 10-30-2001.htm (last visited Nov. 2, 2004).

6. Hamburger, *supra* note 1, at 223.

7. Illinois ex rel. McCollum v. Bd. of Educ., 333 U.S. 203, 235 (1948) (Jackson, J., concurring).

8. 42 U.S.C. § 2000bb (2004) (enacted 1993).

9. 406 U.S. 205 (1972).

10. A *Diverse Educational System*, *in* PORTRAIT OF THE USA (United States Information Agency 1997), *available at* http://usinfo.state.gov/usa/infousa/facts/factover/ch6.htm (last visited Nov. 3, 2004).

11. CUNY GRADUATE CENTER AMERICAN RELIGIOUS IDENTIFICATION SYSTEM, U.S. CENSUS BUREAU, STATISTICAL ABSTRACT OF THE UNITED STATES 67 (U.S. Dep't of Com. 2003).

12. *Religion (13) and Age Groups (8) for Population, for Canada, Provinces, Territories, Census Metropolitan Areas and Census Agglomerations*, 2001 CENSUS (Canada) (2001), *available at* http://www12.statcan.ca/english/census01/products/standard/themes/RetrieveProductTable.cfm?Temporal=2001&PID=68339&APATH=3&GID=431515&METH=1&PTYPE=55430&THEME=56&FOCUS=0

&AID=0&PLACENAME=0&PROVINCE=0&SEARCH=0&GC=99&GK=NA &VID=0&FL=0&RL=0&FREE=0 (last visited Nov. 2, 2004); Cent. Intelligence Agency, United Kingdom, in The World Factbook (2004), *available at* http://www. cia.gov/cia/publications/factbook/geos/uk.html (last modified Oct. 19, 2004). Central Intelligence Agency, *India*, in The World Factbook (2004), *available at* http://www.cia.gov/cia/publications/factbook/geos/in.html (last modified Nov. 2, 2004) (last visited Nov. 5, 2004).

13. W. H. McLeod, The Sikhs: History, Religion, and Society 45, 142 (1989). Women are admitted into the Khalsa as well as men, though they rarely wear the turban. In theory, women are regarded as the equals of men. However, actual practice falls short of the claim. *See* W. H. McLeod, Who is a Sikh? 108–9 (1989).

14. W. H. McLeod, Who is a Sikh? 112–14 (1989); *see also* Michael Rollins, *Sikhs Bring Talent, Strife to New Home: Worship Practices Divide the Community of Immigrants to British Columbia*, Oregonian, Aug. 29, 1999, at A22.

15. Sandeep Singh Brar, *Understanding the Kirpan for Non-Sikhs*, *available at* http://www.sikhs.org/art12.htm (last visited Nov. 3, 2004).

16. *See* Cheema v. Thompson, No. 94-16097, 1994 U.S. App. LEXIS 24160, at * 16 (9th Cir. 1994) (Wiggins, J. dissenting); Clifford Krauss, *A Sikh Boy's Little Dagger Sets Off a Mighty Din*, N.Y. Times, June 5, 2002, at A4 (stating that kirpan in "Sikh faith symbolizes the sovereignty of man and serves as a reminder to go to the defense of others in distress.").

17. Global News Wire, *Punjab Cop's Son Held for Murder*, Times (India), May 27, 2003.

18. Wendy Darroch, *Temple Priest Found Guilty in Stabbing with Dagger*, Toronto Star, May 26, 1989, at A22. Singh was to be sentenced, July 18, 1989, but he was granted a new trial when evidence emerged that another person may have grabbed the kirpan from him and used it in the stabbing. *Priest Gets New Trial in Stabbing*, Toronto Star, Sept. 8, 1989, at A21. Singh admitted his role in the stabbing and pleaded guilty to the lesser charge of assault. Wendy Darroch, *Sikh Priest Jailed for Dagger Attack*, Toronto Star, Feb. 27, 1990, at A8.

19. Paula Schuck, *Sikh Gets 30 Days for Stabbing Relative with Ceremonial Knife*, Toronto Star, July 30, 1007, at B1.

20. Michael Rollins, *Sikhs Bring Talent, Strife to New Home: Worship Practices Divide the Community of Immigrants to British Columbia*, Oregonian, Aug. 29, 1999, at A22; Sudarsan Raghavan, *Sikhs experience violence over Custom of Temple Meals*, Phila. Inq., Mar. 24, 1999, at Lifestyle.

21. *Cheema*, No. 94-16097, 1994 U.S. App. LEXIS 24160; Multani v. Commission Scolaire Marguerite-Bourgeoys, 241 D.L.R. (4th) 336 (2004).

22. For further explanation, *see infra* Part Two, chapters 8 and 10.

23. *Cheema*, 1994 U.S. App. LEXIS 24160, at *11.

24. *Id.* at *9, 11.

25. *Id.* at *16–17.

26. Greg Lucas, *Wilson Veto for Knives at School*, S. F. Chron., Oct. 1, 1994, at A19.

27. *Multani*, 241 D.L.R. at 359.

28. Greg Toppo, *48 School Deaths Highest in Years; Law Enforcement Cites Gangs, Budget Cuts*, USA TODAY, June 28, 2004, at A1. *See also* Douglas E. Thompkins, *School Violence: Gangs and A Culture of Fear*, 567 ANNALS AM. ACAD. POL. & SOC. SCI. 54 (2000).

29. Alison L. Ramsey et. al, *Evaluation of the Gang Resistance and Training (GREAT) Program: A School-Based Prevention Program*, EDUCATION, Dec. 22, 2003, at 297.

30. Jon Yates, *Gangs Not Just Young Boys Network; Recent Violence by Girls Raises Parents' Fears*, CHI. TRIB., May 2, 2004, at 1.

31. Jeffrey J. Mayer, *Individual Moral Responsibility and the Criminalization of Youth Gangs*, 28 WAKE FOREST L. REV. 943, 951 (1993).

32. Levon v. O'Rourke, No. 96 C 7304, 1996 U.S. Dist. LEXIS 19378, at *4–5 (N. D. Ill. Dec. 24, 1996).

33. Cindy Horswell, *Gangs Get A Dressing Down: New Policy at Baytown Junior High School Limits Colors, Sports Attire*, HOUSTON CHRON., Mar 28, 1992, at A1.

34. Todd A. DeMitchell, Richard Fossey, & Casey Cobb, *Dress Codes in the Public Schools: Principals, Policies, and Precepts* 29 J. L. & EDUC. 31, 44–45 (2000).

35. *Uniform Policy: East High School Bets on Dress for Success*, COLUMBUS DISPATCH (Ohio), Jan. 19, 1997, at 2B.

36. U.S. DEPT. OF ED., MANUAL ON SCHOOL UNIFORMS (last updated Feb. 29, 1996), *available at* http://www.ed.gov/updates/uniforms.html (last visited Nov. 5, 2004).

37. No. 96-C-7304, 1996 U.S. Dist. LEXIS 19378, at *4–5, *12, *4, *5, *8 (N. D. Ill. Dec. 24, 1996).

38. *Levon*, No. 96-C-7304, 1996 U.S. Dist. LEXIS 19378, at *22 (quoting Sasnett v. Sullivan, 91 F.3d 1018, 1022 (7th Cir. 1996)).

39. *Id.* at *5.

40. *Id.* at *20–21.

41. Press Release, American Civil Liberties Union, Jewish Student to Wear Star of David Pendant as Mississipi School Board Reverses Policy (Aug. 24, 1999) (on file with author), *also available at* http://archive.aclu.org/news/1999/n082499a.html (last visited Nov. 5, 2004) (hereinafter Press Release, ACLU).

42. Olesen v. Board of Educ. of Sch. Dist. No. 228, 676 F. Supp. 820, 821 (N.D. Ill. 1987) (describing the use of crosses and six-pointed stars by the Simon City Royals, a large Bremen High School gang). The court dismissed the complaint against the Board's policy prohibiting the wearing or display of any gang symbol and Bremen's specific prohibition against the wearing of earrings by male students. *Id.* at 823.

43. Press Release, ACLU, *supra* note 41.

44. *Student Agrees to Hide Wiccan Symbol, Is Readmitted to Classes*, ABILENE REPORTER-NEWS (Tex.) (online), Sep. 5, 2002, *available at* http://texnews.com/1998/2002/texas/texas_Student_a95.html (last visited Nov. 1, 2004).

45. Derek H. Davis, *Reacting to France's Ban: Headscarves and other Religious Attire in American Public Schools*, J. CHURCH & STATE, Apr. 1, 2004, at 221 (hereinafter *Reacting to France's Ban*).

46. *Id.*

47. Menora v. Illinois High School Association, 683 F.2d 1030, 1031 (1982), *cert. denied*, 459 U.S. 1156 (1983); *see also* Keller by Keller v. Gardner Community Consol. Grade School Dist. 72C, 552 F. Supp. 512, (N.D. Ill. 1982).

48. *Menora*, 683 F.2d at 1033.

49. *Id.* at 1035.

50. *Id.* at 1034.

51. *Id.* (emphasis added).

52. *Id.* at 1035.

53. *Menora*, 683 F.2d at 1035.

54. *Id.*

55. *See* Heather Rabkin, *Wearing Hijab Provides Protection, Liberation*, THE DAILY BRUIN (online), Oct. 20, 2004, *at* http://www.dailybruin.ucla.edu/news/articles.asp?id=30445 (last visited Nov. 1, 2004). A burka (also known as burqa or burqua) is either a veil tied over a headscarf or full burka (also called Afghan burka or chador), a top to bottom garment, which also covers the face. Hijab is a head cover worn by Islamic women. Niqab is a face veil worn by Islamic women, together with the hijab. Khimar is literally a covering – a headscarf. Farlex, TheFreeDictionary.com, *at* http://encyclopedia.thefreedictionary.com.

56. *Reacting to France's Ban, supra* note 45 (Candace Ahlfinger speaking for the Waxahachie High School, said, "When we disrupt the educational progress of other students by wearing disruptive clothing, disruptive jewelry, disruptive hairstyles, whatever is disruptive, we are not only hurting one student, we are hurting all.").

57. Joe Cook, *Free Exercise Clause Triumphs – Lafayette School Board Votes to Admit 8 Rastafarian Children with Headgear and Dreadlocks*, American Civil Liberties Union Statement, Sep. 21, 2000, *at* www.laaclu.org/News/2000/free_exercise_clause_triumphs.htm.

58. *Reacting to France's Ban, supra* note 45.

59. Sheema Khan, *Why Does a Head Scarf Have Us Tied Up in Knots?*, GLOBE & MAIL (Ca.), Sept. 26, 2003, *also available at* http://www.caircan.ca/oped_more.php?id=526_0_10_0_C (last visited Nov. 5, 2004).

60. *Probe Launched Over Que. Muslim Student's Hijab*, CTC.CA (online), Sept. 24, 2003, *at* http://www.ctv.ca/servlet/ArticleNews/story/CTVNews/1064344107380_59753307/?hub=Canada (last visited Nov. 5, 2004). See also Khan, *supra* note 59.

61. *Reacting to France's Ban, supra* note 46.

62. Jim Myers, *Settlement Announced in Suit over Head Scarf*, TULSA WORLD, May 20, 2004, at A1.

63. Locke v. Davey, 540 U.S. 712 (2004); Church of Lukumi Babalu Aye, Inc. v. Hialeah, 508 U.S. 520 (1993); Employment Div., Dept. of Human

Resources of Ore. v. Smith, 494 U.S. 872 (1990); Sherbert v. Verner, 374 U.S. 398 (1963).

64. *See Settlement Announced in Suit over Head Scarf, supra* note 62.

65. *See* http://www.usdoj.gov/crt/edo/caselist.html (listing consent decrees); U.S. Dept. of Justice Press Release, *Justice Department Reaches Settlement Agreement with Oklahoma School District in Muslim Student Headscarf Case,* May 19, 2004, *available at* http://www.usdoj.gov/opa/pr/2004/May/04_crt_343.html; Associated Press, *Judge Signs Settlement in Hijab Lawsuit,* TULSA AREA NEWS, May 21, 2004, *also available at http://www.teamtulsa.com/news/local/l5020.shtml* (last visited Nov. 1, 2004).

66. Law No. 2004-228 of Mar. 15, 2004, J.O., Mar. 17, 2004, p. 5190, *also available at* http://www.legifrance.gouv.fr/WAspad/UnTexteDeJorf?numjo=MENX0400001L (last visited Nov. 5, 2004).

67. *See* Elaine Sciolino, *Ban on Head Scarves Takes Effect in France,* N.Y. TIMES, Sept. 3, 2004, at A8.

68. *See* Suzanne Daley, *Europe Wary of Wider Doors for Immigrants,* N.Y. TIMES, Oct. 20, 2001, at A3.

69. Alabama & Coushatta Tribes of Texas v. Trustees of the Big Sandy Independent School District, 817 F. Supp. 1319, 1324–25 (1993), *remanded by,* Alabama & Coushatta v. Trustees, 20 F.3d 469 (5th Cir. 1994); *see also* Chalifoux v. New Caney Independent School Dist., 976 F. Supp. 659 (S.D. Tex. 1997) (holding that the heightened level of scrutiny used in hybrid cases applies).

70. *Alabama & Coushatta Tribes,* 817 F. Supp. at 1323–24.

71. Karr v. Schmidt, 460 F.2d 609 (5th Cir. 1972), *cert. denied,* 409 U.S. 989 (1972).

72. *See* Knight v. Connecticut Dept. of Public Health, 275 F.3d 156 (2d Cir. 2001) (holding in the context of claims involving free exercise and free speech that the Smith's language relating to hybrid claims is nonbinding dictum); Kissinger v. Bd. of Trustees of the Ohio State Univ., College of Veterinary Med., 5 F.3d 177 (6th Cir. 1993) (declining to apply the hybrid rights theory as "completely illogical"). The following Circuits, while not rejecting the hybrid rights theory outright, have not applied strict scrutiny in these cases: EEOC v. Catholic Univ. of Am., 83 F.3d 455 (D.C. Cir. 1996) (requiring an independently viable claim of infringement of a companion right in addition to the free exercise claim); Civil Liberties for Urban Believers v. City of Chicago, 342 F.3d 752 (7th Cir. 2003), *cert. denied,* 124 S. Ct. 2816 (2004) (requiring a colorable claim of infringement of a specific constitutional right in addition to the free exercise claim); Miller v. Reed, 176 F.3d 1202 (9th Cir. 1999) (same); Swanson v. Guthrie Indep. Sch. Dist. No. I-L, 135 F.3d 694 (10th Cir. 1998) (same); Brown v. Hot, Sexy & Safer Prods., 68 F.3d 525 (1st Cir. 1995), cert. denied, 516 U.S. 1159 (1996) (same).

73. TEX. HEALTH & SAFETY CODE ANN. § 481.111(a) (Vernon 2004) ("The provisions of this chapter relating to the possession and distribution of peyote do not apply to the use of peyote by a member of the Native American Church in bona fide religious ceremonies of the church.").

74. School Dist. No. 11-J v. Howell, 517 P.2d 422 (Colo. Ct. App. 1973) held that an application permitting noncompliance with school hair regulation was discriminatory where such application applied only to Indians.

75. Wisconsin v. Yoder, 406 U.S. 205 (1972).

76. *See* Judith G. McMullen, *Behind Closed Doors: Should States Regulate Homeschooling?* 54 S. C. L. Rev. 75, 78 (2002) (noting that religious beliefs are the impetus for homeschooling in approximately 85% of cases)("'These parents believe that God has given them the responsibility and the authority to educate their children.... Since they are called by God to be the primary teachers of their children and to apply God's word to each and every subject, they believe it would be a sin for them to delegate this authority to another school system.'"(quoting Christopher J. Klicka, The Right to Home School 2–3 (2d ed. 1998)).

77. Edwards v. Aguillard, 482 U.S. 578 (1987).

78. *See generally* Marjorie George, Note, *And Then God Created Kansas? The Evolution/Creationism Debate in America's Public Schools,* 149 Pa. L. Rev. 483 (2001). Gabriel Acri, Note, *Persistent Monkey on the Back of the American Public Education System: A Study of the Continued Debate Over the Teaching of Creation and Evolution,* 41 Cath. Law. 39 (2001).

79. *Wisconsin district to teach more than evolution,* CNN.com, November 7, 2004, *at* http://edition.cnn.com/2004/EDUCATION/11/06/evolution.schools.ap/index.html (last visited Nov. 7, 2004).

80. John W. Fountain, *Kansas Puts Evolution Back into Public Schools,* N.Y. Times, Feb. 15, 2001, at A18.

81. Ariel Hart, *Judge in Georgia Orders Anti-Evolution Stickers Removed From Textbooks,* N.Y. Times, Jan. 14, 2005, at A16.

82. *See* James G. Dwyer, *The Children We Abandon: Religious Exemptions to Child Welfare and Educational Laws as Denials of Equal Protection to Children of Religious Objectors,* 74 N.C. L. Rev. 1321, 1350 (1996) ("Approximately one million children in this country are in home schools, and the most common reason parents have for choosing this option is religious opposition to the content and manner of instruction in public schools.").

83. Christopher Klicka, *Biblical Reasons to Home School,* Issue Analysis, National Center for Home Education, May 17, 1999, *at* http://www.hslda.org/docs/nche/000000/00000069.asp (last visited Nov. 7, 2004).

84. *State Laws Concerning Participation of Homeschool Students in Public School Activities,* Aug. 20, 2004, *at* http://www.hslda.org/docs/nche/000000/00000048.asp (last visited Nov. 7, 2004).

85. *Pennsylavnia – Homeschoolers Religious Freedom Case Can Proceed,* Aug. 6, 2003, *at* http://www.hslda.org/hs/state/pa/200408060.asp (last visited Nov. 7, 2004).

86. Pierce v. Society of the Sisters of the Holy Names of Jesus & Mary, 268 U.S. 510, 535 (1925).

87. *See* Franklin v. Bristol Township School Dist. – *Family Files Suit under Religious Protection Act,* Sept. 14, 2004, *at* http://www.hslda.org/Legal/state/pa/20040422HankinvBTSD/default.asp (last visited Nov. 7, 2004); *Newborn v. Franklin*

*School District – Family Files Suit Under Religious Protection Act*, Sept. 14, 2004, *at* http://www.hslda.org/Legal/state/pa/20040205NewbornvFRSD/default.asp (last visited Nov. 7, 2004); *Pennsylavnia – Homeschoolers Religious Freedom Case Can Proceed*, Aug. 6, 2003, *at* http://www.hslda.org/hs/state/pa/200408060.asp (last visited Nov. 7, 2004).

88. United States v. Lee, 455 U.S. 252, 261 (1982).

89. Bowen v. Roy, 476 U.S. 693, 696 (1986).

90. *See* Parham v. J. R., 442 U.S. 584, 630 (1979) (quoting Prince v. Massachusetts, 321 U.S. 158, 170 (1944)) ("In our society, parental rights are limited by the legitimate rights and interests of their children. 'Parents may be free to be become martyrs themselves. But it does not follow they are free, in identical circumstances, to make martyrs of their children before they have reached the age of full and legal discretion when they can make that choice for themselves.'").

91. *A Dark Side to Home Schooling*, CBSNEWS.COM, Oct. 13, 2003, *at* http://www.cbsnews.com/stories/2003/10/13/eveningnews/main577817.shtml (last visited Nov. 7, 2004); *Home Schooling Nightmares*, CBSNEWS.COM, Oct. 14, 2003, *at* http://www.cbsnews.com/stories/2003/10/14/eveningnews/main578007.shtml (last visited Nov. 7, 2004).

92. Fleischfresser v. Directors of School District 200, 15 F.3d 680, 683 (7th Cir. 1994).

93. Press Release, Institute for First Amendment Studies, Institute Joins Impressions Case, Sept. 1992 (on file with author), *also available at* http://www.buildingequality.us/ifas/fw/9209/impressions.html (last visited Nov. 5, 2004).

94. *Fleischfresser*, 15 F.3d at 686–87.

95. *Id.* at 688.

96. *Id.*

97. Mozert v. Hawkins County Board of Educ., 827 F.2d 1058 (6th Cir. 1987), *cert. denied*, 484 U.S. 1066 (1988); *see also* Frances R. A. Paterson, *The Politics of Phonics*, 15 J. CURRICULUM & SUPERVISION 179 (2000) (describing the pattern of lawsuits "[f]rom 1986 to 1994, [in which] *Impressions* was challenged in at least 74 school districts in 16 states.").

98. *Mozert*, 827 F.2d at 1067.

99. Moody v. Cronin, 484 F. Supp. 270 (C.D. Ill. 1979).

100. *Id.* at 276.

101. *Id.* at 277.

## 6. The Prisons and the Military

1. Dan Mihalopoulos, *U.S. Probes Jail Ministry for Muslims*, CHICAGO TRIB., Aug. 10, 2003, at 1 (quoting Dan Pistole) (hereinafter *U.S. Probes Jail Ministry for Muslims*); *see also* ANTI-DEFAMATION LEAGUE, DANGEROUS CONVICTIONS: AN INTRODUCTION TO EXTREMIST ACTIVITIES IN PRISONS, TOPICS IN EXTREMISM 25-6 (2002), *also available at* http://www.adl.org/learn/Ext_Terr/dangerous_convictions.pdf (last visited Nov. 8, 2004) (hereinafter DANGEROUS CONVICTIONS).

2. Facts regarding the Aryan Brotherhood have been gathered from FEDERAL BUREAU OF INVESTIGATION, ARYAN BROTHERHOOD, file number 183-7396 (obtained through the Freedom of Information and Privacy Acts), *also available at* http://foia.fbi.gov/foiaindex/aryanbro.htm (last visited Nov. 8, 2004) [hereinafter ARYAN BROTHERHOOD]; and David Grann, *The Brand*, NEW YORKER, Feb. 16 & 23, 2004, at 156 (hereinafter *The Brand*).

3. *The Brand, supra* note 2, at 158, 171.

4. *Id.* at 160.

5. Andrew Blankstein, *Task Force Thwarts Prison Gang's Growing Reach*, L.A. TIMES, Jan. 30, 2004, at B2.

6. *See* Charles Lane, *Supreme Court Hears Racial Segregation Case*, WASH. POST, Nov. 3, 2004, at A2 (describing California's justification for racial segregation within its prison system); Greg Gittrich, *Bloody Gangs of New York Murderous Youth Violence Surges 80% Across the City*, DAILY NEWS (N.Y.), Feb. 29, 2004, at 8 (describing the different gang affiliations in New York City, and noting that there are about 15,000 gang members "with about a quarter active and not in prison.").

7. DANGEROUS CONVICTIONS, *supra* note 1, at 3.

8. Frank Viviano, *Future Terrorists Train in Prison*, S.F. CHRON., Nov. 3, 2001, at A5.

9. *U.S. Probes Jail Ministry for Muslims, supra* note 1.

10. Department of Defense Instruction 1304.28 § 6.1.5 (June 11, 2004).

11. *See* William T Cavanaugh, Jr., *The United States Military Chaplaincy Program: Another Seam in the Fabric of our Society?*, 59 NOTRE DAME L. REV. 181, 191–92 (1983).

12. *See* Julie B. Kaplan, *Military Mirrors on the Wall: Nonestablishment and the Military Chaplaincy*, 95 YALE L.J. 1210, 1217–18 (1983) (hereinafter Kaplan).

13. "Terrorist Recruitment and Infiltration in the United States: Prisons and Military as an Operational Base": *Hearing before the Senate Comm. on the Judiciary*, 108th Cong. (Oct. 14, 2003) (testimony of Dr. Michael Waller), *available at* http://judiciary.senate.gov/testimony.cfm?id=960&wit_id=2719 (last visited Nov. 9, 2004) (hereinafter Waller).

14. *U.S. Probes Jail Ministry for Muslims, supra* note 1.

15. *Activist Gets 23 Years for Libyan Dealings*, CHI. TRIB., Oct. 16, 2004, at C15.

16. Jerry Markon, *Muslim Activist Sentenced to 23 Years for Libya Contacts*, WASH. POST, Oct. 16, 2004, at A17 (hereinafter Markon).

17. Laurie Goodstein, *Pentagon Says It Will Review Chaplain Policy*, N.Y. TIMES, Sept. 28, 2003, at 1.

18. *Id.*

19. Markon, *supra* note 16.

20. Jerry Seper, *Prisons Breeding Ground for Terror: Moderate Muslim Chaplains in Short Supply, Justice Report Warns*, WASH. TIMES, May 6, 2004, at A11.

21. *See* OFFICE OF THE INSPECTOR GENERAL, U.S. DEP'T OF JUSTICE, A REVIEW OF THE BUREAU OF PRISONS' SELECTION OF MUSLIM RELIGIOUS SERVICES PROVIDERS (2004), *available at* http://www.usdoj.gov/oig/special/0404/final.pdf

(last visited Nov. 9, 2004) (hereinafter Selection of Muslim Religious Services Providers).

22. 395 U.S. 444 (1969).

23. John P. Cronan, *The Next Challenge for the First Amendment: The Framework for an Internet Incitement Standard*, 51 Cath. U. L. Rev. 425 (2002).

24. Selection of Muslim Religious Services Providers, *supra* note 21, at 8–9 (quoting BOP Technical Resource Manual 014.1).

25. For further analysis, *see* Kaplan, *supra* note 12; Katcoff v. Marsh, 755 F.2d 223 (2d Cir. 1985).

26. Waller, *supra* note 13.

27. Rumsfeld v. Padilla, 124 S. Ct. 2711, 2717–18 (2004).

28. *See* Julia Preston, *Staten Island Phone Lets U.S. Eavesdrop on Global Militants*, N.Y. Times, Oct. 2, 2004, at A1.

29. Turner v. Safley, 482 U.S. 78, 84 (1987) (quoting Procunier v. Martinez, 416 U.S. 396, 405 [1974]).

30. Turner, 482 U.S. at 89.

31. *"Protecting Religious Freedom after Boerne v. Flores": Hearing before the Subcomm. on the Constitution of the House Comm. on the Judiciary*, 105th Cong. (July 14, 1997) (testimony of Charles W. Colson), *available at* http://www.house.gov/judiciary/222304.htm (last visited Nov. 9, 2004).

32. *"The Need for Federal Protection of Religious Freedom after Boerne v. Flores": Hearing before the House Comm. on the Judiciary*, 105th Cong. (Mar. 26, 1998) (testimony of Isaac M. Jaroslawicz), *available at* http://www.house.gov/judiciary/222356.htm (last visited Nov. 9, 2004).

33. *Id.*

34. One of the reasons for the lack of opposition to the land-use side existed, because the attorneys general, who tend to be politically ambitious, would not lobby against religious institutions seeking land-use preferences, in part, because these issues are local headaches, not state headaches, and also because religious individuals vote, but, as is often said, prisoners do not vote.

35. *"Protecting Religious Freedom after Boerne v. Flores": Hearing before the Subcomm. on the Constitution of the House Comm. on the Judiciary*, 105th Cong. (July 14, 1997) (testimony of Jeffrey Sutton), *available at* http://www.house.gov/judiciary/222309.htm (last visited Nov. 9, 2004) (hereinafter Jeffrey Sutton).

36. *Id.*

37. 146 Cong. Rec. S7774, 7779 (daily ed. July 27, 2000) (statement of Sen. Reid) (hereinafter Sen. Reid).

38. 146 Cong. Rec. S7991 (daily ed. Sept. 5, 2000) (statement of Sen. Thurmond).

39. Sen. Reid, *supra* note 37.

40. *See* Thomas P. O'Connor & Nathaniel J. Pallone, Religion, the Community, and the Rehabilitation of Criminal Offenders (2003); Stephen T. Hall, *Faith-Based Cognitive Programs in Corrections*, American Correctional Chaplains Association, *at* http://www.correctionalchaplains.org/faith-based/page1.html (last visited Nov. 10, 2004); Robert Toll, *How a Multifaith Chaplaincy Program*

*Operates in a County Detention Facility*, American Correctional Chaplains Association, *at* http://www.correctionalchaplains.org/articles/01-02-2004.html (last visited Nov. 10, 2004); Oregon Department of Corrections Transitional Services Division, *Spirituality, Religion and What Works: Religious Outcomes This Side of Heaven*, http://www.oregon.gov/DOC/TRANS/religious_services/rs_article2.shtml (last visited Nov. 10, 2004).

41. Adam Hochberg, *All Things Considered: Series of Lawsuits Calling for More Religious Freedoms for Prisoners* (National Public Radio broadcast, July 10, 2003), *also available at* 2003 WL 5581034.

42. *See* Jeffrey Sutton, *supra* note 35.

43. Theriault v. Silber, 453 F. Supp. 254, 260 (W.D. Tex. 1978), *appeal dismissed*, 579 F.2d 302 (5th Cir. 1978), *cert. denied*, 440 U.S. 917 (1979); *see also* PAUL W. KEVE, PRISONS AND THE AMERICAN CONSCIENCE: A HISTORY OF U.S. FEDERAL CORRECTIONS 211–12 (1991).

44. Remmers v. Brewer, 494 F.2d 1277 (8th Cir. 1974) (per curiam), *cert. denied*, 419 U.S. 1012 (1974).

45. *Id.* at 1278.

46. *Theriault*, 453 F. Supp. at 264.

47. Goff v. Graves, 362 F.3d 543, 547 (8th Cir. 2004).

48. *Id.* at 548.

49. *Id.* at 549.

50. *See* Yehuda M. Braunstein, Note, *Will Jewish Prisoners Be Boerne Again? Legislative Responses to City of Boerne v. Flores*, 66 FORDHAM L. REV. 2333, 2379 (1988) (arguing that state RFRAs are necessary in part because, "Religion in prison is the most effective form of prisoner rehabilitation . . ."); *see also* O'Lone v. Estate of Shabazz, 482 U.S. 342, 368 (1987) (Brennan, J., dissenting) ("Incarceration by its nature denies a prisoner participation in the larger human community. To deny the opportunity to affirm membership in a spiritual community, however, may extinguish an inmate's last source of hope for dignity and redemption."); Barnett v. Rodgers, 410 F.2d 995, 1002 (D.C. Cir. 1969) ("Religion in prison subserves the rehabilitative function by providing an area within which the inmate may reclaim his dignity and reassert his individuality.").

51. Tim Padgett, *When God Is the Warden: The Nation's First Faith-Based Prison Mixes Religion and Rehab – And Stirs Up Controversy*, TIME, June 7, 2004, at 50.

52. Barbara Bradley, *Morning Edition: 'Morning Edition' Visits Bible-based Prison Program* (National Public Radio broadcast, Sept. 7, 2001), *also available at* http://www.pfm.org/AM/Template.cfm?Section=About_Prison_Fellowship1&template=/CM/HTMLDisplay.cfm&ContentID=2674 (last visited Nov. 9, 2004).

53. The Americans United for Separation of Church and State's complaint is available online at http://www.au.org/site/DocServer/InnerChangeBrief.pdf?docID=163 (last visited Feb. 9, 2005).

54. Larson v. Valente, 456 U.S. 228, 246 (1982).

55. Alan Cooperman, *An Infusion of Religious Funds in Fla. Prisons*, WASH. POST, Apr. 25, 2004, at A1 (hereinafter Cooperman).

56. *See* Mark Chaves, CONGREGATIONS IN AMERICA 93 (2004).

57. Cooperman, *supra* note 55.

58. Megan O'Matz, *Taking the Bible behind Bars Evangelical Christians Mobilize for Two Campaigns Aimed at Carrying the Gospel of Jesus Christ into State Prisons*, SUN-SENTINEL (Ft. Lauderdale, Fla.), Apr. 17, 2004, at 1B.

59. Carlos Campos, *Faith Behind Bars Programs Aim to Uplift, But Foes Say State Oversteps Bounds*, ATLANTA J.-CONST., Aug. 22, 2004, at C4.

60. Goldman v. Weinberger, 475 U.S. 503, 510 (1986).

61. *Id.* at 514 (Brennan, J., dissenting).

62. *Id.* at 524 (Blackmun, J., dissenting).

63. *See id.* at 528–33 (O'Connor, J. dissenting).

64. C. Thomas Dienes, *When the First Amendment Is Not Preferred: The Military and Other "Special Contexts,"* 56 U. CIN. L. REV. 779, 804 (1988).

65. *See* 10 U.S.C. § 774 (1987).

66. Sherwood v. Brown, 619 F.2d 479 (9th Cir. 1980).

## 7. Discrimination

1. Hopkins v. Women's Div., Bd. Of Global Ministries, 238 F. Supp. 2d 174, 181–82 (D.D.C. 2002).

2. 139 CONG. REC. S 2822 (1993).

3. 139 CONG. REC. S 14461 (1993).

4. *Id.*

5. 139 CONG. REC. S 2822 (1993).

6. 139 CONG. REC. D1315 (daily ed. Nov. 16, 1993); *At Least 5 Die, 500 Hurt as Explosion Rips Garage under World Trade Center; Bomb Suspected In Midday Blast*, WASH. POST, Feb. 27, 1993, at A1.

7. Owen Bowcott, *The Nine Victims of IRA Bomb Aimed at Loyalist Paramilitaries*, GUARDIAN (LONDON), October 25, 1993, at 1; *List of Terrorist Incidents, at* http://simple.wikipedia.org/wiki/List_of_terrorist_incidents (last visited Nov. 14, 2004).

8. 139 CONG. REC. S 14350 (Statement of Sen. Hatch).

9. *Coalition for Religious Freedom Calls on Supreme Court to Uphold Constitutionality of Religious Freedom Restoration Act, at* http://www.ajcongress.org/pages/RELS1997/JAN97REL/jan_005.htm (last visited Nov. 14, 2004).

10. TEX. CIV. PRAC. & REM. CODE Ann. § 110.010 (Vernon 2001).

11. 71 PA. CONS. STATE. ANN. § 2406(b) (West 2004).

12. Ashcroft v. ACLU, 124 S. Ct. 2783 (2004) (affirming a five-year-old temporary injunction against enforcement of the Child Online Protection Act, Pub. L. No. 105–277, 112 Stat. 2681–736 (1998) (codified as amended at 47 U.S.C. § 231 (2000)); United States v. Am. Library Ass'n, Inc., 539 U.S. 194 (2003) (upholding the constitutionality of the Children's Internet Protection Act, Pub. L. No. 106–554, 114 Stat. 2763A-335 (2001) (codified as amended at 20 U.S.C. § 9134 (2004) and 47 U.S.C. § 254(h) (2000)); Reno v. ACLU, 521 U.S. 844 (1997) (striking down the Communications Decency Act of 1996, Pub. L. No. 104–104, 110 Stat. 133 (codified as amended at 47 U.S.C. § 223 (2000)). The ACLU also filed an amicus brief

in Ashcroft v. Free Speech Coalition, 535 U.S. 234 (2002) (invalidating the Child Pornography Prevention Act, 18 U.S.C. § 2252, 2256 (1996), which regulated child pornography created with digital technology).

13. Levin v. Yeshiva University, 754 N.E.2d 1099 (N.Y. 2001) (medical students denied campus-subsidized couples housing with their same sex partners).

14. *Religious Freedom Restoration Act of 1991: Hearing on H.R. 2797 Before the House Subcommittee on Civil and Constitutional Rights of the Committee on the Judiciary*, 103rd Cong. 65 (statement of Nadine Strossen, President, and Robert S. Peck, Legislative Counsel, American Civil Liberties Union).

15. *Religious Liberty Protection Act of 1999: Hearing on H.R. 1691 Before the Subcommittee on the Constitution of the House Committee on the Judiciary*, 105th Cong. (1999) (statement of American Civil Liberties Union).

16. I.R.C. § 501. *Exemption from Tax on Corporations, Certain Trusts, Etc.* IRS Rev. Rul. 71-447 states "A private school that does not have a racially nondiscriminatory policy as to students does not qualify for exemption."

17. Bob Jones University v United States, 461 U.S. 574, 576 (1983).

18. *Id.* at 604.

19. 42 U.S.C. § 3607 (2004) states, "Religious organization or private club exemption (a) Nothing in this title shall prohibit a religious organization, association, or society, or any nonprofit institution or organization operated, supervised or controlled by or in conjunction with a religious organization, association, or society, from limiting the sale, rental or occupancy of dwellings which it owns or operates for other than a commercial purpose to persons of the same religion, or from giving preference to such persons, unless membership in such religion is restricted on account of race, color, or national origin. Nor shall anything in this title prohibit a private club not in fact open to the public, which as an incident to its primary purpose or purposes provides lodgings which it owns or operates for other than a commercial purpose, from limiting the rental or occupancy of such lodgings to its members or from giving preference to its members."

20. "[A]pparently there has been some question about the potential effect of S. 2869 on State and local civil rights laws, such as fair housing laws. Although prior legislative proposals implicated civil rights laws in a way that concerned the Department, we believe S. 2869 cannot and should not be construed to require exemptions from such laws." 146 CONG. REC. S 7774 (2000) (letter from Robert Raben, Asst. Att'y. Gen.). *See also* 146 CONG. REC. S 7774 (2000) (letter from Melissa Rogers, General Counsel, Baptist Joint Committee on Public Affairs) ("We greatly appreciate the work of the bill's sponsors in drafting the consensus legislation that will provide important new protections for the freedom of religious exercise without the harmful consequences for civil rights laws.").

21. *But see* Marci A. Hamilton, *The Religious Freedom Restoration Act Is Unconstitutional, Period*, 1 U. PA. J. CONST. L. 1 (1998).

22. 42 U.S.C.A. § 2000e-1(a) (1964) ("This subchapter shall not apply to . . . a religious corporation, association, educational institution, or society with respect to the employment of individuals of a particular religion to perform work connected with the carrying on by such corporation, association, educational

institution, or society of its activities."). *See, e.g.,* Hopkins v. Women's Div., Bd. Of Global Ministries, 238 F. Supp. 2d 174 (D.D.C. 2002) (holding that religious discrimination claim is exempted from antidiscrimination rules).

23. 1959 Cal. Stat. 4074. *See* Maureen E. Markey, *The Price of Landlord's "Free" Exercise of Religion: Tenant's Right to Discrimination Free Housing and Privacy,* 22 FORDHAM URB. L.J. 699, 746 (1995).

24. David A. Thomas, *Fixing Up Fair Housing Laws: Are We Ready for Reform?,* 53 S.C. L. REV. 7, 50 n. 297 (2001).

25. Those in the latter category include: CA, DC, HI, MD, NH, NJ, NM, NY, RI. Here are a few citations: R.I. GEN. LAWS § 34-37-4 (2004); N.Y EXEC. LAW § 296 (2004); N.H. STAT. ANN. §354-A(8) (2004); HAW. REV. STAT. § 368-1 (2003).

26. Smith v. Fair Employment & Hous. Comm'n, 913 P.2d 909, 926 (Cal. 1996); McCready v. Hoffius, 586 N.W. 2d 723, 729 (Mich. 1998). *See also* Stephanie Hammond Knutson, *Note, The Religious Landlord and the Conflict between Free Exercise Rights and Housing Discrimination Laws – Which Interest Prevails?,* 47 HASTINGS L.J. 1669, 1716–17 (1996).

27. Bachman v. St. Monica's Congregation, 902 F.2d 1259 (7th Cir. 1990), *reh'g denied,*902 F.2d 1259 (1990).

28. Swanner v. Anchorage Equal Rights Com'n, 874 P.2d. 274, 280 n. 8 (Alaska 1994) (per curiam); *McCready,* 586 N. W. 2d at 730 ("A compelling state interest in eradicating discrimination in real estate transactions justifies the burden on their beliefs"); *cf.* Attorney Gen. v. Desilets, 636 N.E.2d 233 (Mass. 1994), recognizing a compelling interest test, but stating "The general objective of eliminating discrimi-nation of all kinds referred to in the relevant version of § 4 (6) ("race, religious creed, color, national origin, sex, age, ancestry or marital status" cannot alone provide a compelling State interest that justifies the application of that section in disregard of the defendants' right to free exercise of their religion"); *see also* Markey, *The Price of Landlord's "Free" Exercise of Religion, supra* note 23, at 699.

29. *Compare Swanner,* 874 P.2d at 274 *and McCready* at 586 N.W. 2d at 729 *with* Swanner v. Anchorage Equal Rights Comm'n, 513 U.S. 979 (1994) (Thomas, J., dissenting from denial of certiorari), Donahue v. Fair Employment & Housing Com., 2 Cal. Rptr. 2d 32 (Cal. Ct. App. 1991), *and* State by Cooper v. French, 460 N.W. 2d 2 (Minn. 1990).

30. *Swanner,* 874 P.2d at 282–83; *McCready,* 586 N.W. 2d at 729 (explaining that the Michigan legislature determined the need for equal access to housing regardless of marital status so fundamental as to require the passing of the Civil Rights Act).

31. *Smith,* 913 P.2d at 929.

32. *McCready,* 586 N.W. 2d at 730; *Swanner,* 874 P.2d at 280, n. 9.

33. Hack v. Fellows of Yale College, 237 F.3d 81, 89, 90 (2d Cir. 2000).

34. *State by Cooper,* 460 N.W.2d at 4, 5, 8, 11.

35. *Donahue,* 2 Cal. Rptr. 2d at 50.

36. 42 U.S.C. § 2000e-1 (1964). The Age Discrimination in Employment Act (ADEA) does not have a religious exception. *See, e.g,* De Marco v. Holy Cross High Sch., 4 F.3d 166, 173 (2d Cir. 1993).

37. *See, e.g.*, Killinger v. Samford Univ., 113 F.3d 196 (11th Cir. 1997) (considering numerous factors, university is a religious institution); EEOC v. Kamehameha School/Bishop Estate, 990 F.2d 458, 460 (9th Cir. 1993) (when the statute is properly and narrowly construed, a religious school did not count as a religious organization); EEOC v. Townley Engineering & Mfg. Co., 675 F. Supp. 566 (D. Ariz. 1987) (for-profit corporation whose articles of incorporation made no reference to religion not entitled to Title VII exemption).

38. *See, e.g.*, Bryce v. Episcopal Church in the Diocese of Colo., 289 F.3d 648 (10th Cir. 2002) (court will not take jurisdiction where claim involves fired gay youth minister whose lifestyle was prohibited by church doctrine); EEOC v. Southwestern Baptist Theological Seminary, 651 F.2d 277, 283 (5th Cir. 1981); Smith v. Raleigh Dist. of the N.C. Conf. of the United Methodist Church, 63 F. Supp. 2d 694, 706 (D. N.C. 1999) (hostile environment claim goes forward where employees performed nonreligious tasks); Guinan v. Roman Catholic Archdiocese, 42 F. Supp. 2d 849, 852–53 (S.D. Ind. 1998) (ministerial exception in applicable in ADEA case where teacher did not function in a ministerial capacity).

The Supreme Court upheld Title VII's exemption for religion in year and interpreted the idea of "religious employee" broadly, so that a janitor in a religious organization could be denied the right to sue for discrimination. Corporation of Presiding Bishop of Church of Jesus Christ of Latter-day Saints v. Amos, 483 U.S. 327 (1987).

39. *See, e.g.*, Elvig v. Calvin Presbyterian Church, 375 F.3d 951, 958 (9th Cir. 2004) (holding the claims could not proceed in civil court because that would involve an inquiry into the Church decisions of who shall be a minister); Bollard v. California Province of the Soc'y of Jesus, 196 F.3d 940, 947 (9th Cir. 1999) (allowing the case to proceed because "the Jesuits do not offer a religious justification for the harassment Bollard alleges" and, hence, there is no danger in secular courts passing judgment on religious beliefs or doctrine); Cline v. Catholic Diocese, 206 F.3d 651, 658 (6th Cir. 1999) (Title VII and ministerial exception did not protect the Church from claim based on firing of unwed pregnant woman because the Church cannot discriminate based on pregnancy, which is clearly discrimination based on sex); EEOC v. Pacific Press Pub. Assoc, 676 F.2d 1272, 1279 (9th Cir. 1992) (married female employee's suit against pay according to gender and marital status permitted to go forward, because de minimis burden on religious belief); EEOC v. Fremont Christian School, 781 F.2d 1362, 1368 (9th Cir. 1986) (finding de minimis burden on religious belief where Christian school provided health insurance only to "heads of households"); Dolquist v. Heartland Presbytery, No. 03-2150-KHV, 2004 U.S. Dist. LEXIS 21888 (D. Kan. Oct. 28, 2004); *Smith*, 63 F. Supp. 2d at 710 (hostile environment claims go forward where they do not intrude upon defendant church's spiritual functions).

40. Hartwig v. Albertus Magnus College, 93 F. Supp. 2d 200, 217–18 (D. Conn. 2000) (the contractual claims did not involve impermissible involvement with issues of religious doctrine but rather involved the alleged misrepresentation of Hartwig's status as a priest).

41. Vigars v. Valley Christian Ctr., 805 F. Supp. 802 (N.D. Cal. 1992) (distinguishing between exemption permitted where firing was based on adulterous relationship that violated religious tenets, but not if firing was based on pregnancy, which was not proscribed by religious beliefs); Janet S. Belcove-Shalin, *Ministerial Exception and Title VII Claims: Case Law Grid Analysis*, 2 NEV. L.J. 86, 87 (2002). ("This historical [McClure] holding provided a constitutional mooring for what is variously referred to as "the ministerial exception"... "and what has been construed as a blanket exemption from Title VII judicial review of the employment relationship between a religious organization and its clergy.").

42. McClure v. Salvation Army, 460 F.2d 553, 558–59 (5th Cir. 1972). On appeal, the court held the Free Exercise Clause of the First Amendment precluded the district court from exercising jurisdiction over the minister's claims.

43. Lewis v. Seventh Day Adventists Lake Region Conference, 978 F.2d 940, 942 (6th Cir. 1992).

44. 676 F.2d at 1289.

45. Williams v. Episcopal Diocese, 13 Mass. L. Rep. 289 (Mass. Sup. Ct. 2001).

46. 233 F. Supp. 2d 917 (N.D. Ohio 2002).

47. Rosati v. Toledo, 233 F. Supp.2d 917 (N.D. Ohio 2002).

48. *See, e.g., Hopkins,* 238 F. Supp. 2d 174 (holding that church can avoid religious discrimination claim under Title VII exemption, but not claims regarding racial discrimination); *Guinan,* 42 F. Supp. 2d 849 (age discrimination claim stands where teacher does not function as a minister or clergy member, rejecting claims under ministerial exception and RFRA).

49. *Southwest Baptist Theological Seminary,* 651 F.2d at 284.

50. *Pacific Press Pub. Assoc.,* 676 F.2d at 1278 (Title VII, sec. 702 applies only to employees whose duties "go to the heart of the church's function").

51. EEOC v. Mississippi College, 626F.2d 477 (5th Cir. 1980) (religious college does not get benefit of Title VII, sec. 702 exemption, because it is not a church).

52. McKelvey v. Pierce, 800 A.2d 840 (N.J. 2002).

53. *Id.* at 857 (quoting Sanders v. Casa View Baptist Church, 134 F.2d 331, 335–36 (5th Cir. 1998)).

54. Dunn v. Bd. of Incorporators of the African Methodist Episcopal Church, No. 00-CV02547-D, 2002 U.S. Dist. LEXIS 2464 (N.D. Tex. 2002).

55. Young v. Northern Ill. Conference United Methodist Church, 818 F. Supp. 1206 (N.D. Ill. 1993), *aff'd,* 21 F.3d 184 (7th Cir. 1994), *cert. denied,* 513 U.S. 929 (1994).

56. Elvig v. Calvin Presbyterian Church, 375 F.3d 951, 953, 953–54, 965 (9th Cir. 2004). *See also* Petruska v. Gannon Univ., No. 04-80, 2004 U.S. Dist. LEXIS 26085 (W.D. Pa. Dec. 27, 2004).

57. Bollard v. California Province of Society of Jesus, No. C 97-3006 SI, 1998 WL 273011 (N.D. Cal. May 15, 1998), *rev'd and remanded by* Bollard v. California Province of the Soc'y of Jesus, 196 F.3d 940 (9th Cir. 1999).

58. *Id.* at *1 (N.D.Cal. May 15, 1998).

59. *Bollard*, 196 F.3d at 944, 948. Bollard settled his claim against the Jesuits for an undisclosed amount after the case was remanded to trial. *Ex-Jesuit Seminarian Settled Sex-Harass Suit*, S. F. CHRON., Aug. 2, 2000, at A24.

60. Dolquist v. Heartland Presbytery, No. 03-2150-KHV, 2004 U.S. Dist. LEXIS 21888, *7 (D. Kan. Oct. 28, 2004).

61. *Id.* at *37.

## 8. Boerne v. Flores: The Case that Fully Restored the Rule of Law for Religious Entities

1. Wisconsin v. Yoder, 406 U.S. 205, 221 (1972); Sherbert v. Verner, 374 U.S. 398, 406–7 (1963).

2. Katzenbach v. Morgan, 384 U.S. 641, 652 (1966).

3. In the interest of full disclosure, I represented the City of Boerne, Texas, in Boerne v. Flores, 521 U.S. 507 (1997), in which the City prevailed. My personal involvement in the case, however, is only tangentially relevant to the doctrinal analysis in this chapter. The City of Boerne, Texas was settled by German immigrants and is pronounced Ber-knee.

4. THOMAS JEFFERSON, "Notes on the State of Virginia (1787)," *in* 2 THE WRITINGS OF THOMAS JEFFERSON, at 221 (Albert Ellery Bergh ed., 1905).

5. JOHN STUART MILL, ON LIBERTY, *reprinted in* Vol. XXV, Part 2 THE HARVARD CLASSICS (1909–14), *available at* http://www.bartleby.com/25/2/4.html (last visited Jan. 7, 2005).

6. This is true in the history leading up to the Constitution, and in the Supreme Court case across the spectrum of constitutional topics. *See* BERNARD BAILYN, THE IDEOLOGICAL ORIGINS OF THE AMERICAN REVOLUTION 77 (1967) ("Liberty, that is, was the capacity to exercise "natural rights' within limits set, not by the mere will or desire of men in power but by nonarbitrary law – law enacted by legislatures containing within them the proper balance of forces"); GORDON S. WOOD, THE CREATION OF THE AMERICAN REPUBLIC 1776–87 60–61 (1969); *Boerne*, 521 U.S. at 539–41 (Scalia, J., concurring) ("Religious exercise shall be permitted *so long as it does not violate general laws governing conduct*") (emphasis in original) (citing the Maryland Act Concerning Religion of 1649, negating a license to act in a manner "unfaithful to the Lord Proprietary"; the Rhode Island Charter of 1663, requiring people to "behave" in other than a "peaceable and quiet" manner; the earliest New York, Maryland, and Georgia Constitutions prohibiting interference with the "peace [and] safety of the State"; the first New Hampshire Constitution forbidding anyone from "disturb[ing]" the public peace"; the Northwest Ordinance of 1787 prohibiting citizens from "demean[ing]" oneself in other than a "peaceable and orderly manner").

The importance of "ordered liberty" in Supreme Court jurisprudence cannot be overrstated. *See infra* note 17.

7. 98 U.S. 145 (1879).

8. *Reynolds*, 98 U.S. at 164 (quoting 8 JEFFERSON WORKS 113).

9. *Id.* at 166–67.

10. I have called it the no-harm principle. *See* Marci A. Hamilton, *Religious Institutions, the No-Harm Doctrine, and the Public Good*, 2004 B.Y.U. L. REV. 1099.

11. *Reynolds*, 98 U.S. at 164 (quoting 8 JEFFERSON WORKS 113).

12. JOHN LOCKE, A LETTER CONCERNING RELIGIOUS TOLERATION 50 (Bobbs-Merrill 2d ed. 1955) (1689) ("[L]iberty of conscience is every man's natural right, equally belonging to dissenters as to themselves;... nobody ought to be compelled in matters of religion either by law or force. The establishment of this one thing would take away all ground of complaints and tumults upon account of conscience.").

13. JOHN LOCKE, TWO TREATISES OF GOVERNMENT (Mark Goldie ed. 1993) (1689) (hereinafter LOCKE, TWO TREATISES), in which he discusses a "no-harm" principle ("If human beings belong to God, they cannot belong to one another, or even to themselves. Since God is the true proprietor, no one else has the right to damage or destroy his property"). *See also* Russell L. Caplan, *The History and Meaning of the Ninth Amendment*, 69 VA. L. REV. 223, 230 (1983) (hereinafter Caplan) ("Under [Locke's] theory, individuals are born into a "state of nature," that is, without organized government, and agree out of "strong Obligations of Necessity, Convenience, and Inclination" to live in political communities. In so contracting, individuals must give up some of their natural rights so that the rest of those rights may be more effectively secured. The sole legitimate purpose of government, therefore, is the good of the contracting parties – the public. Accordingly, government has a right only to act for the benefit of the governed, to protect its citizens from rebellion within and invasion without").

14. LOCKE, TWO TREATISES, *supra* note 13, at 164; *see also* Caplan, *supra* note 13, at 230.

15. *Reynolds*, 98 U.S. at 164.

16. MILL, ON LIBERTY, *supra* note 5, *available at* http://www.bartleby.com/25/2/ (last viewed May 11, 2004).

17. *See* Sell v. U.S. 539 U.S. 166 (2003); Chavez v. Martinez, 538 U.S. 760 (2003); Tyler v. Cain, 533 U.S. 656 (2001); County of Sacramento v. Lewis, 523 U.S. 833 (1998); Washington v. Glucksberg, 521 U.S. 702 (1997); Kansas v. Hendricks, 521 U.S. 346 (1997); O'Dell v. Netherland, 521 U.S. 151 (1997); Carlisle v. U.S., 517 U.S. 416 (1996); Goeke v. Branch, 514 U.S. 115 (1995); Gilmore v. Taylor, 508 U.S. 333 (1993); Graham v. Collins, 506 U.S. 461 (1993); Riggins v. Nevada, 504 U.S. 127 (1992); Milkovich v. Lorain Journal Co., 497 U.S. 1 (1990); Butler v. McKellar, 494 U.S. 407 (1990); Stanford v. Kentucky, 492 U.S. 361 (1989); Michael H. v. Gerald D., 491 U.S. 110 (1989); Teague v. Lane, 489 U.S. 288 (1989); Yates v. Aiken, 484 U.S. 211 (1988); U.S. v. Salerno, 481 U.S. 739 (1987); Memphis Community School Dist. v. Stachura, 477 U.S. 299 (1986); Bowen v. Roy, 476 U.S. 693 (1986); U.S. v. Bagley, 473 U.S. 667 (1985); Dun & Bradstreet, Inc. v. Greenmoss Builders, 472 U.S. 749 (1985); Kolender v. Lawson, 461 U.S. 352 (1983); Moore v. City of East Cleveland, Ohio, 431 U.S. 494 (1977); Ingraham v. Wright, 430 U.S.

651 (1977); Whalen v. Roe, 429 U.S. 589 (1977); Stone v. Powell, 428 U.S. 465 (1976); U.S. v. Janis, 428 U.S. 433 (1976); Paul v. Davis, 424 U.S. 693 (1976); Gertz v. Robert Welch, Inc., 418 U.S. 323 (1974); Paris Adult Theatre I v. Slaton, 413 U.S. 49 (1973); Roe v. Wade, 410 U.S. 113 (1973); Wisconsin v. Yoder, 406 U.S. 205 (1972); Coolidge v. New Hampshire, 403 U.S. 443 (1971); Williams v. U.S., 401 U.S. 646 (1971) (plurality opinion); Duncan v. State of La., 391 U.S. 145 (1968); Tehan v. U.S. ex rel. Shott, 382 U.S. 406 (1966); Ker v. State of Cal., 374 U.S. 23 (1963); Gideon v. Wainwright, 372 U.S. 335 (1963); Mapp v. Ohio, 367 U.S. 643 (1961); Elkins v. U.S., 364 U.S. 206 (1960); Ohio v. Price, 364 U.S. 263 (1960) (per curiam); Napue v. Illinois, 360 U.S. 264 (1959); Bartkus v. Illinois, 359 U.S. 121 (1959); Leland v. Oregon, 343 U.S. 790 (1952); Rochin v. California, 342 U.S. 165 (1952); Stefanelli v. Minard, 342 U.S. 117 (1951); Kovacs v. Cooper, 336 U.S. 77 (1949); Bute v. Illinois, 333 U.S. 640 (1948); Screws v. U.S., 325 U.S. 91 (1945).

18. *See generally* THE WORKS OF JOHN WITHERSPOON, LECTURES ON MORAL PHILOSOPHY (1805).

19. 7 THE WORKS OF JOHN WITHERSPOON 100, 148 (lecture 16) (1805). Witherspoon, a signer of the Declaration of Independence and president of Princeton, was influential in the development of many of the Framers, including James Madison.

20. Lee v. Weisman, 505 U.S. 577, 590–91 (1992) ("To endure the speech of false ideas or offensive content and then to counter it is part of learning how to live in a pluralistic society, a society which insists upon open discourse towards the end of a tolerant citizenry. And tolerance presupposes some mutuality of obligation."); *Smith*, 494 U.S. at 879 ("the right of free exercise does not relieve an individual of the obligation to comply with a 'valid and neutral law of general applicability on the ground that the law proscribes (or prescribes) conduct that his religion prescribes (or proscribes).'" (quoting United States v. Lee, 455 U.S. 252, 263, n. 3 (1982) (Stevens, J., concurring in judgment)).

21. 512 U.S. 687 (1994).

22. 406 U.S. 205 (1972).

23. *Smith*, 494 U.S. at 881.

24. *Lee*, 455 U.S. at 259–60.

25. ROBERT NOZICK, ANARCHY, STATE, & UTOPIA 32–35 (1974).

26. Church of Lukumi Babalu Aye v. City of Hialeah, 508 U.S. 520, 547 (1993).

27. Abington School Dist. v. Schempp, 374 U.S. 203, 305 (1963) (Goldberg, J. concurring).

28. SARAH BARRINGER GORDON, THE MORMON QUESTION: POLYGAMY AND CONSTITUTIONAL CONFLICT IN NINETEENTH CENTURY AMERICA 157 (2002).

29. U.S. CONST. art. III § 2 states:

> The judicial power shall extend to all cases, in law and equity, arising under this Constitution, the laws of the United States, and treaties made, or which shall be made, under their authority . . . to controversies to which the United States shall be a party; – to controversies between two or more states; – between a state and citizens of another state; – between citizens of different states; – between citizens of the same state claiming lands under grants of different states, and between a state, or the citizens thereof, and foreign states, citizens or subjects.

30. *Lee*, 455 U.S. at 259–60.

31. Bob Jones Univ. v. United States, 461 U.S. 574, 604 (1983).

32. Tony & Susan Alamo Foundation v. Secretary of Labor, 471 U.S. 290, 306 (1985).

33. Goldman v. Weinberger, 475 U.S. 503, 509–10 (1986).

34. Bowen v. Roy, 476 U.S. 693, 700–701 (1986).

35. Lyng v. Northwest Indian Cemetery Protective Assn., 485 U.S. 439, 452 (1988).

36. Hernandez v. Commissioner, 490 U.S. 680, 683 (1989).

37. Jimmy Swaggart Ministries v. Board of Equalization, 493 U.S. 378, 394 (1990).

38. O'Lone v. Estate of Shabazz, 482 U.S. 342, 345 (1987).

39. *Smith*, 494 U.S. at 885. In addition to this list of cases in which the Court upheld neutral, generally applicable laws against free-exercise challenges, the Court also refused to read into the requirements of the civil rights act a duty to accommodate Sabbatarians. *See* Trans World Airlines v. Hardison, 432 U.S. 63, 81 (1977) ("It would be anomalous to conclude that by 'reasonable accommodation' Congress meant that an employer must deny the shift and job preference of some employees, as well as deprive them of their contractual rights, in order to accommodate or prefer the religious needs of others, and we conclude that Title VII does not require an employer to go that far."). This is especially interesting in light of the fact that the only arena wherein the Court consistently found free-exercise violations between 1963 and 1990 involved Sabbatarians challenging the laws governing unemployment compensation. *See, e.g., Sherbert*, 374 U.S. 398; *see also* Frazee v. Ill. Dep't of Employment Sec., 489 U.S. 829 (1989).

40. *Smith*, 494 U.S at 878–79, 885.

41. *Lukumi*, 508 U.S. at 547, 523 (internal citations omitted).

42. *Smith*, 494 U.S. at 890.

43. *Lukumi*, 508 U.S. 520.

44. McDaniel v. Paty, 435 U.S. 618, 628–29 (1978).

45. Locke v. Davey, 124 S. Ct. 1307, 1312–13 (2004) (citing Hobbie v. Unemployment Appeals Comm'n of Fla., 480 U.S. 136 (1987); Thomas v. Review Bd. of Indiana Employment Security Div., 450 U.S. 707 (1981); *Sherbert*, 374 U.S. 398 (1963)).

46. *See* Fowler v. Rhode Island, 345 U.S. 67 (1953), where the appellant was a minister of Jehovah's Witnesses who was arrested for addressing a religious meeting in a public park, in violation of an ordinance of the City of Pawtucket, R.I. Appellant contended that the ordinance as applied violated the First and Fourteenth Amendments. On oral argument before the Court, the State conceded that the ordinance did not prohibit church services in public parks and that Catholics and Protestants could conduct religious services without violating the ordinance. The Court held that the ordinance, as construed and applied by the State, amounted to unlawful discrimination because the religious services were of Jehovah's Witnesses.

47. *See* Brief for Respondent at *15, *Davey*, 124 S. Ct. 1307, *available at* 2002 U.S. Briefs 1315 (LEXIS) ("The state's express, discriminatory disqualification of otherwise eligible scholarship recipients, solely because they declare a major in theology taught from a religious point of view, violates the Free Exercise Clause of the First Amendment"); Brief for Amici Curiae The Beckett Fund for Religious Liberty, et. al. at *3, *Davey*, 124 S. Ct. 1307, *available at* 2002 U.S. Briefs 1315 (LEXIS) ("The Washington State law at issue in this case disqualifies a student from an otherwise available government benefit, only because the student would use the benefit for a religious purpose. That is the core constitutional offense identified by the court below, and this Court may affirm [the invalidation of the statute] on that basis alone.").

48. *Davey*, 124 S. Ct. at 1312.

49. *Frazee*, 489 U.S. at 835; *Hobbie*, 480 U.S. at 141; *Thomas*, 450 U.S. at 718; *Yoder*, 406 U.S. at 221; *Sherbert*, 374 U.S. at 406–7.

50. Justice Brennan's opinion in *Sherbert*, 374 U.S. 398, was the first case to introduce this new rule, and its reasoning was the template against which the succeeding unemployment compensation cases were decided. *See, e.g., Hobbie*, 480 U.S. at 139–40 (author for majority); *Thomas*, 450 U.S. at 713–14 (joined in majority). He also joined the majority in *Yoder*, 406 U.S. 205, where he also joined the concurrences of Justices Byron White and Potter Stewart, which argued that a different case would be presented if an Amish child wished to attend school beyond the eighth grade, despite the parents' religious beliefs, *id.* at 237 (Stewart, J., concurring), or if the "religion forbade their children from attending any school at any time and from complying in any way with the educational standards set by the State." *Id.* at 238 (White, J., concurring).

51. *Smith*, 494 U.S. 872, which rejected the application of strict scrutiny to generally applicable, neutral laws, was decided on April 17, 1990, only three months before Brennan retired on July 20, 1990. *See* Members of the Supreme Court of the United States, *at* http://www.supremecourtus.gov/about/members.pdf (last viewed May 18, 2004).

52. *Frazee*, 489 U.S. at 835; *Hobbie*, 480 U.S. at 141; *Thomas*, 450 U.S. at 718; *Sherbert*, 374 U.S. at 406–7.

53. *Yoder*, 406 U.S. at 221.

54. 374 U.S. 398, 400–401 (quoting S. C. Code, tit. 68, §§ 68-1 to 68-404), 404 (1963).

55. 450 U.S. 707, 709, 709 n. 1 (quoting Indiana Code § 22-4-15-1 [Supp. 1978]) (1981).

56. 480 U.S. 136, 137–138 (quoting Fla. Stat. § 443.021 [1985]) (1987).

57. 489 U.S. 829, 830–831 (quoting Frazee v. Ill. Dep't of Employment Sec., 512 N. E. 2d 789 [Ill. 1987]), 834 (1989).

58. *See, e.g.,* Weiss, *Privilege, Posture and Protection: "Religion" in the Law,* 73 YALE L.J. 593 (1964); J. Morris Clark, *Guidelines for the Free Exercise Clause,* 83 HARV. L. REV. 327, 329 (1969) ("In common sense terms the Sherbert decision seems correct enough.... Yet by its holding that some religious practices

364 / NOTES TO PAGES 218–219

are protected even from laws not intended to affect the communicative aspects of belief, Sherbert introduced a new range of complexity into the free exercise clause.").

59. *See generally* Kent Greenawalt, *Religion as a Concept in Constitutional Law*, 72 CAL. L. REV. 753 (1984); Philip E. Johnson, *Concepts and Compromise in First Amendment Religious Doctrine*, 72 CAL. L. REV. 817 (1984); Note, *Toward a Constitutional Definition of Religion*, 91 HARV. L. REV. 1056, 1077–82 (1978) (discussing and rejecting criticisms of *Sherbert*).

60. *See, e.g.*, Douglas Laycock, *Continuity and Change in the Threat to Religious Liberty: The Reformation Era and the Late Twentieth Century*, 80 MINN. L. REV. 1047, 1099 (1996) ("When the evil is human suffering, the sufferer is penalized because of his religious practice, and the State inflicts the suffering, focusing on the State's motive seems to miss the point."); Michael W. McConnell, *The Origins and Historical Understanding of Free Exercise of Religion*, 103 HARV. L. REV. 1409, 1516 (1990) (hereinafter McConnell, *Origins*) ("the Court should extend its protection to religious groups that, because of their inability to win accommodation in the political process, are in danger of forced assimilation into our secularized Protestant culture.... The free-exercise clause also makes an important statement about the limited nature of governmental authority. While the government is powerless and incompetent to determine what particular conception of the divine is authoritative, the free-exercise clause stands as a recognition that such divine authority may exist and, if it exists, has a rightful claim on the allegiance of believers who happen to be American citizens."); Stephen M. Feldman, *Religious Minorities and the First Amendment: The History, the Doctrine, and the Future*, 6 U. PA. J. CONST. L. 222, 270 (2003) ("A free-exercise claimant's religious interests should be presumed to outweigh all countervailing governmental interests unless the government shows that its interests are of overriding (or compelling) importance and cannot be satisfied in any other manner. Quite evidently, this presumption would reinstitute the strict scrutiny or compelling state interest test that the Court at least claimed to apply for many years in free-exercise cases. The reason for reintroducing this presumption is powerful: the Court might all too easily permit the sacrifice of outsiders' sincere religious interests for the mere convenience of the government or democratic majorities (the religious mainstream).").

61. 406 U.S. 205 (1972).

62. *Yoder*, 406 U.S. at 228–29.

63. *See* Ellis West, *The Case Against a Right to Religious-Based Exemptions*, 4 NOTRE DAME J. L. ETHICS & PUB. POL'Y 591, 624 (1989) (rejecting constitutionally compelled exemptions, but not legislative exemptions); William P. Marshall, *The Case Against the Constitutionally Compelled Free Exercise Exemption*, 40 CASE W. RES. L. REV. 357 (1990). The historical case against mandatory exemptions was initiated in the well-respected article, Philip A. Hamburger, *A Constitutional Right of Religious Exemption: An Historical Perspective*, 60 GEO. WASH. L. REV. 915 (1992).

64. McConnell, *Origins*, *supra* note 60.

65. *Id.* at 1415.

66. *See generally* Frederick M. Gedicks, *An Unfirm Foundation: The Regrettable Indefensibility of Religious Exemptions*, 20 U. ARK. LITTLE ROCK L.J. 555, 574 (1998) ("[T]he historical moment for exemptions has come and gone. There no longer exists a plausible explanation of why religious believers – and only believers – are constitutionally entitled to be excused from complying with otherwise legitimate laws that burden practices."); Marshall, *supra* note 63; Hamburger, *supra* note 63; West, *supra* note 63, at 624 (rejecting constitutionally compelled exemptions, but not legislative exemptions); *see also* Gedicks, *supra* note 66, at 950–51 ("[I]n the long run, no effective defense is possible [for judicially mandated exemptions]. To the extent that a residuum of religious exemptions persists under state law, ... I say enjoy them while they last.").

67. *See, e.g.,* II JOHN CALVIN, INSTITUTES OF THE CHRISTIAN RELIGION, bk. IV, ch.XX, §32, at 1520:

> But in that obedience which we have shown to be due the authority of rulers, we are always to make this exception, indeed, to observe it as primary, that such obedience is never to lead us away from obedience to him.

68. *See* Marci A. Hamilton, *Religion, the Rule of Law, and the Good of the Whole: A View from the Clergy*, 18 J. L. & POLITICS 387, 396–408 (2002).

69. POLITICAL SERMONS OF THE AMERICAN FOUNDING ERA, 1730–1805, at 147–48 (Ellis Sandoz ed., 1991) (Charles Chauncy 1747).

70. 494 U.S. 872 (1990).

71. *See* Oral Argument in *Smith*, 494 U.S. 872, *available at* 1989 U.S. TRANS LEXIS 94, at *36. Respondents argued that "it is our belief that the state cannot meet any of the burdens in this case. The compelling state interest is the regulation of drug abuse generally, but we do not have any evidence in this case that peyote has been abused or that it contributes to the drug abuse problem. In fact, all of the evidence is to the contrary. We have the findings, for instance, of the federal agency charged with enforcement of the drug laws in this country, which found that and concluded that the religious use of peyote by the Native American Church does not cause a law enforcement problem in this country."

72. *See* Reply Brief for Petitioners, *Smith*, No. 88–1213, 494 U.S. 872 ("Unlike Yoder, the practice at issue here directly affects physical and mental health. The State's health interests in preventing the use of peyote is no different from its interests in preventing the use of mescaline, psilocybin, and LSD, all of which have substantially the same hallucinogenic properties as peyote. Unlike the Amish's practices, the state cannot accommodate religiously motivated drug use without substantially compromising its interests in the health and safety of its citizens." (footnote omitted)).

73. *Smith*, 494 U.S. at 878–79.

74. *Smith*, 494 U.S. at 890.

75. *See, e.g.,* Michael W. McConnell, *Free Exercise Revisionism and the Smith Decision*, 57 U. CHI. L. REV. 1109, 1129 (1990) (hereinafter McConnell, *Free Exercise Revisionism*) ("The rhetoric of [*Smith*] is certainly impolitic, leaving the Court open to the charge of abandoning its traditional role as protector of minority rights against majoritarian oppression."); Douglas Laycock, *The Remnants of Free*

*Exercise,* 1990 SUP. CT. REV. 1, 15 (criticizing Smith's reliance on exemptions in part because "Legislators are under no obligation to be principled. Subject only to their oath to uphold the Constitution, they are free to reflect majority prejudices, to respond to the squeakiest wheel among minorities, to trade votes and make compromises, and to ignore problems that have no votes in them."); Gordon, *infra* note 83, at 110 (calling Smith's invocation of exemptions "Small comfort. 'Discrete and insular minorities' often cannot protect themselves adequately in the legislative process. The right to practice one's religion should not be reduced to a question of political influence, completely subject to the whims of transient and shifting majorities," quoting United States v. Carolene Prods. Co., 304 U.S. 144, 153 n. 4 (1938)).

76. *Smith,* 494 U.S. at 879 (quoting United States v. Lee, 455 U.S. 252, 263, n. 3 (1982) (Stevens, J. concurring in judgment)).

77. *Yoder,* 406 U.S. at 216–17. For this reason, *Yoder* is an early harbinger of Chief Justice Burger's later decision in Bowers v. Hardwick, 478 U.S. 186 (1986), where he employed biblical passages to interpret the 14th Amendment's Equal Protection Clause. *Bowers* was overruled in Lawrence v. Texas, 539 U.S. 558, 578 (2003).

78. *See, e.g.,*Knight v. Conn. Dep't of Pub. Health, 275 F.3d 156, 167 (2d Cir. 2001) ("The allegation that a state action that regulates public conduct infringes on more than one of a public employee's constitutional rights does not warrant more heightened scrutiny than each claim would warrant when viewed separately."); Swanson by & Through Swanson v. Guthrie Indep. Sch. Dist. No. I-L, 135 F.3d 694, 699 (10th Cir. 1998) ("It is difficult to delineate the exact contours of the hybrid-rights theory discussed in Smith. As we discuss below, however, we believe that simply raising such a claim is not a talisman that automatically leads to the application of the compelling-interest test. We must examine the claimed infringements on the party's claimed rights to determine whether either the claimed rights or the claimed infringements are genuine."); Kissinger v. Board of Trustees of Ohio State Univ., 5 F.3d 177, 180 (6th Cir. 1993) ("We do not see how a state regulation would violate the Free Exercise Clause if it implicates other constitutional rights but would not violate the free Exercise Clause if it did not implicate other constitutional rights.... At least until the Supreme Court holds that legal standards under the Free Exercise Clause vary depending on whether other constitutional rights are implicated, we will not use a stricter legal standard . . . to evaluate generally applicable, exceptionless state regulations under the Free Exercise Clause.").

79. *Smith,* 494 U.S. at 907 (Blackmun, J. dissenting) ("This Court over the years painstakingly has developed a consistent and exacting standard to test the constitutionality of a state statute that burdens the free exercise of religion. Such a statute may stand only if the law in general, and the State's refusal to allow a religious exemption in particular, are justified by a compelling interest that cannot be served by less restrictive means.").

80. Douglas Laycock, *The Supreme Court's Assault on Free Exercise, and the Amicus Brief that Was Never Filed,* 8 J.L. & RELIGION 99, 102 (1990).

81. McConnell, *Free Exercise Revisionism, supra* note 75, at 1120.

82. Steven D. Smith, *Free Exercise Doctrine and the Discourse of Disrespect*, 65 U. Colo. L. Rev. 519, 575 (1994).

83. Harry F. Tepker, Jr., *Hallucinations of Neutrality in the Oregon Peyote Case*, 16 Am. Indian L. Rev. 1 (1991).

84. James D. Gordon III, *Free Exercise on the Mountaintop*, 79 Cal. L. Rev. 91, 114–15 (1991).

85. Robert L. Stern, et. al., Supreme Court Practice 313–14 (8th ed. 2002).

86. The following colloquy from the oral argument is telling:

QUESTION [BY JUSTICE]: I mean, we granted certiorari on the question presented, which is whether the Free Exercise Clause of the First Amendment protects a person's religiously motivated use of peyote from the reach of the state's general criminal law prohibition. And you say maybe it is not so much a question of criminal law, but you agree that the First Amendment issue is here.

. . .

MR. DORSAY: Yes, but we think it is disposed of, and we need to keep reemphasizing this by Sherbert and Thomas, that the criminality is irrelevant. If the criminality is relevant, we still believe that the state has not met their test under the First Amendment. And I would be glad to move to that issue. Transcript of oral argument in *Smith*, 494 U.S. 872, 1989 U.S. TRANS LEXIS 94, at *35–42.

The representative of Galen and Black, Mr. Dorsay, argued: The state has failed to meet its burden under the First Amendment to justify what we believe would be the total destruction of this religion, and that is because of the test that has been established by this Court in First Amendment cases. There is a sincere religious belief, it is a bonafide religion; that is conceded by the state. But once that is shown, the state must show, as Justice O'Connor summarized in the Goldman case, that the interest will in fact be substantially harmed by granting the type of exemption requested, and that the state interest will be undermined by granting the exemption, and there is no less restrictive alternative that can be granted in this case. And it is our belief that the state cannot meet any of the burdens in this case. The compelling state interest is the regulation of drug abuse generally, but we do not have any evidence in this case that peyote has been abused or that it contributes to the drug abuse problem.

. . .

QUESTION BY JUSTICE: [W]hy can't the state say we don't want Native American Church members to use it either. We think this is dangerous. It is harmful to people. We don't want children to be brought into this church and taught to use this thing, it is harmful to them. It is a Schedule I substance; we have made that determination.

. . .

MR. DORSAY: Because the First Amendment, I believe, requires something more than a mere legislative statement that we believe it may be harmful.

. . .

QUESTION BY JUSTICE: How about marijuana use by a church that uses that as part of its religious sacrament?
MR. DORSAY: Well, see, I think we can get into a lot of examples, and I don't want to go down that road too far because we don't –
QUESTION BY JUSTICE: I'll bet you don't. (Laughter)

87. William P. Marshall, *In Defense of Smith and Free Exercise Revisionism*, 58 U. CHI. L. REV. 308, 308–9 (1991).

88. *See* Religious Freedom Restoration Act of 1990: Hearing before the Subcommittee on Civil and Constitutional Rights of the House Committee on the Judiciary, 101st Cong., 2d Sess. (Sept. 27, 1990).

89. The one exception was Sen. Harry Reid of Nevada, who in the final stages before RFRA was passed, requested an amendment to exempt the prisons. The amendment failed. See 139 Cong. Rec. S14, 461–68 (daily ed. Oct. 27, 1993); 139 Cong. Rec. S14, 350–68 (daily ed. Oct. 26, 1993).

90. 42 U.S.C. § 2000bb-1 (1993). RFRA was nothing but an attempt by Congress to impose the reasoning of *Sherbert* and *Yoder* on all classes of neutral, generally applicable laws, even though the Court had never traveled that far from the rule of law. Congress stated in their findings and declared purposes that:

(a) Findings. The Congress finds that –
    (1) the framers of the Constitution, recognizing free exercise of religion as an unalienable right, secured its protection in the First Amendment to the Constitution;
    (2) laws "neutral" toward religion may burden religious exercise as surely as laws intended to interfere with religious exercise;
    (3) governments should not substantially burden religious exercise without compelling justification;
    (4) in Employment Division v. Smith, 494 U.S. 872 (1990) the Supreme Court virtually eliminated the requirement that the government justify burdens on religious exercise imposed by laws neutral toward religion; and
    (5) the compelling interest test as set forth in prior Federal court rulings is a workable test for striking sensible balances between religious liberty and competing prior governmental interests.
(b) Purposes. The purposes of this Act are –
    (1) to restore the compelling interest test as set forth in Sherbert v. Verner, 374 U.S. 398 (1963) and Wisconsin v. Yoder, 406 U.S. 205 (1972) and to guarantee its application in all cases where free exercise of religion is substantially burdened; and
    (2) to provide a claim or defense to persons whose religious exercise is substantially burdened by government.

42 U.S.C. 2000bb (1993).

91. *Smith*, 494 U.S. at 890.

92. Robert C. Post & Reva B. Siegel, *Equal Protection by Law: Federal Antidiscrimination Legislation after Morrison and Kimel*, 110 YALE L.J. 441 (2000).

93. Larry D. Kramer, *No Surprise. It's an Activist Court*, N.Y. TIMES, Dec. 12, 2000, at A33. ("But perhaps the most *audacious* instance of judicial activism is the way the court has extended the doctrine of judicial review itself.") (referring to *Boerne*).

94. Nev. Dep't of Human Res. v. Hibbs, 538 U.S. 721 (2003).

95. Tennessee v. Lane, No. 02–1667, 541 U.S. 509 (2004).

96. Civil Rights Act of 1957, PL 85–315, 71 Stat. 634; Civil Rights Act of 1960, PL 86–449, 74 Stat. 86; Civil Rights Act of 1964, PL 88–352, 78 Stat. 241; Voting Rights Act of 1965, PL 89–110, 79 Stat. 437.

97. 42 U.S.C. § 2000b states:

> Whenever the Attorney General receives a complaint in writing signed by an individual to the effect that he is being deprived of or threatened with the loss of his right to the equal protection of the laws, on account of his race, color, religion, or national origin, by being denied equal utilization of any public facility which is owned, operated, or managed by or on behalf of any State or subdivision thereof, other than a public school or public college as defined in section 2000c of this title, and the Attorney General believes the complaint is meritorious and certifies that the signer or signers of such complaint are unable, in his judgment, to initiate and maintain appropriate legal proceedings for relief and that the institution of an action will materially further the orderly progress of desegregation in public facilities, the Attorney General is authorized to institute for or in the name of the United States a civil action in any appropriate district court of the United States against such parties and for such relief as may be appropriate, and such court shall have and shall exercise jurisdiction of proceedings instituted pursuant to this section. The Attorney General may implead as defendants such additional parties as are or become necessary to the grant of effective relief hereunder.

Similar language was included in all previous versions of the Civil Rights Act.

98. 347 U.S. 873 (1954).

99. Loving v. Virginia, 388 U.S. 1 (1967).

100. McLaughlin v. Florida, 379 U.S. 184 (1964).

101. Anderson v. Martin, 375 U.S. 399 (1964).

102. Garner v. Louisiana, 368 U.S. 157 (1961); *see also* Bell v. Maryland, 378 U.S. 226 (1963) (public accommodation law supersedes criminal trespass law used to convict African-American students who participated in a "sit-in" at private restaurant that refused to serve them).

103. Johnson v. Virginia, 373 U.S. 61 (1963).

104. Whitus v. Georgia, 385 U.S. 545 (1966).

105. Heart of Atlanta Motel v. United States, 379 U.S. 241 (1964).

106. Burton v. Wilmington Parking Authority, 365 U.S. 715 (1961).

107. Cooper v. Aaron, 358 U.S. 1 (1958).

108. Reitman v. Mulkey, 387 U.S. 369 (1967).

109. U.S. CONST. art. V provides:

> The Congress, whenever two thirds of both Houses shall deem it necessary, shall propose Amendments to this Constitution, or, on the Application of the Legislatures of two thirds of the several States, shall call a Convention for proposing Amendments, which, in either Case, shall be valid to all Intents and Purposes, as Part of this Constitution, when ratified by the Legislatures of three fourths of the several States, or by Conventions in three fourths thereof, as the one or the other Mode of Ratification may be proposed by the Congress; Provided that no Amendment which may be made prior to the Year One thousand eight hundred and eight shall in any Manner affect the first and fourth Clauses in the Ninth

Section of the first Article; and that no State, without its Consent, shall be deprived of its equal Suffrage in the Senate.

110. EEOC v. Wyoming, 460 U.S. 226 (1983).

111. *Id.* at 262 (Burger, C.J., dissenting).

112. William Cohen, *Congressional Power to Interpret Due Process and Equal Protection*, 27 STAN. L. REV. 603, 606 (1975).

113. *See id.* at 614; see also Matt Pawa, Comment, *When the Supreme Court Restricts Constitutional Rights, Can Congress Save Us? An Examination of Section 5 of the Fourteenth Amendment*, 141 U. PA. L. REV. 1029, 1062 (1993); *but see generally* Lawrence H. Tribe, *A Constitution We Are Amending: In Defense of a Restrained Judicial Role*, 97 HARV. L. REV. 433 (1983).

114. *See* 103 Cong. Rec. S6,867 (1994) (statement of Sen. Cochran quoting Douglas Laycock).

115. Further proof of the widespread and entrenched dogma regarding Congress's power to enact laws like RFRA, resides in the fact that on the law and religion listserv, where church/state scholars debate various issues, the betting on *Boerne* was heavily in favor of Professor Laycock's position. As I understand it, my client, the City of Boerne, received only one vote in support, and that was by someone who was simply willing to take the bet. As it turned out, he was also willing to take the case of beer when the City of Boerne won.

116. Douglas Laycock, *Conceptual Gulfs in City of Boerne v. Flores*, 39 WM. & MARY L. REV. 743, 743 (1998) ("Marci Hamilton and others who doubted the validity of the Religious Freedom Restoration Act plainly had a much better sense than I of the Court's political mood. The city's brief contained twenty-nine citations to dissenting opinions, most of them for key points. But Professor Hamilton's judgment was exactly right; the former dissenters now had the votes to change the law. Moreover, something about the facts or politics of RFRA provoked at least the acquiescence of Justices who I suspect would not have joined the earlier dissents on which she relied.")

117. 384 U.S. 641 (1966).

118. U.S. Const. amend. XIV § 5.

119. Lassiter v. Northhampton County Bd. Of Elections, 360 U.S. 45, 51–53 (1959).

120. While not using the term "prophylactic" explicitly in this opinion, the term was part of the jurisprudence that Brennan subscribed to at the time. *See, e.g.*, Estes v. State of Texas, 381 U.S. 532, 616 (1965) (White, J. dissenting, in which Brennan, J. joins) ("Serious threats to constitutional rights in some instances justify a prophylactic rule dispensing with the necessity of showing specific prejudice in a particular case.").

121. *Katzenbach*, 383 U.S. at 309.

122. *Katzenbach*, 383 U.S. at 668 (Harlan, J., dissenting).

123. 383 U.S. at 651 n. 10.

124. Archibald Cox, *Foreword: Constitutional Adjudication and the Promotion of Human Rights*, 80 HARV. L. REV. 91, 110–11 (1966).

125. Cohen, *supra* note 112, at 606–7.

126. Eugene Gressman & Angela C. Carmella, *The RFRA Revision of the Free Exercise Clause*, 57 OHIO ST. L.J. 65, 118–19 (1996) ("The 'ratchet theory,' which at the time of its birth in *Morgan*led to a spirited dissent by Justices Harlan and Stewart, has never been revisited, followed, or clarified by the Court.").

127. 400 U.S. 112 (1970).

128. 446 U.S. at 220–21.

129. 400 U.S. 112 (1970).

130. 460 U.S. at 262 (quoting Oregon v. Mitchell, 400 U.S. 112, 205 (1970)).

131. Gressman & Carmella, *supra* note 126, at 131–32.

132. *Id.* at 118–19; *see also* Daniel O. Conkle, *The Religious Freedom Restoration Act: The Constitutional Significance of an Unconstitutional Statute*, 56 MONT. L. REV. 39, 46 (1995).

133. *Boerne*, 521 U.S. at 519.

134. *Id.* at 530.

135. *Id.* at 532.

## 9. The Decline of the Special Treatment of Religious Entities and the Rise of the No-Harm Rule

1. HAROLD J. BERMAN, LAW AND REVOLUTION: THE FORMATION OF THE WESTERN LEGAL TRADITION 267 (1983) (hereinafter BERMAN, LAW AND REVOLUTION).

2. A. R. HOGUE, ORIGINS OF THE COMMON LAW, 5, 186–90 (1966).

3. See *infra* notes 144–151 and accompanying text (discussing no-harm principle in works of John Locke, James Madison, and Thomas Jefferson).

4. *See, e.g.*, Craigdallie v. Aikman, 1 Dow 1, 3 Eng. Rep. 601 (H. L. 1813) (Scot.); The Reverend G. H. Forbes, of the Scotch Episcopal Church v. The Right Reverend Bishop Eden, Primus of the Scotch Episcopal Church, L. R. 1 Sc. 568 (1867) ("Per Lord Colonsay: A Court of Law will not interfere with the rules of a voluntary association, *unless to protect some civil right or interest which is said to be infringed by their operation*.") (emphasis added).

5. The Feoffees of Heriot's Hospital v. Ross, 1846, 12 Clark & Fin. 507, 8 Eng. Rep. 1508 (introducing the doctrine of charitable immunity); Duncan v. Findlater, 1839, 6 Clark & Fin. 894, 7 Eng.Rep. 934 (similar dicta from the same judge in this earlier case); Holliday v. St. Leonard, 1861, 11 C.B., N.S., 192 (following Duncan's case); McDonald v. Massachusetts General Hospital, 1876, 120 Mass.432, 21 Am.Rep. 529 (first American case adopting the charitable immunity rule of Holliday's case); Perry v. House of Refuge, 1885, 63 Md. 20, 52 Am.Rep. 495 (charitable immunity rule of Heriot's case adopted by Maryland).

6. See Bradley C. Canon & Dean Jaros, *The Impact of Changes in Judicial Doctrine: The Abrogation of Charitable Immunity*, 13 LAW & SOC'Y REV. 969, 971 (1979) (hereinafter Canon & Jaros).

7. *See, e.g.*, Elizabeth Stewart Poisson, Comment, *The Impropriety of Statutory Caps on Pain and Suffering Damages in the Medical Liability System*, 82 N. C. L.

REV. 759 (2004); M. King Hill III & Katherine D. Williams, *State Laws Limiting Liability for Noneconomic Damages: How Courts Have Dealt with the Related Legal and Medical Issues in Asbestos Personal Injury Cases*, 27 U. BALT. L. REV. 317 (1998); Nancy L. Manzer, Note, *Tort Reform Legislation: A Systematic Evaluation of Caps on Damages and Limitations on Joint and Several Liability*, 73 CORNELL L. REV. 628 (1988); George L. Priest, *The Current Insurance Crisis and Modern Tort Law*, 96 YALE L.J. 1521, 1587–88 (1987).

8. *See, e.g.*, Michel Rosenfeld, *The Rule of Law and the Legitimacy of Constitutional Democracy*, 74 S. CAL. L. REV. 1307, 1345–46 (2001) (noting that that the common law "is grounded in a common well of values, a widely shared sense of justice and fairness, and dedication to elaborating a pragmatically oriented, empirically-based working legal order that insures stability through steadfast adherence to core principles."); *id.* at 1349 ("At least under certain propitious circumstances, therefore, the rule of law can promote both predictability and fairness; this seems equally possible in an Anglo-American common law setting as in a continental civil law system."); Charles H. Koch, Jr., *Envisioning a Global Legal Culture*, 25 MICH J. INT'L L.J. 1, 54 (2003) ("the common law judge is charged with applying the 'law' in order to render individual fairness, but is also committed to treating like cases alike.

9. *See* Locke v. Davey, 124 S. Ct. 1307, 1309 (2004); City of Boerne v. Flores, 521 U.S. 507 (1997); Employment Div. v. Smith, 494 U.S. 872 (1990); Jimmy Swaggart Ministries v. Board of Equalization, 493 U.S. 378 (1990); Braunfeld v. Brown, 366 U.S. 599 (1961); Reynolds v. U.S., 98 U.S. 145 (1878).

10. Religious institutions being sued or prosecuted for childhood sexual abuse have repeatedly asserted so-called "privileges" over the law, claiming that they need not provide internal documents, despite their relevance. The Catholic Church has asserted numerous privileges that purportedly prevent the state from seeing employee files in grand jury proceedings. *See, e.g.*,William Lobdell and Jean Guccione, *A Novel Tack by Cardinal*, L.A. TIMES, Mar. 14, 2004, at A1.

11. Wayne A. Logan, *Criminal Law Sanctuaries*, 38 HARV. C.R. - C.L. L. REV. 321, 323–24 (2003) (hereinafter Logan). The practice of sanctuary may date back much farther. The Bible explicitly mentions sanctuary three times and temples in ancient Greece afforded sanctuary to criminals. *Id.* Roman temples, on the other hand, offered only a temporary refuge before turning criminals over to civil authorities. *Id.* at 324.

12. *See* NORMAN MACLAREN TRENHOLME, THE RIGHT OF SANCTUARY IN ENGLAND: A STUDY IN INSTITUTIONAL HISTORY 5, 325 (1903) (hereinafter TRENHOLME).

13. *Id.* at 47 (1903).

14. *See* Logan, *supra* note 11, at 326.

15. *See* TRENHOLME, *supra* note 12, at 43 (noting that, during the 13th and 14th centuries, the law forced clergymen to surrender to ecclesiastical courts for "spiritual offenses" and to secular authorities for common law crimes. Once in the secular courts, however, they would be permitted to invoke the benefit of clergy,

which sent them to the ecclesiastical courts, where they escaped the most severe punishments).

16. *See* Logan, *supra* note 11, at 328.

17. STEPHEN, *infra* note 82, at 491–92.

18. *See* Logan, *supra* note 11, at 329.

19. *Id.*

20. *See* C. WARREN HOLLISTER, THE MAKING OF ENGLAND: 55 B.C. TO 1399, 149–50, 162–64 (7th ed. 1996) (hereinafter HOLLISTER); RICHARD BARBER, HENRY PLANTAGENT 30, 106–10 (1967) (hereinafter BARBER).

21. *See* EDWARD A. FREEMAN, 4 THE HISTORY OF THE NORMAN CONQUEST OF ENGLAND: ITS CAUSES AND RESULTS 392 (1871); GEORGE W. DALZELL, BENEFIT OF CLERGY IN AMERICA & RELATED MATTERS 13 (1955) (hereinafter DALZELL); HOLLISTER, *supra* note 20, at 115. William the Conqueror divided the ecclesiastical courts from the secular courts, decreeing that "no bishop or archdeacon shall any longer hold pleas involving episcopal laws in the hundred [court]," that instead bishops were to maintain separate courts of their own in which to try civil matters such as marriage, wills, and debts, and criminal offenses committed by or upon all members of the church. RICHARD WINSTON, THOMAS BECKET 17 (1967) (quoting H. I. STUBBS, HISTORICAL INTRODUCTIONS TO THE ROLLS SERIES (ed. Arthur Hassell, 1902) (hereinafter WINSTON). In the 12th and 13th centuries, canon law claimed jurisdiction over criminal and civil cases arising out of sin and breach of faith, as well as over clerics and church property; secular law had jurisdiction over criminal and civil cases arising out of seisin of freehold land and breach of the king's peace. *See* BERMAN, LAW AND REVOLUTION, *supra* note 1, at 516.

22. *See* Peter D. Jason, *The Courts Christian in Medieval England*, 37 CATH. LAW. 339, 342 n. 27 (1997) (citing Z. N. BROOKE, THE ENGLISH CHURCH AND THE PAPACY 188–89 (1968) ("Overall, Stephen failed to preserve the barrier against papal authority over the English Church. Therefore, when Henry II succeeded Stephen, he was faced with the challenge of overcoming the increased authority of the Church.").

23. Unless otherwise noted, the account of the feud between Henry II and Thomas Becket in the following paragraphs can be found in HOLLISTER, *supra* note 20, at 160–64; BARBER, *supra* note 20, at 110–21; WINSTON, *supra* note 21, at 166–91, 318–21.

24. HENRY C. LEA, STUDIES IN CHURCH HISTORY 187 (1869).

25. *See* HOLLISTER, *supra* note 20, at 161.

26. *See* WINSTON, *supra* note 21, at 319–20.

27. *See* HOLLISTER, *supra* note 20, at 162; BARBER, *supra* note 20, at 110–11; WINSTON, *supra* note 22, at 167–68. As archbishop of Canterbury, Becket (who had previously served as Henry's royal chancellor) was the head of the English Church, responsible for the crowning of kings and direct relations with Rome. *See* HOLLISTER, *supra* note 20, at 161–63.

28. Henry ordered Becket to stand trial in the royal court for various offenses allegedly committed when he was Henry's chancellor. Claiming clerical immunity

from royal jurisdiction, Becket fled the country to appeal his case to the pope, which violated the prohibition of unlicensed appeals to Rome. *See* HOLLISTER, *supra* note 20, at 162; BARBER, *supra* note 20, at 116–21; WINSTON, *supra* note 21, at 175–91.

29. *See* BERMAN, LAW AND REVOLUTION, *supra* note 1, at 262 ("Interdict was a partial or total suspension of public services and sacraments; it could extend to one or more persons or to a whole locality or kingdom.").

30. *See* WINSTON, *supra* note 21, at 319–20 (quoting 3 MATERIALS FOR THE HISTORY OF THOMAS BECKET, ARCHBISHOP OF CANTERBURY 119 [James Craigie Robertson, ed. 1875]).

31. *See* HOLLISTER, *supra* note 20, at 163; BARBER, *supra* note 20, at 140–41; WINSTON, *supra* note 21, at 302–5.

32. *See* HOLLISTER, *supra* note 20, at 163, 164; BARBER, *supra* note 20, at 161–65; WINSTON, *supra* note 21, at 375.

33. *See* 2 THE REPORTS OF JOHN SPELMAN 327 (J.H. Baker ed. 1978) (stating that benefit of clergy appeared in 1170).

34. DALZELL, *supra* note 21, at 11.

35. *See* Phillip M. Spector, *The Sentencing Rule of Lenity*, 33 U. TOL. L. REV. 511, 515 (2002) (hereinafter Spector).

36. *See* DALZELL, *supra* note 21, at 11 ("church tribunal could not enter a 'judgment of blood," i.e., a capital sentence or an attainder").

37. R. H. HELMHOLZ, THE SPIRIT OF THE CLASSICAL CANON LAW 158–59 (1996).

38. DALZELL, *supra* note 21, at 11; R. H. HELMHOLZ, *Crime, Compurgation and the Church Courts, in* CANON LAW AND THE LAW OF ENGLAND 137 (1987) ("Too many accused persons successfully underwent purgation for the method to inspire confidence as a factfinding device . . . Almost every person who came before the ecclesiastical courts accused of theft, murder, or other secular offense, and who went on to purgation, did so successfully.").

39. DALZELL, *supra* note 21, at 11.

40. *See* Spector, *supra* note 35, at 515.

41. DALZELL, *supra* note 21, at 13.

42. *Id.* at 12 ("From the tie of the first Plantagenet the toleration of a class of privileged criminals was persistently assailed as iniquitous."). *See also* LEA, *supra* note 24, at 186–91.

43. *See* Spector, *supra* note 35, at 515, n. 22 (noting that in 1350, the privilege was statutorily extended to "all manner of clerks, as well secular as religious.") This statute was intended to extend the privilege to "inferior Orders" of the clergy rather than to laypersons. *Id.* Judges nonetheless interpreted "secular clerks" to include all literate males. *Id.* at 515.

44. Frank Riebli, Note, *The Spectre of Star Chamber: The Role of an Ancient English Tribunal in the Supreme Court's Self-Incrimination Jurisprudence*, 29 HASTINGS CONST. L.Q. 807, 826 (2002) (hereinafter Riebli).

45. 1 WILLIAM S. HOLDSWORTH, A HISTORY OF ENGLISH LAW 608 (A.L. Goodhart & H.G. Hanbury eds., 7th ed. 1956) (hereinafter HOLDSWORTH).

46. *Id.* at 605–08.

47. *Id.* at 24.

48. John H. Langbein, *Shaping the Eighteenth Century Criminal Trial: A View from the Ryder Sources*, 50 U. CHI. L. REV. 1, 40, 45 (1983) (hereinafter Langbein).

49. *See* DALZELL, *supra* note 21, at 24 (discussing 18 Eliz., ch. 7, §§2–3 (1576)).

50. Langbein, *supra* note 48, at 38 n. 147 (1983) (citing 18 Eliz., ch. 7, §§ 2–3 (1576), *discussed in* WILLIAM BLACKSTONE, 4 COMMENTARIES ON THE LAWS OF ENGLAND 368 (Sir George Tucker, ed., 1803); J. F. STEPHEN, *infra* note 82, at 462.

51. *See* Spector, *supra* note 35, at 516.

52. BLACKSTONE, *supra* note 50, at 368–69.

53. *Id.* at 36.

54. DALZELL, *supra* note 21, at 49.

55. E. MORGAN, ROGER WILLIAMS: THE CHURCH AND THE STATE 67 (1967). Because there were no high officials of the Anglican church in the New World, there were no ecclesiastical courts. Matters still subject to ecclesiastical jurisdiction in England – marriage, divorce, probate – became purely civil matters in the colonies. *Id.*

56. Langbein, *supra* note 48, at 38.

57. *See, e.g.,* Craigdallie v. Aikman, 1 Dow 1, 3 Eng. Rep. 601 (1813); The Reverend G. H. Forbes, of the Scotch Episcopal Church v. The Right Reverend Bishop Eden, Primus of the Scotch Episcopal Church, L.R. 1 Sc&Div 568 (1867).

58. *See, e.g., Craigdallie, The Reverend G. H. Forbes*, 1 Dow 1, 3 Eng. Rep. 601 (1813).

59. In many jurisdictions, the Catholic Church has attempted to resist grand jury subpoenas for documents on the ground of a First Amendment "privilege." *See* William Lobdell & Larry B. Stammer, *Mahony Criticized by National Review Panel*, L.A. TIMES, Feb. 28, 2004, at A1, *see also*, Peter Shinkle & Hannah Bergman, *Diocesan Cooperation Varies across Country*, ST. LOUIS POST-DISPATCH, Jun. 21, 2003, at 12 (Los Angeles and Metuchen, N.J. bishops refusing to cooperate, while St. Louis bishop and new Boston bishop are cooperating); James F. McCarty, *Bishop Pilla Walks Tightrope in Priest Sex Abuse Scandal*, CLEVELAND PLAIN DEALER, May 5, 2002, at A1 (describing church lawyers' tactics to avoid grand jury subpoenas). One jurisdiction, however, fully cooperated without raising such defenses); Stephen Kurkjian, *N.H. Diocese Admits Likely Violations*, BOSTON GLOBE, Dec. 11, 2002, at A1 (reporting the settlement of the N.H. Diocese sexual abuse claims and the bishop's statement that, "The Diocese of Manchester has reached a legally binding mutual agreement with the Office of the Attorney General of New Hampshire which involves acknowledgment by the diocese that the state has evidence likely to sustain a criminal conviction against the diocese for a failure in its duty to care for young people").

60. *See* Canon & Jaros, *supra* note 6, at 971–72. Charitable organizations are those that serve the public, not just their members. *See* Tremper, *supra* note 14, at 408–9.

376 / NOTES TO PAGES 248–250

61. *See* Charles Robert Tremper, *Compensation for Harm from Charitable Activity*, 76 CORNELL L. REV. 401, 401–02 (1991) (hereinafter Tremper); Canon & Jaros, *supra* note 6, at 971.

62. RESTATEMENT (SECOND) OF TORTS § 895E (1979); *See also* McDonald v. Massachusetts, 120 Mass. 432, 434–35 (1876).

63. RESTATEMENT (SECOND) OF TORTS § 895E (1979).

64. *See* Benjamin S. Birnbaum, Comment, *Cashman v. Merident Hospital, 169 Atl. 915 (Conn.)*, 14 BOSTON UNIV. L. REV. 477, 478 (1934).

65. Canon & Jaros, *supra* note 6, at 971.

66. The Feoffees of Heriot's Hospital v. Ross, 12 Clark & Fin. 507, 8 Eng. Rep. (1508).

67. 120 Mass. 432, 21 Am. Rep. 529 (1876), *overruled in part by* Colby v. Carney Hospital, 254 N.E.2d 407, 408 (Mass. 1969) stating:

> In the past on many occasions we have declined to renounce the defence of charitable immunity set forth in McDonald v. Massachusetts Gen. Hosp., 120 Mass. 432. Now it appears that only three or four States still adhere to the doctrine.... Accordingly, we take this occasion to give adequate warning that the next time we are squarely confronted by a legal question respecting the charitable immunity doctrine it is our intention to abolish it.

68. Canon & Jaros, *supra* note 6, at 971.

69. *Id. See also* Mersey Docks Trustees v. Gibbs, L.R. 1 H.L. 93 (1866); Foreman v. Mayor of Canterbury, L.R. 6 Q.B. 214 (1871).

70. Hillyer v. St. Bartholomew's Hospital, (1909) 2 K.B. 820.

71. Tremper, *supra* note 61, at n. 107 (describing rejected theories behind charitable immunity).

72. 130 F.2d 810, 815 (D.C. Cir. 1942).

73. Tremper, *supra* note 61, at 422 (emphasis added). The doctrine of charitable immunity established by common law still exists, to varying degrees, in nine states: Alabama, Arkansas Georgia, Maine, Maryland, New Jersey, Virginia, Utah, and Wyoming. NONPROFIT RISK MANAGEMENT CENTER, STATE LIABILITY LAWS FOR CHARITABLE ORGANIZATIONS AND VOLUNTEERS 8 (2001) (hereinafter NONPROFIT RISK MANAGEMENT CENTER). In the face of the clergy sexual abuse cases, there is a movement to repeal it. For example, a New Jersey senate committee has approved S-540, an amendment to the state's charitable immunity statute, which would bar immunity for charitable organizations in damage suits alleging negligent hiring or supervision of an employee which resulted in sexual abuse of a minor. *See* Valerie L. Brown, et al., *2004 Capitol Report*, 13 N.J. LAWYER, Apr. 5, 2004, at 708.

74. *Jefferson Hosp. Ass'n.*, 337 Ark. at 211 (Giving narrow construction to protect "[t]he essence of the doctrine[, ] that agencies, trusts, etc., created and maintained exclusively for charity may not have their assets diminished by execution in favor of one injured by acts of persons charged with duties under the agency or trust.").

75. In 1997, Congress enacted the Volunteer Protection Act, 42 U.S.C. § 14501 et. seq., which immunizes volunteers from tort liability in certain, limited circumstances. The majority of state statutes follow this approach, with the VPA

preempting those state laws that protect volunteers more narrowly. 42 U.S.C. § 14502. Rep. Inglis (S.C.), one of the bill sponsors, stated on the floor of the House of Representatives that:

> [T]here are 124 separate charitable organizations that support this legislation very strongly. They range from the American Association of University Women to the American Heart Association, to the American Red Cross, to the American Symphony Orchestra League, to B'nai Brith International, the Girl Scout Council USA, the National Association of Retired Federal Employees, the National Easter Seal Society, the Salvation Army, Save the Children, United Way, the YMCA. Any national organization that one can think of probably is a strong supporter of this legislation.

105 CONG. REC. H.R. 911, H3097 (daily ed. May 21, 1997) (statement of Rep. Inglis), *available at* http://thomas.loc.gov (last viewed Mar. 8, 2004). Britain has not followed the United States' lead on volunteer immunity. *See* Tash Shifron, *Volunteer Bill 'Could Be Deterrent,'* GUARDIAN, Mar. 5, 2004, *available at* http://society.guardian.co.uk/print/0,3858,4873706-106647,00.html (last viewed Mar. 8, 2004) (the chief executive of Volunteering England has said, "[w]e have serious concerns that a bill intended to support and encourage volunteering could have exactly the opposite effect.").

76. Those states are Colorado, Massachusetts, and South Carolina. NONPROFIT RISK MANAGEMENT CENTER, *supra* note 73, at 9.

77. HOLDSWORTH, *supra* note 45, at 584 ("As the state grew into conscious life it was inevitable that occasions for disputes between the temporal and spiritual powers should arise.").

78. *Id.* (noting that, "from that time on, the professional jealousy of the common lawyers led them to restrict the jurisdiction of the ecclesiastical courts whenever it was possible to restrict it.").

79. *Id.* at 587.

80. THEODORE F.T. PLUCKNETT, A CONCISE HISTORY OF THE COMMON LAW 41 (1929) (hereinafter PLUCKNETT).

81. *Id.* (noting that, by the time Edward VI (1547–1553), the Reformation was used as a political weapon against Rome, and after the brief reign of Catholic Mary (1554–1558), Elizabeth made the Reformation "the permanent basis of English political and religious life.")

82. R. H. HELMHOLZ, CANON LAW AND THE LAW OF ENGLAND 320–21 (1997); *See also id.* at 316–317 (ecclesiastical jurisdiction over testamentary debt and probate began a slow decline in the mid-16th century; R. H. HELMHOLZ, IN SELECT CASES ON DEFAMATION TO 1600 xxxvii–xlii (Selden Soc'y No. 101, 1985) (royal courts began to prohibit the church courts from hearing defamation cases involving secular crimes and began to hear such cases on their own in the 16th century); Edward P. Steegmann, Note, *Of History and Due Process,* 63 IND. L. J. 369, 397 (1988) (citing J. F. STEPHEN, 2 A HISTORY OF THE CRIMINAL LAW OF ENGLAND, ch. 25 (London 1883) (hereinafter STEPHEN) (sodomy made a secular offense by statute in 1533); Jeremy D. Weinstein, Note, *Adultery, Law, and the State:* A History, 31 HASTINGS L.J. 195, 225 (1986) (citing W. BLACKSTONE, 4 COMMENTARIES 64–65) (Puritans of

the Commonwealth made adultery a capital offense in 1650, although this was nullified in 1660 with the Restoration). Conversely, the Church retained jurisdiction over other matters well beyond the Reformation. *See, e.g.*, R. H. HELMHOLZ, MARRIAGE LITIGATION IN MEDIEVAL ENGLAND 3 (1974) (jurisdiction over marriage and marital disputes not withdrawn from the Church until 1857); R. H. HELMHOLZ, CANON LAW AND THE LAW OF ENGLAND 210 (1997) (jurisdiction over bastardy litigation not withdrawn until the nineteenth century).

83. In 1576, the ecclesiastical courts were relieved of their jurisdiction over clergy who committed crimes. DALZELL, *supra* note 21, at 24 (discussing 18 Eliz., ch. 7, §§2–3 (1576)). In 1641, the Puritan-dominated Long Parliament abolished all criminal jurisdiction of the ecclesiastical courts. *See* HOLDSWORTH, *supra* note 45, at 611.

84. *See* BERMAN, LAW AND REVOLUTION, *supra* note 1, at 268.

85. *Id.* at 266–67.

86. *See* PLUCKNETT, *supra* note 80, at 43–44, 46; *see generally* R. H. HELMHOLZ, *Canon Law and the English Common Law, in* CANON LAW AND THE LAW OF ENGLAND 2 (discussing approaches to the relationship between the two systems during the rise of the common law).

87. *See* HOLDSWORTH, *supra* note 45, at 588 ("The wealth and corruption of the church, and more particularly the abuses of the ecclesiastical courts, were exciting extreme unpopularity."); FRANK LAMBERT, THE FOUNDING FATHERS AND THE PLACE OF RELIGION IN AMERICA 34–35 (2003) (hereinafter LAMBERT) ("Whether or not the Church . . . was in as deplorable condition as its critics made out is beside the point; the fact is, widespread opinion that it was corrupt constituted the greater reality that shaped events."); WILL DURANT, THE REFORMATION: A HISTORY OF EUROPEAN CIVILIZATION FROM WYCLIF TO CALVIN, 1300–1564, 584 (1957) (hereinafter DURANT, THE REFORMATION) (referring to "the collapse of the spiritual and moral authority of the priesthood.").

88. Of the Reformers, John Calvin in particular addressed the faults of the 16th-century Catholic Church as a problem in the structure of the church, with his primary concern being the lack of accountability of the clergy to the members or the higher good. It was his view that the Church had deviated from the ancient church's structures of accountability. *See, e.g.*, II JOHN CALVIN, INSTITUTES OF THE CHRISTIAN RELIGION, bk. IV, ch. IV, §§ 1–2, at 1068–70 (describing ancient practice of electing bishops and their accountability to "the assembly of his brethren"); *Id.* at bk. IV, ch. VII, § 21, at 1141 (criticizing contemporary pope for ruling in a "tyrannical fashion" and considering "his own whim as law. . . . [I]t is utterly abhorrent not only to a sense of piety but also of humanity.").

89. *See* CHEYNEY, *infra* note 110, at 383–84.

90. "The Act of Supremacy [26 Henry VIII. C.I.] recognized the king as 'the only Supreme Head in earth of the church of England,' having full power to correct all 'errors, heresies, abuses, offences, contempts, and enormities,' which by any manner of spiritual authority ought to be reformed; and the form of oath

taken under the provisions of this Act denied to the Pope any other authority than that of Bishop of Rome." HOLDSWORTH, *supra* note 45, at 591–92 (citing Report of Ecclesiastical Commission 1883, 72). The ecclesiastical authorities lost all power save that granted by the King, and ecclesiastical judges need no longer needed to be clerics, a move that displaced Rome's canon law. *Id.* at 592.

91. Riebli, *supra* note 44, at 826 (quoting LEONARD W. LEVY, ORIGINS OF THE FIFTH AMENDMENT 96 (1986)).

92. *See* DURANT, THE REFORMATION, *supra* note 87, at 579 (Somerset "favored a Protestant policy."); *id.* at 581, 585 (noting that in 1550, under Warwick (who was made duke of Northumberland in 1551), "the protectorate was now definitely Protestant."); *id.* at 585 ("Religious persecution, so long of heretics by Catholics, was now in England, as in Switzerland and Lutheran Germany, of heretics and Catholics by Protestants.").

93. Although "numerically a minority," the Protestants were "financially powerful," and nearly every influential family held property taken from the Catholic Church. *See* DURANT, THE REFORMATION, *supra* note 87, at 590; *id.* at 588 (London, however, was a "half-Protestant city.").

94. *See id.* at 595 ("To her simple faith these heresies seemed mortal crimes, far worse than treason.").

95. *Id.* at 598 ("[Cranmer's] death marked the zenith of the persecution. Some 300 persons died in its course, 273 of them in the last four years of her reign.").

96. ROBERT E. RODES, JR., LAW AND MODERNIZATION IN THE CHURCH OF ENGLAND: CHARLES II TO THE WELFARE STATE 81 (1991) (hereinafter RODES).

97. Holdsworth writes:

The Act of Supremacy (26 Henry VIII. C.I.) recognized the king as 'the only Supreme Head in earth of the church of England,' having full power to correct all 'errors, heresies, abuses, offences, contempts, and enormities,' which by any manner of spiritual authority ought to be reformed; and the form of oath taken under the provisions of this Act denied to the Pope any other authority than that of Bishop of Rome.

HOLDSWORTH, *supra* note 45, at 591–92 (citing Report of Ecclesiastical Commission 1883, 72).

98. RODES, *supra* note 96, at 81.

99. 7 THE CAMBRIDGE MODERN HISTORY 13 (W. Ward, et al. eds., 1934).

100. Riebli, *supra* note 44, at 826.

101. *See* BERMAN, LAW AND REVOLUTION II, *infra* note 108, at 104, and accompanying text.

102. HOLDSWORTH, *supra* note 45, at 597.

103. *Id.* at 611; BERMAN, LAW AND REVOLUTION, *supra* note 1, at 113.

104. 2 THE CAMBRIDGE MODERN HISTORY 532–33 (W. Ward, et al. eds., 1934).

105. CHEYNEY, *infra* note 110, at 325; DURANT, THE REFORMATION, *supra* note 87, at 598. The official website of the British monarchy places the figure at

300 executed in three years. *See Kings and Queens of England (to 1603), at* http://www.royal.gov.uk/output/Page45.asp (last visited Apr. 30, 2004).

106. 2 THE CAMBRIDGE MODERN HISTORY 586 (W. Ward, et al. eds., 1934).

107. *See* John Coffey, PERSECUTION AND TOLERATION IN PROTESTANT ENGLAND: 1558–1689 169–70 (2000).

108. *See* RUSSELL CHAMBERLIN, THE TOWER OF LONDON 68–71 (1989).

109. *See id.* at 78.

110. *See* HAROLD J. BERMAN, LAW AND REVOLUTION II: THE IMPACT OF THE PROTESTANT REFORMATIONS ON THE WESTERN LEGAL TRADITION 209–10, 215–16 (2003) (hereinafter BERMAN, LAW AND REVOLUTION II). Between 1630 and 1640, an estimated 20,000 religious dissenters fled to the Massachusetts Bay Colony, and a similar number emigrated to the Netherlands. *Id.* at 216.

111. *See infra* note 129.

112. LAMBERT, *supra* note 87, at 38–39. Early attempts at colonization were unsuccessful – settlements founded in Virginia between 1585 and 1587, and again in 1602, were either abandoned or destroyed. *See* EDWARD P. CHEYNEY, A SHORT HISTORY OF ENGLAND 354–55 (1919). Jamestown, founded in 1607 in Virginia, was the first permanent English settlement in America. *Id.* at 403.

113. HOLDSWORTH, *supra* note 45, at 611.

114. JAMES MADISON, *Memorial and Remonstrance, in* 8 THE PAPERS OF JAMES MADISON, at 301–2 (William T. Hutchinson, et al. eds., 1962).

115. *See generally* CHRISTIAN PERSPECTIVES, *infra* note 151 (discussing the paradox of hope and distrust at the base of constitutional vision).

116. THE SELECTED WRITINGS OF JOHN WITHERSPOON: LANDMARKS IN RHETORIC AND PUBLIC ADDRESS 135–36 (Thomas Miller ed., 1990). Witherspoon, whose stamp on the Constitution is visible, was also mentor to a number of other Framers. *See generally,* MARCI A. HAMILTON, WHY THE PEOPLE DO NOT RULE (unpublished manuscript, on file with the author).

117. WILL DURANT, THE AGE OF FAITH: A HISTORY OF MEDIEVAL CIVILIZATION - CHRISTIAN, ISLAMIC, AND JUDAIC – FROM CONSTANTINE TO DANTE: A.D. 325–1300 779 (1950) (hereinafter DURANT, THE AGE OF FAITH).

118. *See* WADE ROWLAND, GALILEO'S MISTAKE: A NEW LOOK AT THE EPIC CONFRONTATION BETWEEN GALILEO AND THE CHURCH (2003).

119. *See* DURANT, THE AGE OF FAITH, *supra* note 117, at 782.

120. *Id.* at 208–9 (1957).

121. 2 THE CAMBRIDGE MODERN HISTORY 650 (W. Ward, et al. eds., 1934).

122. *See* DURANT, THE AGE OF FAITH, *supra* note 117, at 209.

123. *See* JOHN EDWARD LONGHURST, THE AGE OF TORQUEMADA 85 (1964), *available at* http://libro.uca.edu/torquemada/torquemada.htm (last visited April 25, 2004).

124. *See* CHARLES H. LEA, 4 A HISTORY OF THE INQUISITION OF SPAIN 467–68 (1907) (Spanish Inquisition ended in 1834); 7 THE CAMBRIDGE MODERN HISTORY 208–9 (W. Ward, et al. eds., 1934) (Declaration of Independence signed in 1776).

125. *See* RODES, *supra* note 96, at 87. The original Act of Uniformity, passed by the Elizabeth's Parliament in 1571, required that all Church of England prayers, services, and rites conform to the Book of Common Prayer. *See* LAMBERT, *supra* note 87, at 40.

126. RODES, *supra* note 96, at 88–89, 93, 147.

127. Carl H. Esbeck, Symposium, *The Church-State Settlement in the Early American Republic*, 2004 B.Y.U.L. REV. 1385 (2004).

128. *See* Marci A. Hamilton, *Religion, the Rule of Law, and the Good of the Whole: A View from the Clergy*, 18 J.L. & POLITICS 387, 394, n.22 (2002) (hereinafter Hamilton, Religion, the Rule of Law, and the Good of the Whole); *See also* ALICE M. BALDWIN, THE NEW ENGLAND CLERGY AND THE AMERICAN REVOLUTION 22–31 (2d ed. 1965) (detailing the social impact of the works of New England clergy before 1763); FRANCIS J. BREMER, SHAPING NEW ENGLAND: PURITAN CLERGYMEN IN SEVENTEENTH CENTURY ENGLAND AND NEW ENGLAND 82–88 (1994) (noting the influence of the clergy on education and government in 17th-century New England); BERNARD BAILYN, THE IDEOLOGICAL ORIGINS OF THE AMERICAN REVO-LUTION 246–50 (1967) (hereinafter BAILYN) (discussing the predominant religions in the colonies before the Revolutionary War); GORDON S. WOOD, THE AMERICAN REVOLUTION: A HISTORY 129–35 (2002) (detailing impact of Protestant ministers at the forefront of the Revolutionary movement); James T. McHugh, *A Liberal Theocracy: Philosophy, Theology, and Utah Constitutional Law*, 60 ALB. L. REV. 1515, 1520 n. 16 (1997) (citing ALICE M. BALDWIN, THE NEW ENGLAND CLERGY AND THE AMERICAN REVOLUTION 22–31 (2d ed. 1965) which details the social impact of the works of New England clergy before 1763)).

129. The Reformation was instituted by Martin Luther and John Calvin, because they believed that the Roman Catholic Church had turned away from all that is holy and become infested with evil. II JOHN CALVIN, INSTITUTES OF THE CHRISTIAN RELIGION, bk. IV, §§ 21–30, at 1141, 1144, 1147 (referring to "corruption of the present-day-papacy"; "kingdom of Antichrist"; "moral abandonment of the popes"). They were Church insiders, who initially acted in order to reform the Church itself, but the Church proved incapable of sufficiently rapid change to avoid having many of its members leave the Church to follow Luther, Calvin, or other reformation leaders, into new churches. The instinct to schism, in response to the perceptions of corruption, has never left the Protestant movement, which has resulted in the thousands of modern-day sects that continue to divide. *See generally* STEVE BRUCE, A HOUSE DIVIDED: PROTESTANTISM, SCHISM, AND SECULARIZATION (1990).

130. I CALVIN: INSTITUTES OF THE CHRISTIAN RELIGION, bk. II, ch. V, § 19, at 340 (John T. McNeill ed., 1975).

131. Calvin wrote that the "principal use" of the law was to help believers know the will of God and to incite them to obedience:

[The law] is the best instrument for enabling them daily to learn with greater truth and certainty what the will of the Lord is. . . . Then, because we need not doctrine merely, but exhortation also, the servant of God will derive this further advantage of from the Law: by frequently meditating upon it, he will be excited to obedience, and confirmed in it, and so drawn away form the slippery paths of sin.

I CALVIN: INSTITUTES OF THE CHRISTIAN RELIGION, bk. II, ch. VII, § 12 at. 360–61 ("Even the believers have need of the law."). The depravity of humans, however, never made obedience to the law alone sufficient to ensure redemption. *Id.* at §3 at 351–52.

132. REV. WILLIAM RALPH INGE, PROTESTANTISM 3–5 (1927). *See also* 1 EMILE G. LEONARD, A HISTORY OF PROTESTANTISM: THE REFORMATION 316 (H. H. Rowley ed., Joyce M. H. Reid trans., 1965) (noting that Farel agreed with Luther in condemning institutionalism, saying "sects, organizations and institutions are born of the flesh"); 1 REV. J. A. WYLIE, THE HISTORY OF PROTESTANTISM 2 (London, Cassell, Petter & Galpin) ("[Protestants] replaced the authority of the Infallability with the authority of the Word of God. The long and dismal obscuration of centuries they dispelled, that the twin stars of liberty and knowledge might shine forth . . . and human society . . . might, after its halt of a thousand years, resume its march towards a higher goal").

133. *See* DURANT, THE REFORMATION, *supra* note 87, at 329–33. On the eve of the Reformation in Germany, the Catholic Church was rife with abuses: there had been a breakdown of monastic discipline and clerical celibacy, greedy ecclesiastical authorities increased clerical rents, incomes, and taxes; the higher ecclesiastical orders brazenly displayed their wealth, to the chagrin of the people; "mercenary abuse of sacred things" was common; and hush money was often sent to Rome.

134. *See* CHARLES P. HANSON, NECESSARY VIRTUE: THE PRAGMATIC ORIGINS OF RELIGIOUS LIBERTY IN NEW ENGLAND 11 (1998); *see generally* PHILIP HAMBURGER, THE SEPARATION OF CHURCH AND STATE (2003).

135. II JOHN CALVIN, INSTITUTES OF THE CHRISTIAN RELIGION, *supra* note 86, at bk. IV, ch. 7, § 19.

136. Leonard J. Kramer, *Presbyterians Approach the American Revolution*, 31 J. PRESBYTERIAN HIST. SOC. 72 (1953) (quoting minutes of the Synod of New England, 1776–82).

137. *See, e.g.,* Richard A. Epstein, *The Harm Principle – And How It Grew*, 45 U. TORONTO L.J. 369, 370–71 (1995).

138. *See* M.N.S. SELLERS, AMERICAN REPUBLICANISM 133–41 (1994); M.N.S. SELLERS, THE SACRED FIRE OF LIBERTY 101–2 (1998).

139. JOHN STUART MILL, ON LIBERTY 87 (David Spitz ed., 1975).

140. *Id* at 11, 18.

141. *See generally* H. L. A. HART, LAW, LIBERTY, AND MORALITY (1962); RICHARD A. EPSTEIN, PRINCIPLES FOR A FREE SOCIETY: RECONCILING INDIVIDUAL LIBERTY WITH THE COMMON GOOD (1998). Hart believed that "[r]ecognition of individual liberty as a value involves, as a minimum, acceptance of the principle that the individual may do what he wants, even if others are distressed when they learn what it is that he does – unless, of course, there are other good grounds for forbidding it." *Id.*

142. *See generally* JOEL FEINBERG, THE EXPRESSIVE FUNCTION OF PUNISHMENT, IN DOING AND DESERVING (1970); JOEL FEINBERG, 1 THE MORAL LIMITS OF CRIMINAL LAW 214 (1988).

143. *See* Angela C. Carmella, *The Protection of Children and Young People: Catholic and Constitutional Visions of Responsible Freedom*, 44 B.C.L. REV. 1031, 1044 (2003) ("There is one condition attached to all exercises of freedom: that the use of the freedom will not breach minimal responsibilities owed to the larger society as those responsibilities are embodied in legitimate laws.").

144. THOMAS JEFFERSON, NOTES ON THE STATE OF VIRGINIA (1787), *in* 2 THE WRITINGS OF THOMAS JEFFERSON, at 221 (Albert Ellery Bergh ed., 1905).

145. THOMAS JEFFERSON, *An Act for Establishing Religious Freedom, Passed in the Assembly of Virginia in the Beginning of the Year 1786*, *in* 2 THE WRITINGS OF THOMAS JEFFERSON, *supra* note 144, at 312. On the absolute right to believe, *see also* Letter to Benjamin Rush, *supra* note 144, at 381 (referring to "the common right of independent opinion, by answering questions of faith, which the laws have left between god and himself").

146. Letter from Thomas Jefferson to James Madison (Jul. 31, 1788), *in* THE PAPERS OF THOMAS JEFFERSON (Julian P. Boyd, et al. eds., 1950).

147. ADRIENNE KOCH, MADISON'S "ADVICE TO MY COUNTRY" 15 (1966) (quoting James Madison).

148. Letter from James Madison to William Bradford (Apr. 1, 1774), *in* 1 THE PAPERS OF JAMES MADISON, at 112–13 (William T. Hutchinson, et al. eds., 1962).

149. Letter from James Madison to William Bradford (Jan. 24, 1774), *in* 1 THE PAPERS OF JAMES MADISON, *supra* note 148, at 112–13, 106.

150. *See, e.g.*, JAMES MADISON, *Memorial and Remonstrance*, *in* 8 THE PAPERS OF JAMES MADISON, *supra* note 148, at 301–2 ("Because experience witnesseth that ecclesiastical establishments, instead of maintaining the purity and efficacy of Religion, have had a contrary operation. During almost fifteen centuries has the legal establishment of Christianity been on trial. What have been its fruits? More or less in all places, pride and indolence in the Clergy, ignorance and servility in the laity, in both, superstition, bigotry and persecution"); JEFFERSON, *supra* note 145, at 221–22 ("Had not the Roman government permitted free enquiry, Christianity could never have been introduced. Had not free enquiry been indulged, at the aera of the reformation, the corruptions of Christianity could not have been purged away. If it be restrained now, the present corruptions will be protected, and new ones encouraged.").

151. *See generally* Marci A. Hamilton, *The Calvinist Paradox of Distrust and Hope at the Constitutional Convention*, *in* CHRISTIAN PERSPECTIVES ON LEGAL THOUGHT (Michael. W. McConnell et al. eds., 2001) (hereinafter CHRISTIAN PERSPECTIVES).

152. KERRY S. WALTERS, THE AMERICAN DEISTS: VOICES OF REASON AND DISSENT IN THE EARLY REPUBLIC 106–40 (1992). Jefferson, of course, was not solitary in his beliefs. Deists dominated the colleges during the latter 18th century. *Id.*

153. *See* Fawn M. Brodie, Thomas Jefferson: An Intimate History 372 (1974).

154. Letter from Thomas Jefferson to Benjamin Rush, (Apr. 21, 1803), *in* 10 The Writings of Thomas Jefferson, 380 (Albert Ellery Bergh, ed., 1905).

155. *See generally* Philip Hamburger, Separation of Church and State, *supra* note 134.

156. *See* R. H. Helmholz, The Spirit of the Classical Canon Law 316-21 (1996); 1 William S. Holdsworth, A History of English Law 588 (A.L. Goodhart & H.G. Hanbury eds., 7th ed. 1956); Will Durant, The Reformation: A History of European Civilization from Wyclif to Calvin 1300–1564, at 584 (1957).

157. The Reformation was instituted by Martin Luther and John Calvin because they believed that the Roman Catholic Church had turned away from all that is holy and become infested with evil. *See, e.g.*, 2 John Calvin, Institutes of the Christian Religion, bk. IV, ch. IV, 1–2, at 1141, 1144, 1147 (referring to "corruption of the present-day papacy"; "kingdom of Antichrist"; and "moral abandonment of the popes"). They were Church insiders who initially acted in order to reform the Church itself, but the Church proved incapable of sufficiently rapid change to avoid having many of its members leave the Church to follow Luther, Calvin, or other reformation leaders into new churches. The instinct to schism, in response to the perceptions of corruption, has never left the Protestant movement, resulting in the thousands of modern-day sects that continue to divide. *See generally* Steve Bruce, A House Divided: Protestantism, Schism, and Secularization (1990).

158. Hamilton, *supra* note 114.

159. Frederick Nymeyer, *A Great Netherlander Who Had One Answer to the Problem of 'Liberty' Destroying Liberty, Namely Sphere Sovereignty*, in Progressive Calvinism (Feb. 1956), *available at* http://www.visi.com/~contra_m/pc/1956/2-2great.html (last visited Mar. 8, 2004).

160. David H. McIlroy, *Subsidiarity and Sphere Sovereignty: Christian Reflections on the Size, Shape and Scope of Government*, 45 J. Church & State 739, 754–59 (2003).

161. Abraham Kuyper, *Sphere Sovereignty*, New Church Speech, October 20, 1880 (cited in McIlroy, *supra* note 160, at 755).

162. *Id.*; Abraham Kuyper, Lectures on Calvinism 124–25 (William B. Eerdmans ed., 1987) (1898–99), *also available at* http://www.kuyper.org/stone/lecture4.html (last visited May 28, 2004).

163. McIlroy, *supra* note 160, at 757–59; *see also* Johan D. van der Vyver, *Sphere Sovereignty of Religious Institutions: A Contemporary Calvinistic Theory of Church-State Relations*, at 24 (1999) *available at* http://www.uni-trier.de/~ievr/konferenz/papers/vanvyver.pdf (last visited Mar. 8, 2004) ("Persons engaged in government [have] the right and an obligation to scrutinize the conduct of their subjects.... Unbecoming conduct should not escape the power of the sword simply because it was committed in the name of religion.").

164. *See* Johan D. van der Vyver, *Review, Culture and Equality: An Egalitarian Critique of Multiculturalism: By Brian Barry*, 17 CONN. J. INT'L L. 323, 329 (2002).

165. *See generally* Hamilton, *Religion, the Rule of Law, and the Good of the Whole, supra* note 128.

166. Cass R. Sunstein, *American Advice and New Constitutions*, 1 CHI. J. INT'L L. 173, 178 (2000) (noting that while we cannot overestimate the significance of the constitutional text, we also cannot underestimate the "need for a culture that is committed, first to the rule of law and constitutional limitations"); Guillermo Garcia-Montufar & Elvira Martinez Coco *Antecedents, Perspectives, and Projections of a Legal Project about Religious Liberty in Peru* 1999 B.Y.U.L. REV. 503; American Bar Association, *Central Eastern European Law Initiative, available at* http://www.abanet.org/ceeli/home.html (last visited June 10, 2004) (ABA/CEELI "advances the rule of law in the world by supporting the legal reform process in Central and Eastern Europe and the New Independent States of the former Soviet Union").

167. To be sure, many of the sermons used in this chapter were delivered by Calvinists, who would have a predisposition to the virtues of the rule of law. These views, however, were not exclusive to Calvinists, and appealed to Calvinists of all sorts, including Congregationalists, Anglicans, and Presbyterians, as well as the many Baptists influenced by Calvinist perspectives. *See, e.g.,* GREGORY A. WILLS , DEMOCRATIC RELIGION: FREEDOM, AUTHORITY, AND CHURCH DISCIPLINE IN THE BAPTIST SOUTH, 1785–1900 103 (1997); *see also* ROBERT BAYLOR SEMPLE, THE HISTORY OF THE BAPTISTS OF VIRGINIA 60 (1810).

168. Unless otherwise indicated, sermons are drawn from Ellis Sandoz's extremely useful collection, POLITICAL SERMONS OF THE AMERICAN FOUNDING ERA, 1730–1805 (Ellis Sandoz ed., 1991) (hereinafter POLITICAL SERMONS). *Id.* at 334–35 (Isaac Backus 1773) ("God has appointed two kinds of government in the world, which are distinct in their nature, and ought never to be confounded together; one of which is called civil, the other ecclesiastical government."). *See also* HAMBURGER, SEPARATION OF CHURCH AND STATE, *supra* note 134, at 21 (stating that Christians "often took for granted that church and state were distinct institutions, with different jurisdictions and powers").

169. POLITICAL SERMONS, *supra* note 168, at 80 (Elisha Williams 1774); *See also id.* at 81–82 (urging obedience to laws involving "those things which are the objects of the civil magistrate's power, *viz.* the civil interests of the people" but not on "matters of religion").

170. *Id.* at 58; *see also id.* at 337 (Isaac Backus 1773) ("the state is armed with the sword to guard the peace, and the civil rights of all persons and societies, and to punish those who violate the same"); Jonas Clarke, A Sermon 29 (1781), *cited in* Phillip A. Hamburger, *A Constitutional Right of Religious Exemption: An Historical Perspective*, 60 GEO. WASH. L. REV. 915, at 943 n. 112 (1992) ("[A]s by the social compact, the whole is engaged for the protection and defense of the life, liberty and property of each individual").

171. POLITICAL SERMONS, *supra* note 168, at 147–48 (Charles Chauncey 1747).

172. HARRY S. STOUT, THE NEW ENGLAND SOUL: PREACHING AND RELIGIOUS CULTURE IN COLONIAL NEW ENGLAND 273 (1986) (hereinafter NEW ENGLAND SOUL).

173. POLITICAL SERMONS, *supra* note 168, at 72, 67.

174. *Id.* at 58; *see also id.* at 1064 (Israel Evans 1791) ("*We the people* are the source of all legislative authority.").

175. Gersham C. Lyman, A Sermon 12, 19 (1784), *cited in* Hamburger, *Constitutional Right of Religious Exemption, supra* note 170, at 942 n. 112 ("It is a most inconsistent and distracted piece of conduct, to set up rulers, and then disobey their just & needful laws.").

176. A Declaration of Certain Fundamental Rights and Liberties of the Protestant Episcopal Church of Maryland, *in* 1 ANSON P. STOKES, CHURCH AND STATE IN THE UNITED STATES 741 (1950), *cited in* Hamburger, *Constitutional Right of Religious Exemption, supra* note 170, at 935 n. 84. *See also* Noah Hobart, Civil Government The Foundation of Social Happiness 42 (1751), *cited in* Hamburger, *Constitutional Right of Religious Exemption, supra* note 170, at 942 n. 96 (stating that the government should not "inflict temporal Punishments" for ecclesiastical errors that "do not affect the Peace and Happiness of Civil Society").

177. POLITICAL SERMONS, *supra* note 168, at 337 (Isaac Backus 1773).

178. Samuel Stillman, A Sermon 20, 27–28 (Mass. Election sermon, 1779), *cited in* Hamburger, *Constitutional Right of Religious Exemption, supra* note 170, at 942 n. 111; *see also* The Constitution of the Presbyterian Church in the United States of America (adopted 1788).

179. The Constitution of the Reformed Dutch Church, in the United States of America 190 (1793), *cited in* Hamburger, A *Constitutional Right of Religious Exemption, supra* note 170, at 942 n. 111 (1992).

180. POLITICAL SERMONS, *supra* note 168, at 143 (Charles Chauncy 1747), *Id.* at 335 (Isaac Backus 1773) ("God has appointed two kinds of government.").

181. *Id.* at 922 (Elizur Goodrich 1787); *see also* AARON HUTCHINSON, A WELL TEMPERED SELF-LOVE A RULE OF CONDUCT TOWARDS OTHERS 37–38 (1779) ("it is folly and stupidity for a man to plead conscience for breaking the moral law, which is a transcript of the moral perfections of God, and written upon the hearts of all by nature."); GORDON S. WOOD, THE CREATION OF THE AMERICAN REPUBLIC 1776–1787 69 (1969) (quoting Samuel Magaw, A Discourse Preached in Philadelphia (Oct. 8, 1775) ("[T]he practice of all the social virtues is the law of our nature, and the law of our nature is the law of God.").

182. James D. Gordon III, *The New Free Exercise Clause*, 26 CAP. U. L. REV. 65, 92 (1997); David E. Steinberg, *Rejecting the Case against the Free Exercise Exemption: A Critical Assessment*, 75 B.U.L. REV. 241 (1995); Michael W. McConnell, *The Origins and Historical Understanding of Free Exercise of Religion*, 103 HARV. L. REV. 1409, 1461–66 (1990); Douglas Laycock, *Formal, Substantive, and Disaggregated Neutrality toward Religion*, 39 DEPAUL L. REV. 993, 1002 (1990).

183. Olmstead v. United States, 277 U.S. 438, 478 (1928) (Brandeis, J., dissenting) ("The makers of our Constitution . . . conferred, as against the Government, the

right to be let alone – the most comprehensive of rights and the most valued by civilized men.").

184. NEW ENGLAND SOUL, *supra* note 172, at 213.

185. POLITICAL SERMONS, *supra* note 168, at 914 (Elizur Goodrich 1787).

186. WOOD, THE CREATION OF THE AMERICAN REPUBLIC, *supra* note 181, at 69, 61.

187. *Id.* at 60.

188. POLITICAL SERMONS, *supra* note 168, at 331–32 (Isaac Backus 1773).

189. Jonas Clarke, A Sermon 29 (Mass. election sermon 1781), *in* Hamburger, *Constitutional Right of Religious Exemption, supra* note 170, at 943 n. 112. *See also* WOOD, THE CREATION OF THE AMERICAN REPUBLIC, *supra* note 181, at 118 (referring to "common emphasis on the usefulness and goodness of devotion to the general welfare of the community"); AMERICAN STATE PAPERS 113 (Presbyterians stating that the "end of civil government is security to the temporal liberty and property of mankind . . . ").

190. Jonathan Edwards, *An Humble Attempt to Promote Explicit Agreement and Visible Union of God's People in Extraordinary Prayer*, Works, III, *reprinted in* A. Heimert, THE GREAT AWAKENING: DOCUMENTS ILLUSTRATING THE CRISIS AND ITS CONSEQUENCES 567 (1967). This view certainly did not die with the passing of the 18th century. *See, e.g.*, James W. Gordon, *Religion and the First Justice Harlan: A Case Study in Late Nineteenth-Century Presbyterian Constitutionalism*, 85 MARQ. L. REV. 317, 346, 369, 371 (2001) (discussing Justice Harlan's view of the role of the religious believer in aiming for the public good) (hereinafter Gordon); Sydney Ahlstrom, A RELIGIOUS HISTORY OF THE AMERICAN PEOPLE 275–77 (1972), *cited in* Gordon, *supra*, at 366–67.

191. 7 THE WORKS OF JOHN WITHERSPOON 100 (1805).

192. POLITICAL SERMONS, *supra* note 168, at 334 (Isaac Backus 1773). The New York *Evening Post* echoed these views in 1747. *See* BAILYN, *supra* note 128, at 77 (1967) ("Liberty, that is, was the capacity to exercise 'natural rights' within limits set, not by the mere will or desire of men in power but by non-arbitrary law-law enacted by legislatures containing within them the proper balance of forces.").

193. POLITICAL SERMONS, *supra* note 168, at 1063 (Israel Evans 1791).

194. Moses Hemmenway, A Sermon 27, 30 (1784), *cited in* Hamburger, *Constitutional Right of Religious Exemption, supra* note 170, at 934 n. 84.

195. POLITICAL SERMONS, *supra* note 168, at 67 (Elisha Williams 1744); *id.* at 339 (Isaac Backus 1773) ("God always claimed it as his sole prerogative to determine by his own laws, what his worship shall be, who shall minister in it, and how they shall be supported, so it is evident that this prerogative has been, and still is, encroached upon in our land.").

196. POLITICAL SERMONS, *supra* note 168, at 1089 (John Leland 1791).

197. THE WRITINGS OF THE LATE ELDER JOHN LELAND 228 (1845) (hereinafter LELAND WRITINGS). Thomas Jefferson made the same point in 1782, saying that "[t]he legitimate powers of government extend to such acts only as are injurious to others." THOMAS JEFFERSON, NOTES ON THE STATE OF VIRGINIA 152 (1964).

198. POLITICAL SERMONS, *supra* note 168, at 1089 (John Leland 1791).

199. Caleb Blood, A Sermon (1792), *cited in* Hamburger, *Constitutional Right of Religious Exemption, supra* note 170, at 918 n. 15.

200. John Leland, *The Yankee Spy, in* LELAND WRITINGS, *supra* note 180, *cited in* Hamburger, *Constitutional Right of Religious Exemption, supra* note 170, at 942 n. 111.

201. HAMBURGER, SEPARATION OF CHURCH AND STATE, *supra* note 134, at 69 (*citing* William Balch, A Sermon (1749) "requiring Submission and Obedience to lawful Authority in the People, as well as Integrity and a public Spirit in Rulers"). Noah Webster extended the concept of subjugation to the law to clergy members as well. *Id.* at 88.

202. Samuel Stillman, *cited in* Hamburger, *Constitutional Right of Religious Exemption supra* note 170, at 942 n. 111. This reasoning appeared a century earlier in the works of Roger Williams, 3 THE COMPLETE WRITINGS OF ROGER WILLIAMS 127 (1963). These views also were explicitly embraced by the Supreme Court and especially Justice Harlan a century later. *See* Reynolds v. United States, 98 U.S. 145 (1878); Gordon, *supra* note 190, at 346.

203. ISAAC BACKUS, ISAAC BACKUS ON CHURCH, STATE, AND CALVINISM: PAMPHLETS, 1754–1789, app. 3, at 487 (W. McLoughlin, ed. 1968).

204. McConnell, *supra* note 182, at 1415 ("Constitutionally compelled exemptions were within the contemplation of the framers and ratifiers as a possible interpretation of the free exercise clause"); Michael W. McConnell, *The Problem of Singling out Religion,* 50 DEPAUL L. REV. 1 (2000); Michael W. McConnell, *Free Exercise Revisionism and the Smith Decision,* 57 U. CHI. L. REV. 1109 (1990); Douglas Laycock, *Towards a General Theory of the Religion Clauses: The Case of Church Labor Relations and the Right to Church Autonomy,* 81 COLUM. L. REV. 1373 (1981); *see also* Ira C. Lupu, *Reconstructing the Establishment Clause: The Case Against Discretionary Accommodation of Religion,* 140 U. PA. L. REV. 555 (1991).

205. *See generally* Marci A. Hamilton, Symposium, *Religious Institutions, The No-Harm Doctrine, and the Public Good,* 2004 B. Y. U. L. REV. 1099 (2004); Frederick M. Gedicks, *An Unfirm Foundation: The Regrettable Indefensibility of Religious Exemptions,* 20 U. ARK. LITTLE ROCK L. J. 555, 574 (1998) ("[T]he historical moment for exemptions has come and gone. There no longer exist a plausible explanation of why religious believers – and only believers – are constitutionally entitled to be excused from complying with otherwise legitimate laws that burden practices."); William P. Marshall, *The Case against the Constitutionally Compelled Free Exercise Exemption,* 40 CASE W. RES. L. REV. 357 (1990); Hamburger, *A Constitutional Right of Religious Exemption, supra* note 170; Ellis West, *The Case against a Right to Religious-Based Exemptions,* 4 NOTRE DAME J. L. ETHICS & PUB. POL'Y 591, 624 (1989) (rejecting constitutionally compelled exemptions, but not legislative exemptions); *see also* Frederick Mark Gedicks, *Towards a Defensible Free Exercise Doctrine,* 68 GEO. WASH. L. REV. 925, 950–51 (2000) ("[I]n the long run, no effective defense is possible [for judicially mandated exemptions]. To the extent that

a residuum of religious exemptions persists under state law, . . . I say enjoy them while they last.").

206. The Warren Court's distortion of the Free Exercise Clause from a principle of no harm to a virtually unfettered individual right was contrary to the intent of the First Amendment and fundamental common sense. *See, e.g.,* Sherbert v. Verner, 374 U.S. 398, 423 (1963) (Harlan, J., dissent) ("Those situations in which the Constitution may require special treatment on account of religion are, in my view, few and far between, and this view is amply supported by the course of constitutional litigation in this area").

207. *Boerne,* 521 U.S. at 539 (1997) (Scalia, J., concurring).

208. *Id.* (emphasis in original).

209. Queen v. Lane, 6 Mod. 128, 87 Eng. Rep. 884, 885 (Q. B. 1704).

210. *See, e.g.,* Kathleen Brady, Symposium, *Religious Organizations and Free Exercise: The Surprising Lessons of Smith,* 2004 B. Y. U. L. Rev. 1638 (2004); to a lesser extent, Ira C. Lupu & Robert W. Tuttle, *Symposium, Sexual Misconduct and Ecclesiastical Immunity,* 2004 B. Y. U. L. Rev. 1789 (2004).

211. *See* Zelman v. Simmons-Harris, 536 U.S. 369 (2002); Good News Club v. Milford, 533 U.S. 98 (2001).

## 10. The Path to the Public Good

1. 521 U.S. 507 (1997).

2. Aristotle, Ethica Nicomachea (W.D. Ross, trans.), *in* IX The Works of Aristotle Translated Into English (W.D. Ross, ed. 1925).

3. 406 U.S. 205 (1972).

4. *See generally* Marci A. Hamilton, *The Calvinist Paradox of Distrust and Hope at the Constitutional Convention,* in Christian Perspectives on Legal Thought (Michael. W. McConnell et al., eds., 2001) (hereinafter Hamilton, *Distrust and Hope*).

5. For example, the dual sovereignty of federalism was intended to divide power between the federal government and the states, with each checking the other. *See* Federalist No. 46 (James Madison) ("The federal and State governments are in fact but different agents and trustees of the people, constituted with different powers, and designed for different purposes."); *see id.* (noting that federal and state governments each possess a different "disposition and faculty" with which to "resist and frustrate the measures of the other.") Similarly, the three federal branches were assigned discrete powers and the power to check the other branches. *See* Federalist No. 47 (Madison) ("the preservation of liberty requires . . . that the three great departments of power should be separate and distinct."); Federalist No. 51 (Madison) ("[T]he defect must be supplied, by so contriving the interior structure of the government, as that its several constituent parts may, by their mutual relations, be the means of keeping each other in their proper places.").

6. Articles of Confederation, art. II (U.S. 1781).

7. GORDON S. WOOD, THE CREATION OF THE AMERICAN REPUBLIC 1776–87 359 (1969) (hereinafter WOOD, THE CREATION).

8. See II THE RECORDS OF THE FEDERAL CONVENTION OF 1787 288 (Max Farrand, ed. 1966) (hereinafter II RECORDS) ("What led to the appointment of this convention? The corruption & mutability of the Legislative Councils of the States.") (Mercer); id. at 74 ("Experience in all the States had evidenced a powerful tendency in the Legislature to absorb all power into its vortex.") (Madison).

9. See Marci A. Hamilton, Symposium, Direct Democracy and The Protestant Ethic, 13 J. CONTEMP. LEGAL ISSUES 411, 418–422 (2004) (hereinafter Hamilton, Direct Democracy); see also MARCI A. HAMILTON, WHY THE PEOPLE DO NOT RULE (Aug. 2004) (unpublished manuscript, on file with the author) (hereinafter HAMILTON, WHY THE PEOPLE DO NOT RULE).

10. See BERNARD BAILYN, THE IDEOLOGICAL ORIGINS OF THE AMERICAN REVO-LUTION 57–60 (1967); WOOD, THE CREATION, supra note 7, at 135; see also Hamilton, Direct Democracy, supra note 9; see generally Hamilton, Distrust and Hope, supra note 4.

11. See M.N.S. SELLERS, THE SACRED FIRE OF LIBERTY: REPUBLICANISM, LIBER-ALISM AND THE LAW 39–40 (1998) (hereinafter SELLERS, SACRED FIRE) (discussing historical influences on the framing generation's choice of a republican form of representative government and concluding they chose it because, "[t]his concep-tion of liberty as subjection to equal laws made by common consent, for the general welfare, maintained the old republican connection between political rights and substantive freedom."); WOOD, THE CREATION, supra note 7, at 164 ("Only with the presence of the democracy in the Constitution [through an elected legislature] could any government remain faithful to the public good."); HAMILTON, WHY THE PEOPLE DO NOT RULE, supra note 9 (discussing Calvin's influence on the Framer's, and Calvin's notion that "[r]epresentatives were to be watched by the people and tethered to their common good, yet they bore the independent duty to make decisions serving the people on behalf of God.").

12. See Donald S. Lutz, Symposium, Religious Dimensions in the Development of American Constitutionalism, 39 EMORY L.J. 21, 23–24 (1990).

13. See generally Hamilton, Direct Democracy, supra note 9; Hamilton, Distrust and Hope, supra note 4; see also HAMILTON, WHY THE PEOPLE DO NOT RULE, supra note 9.

14. U.S. CONST. amend. I.

15. U.S. CONST. amend. I. ("Congress shall make no law respecting an es-tablishment of religion, or prohibiting the free exercise thereof..."); see gener-ally LEONARD W. LEVY, THE ESTABLISHMENT CLAUSE: RELIGION AND THE FIRST AMENDMENT (1983).

16. See James Madison, Memorial and Remonstrance, in 8 THE PAPERS OF JAMES MADISON 301–302 (Robert A. Rutland, et al., eds. 1962).

17. BERNARD LEWIS, ISLAM AND THE WEST 186 (1993).

18. Jones v. Wolf, 443 U.S. 595, 602–603 (1979); cf. Employment Div. v. Smith, 494 U.S. 872, 885 (1990).

19. Gillette v. United States, 401 U.S. 437, 461 (1971).

20. *See, e.g.*, Kathleen Brady, Symposium, *Religious Organizations and Free Exercise: The Surprising Lessons of Smith*, 2004 B.Y.U. L. REV. 1633 (2004); to a lesser extent, Ira C. Lupu & Robert W. Tuttle, Symposium, *Sexual Misconduct and Ecclesiastical Immunity*, 2004 B.Y.U. L. REV. 1789 (2004).

21. *See* Zelman v. Simmons-Harris, 536 U.S. 369 (2002); Good News Club v. Milford, 533 U.S. 98 (2001).

22. *Smith*, 494 U.S. at 890.

23. DEA Briefs & Background, Drugs and Drug Abuse, Drug Descriptions, Peyote & Mescaline, *at* http://www.usdoj.gov/dea/concern/peyote.html (last visited Sept. 11, 2004).

24. *See* National Prohibition Act of 1919, ch. 85, tit. II, § 3, 41 Stat. 305, 308–09 (1919).

25. Terrence A. Gerace, *The Toxic-Tobacco Law: "Appropriate Remedial Action,"* 20 J. PUB. HEALTH L. 394, 400 (1999).

26. Goldman v. Weinberger, 475 U.S. 503, 509–510 (1986).

27. 10 U.S.C. § 774 (1987).

28. Sherwood v. Brown, 619 F.2d 47 (9th Cir. 1980), *cert. denied*, 449 U.S. 919 (1980).

29. 42 U.S.C. § 2000(e)(1) (1964).

30. 118 Cong. Rec. 4503 (1972) (statement of Sen. Ervin) ("[T]his amendment is to take the political hands of Caesar off the institutions of God, where they have no place to be.").

31. 42 U.S.C. § 2000(e)(1) (1964). The exemption was expanded in 1972 to exempt employees of religious organizations that were engaged in "activities" and not just "religious activities." H.R. REP. No.92–238 & Conference Report No. 92–899, *see* 1972 U.S. Code Cong. & Adm. News, at 2137, 2180.

32. Corporation of Presiding Bishop of the Church of Jesus Christ of Latter Day Saints v. Amos, 483 U.S. 327, 338 (1987).

33. *See* Marci A. Hamilton, *Religious Institutions, the No-Harm Rule, and the Public Good*, 2004 B.Y.U. L. REV. 1099 (2004).

34. The Military Selective Service Act provides: "Nothing contained in this title shall be construed to require any person to be subject to combatant training and service in the armed forces of the United States who, by reason of religious training and belief, is conscientiously opposed to participation in war in any form." 50 U.S.C. Appx. § 456(j) (2004).

35. *See* Russell, *Development of Conscientious Objector Recognition in the United States*, 20 GEO. WASH. L. REV. 409, 412–414 (1952) (citing colonial laws exempting Quakers from compulsory service).

36. *See, e.g.*, Welsh v. United States, 398 U.S. 333, 342–44 (1970).

37. 50 U.S.C. Appx. § 456(j) (2004).

38. II RECORDS, *supra* note 8, at 287–88.

39. I have written in more detail about this in HAMILTON, WHY THE PEOPLE DO NOT RULE, *supra* note 9; Hamilton, *Direct Democracy*, *supra* note 9; Marci

A. Hamilton, *Discussion and Decisions: A Proposal to Replace the Myth of Self-Rule with an Attorneyship Model of Representation*, 69 N.Y.U. L. Rev. 477 (1994) (hereinafter Hamilton, *Discussion and Decisions*).

40. Mortimer Sellers, *Republicanism, Liberalism, and the Law*, 86 Ky. L.J. 1, 3 (1997).

41. *See* Stephan Thernstrom & Abigail Thernstrom, America in Black and White: One Nation, Indivisible 310–36 (1997).

42. 347 U.S. 483 (1954).

43. Geoffrey R. Stone, et al., Constitutional Law 456 (4th ed. 2001)

44. *See* Morgan v. Hennigan, 379 F. Supp. 410 (D. Mass. 1974), *aff'd*, 509 F.2d 580 (1st Cir. 1974), *cert. denied*, 421 U.S. 963 (1975).

45. *See* Keyes v. School Dist. No. 1, 413 U.S. 189 (1973).

46. *See* Milliken v. Bradley, 418 U.S. 717 (1974) (reversing and remanding the Detroit desegregation plan implemented by District Court Judge).

47. Katzenbach v. Morgan, 384 U.S. 641 (1966).

48. Loving v. Virginia, 388 U.S. 1 (1967) (holding that miscegenation statutes preventing marriages between persons solely on basis of racial classification violate equal protection and due process clauses of Fourteenth Amendment).

49. Shelley v. Kraemer, 334 U.S. 1 (1948) (upholding restrictive covenants barring ownership or occupancy of property by Blacks).

50. Reitman v. Mulkey, 387 U.S. 369 (1967) (holding that provision of California's constitution prohibiting the state from denying property owners the right to decline to sell or rent to anyone at their discretion impermissibly involves the state in private racial discrimination).

51. *See* The New Rules Project, The New England Town Meeting, *at* http://www.newrules.org/gov/townmtg.html (last visited Aug. 20, 2004) (showing the rules and definitions for town meetings in Marshfield); *see also generally* Frank M. Bryan, Real Democracy (2003).

52. *See* Hamilton, Why the People Do Not Rule, *supra* note 9.

53. *See* Mancur Olson, The Logic of Collective Action 144 (2d ed. 1971); *see also* Jeffrey M. Berry, The New Liberalism: The Rising Power of Citizen Groups 154 (1999) ("The dominant scholarly explanation of interest group mobilization – then and now – is Mancur Olson's selective incentive theory of collective action.").

54. Sellers, Sacred Fire, *supra* note 11, at 104.

55. *See* Peter Smith, *Protestants Are Close to Losing Majority Status*, Louisville Courier-J., Jul. 21, 2004, at 1A.

56. *See generally* Hamilton, Why the People Do Not Rule, *supra* note 9.

57. *See generally id.*; Hamilton, *Direct Democracy, supra* note 9; Hamilton, *Discussion and Decisions, supra* note 39.

58. *See* Olson, *supra* note 53, at 144; *see also* Berry, *supra* note 53, at 154.

59. *See generally* Diana L. Eck, A New Religious America (2001).

60. Maria Jow Parejo Guzman, *The Anomolous European Rights to Life and Death: Understanding the Struggle for Recognition of Religious Minority Rights by*

*Examining the Cultural Identity of Spain and Other European Communities,* 35 TEXAS TECH. L. REV. 297, 308 (2004); *see also* Nathan A. Adams, IV, *A Human Rights Imperative: Extending Religious Liberty Beyond the Border,* 33 CORNELL INT'L L. REV. 1 (2000).

61. Church of Lukumi Babalu Aye v. City of Hialeah, 508 U.S. 520, 533 (1993).

62. *Id.; see also* Corp. of Presiding Bishop of the Church of Jesus Christ of Latter-day Saints v. Amos, 483 U.S. 327, 330 (1987) (upholding exemption from Title VII for the secular, non-profit activities of a religious organization).

63. For further elaboration of this concept, *see generally* Hamilton, *Direct Democracy, supra* note 9.

64. *Smith,* 494 U.S. at 878–79.

65. Douglas Laycock, *Free Exercise and the Religious Freedom Restoration Act,* 62 FORDHAM L. REV. 883, 884 (1994).

66. Press Release, The Pew Research Center, Religion and Politics: Contention and Consensus 42 (Jul. 24, 2003) (hereinafter Press Release, The Pew Research Center) (on file with author), *also available at* http://pewforum.org/publications/surveys/religion-politics.pdf (last visited Aug. 25, 2004) (answer to Question 17: "What is your religious preference – do you consider yourself Christian, Jewish, Muslim, other non-Christian such as Buddhist or Hindu, atheist, agnostic, something else, or don't you have a religious preference?" 82% of respondents in March 2002 identified themselves as Christian, 1% as Jewish, 1% as other non-Christian, 2% as an unlisted religion, 2% were agnostic, 1% were atheists. Only 10% said they didn't have a religious preference.).

67. Michael W. McConnell, *Free Exercise Revisionism and the Smith Decision,* 57 U. CHI. L. REV. 1109, 1142–43 (1990) (hereinafter McConnell, *Free Exercise Revisionism and the Smith Decision*).

68. Hall v. Baptist Mem'l Health Care Corp., 215 F.3d 618 (6th Cir. 2000).

69. *See* First Covenant Church v. Seattle, 840 P.2d 174, 184–85 (Wash. 1992) (holding an exemption from city's zoning ordinances that exempted structural changes for liturgical purposes was still unconstitutional because it requires the city to determine "what is liturgy and what is a valid religious purpose . . . foster[ing] exactly the kind of religious entanglement the constitution seeks to avoid."); Society of Jesus of New England v. Boston Landmarks Comm'n, 564 N.E.2d 571 (Mass. 1990) (holding landmark commission approval of interior renovations of church violated the Massachusetts Constitution and not reaching the federal question).

70. *See, e.g.,* CAL. EVID. CODE § 5193 (Deering 2004) ("A parent or guardian of a pupil has the right to excuse their child from all or part of comprehensive sexual health education, HIV/AIDS prevention education, and assessments related to that education . . . "); R.I. GEN. LAWS § 16-22-17 (2003) ("A parent or legal guardian may exempt his or her child from the [HIV/AIDS education] program by written directive to the principal of the school . . . "); S.C. CODE ANN. § 59-32-50 (Law. Co-op. 1976) ("A public school principal, upon receipt of a statement signed by a student's parent or legal guardian stating that participation by the student in the health education program conflicts with the family's beliefs, shall exempt that

student from any portion or all of the units on reproductive health, family life, and pregnancy prevention where any conflicts occur."); IOWA CODE ANN. § 279.50 (West 1996) ("A pupil shall not be required to take instruction in human growth and development if the pupil's parent or guardian or files with the appropriate principal a written request that the pupil be excused from the instruction."); N.C. GEN. STAT. ANN. § 115C-81(e1)(7) (Bender 2004) ("Local boards of education shall adopt policies to provide opportunities either for parents and legal guardians to consent or for parents and legal guardians to withhold their consent to the students' participation in any or all of these [i. STD and pregnancy prevention, ii. Abstinence until marriage, iii. Comprehensive sexual education] programs.").

71. Ford v. McGinnis, 352 F.3d 582, 598 n.17 (2d Cir. 2003) (in case of Muslim inmate denied religious meal, "we hold as a matter of law that the prison officials' conduct was not objectively reasonable"); *see also* Jackson v. Mann, 196 F.3d 316, 320 (2d Cir. 1999) (in case of Jewish inmate denied access to kosher meal program, the court noted that "prison officials must provide a prisoner a diet that is consistent with his religious scruples") (quoting Bass v. Coughlin, 976 F.2d 98, 99 (2d Cir.1992) (per curiam)); Love v. Reed, 216 F.3d 682, 690 (8th Cir. 2000) (in case of inmate practicing "Hebrew religion" who wished to observe the Sabbath, prison's "failure to provide the requested accommodation . . . substantially burdens [inmate's] ability to freely exercise his religion.").

72. 42 U.S.C. § 300a-7 (2004).

73. 26 U.S.C.S. § 501(c)(3) (2004).

74. STEPHEN L. CARTER, THE CULTURE OF DISBELIEF: HOW AMERICAN LAW AND POLITICS TRIVIALIZE RELIGIOUS DEVOTION (1993).

75. *See* MARTIN E. MARTY, RELIGION AND REPUBLIC 71–72 (1987) (describing advent of secularization in law and commenting that Supreme Court decisions in the 1960s and 1970s drained "the last trace of religious substance" from the law); *see also generally* MARTIN E. MARTY, THE INFIDEL: FREE THOUGHT AND AMERICAN RELIGION (1961).

76. Kathleen A. Shaw, *Priests Huddle on Role in Election*, TELEGRAM & GAZETTE (Worcester, MA), Sept. 10, 2004, at B7.

77. *See generally* Marci Hamilton, *Protecting Religious Institutions' Right to Political Speech*, FINDLAW'S WRIT, Aug. 15 2002, *at* http://writ.news.findlaw.com/hamilton/20020815.html (last visited Sept. 12, 2004). There is a bill pending in both Houses of Congress that would affect the repeal.

78. *Smith*, 494 U.S. at 872.

79. 139 Cong. Rec. S 14350, 103rd Cong., 1st Sess. Oct. 26, 2993 (statement of Sen. Hatch).

80. McConnell, *Free Exercise Revisionism and the Smith Decision, supra* note 67, at 1152.

81. *See generally* Kent Greenawalt, *Religion and American Political Judgments*, 36 WAKE FOREST L. REV. 401 (2001).

82. Bill Broadway, *Claim of 'Post-Denominational Era' Defied*, WASH. POST, Mar. 14, 2001, at A3 (citing Hartford Institute for Religion Research study).

83. The 2000 Census reported a total U.S. population of 281,421,906. POPULA-
TION DIVISION, U.S. CENSUS BUREAU, ANNUAL ESTIMATES OF THE POPULATION OF
THE UNITED STATES AND STATES, AND FOR PUERTO RICO: APRIL 1, 2000 TO JULY
1, 2003 (Dec. 18, 2003) (revised May 11, 2004), *available at* http://www.census.gov/
popest/states/tables/NST-EST2003-01.pdf (last visited Aug. 29. 2004).

84. Stephen D. Smith, *The Rise and Fall of Religious Freedom in Constitutional
Discourse*, 140 U. PA. L. REV. 149, 232, 237 (1991).

85. Christopher L. Eisgruber & Lawrence G. Sager, *The Vulnerability of
Conscience: The Constitutional Basis for Protecting Religious Conduct*, 61 U. CHI.
L. REV. 1245, 1315 (1994).

86. Christopher L. Eisgruber & Lawrence G. Sager, *Why the Religious Freedom
Restoration Act is Unconstitutional*, 69 N.Y.U. L. REV. 437, 456–57 (1994).

87. *Id.*

88. McConnell, *Free Exercise Revisionism and the Smith Decision, supra* note
67, at 1150.

89. MODEL RULES OF PROF'L CONDUCT AND CODE OF JUDICIAL CONDUCT
Canon 3(B)(5) (1999).

90. 28 U.S.C. § 453 (2004).

91. 28 U.S.C. § 455(a) (2004).

92. Tennessee Valley Auth. v. Hill, 437 U.S. 153, 195 (1978).

93. *See* Jesse Choper, *The Supreme Court and the Political Branches: Democratic Theory and Practice*, 122 U. PA. L. REV. 810, 814 (1974); RICHARD A. POSNER,
OVERCOMING LAW 134 (1995).

> I reject an expanded judicial role because it must eventually lead to the ridiculous
> conclusion that members of the judiciary not only must be experts on topics
> ranging from anatomy to zoology, but that they also are capable of resolving
> differences of opinion within each of those disciplines.... It is far more probable
> that over time such judges will substitute their personal preferences for those of
> the framers or legislators.

WILLIAM GANGI, SAVING THE CONSTITUTION FROM THE COURTS 275 (1995). *See
also* Norman Ornstein, *The Role of the Legislature in a Democracy*, FREEDOM
PAPER NO. 3, (Wayne Hall ed., 1992), *available at* http://usinfo.state.gov/products/
pubs/archive/freedom/freedom3.htm#lesson (last visited Aug. 25, 2004).

94. That is in fact happening in the context of children's interests. Religious
organizations have been successful in obtaining state and federal laws that exempt faith-healing parents from the force of the laws that protect children. *See*
Rita Swan, Ph.D., Symposium, *Moral, Economic, and Social Issues in Children's
Health Care: On Statutes Depriving a Class of Children of Rights to Medical
Care: Can this Discrimination be Litigated?*, 2 QUINNIPIAC HEALTH L.J. 73, 79–80
(1988). Children's rights, however, have become internationally recognized and
the argument for giving such latitude to parents to harm their children, even if
religiously motivated, have lost a significant degree of force. *See, e.g., Weld Ap-
proves Child Abuse Law*, BOSTON GLOBE, Dec. 29, 1993, at Metro-24 (reporting the
passage of legislation that "repeals a statutory provision that states a child shall not

be deemed neglected if treated with spiritual healing alone."); CAL. PEN. CODE § 11166(a)(2)(c)(1)-(2) (Bender 2004) (Duty to report statute excludes reporting information received during "penitential communication" but clarifies that " [n]othing in this subdivision shall be construed to modify or limit a clergy member's duty to report known or suspected child abuse or neglect when the clergy member is acting in some other capacity that would otherwise make the clergy member a mandated reporter.").

95. *Smith*, 494 U.S. at 890.

96. Press Release, The Pew Research Center, Religion and Politics: Contention and Consensus, *supra* note 66.

97. The investigation by Oregon's medical examiner showed that the deaths of at least 21 of the 78 children who died since 1955 probably could have been prevented with medical treatment. Mark Larabee & Peter D. Sleeth, *Followers Children Needed Medical Care, Experts Say*, CLEVELAND PLAIN DEALER, Jun. 28, 1998, at 21A.

98. Mark Larabee, *Bill Aims to Lift All Oregon Religious Shields*, OREGONIAN, Jan. 22, 1999, at C6.

99. Mark Larabee, *Balancing Rights Makes Faith-Healing Bills Thorny*, OREGONIAN, Jun. 28, 1999, at A1.

100. *Id.*

101. In 1844, Karl Marx said, "Religion is the sigh of the oppressed creature, the heart of a heartless world, and the soul of soulless conditions. It is the opium of the people." KARL MARX, CRITIQUE OF HEGEL'S 'PHILOSOPHY OF RIGHT' 131 (Joseph O'Malley ed., Annette Jolin & Joseph O'Malley trans., 1970). Thomas Mann paraphrased Marx in 1930, saying, "Fanaticism turns into a means of salvation, enthusiasm into epileptic ecstacy, politics becomes an opiate for the masses, a proletarian eschatology; and reason veils her face." THOMAS MANN, An Appeal to Reason, *in* ORDER OF THE DAY, POLITICAL ESSAYS AND SPEECHES OF TWO DECADES 57 (Helen T. Lowe-Porter trans., 1942).

102. C.B. MACPHERSON, THE POLITICAL THEORY OF POSSESSIVE INDIVIDUALISM: HOBBES TO LOCKE 3 (1962).

103. *See generally* various authors, Symposium, *Foundations of Church Autonomy*, 2004 B.Y.U. L. Rev.

104. FRIEDRICH NIETZSCHE, BEYOND GOOD AND EVIL 52 (Helen Zimmern trans., 1967) ("Granted, finally, that we succeeded in explaining our entire instinctive life as the development and ramification of one fundamental form of will – namely, the Will to Power, as *my* thesis puts it; granted that all organic functions could be traced back to this Will to Power, and that the solution of the problem of generation and nutrition – it is one problem – could also be found therein: one would thus have acquired the right to define *all* active force unequivocally as *Will to Power*. The world seen from within, the world defined and designated according to its 'intelligible character' – it would simply be 'Will to Power' and nothing else.") (emphasis in original).

105. Ira C. Lupu, *Free Exercise Exemption and Religious Insitutions: The Case of Employment Discrimination*, 67 B.U. L. REV. 391, 403 (1987).


Epilogue

1. Brochure, U.S. Conference of Catholic Bishops, The Challenge of Faithful Citizenship: A Catholic Call to Political Responsibility (2004), *available at* http://www.usccb.org/faithfulcitizenship/pdf/brochure.pdf (last visited Jan. 8, 2004).

2. Carol Eisenberg, *Religious Political Revival*, NEWSDAY (N.Y.), Nov. 5, 2004, at A28.

3. Emma Schwartz, *Falwell's School Joins Others in Teaching Law to Their Flocks*, L.A. TIMES, Nov. 21, 2004, at A24; *see also* Adam Liptak, *Giving the Law a Religious Perspective*, N.Y. TIMES, Nov. 23, 2004, at A16.

4. BERNARD GOLDBERG, ARROGANCE: RESCUING AMERICA FROM THE MEDIA 27 (2003).

5. Rukhl Schaechter & Eric J. Greenberg, *Major Rabbinical Council Slammed for Releasing Names in Sexual Abuse Case*, FORWARD (N.Y.), Dec. 17, 2004.

6. Rebecca Ruiz, *Satanists Not so Spooky, Say Supporters*, NORTH GATE NEWS ONLINE (Berkeley, Cal.), Oct. 27, 2004, *at* http://journalism.berkeley.edu/ngno/stories/003517.html (last visited Jan. 8, 2004).

7. *Id.*

8. John R. Llewellyn, Believer Beware: A Dissertation Dealing with Government Ineptness in Combating Coerced Sexual Exploitation – and the Dire Need for New Legislation (2004) (unpublished manuscript on file with the author).

9. Laurie Goodstein, *Murder and Suicide Reviving Claims of Child Abuse in Cult*, N.Y. TIMES, Jan. 15, 2005, at A12.

# INDEX